Taste *of* Home

GRANDMA'S FAVORITES

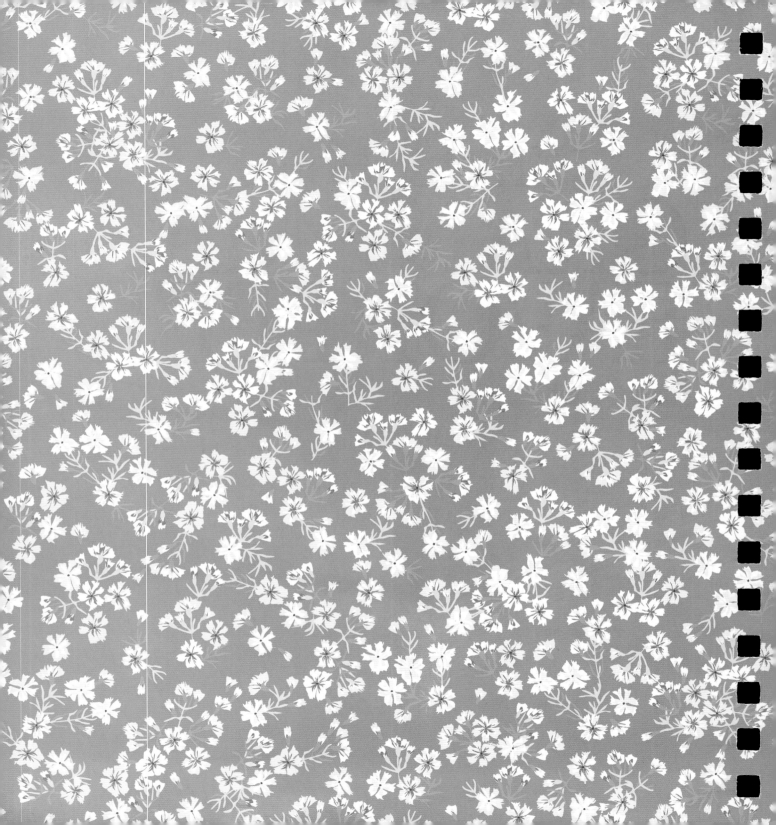

GRANDMA'S FAVORITES

TASTE OF HOME BOOKS • RDA ENTHUSIAST BRANDS, LLC • MILWAUKEE, WI

Visit us at tasteofhome.com for other
Taste of Home books and products.

ISBNs:
978-1-61765-868-6 (Wire Bound)
978-1-61765-917-1 (Paperback)

LOCC: 2019904320

Deputy Editor: Mark Hagen
Senior Art Director: Raeann Thompson
Senior Designer: Courtney Lovetere
Designer: Arielle Jardine
Copy Editor: Ann Walter

Cover Photographer: Mark Derse
Cover Senior Set Stylist: Melissa Franco
Cover Senior Food Stylist: Shannon Norris

Pictured on front cover:
Lemon Layer Cake, p. 358

Pictured on title page:
Great-Grandma's Oatmeal Cookies, p.328

Pattern:
Eva Marina/Shutterstock

Pictured on back cover:
Warm Fava Bean & Pea Salad, p. 300;
Traditional Meat Loaf, p. 271;
Yogurt Yeast Rolls, p. 122

Printed in China
1 3 5 7 9 10 8 6 4 2

CONTENTS

RECIPES
MADE WITH

♥

When you think of finger-licking, stick-to-your-ribs, all-time comfort foods, Grandma's house quickly comes to mind. From the aroma of freshly baked breads to the satisfaction of a bubbling casserole and the anticipation of a rich chocolate dessert, Grandma's kitchen never disappoints.

Now you can relish these much-loved specialties in your own home when you explore the 475 recipes in *Taste of Home Grandma's Favorites*. From savory to sweet, you'll find delight in forgotten foods, add heartwarming flair to weeknight suppers and bring Grandma's special touch to holidays and other celebrations. You'll also enjoy...

Grandma's Favorite Breakfasts. Remember sleepovers at Grandma's? The best food was always waiting first thing in the morning. Relive those moments with these eye-opening classics.

Grandma's Favorite Main Courses. You can't go wrong when your meal features meat loaf, potpie, roasted chicken or from-scratch spaghetti sauce. Don't forget hearty roasts, tangy hams and fish that's fried to perfection in a cast-iron skillet.

Grandma's Favorite Sunday Dinners. Surprise everyone at the table when you serve one of these complete menus inspired by Sunday meals with Grandma. The planning is done—let a deliciously delightful night begin!

Grandma's Favorite Desserts. Crisps and cobblers, tarts and tortes...here you'll find all the sweets you crave, as well as crispy cookies, decadent brownies and so many other much-loved treats.

Relive those glorious moments around the table, create new memories in your kitchen and savor the goodness of the home-cooked foods you've always adored. It's easy with this all-new keepsake, *Taste of Home Grandma's Favorites*.

BREAKFASTS

Whether made for a weekend sleepover or holiday brunch, Grandma's eye-opening breakfasts continuously warmed hearts and satisfied tummies. Enjoy those sunny dishes once again with this collection of all-time classics.

RHUBARB & STRAWBERRY COFFEE CAKE

Vanilla cake with cream cheese filling and strawberry rhubarb sauce makes a grand finale for family brunches. That's how we honor moms and grandmas at our house.
—Danielle Lee, Sewickley, PA

Prep: 50 min. • **Bake:** 50 min. + cooling
Makes: 12 servings

- 1½ tsp. cornstarch
- 3 Tbsp. sugar
- ¾ cup chopped fresh strawberries
- ¾ cup chopped fresh or frozen rhubarb
- 1 Tbsp. water

FILLING
- 1 pkg. (8 oz.) cream cheese, softened
- ¼ cup sugar
- 1 large egg, lightly beaten

CAKE
- 2 cups all-purpose flour
- ¾ cup sugar
- ½ cup cold butter, cubed
- ½ tsp. baking powder
- ½ tsp. baking soda
- ¼ tsp. salt
- 1 large egg, room temperature, lightly beaten
- ¾ cup fat-free sour cream
- 1 tsp. vanilla extract

1. Preheat oven to 350°. Line the bottom of a greased 9-in. springform pan with parchment; grease parchment. In a small saucepan, mix the cornstarch and sugar; stir in strawberries, rhubarb and water. Bring to a boil. Reduce the heat; simmer, uncovered, until thickened, 6-8 minutes, stirring occasionally. For filling, in a small bowl, beat cream cheese and sugar until smooth. Beat in egg.

2. In a large bowl, combine flour and sugar; cut in butter until crumbly. Reserve ¾ cup for topping. Stir baking powder, baking soda and salt into remaining flour mixture. In a small bowl, whisk egg, sour cream and vanilla until blended; gently stir into flour mixture (do not overmix).

3. Spread batter onto bottom and ½ in. up sides of prepared pan. Spread filling over crust, leaving a ½-in. border around edge of pan. Spoon strawberry mixture over top; sprinkle with reserved crumb mixture.

4. Bake until edges are golden brown, 50-60 minutes. Cool on a wire rack for 20 minutes. Loosen sides from pan with a knife. Cool completely. Remove rim from pan. Refrigerate leftovers.

Freeze option: Securely wrap cooled cake in plastic wrap and foil, then freeze. To use, thaw in refrigerator.

1 slice: 320 cal., 15g fat (9g sat. fat), 75mg chol., 274mg sod., 41g carb. (22g sugars, 1g fiber), 6g pro.

BACON-EGG ENGLISH MUFFIN

I stack some cheese, Canadian bacon and poached eggs on an English muffin to make this appealing eye-opener. Perfect for one or two, this delicious open-faced sandwich is special enough for guests as well.
—Terry Kuehn, Waunakee, WI

Takes: 15 min. • **Makes:** 2 servings

- 1 **Tbsp. white vinegar**
- 2 **large eggs**
- 1 **Tbsp. cream cheese, softened**
- 1 **English muffin, split and toasted**
- 2 **slices process American cheese**
- 2 **slices Canadian bacon**

1. Place 2-3 in. of water in a large skillet with high sides; add the vinegar. Bring to a boil; reduce heat and simmer gently. Break cold eggs, one at a time, into a custard cup or saucer; holding the cup close to the surface of the water, slip the egg into water. Cook, uncovered, until whites are completely set, about 4 minutes.

2. Meanwhile, spread cream cheese over muffin halves. Top with cheese slices and Canadian bacon. Using a slotted spoon, lift eggs out of water and place over bacon.

1 serving: 273 cal., 15g fat (7g sat. fat), 247mg chol., 828mg sod., 16g carb. (3g sugars, 1g fiber), 19g pro.

PEPPERONI HOPPLE-POPPLE

My grandma and I created this kid-friendly version of a German breakfast dish. Serve it with toast or English muffins.
—Jaycee Gfeller, Russell, KS

- -

Takes: 30 min. • **Makes:** 6 servings

- 2½ cups frozen shredded hash brown potatoes
- ⅓ cup chopped onion
- 3 Tbsp. butter
- 5 large eggs
- ½ cup whole milk
- 1 tsp. Italian seasoning
- ½ tsp. salt
- ½ tsp. pepper
- 25 slices pepperoni
- 1 cup shredded Mexican cheese blend

1. In a large skillet, cook potatoes and onion in butter until tender and lightly browned. Meanwhile, in a large bowl, beat eggs, milk, Italian seasoning, salt and pepper.
2. Pour over potato mixture. Sprinkle with pepperoni. Cover and cook on medium-low heat until the eggs are set, 10-12 minutes. Remove from the heat. Sprinkle with the cheese; cover and let stand for 2 minutes. Cut into wedges.
1 piece: 267 cal., 20g fat (11g sat. fat), 219mg chol., 608mg sod., 9g carb. (2g sugars, 1g fiber), 12g pro.

OLD-WORLD PUFF PANCAKE

My grandmother taught my mom how to make this dish, which was popular during the Depression. Then, cooks measured ingredients in pinches, dashes and dibs. But through the years, accurate amounts were noted. My wife and I enjoy this dish today, particularly for brunch.
—Auton Miller, Piney Flats, TN

- -

Takes: 30 min. • **Makes:** 4 servings

- 2 Tbsp. butter
- 3 large eggs
- ¾ cup whole milk
- ¾ cup all-purpose flour
- 2 tsp. sugar
- 1 tsp. ground nutmeg

Confectioners' sugar
Lemon wedges
Optional: Syrup and fresh raspberries

1. Place butter in a 10-in. ovenproof skillet; place in a 425° oven until butter is melted, 2-3 minutes. In a blender, process the eggs, milk, flour, sugar and nutmeg until smooth. Pour into prepared skillet.
2. Bake at 425° until puffed and browned, 16-18 minutes. Dust with confectioners' sugar. Serve with lemon wedges and, if desired, syrup and raspberries.
1 slice: 178 cal., 5g fat (2g sat. fat), 144mg chol., 74mg sod., 23g carb. (5g sugars, 1g fiber), 9g pro.

APPLE PAN GOODY

Dotted with dried cranberries, this heirloom apple bake is sweetened with brown sugar and a little cinnamon. We enjoy it on breakfast buffets, but it also makes a fun side dish, particularly with a pork entree.
—Jeanne Bredemeyer, Orient, NY

- -

Prep: 20 min. • **Bake:** 20 min.
Makes: 8 servings

   4   to 5 medium tart apples,
        peeled and sliced
   ¾   cup dried cranberries
   6   Tbsp. brown sugar
   1   tsp. ground cinnamon, divided
   3   Tbsp. butter
   6   large eggs
   1½ cups orange juice
   1½ cups all-purpose flour
   ¾   tsp. salt
   2   Tbsp. sugar
        Maple syrup, optional

1. In a large skillet, saute the apples, cranberries, brown sugar and ¾ tsp. cinnamon in butter until apples begin to soften, about 6 minutes. Transfer to a greased 13x9-in. baking dish.
2. Place the eggs, orange juice, flour and salt in a blender; cover and process until smooth. Pour over apple mixture. Sprinkle with sugar and remaining cinnamon.
3. Bake, uncovered, at 425° until a knife inserted in the center comes out clean, 20-25 minutes. Serve with syrup if desired.
1 cup: 316 cal., 8g fat (4g sat. fat), 171mg chol., 316mg sod., 54g carb. (32g sugars, 2g fiber), 7g pro.

COUNTRY POTATO PANCAKES

These potato pancakes are so versatile. They can be a side dish for just about any meal or the main course for a light breakfast. We enjoy them often.
—Lydia Robotewskyj, Franklin, WI

- -

Takes: 30 min. • **Makes:** about 24 pancakes

   3   large potatoes (about
        2 lbs.), peeled
   2   large eggs, lightly beaten
   1   Tbsp. grated onion
   2   Tbsp. all-purpose flour
   1   tsp. salt
   ½   tsp. baking powder
        Vegetable oil for frying

1. Finely grate potatoes. Drain any liquid. Add the eggs, onion, flour, salt and baking powder. In a frying pan, add oil to the depth of ⅛ in.; heat over medium-high (375°).
2. Drop batter by heaping tablespoonfuls in hot oil. Flatten into patties. Fry until golden brown, turning once. Serve immediately.
2 pancakes: 257 cal., 8g fat (1g sat. fat), 31mg chol., 242mg sod., 41g carb. (2g sugars, 5g fiber), 6g pro.

TEST KITCHEN TIP
Warm leftover pancakes in the oven and have them as a snack with smoked salmon or a little bit of applesauce.

BLUEBERRY CRUNCH BREAKFAST BAKE

Blueberries in season make this a very special breakfast, but I find that frozen berries can work just as well. My dear grandmother used to make this with strawberries, and I always loved to eat it at her house.
—Marsha Ketaner, Henderson, NV

Prep: 15 min. • **Bake:** 30 min.
Makes: 12 servings

- 1 loaf (16 oz.) day-old French bread, cut into 1-in. slices
- 8 large eggs
- 1 cup half-and-half cream
- ½ tsp. vanilla extract
- 1 cup old-fashioned oats
- 1 cup packed brown sugar
- ¼ cup all-purpose flour
- ½ cup cold butter
- 2 cups fresh or frozen blueberries
- 1 cup chopped walnuts

1. Arrange half of the bread slices in a greased 13x9-in. baking dish.
2. In a large bowl, whisk the eggs, cream and vanilla. Slowly pour half of the cream mixture over the bread. Top with remaining bread and egg mixture. Let stand until liquid is absorbed, about 5 minutes.
3. Meanwhile, in a small bowl, combine the oats, brown sugar and flour; cut in butter until crumbly. Sprinkle over top. Top with blueberries and walnuts.
4. Bake, uncovered, at 375° until a knife inserted in the center comes out clean, 30-35 minutes. Let stand for 5 minutes before serving.

1 serving: 427 cal., 21g fat (8g sat. fat), 154mg chol., 351mg sod., 50g carb. (23g sugars, 3g fiber), 12g pro.

APRICOT-ALMOND TEA RINGS

Apricots and almonds are the perfect pairing in this luscious iced ring. It's a great breakfast treat to serve your family and a perfect centerpiece for a coffee date with your friends.
—Ann Hillmeyer, Sandia Park, NM

- -

Prep: 45 min. + rising
Bake: 20 min. + cooling
Makes: 2 rings (8 slices each)

- 2 pkg. (¼ oz. each) active dry yeast
- ¼ cup warm water (110° to 115°)
- 1¼ cups warm 2% milk (110° to 115°)
- ½ cup butter, softened
- ⅓ cup sugar
- ½ tsp. salt
- ½ cup mashed potato flakes
- 2 large eggs, room temperature
- 3½ to 4 cups all-purpose flour

FILLING
- 1½ cups apricot preserves
- ⅔ cup sugar
- 5 oz. almond paste
- ⅓ cup butter, softened

ICING
- 1⅓ cups confectioners' sugar
- ½ tsp. vanilla extract
- 2 to 3 Tbsp. 2% milk
- ⅓ cup sliced almonds, toasted

1. In a large bowl, dissolve yeast in warm water. In another bowl, combine milk, butter, sugar, salt, potato flakes and eggs. Let stand 1 minute. Add milk mixture and 3 cups flour to yeast mixture; beat until smooth. Add enough remaining flour to form a soft dough.

2. Turn onto a floured surface; knead until smooth and elastic, about 6-8 minutes. Place in a greased bowl, turning once to grease the top. Cover and let rise in a warm place until doubled, about 1 hour.

3. Place preserves, sugar, almond paste and butter in a food processor; cover and process until blended. Punch dough down. Divide in half. On a lightly floured surface, roll each portion into 14x7-in. rectangle. Spread filling evenly to within ½ in. of edges. Roll up jelly-roll style, starting with a long side; pinch seams to seal.

4. Place the rolls, seam side down, on 2 parchment-lined baking sheets. Pinch the ends together to form 2 rings. With scissors, cut from the outside edge to two-thirds of the way toward center of rings at 1-in. intervals. Separate strips slightly; twist to allow filling to show. Let rise until doubled, 35-40 minutes.

5. Preheat oven to 375°. Bake until lightly browned, 18-22 minutes. Remove from pans to wire racks to cool. Combine the confectioners' sugar, vanilla and enough milk to reach a drizzling consistency. Drizzle over the warm tea rings and sprinkle with toasted sliced almonds.

1 slice: 425 cal., 14g fat (7g sat. fat), 53mg chol., 178mg sod., 70g carb. (38g sugars, 2g fiber), 6g pro.

Cinnamon-Pecan Tea Ring: Omit filling ingredients and toasted sliced almonds in icing. Cream ½ cup softened butter, ¼ cup packed brown sugar and 1½ tsp. ground cinnamon. Spread over each rectangle to within ½ in. of edges. Sprinkle with ¾ cup chopped pecans.

APPLE-HONEY DUTCH BABY

I love to make this on Sunday mornings. It's so impressive when it's served warm right out of the oven, and the honey and apple filling is yummy.
—Kathy Fleming, Lisle, IL

- -

Takes: 30 min. • **Makes:** 4 servings

- 3 large eggs, room temperature
- ¾ cup 2% milk
- ¾ cup all-purpose flour
- 1 Tbsp. sugar
- 2 Tbsp. butter

TOPPING

- 1 Tbsp. butter
- 2 large apples, sliced
- ½ cup honey
- 2 to 3 tsp. lemon juice
- ½ tsp. ground cardamom
- 1 tsp. cornstarch
- 2 tsp. cold water

1. Preheat oven to 400°. In a large bowl, whisk together the first 4 ingredients until smooth. Place butter in a 10-in. ovenproof skillet; heat in oven until butter is melted, 2-3 minutes.
2. Tilt pan to coat bottom and sides. Pour batter into hot skillet. Bake until puffed and edges are lightly browned, 16-20 minutes.
3. Meanwhile, in a large saucepan, heat the butter for topping over medium heat; saute apples until lightly browned. Stir in honey, lemon juice and cardamom. Mix cornstarch and water until smooth; stir into the apple mixture. Bring to a boil; cook and stir until thickened, 1-2 minutes. Spoon into pancake; serve immediately.
1 serving: 429 cal., 14g fat (7g sat. fat), 166mg chol., 146mg sod., 72g carb. (50g sugars, 3g fiber), 9g pro.

SPINACH FETA STRATA

My family loves this hearty dish. I enjoy the fact that it's nearly from scratch but saves time with frozen chopped spinach. Best of all, I can make it the night before.
—Pat Lane, Pullman, WA

- -

Prep: 10 min. + chilling • **Bake:** 40 min.
Makes: 12 servings

- 10 slices French bread (1 in. thick) or 6 croissants, split
- 6 large eggs, lightly beaten
- 1½ cups 2% milk
- 1 pkg. (10 oz.) frozen chopped spinach, thawed and squeezed dry
- ½ tsp. salt
- ¼ tsp. ground nutmeg
- ¼ tsp. pepper
- 1½ cups shredded Monterey Jack cheese
- 1 cup crumbled feta cheese

1. In a greased 3-qt. or 13x9-in. baking dish, arrange French bread or croissant halves with sides overlapping.
2. In a large bowl, combine the eggs, milk, spinach, salt, nutmeg and pepper; pour over bread. Sprinkle with cheeses. Cover and refrigerate for 8 hours or overnight.
3. Remove from the refrigerator 30 minutes before baking. Bake, uncovered, at 350° until a knife inserted in the center comes out clean, 40-45 minutes. Let stand for 5 minutes before cutting. Serve warm.
1 serving: 190 cal., 10g fat (5g sat. fat), 128mg chol., 443mg sod., 13g carb. (2g sugars, 2g fiber), 12g pro.

CORNFLAKE-COATED CRISPY BACON

I've loved my aunt's crispy coated bacon ever since I was a child. Now I've shared the super simple recipe with my own children. We still enjoy big panfuls for special occasions as well as Sundays throughout the year!
—Brenda Severson, Norman, OK

- -

Prep: 20 min. • **Bake:** 25 min.
Makes: 9 servings

- ½   cup evaporated milk
- 2   Tbsp. ketchup
- 1   Tbsp. Worcestershire sauce
     Dash pepper
- 18   bacon strips (1 lb.)
- 3   cups crushed cornflakes

Preheat oven to 375°. In a large bowl, combine milk, ketchup, Worcestershire sauce and pepper. Add bacon strips, turning to coat. Dip the strips in crushed cornflakes, patting to help coating adhere. Place bacon on 2 racks; place each rack on an ungreased 15x10x1-in. baking pan. Bake until golden and crisp, rotating pans halfway through baking, 25-30 minutes.

2 bacon strips: 198 cal., 7g fat (3g sat. fat), 20mg chol., 547mg sod., 26g carb. (4g sugars, trace fiber), 8g pro.

BACON & ASPARAGUS FRITTATA

Especially during the summertime, this makes a nice breakfast or even a light dinner. Serve it with toast or muffins in the morning, and with rice in the evening. It's quick and easy, but it always wins me many compliments from guests.
—Gwen Clemon, Soldier, IA

- -

Prep: 10 min. • **Cook:** 25 min.
Makes: 6 servings

- 12 oz. bacon
- 2 cups sliced fresh asparagus (cut in ½-in. pieces)
- 1 cup chopped onion
- 2 garlic cloves, minced
- 10 large eggs, beaten
- ¼ cup minced parsley
- ½ tsp. seasoned salt
- ¼ tsp. pepper
- 1 large tomato, thinly sliced
- 1 cup shredded cheddar cheese

1. In a 9- or 10-in. ovenproof skillet, cook bacon until crisp. Drain, reserving 1 Tbsp. drippings. Heat reserved drippings on medium-high. Add asparagus, onion and garlic; saute until onion is tender. Crumble bacon; set aside a third. In a large bowl, combine remaining bacon, eggs, parsley, salt and pepper..
2. Pour egg mixture into skillet; stir. Top with tomato, cheese and reserved bacon. Cover and cook over medium-low until the eggs are nearly set, 10-15 minutes. Preheat broiler; place skillet 6 in. from heat. Broil until lightly browned, about 2 minutes. Serve immediately.
1 piece: 344 cal., 24g fat (10g sat. fat), 351mg chol., 738mg sod., 7g carb. (3g sugars, 2g fiber), 23g pro.

TEST KITCHEN TIP
Looking to feed a larger crowd? You can make this in a 12-in. skillet by increasing each ingredient by 50 percent and baking it for 20-25 minutes.

MUSHROOM & SMOKED SALMON TARTS

I love that this recipe actually makes two tarts for a large brunch with family and friends. I often cut the tarts into narrow slices for appetizers as well. Get creative and work in cooked chicken or ham in place of the salmon if you'd like.
—Jacquelyn Benson, South Berwick, ME

- -

Prep: 30 min. + chilling
Bake: 15 min.
Makes: 2 tarts (6 servings each)

2	sheets refrigerated pie crust
1	Tbsp. olive oil
1	medium red onion, thinly sliced
1	Tbsp. butter
4	cups sliced fresh mushrooms (about 10 oz.)
⅔	cup smoked salmon or lox
⅓	cup crumbled feta cheese
8	large eggs, divided use
4	tsp. drained capers, divided
½	tsp. salt, divided
½	tsp. pepper, divided
2	tsp. snipped fresh dill, optional, divided

1. Unroll crusts into two 9-in. fluted tart pans with removable bottoms; trim edges. Refrigerate 30 minutes. Preheat oven to 400°.
2. Line unpricked crusts with a double thickness of foil. Fill with pie weights, dried beans or uncooked rice. Bake on a lower oven rack until edges are golden brown, 10-15 minutes. Remove foil and weights; bake until the bottoms are golden brown, 2-4 minutes longer. Cool on a wire rack. Reduce oven setting to 375°.
3. In a large skillet, heat oil over medium-high heat. Add onion; cook and stir until tender and lightly browned, 5-7 minutes. Remove from pan. Add the butter and mushrooms; cook and stir until the mushrooms are tender, 6-8 minutes. Cool slightly.
4. Place the tart pans on separate baking sheets. Divide the onion and mushrooms between crusts; top with the salmon and cheese. In a bowl, whisk 4 eggs, 2 tsp. capers and ¼ tsp. each salt and pepper; if desired, stir in 1 tsp. dill. Pour over 1 of the tarts. Repeat with remaining ingredients for second tart.
5. Bake until a knife inserted in the center comes out clean, 15-20 minutes. Let stand 5 minutes before cutting.: Tarts may also be prepared in two 9-in. springform pans or pie plates; bake as directed.

1 slice: 239 cal., 15g fat (6g sat. fat), 136mg chol., 382mg sod., 18g carb. (2g sugars, 1g fiber), 8g pro.

OLD-FASHIONED FRUIT BAKE

Pop this old-world dish in the oven and mouths will water in anticipation— the cinnamony aroma is tantalizing! The fruit comes out tender and slightly tart, while the pecan halves add a delightful crunch.
—Bonnie Baumgardner, Sylva, NC

- -

Prep: 15 min. • **Bake:** 45 min.
Makes: 12 servings

1   **medium apple, peeled
    and thinly sliced**
1   **tsp. lemon juice**
1   **can (20 oz.) pineapple chunks**
1   **can (29 oz.) peach halves, drained**
1   **can (29 oz.) pear halves, drained**
1   **jar (6 to 8 oz.) maraschino cherries**
½   **cup pecan halves**
⅓   **cup packed brown sugar**
1   **Tbsp. butter, melted**
1   **tsp. ground cinnamon**

1. Preheat oven to 325°. Toss apple slices with lemon juice. Arrange in a greased 2½-qt. baking dish. Drain the pineapple, reserving ¼ cup juice. Combine pineapple, peaches and pears; spoon over apples. Top with cherries and pecans; set aside.
2. In a small saucepan, combine the brown sugar, butter, cinnamon and the reserved pineapple juice. Cook and stir over low heat until sugar is completely dissolved and butter is melted. Pour over fruit. Bake, uncovered, until the apples are tender, about 45 minutes. Serve warm.
¾ cup: 220 cal., 4g fat (1g sat. fat), 3mg chol., 21mg sod., 49g carb. (44g sugars, 3g fiber), 1g pro.

MAPLE BACON FRENCH TOAST BAKE

Our family loves Sunday brunch. Each season I try to bring a little different flavor to the table. Here's the French toast bake for the fall. Whole or 2% milk works best, but it's also wonderful with almond milk.
—Peggie Brott, Colorado Springs, CO

Prep: 35 min. + chilling
Bake: 50 min. + standing
Makes: 12 servings

- 8   cups cubed bread
- 8   large eggs
- 2   cups 2% milk
- ½   cup packed brown sugar
- ⅓   cup maple syrup
- ½   tsp. ground cinnamon
- 1   lb. bacon strips, cooked and crumbled

1. Place bread in a greased 13x9-in. baking dish. In a large bowl, whisk the eggs, milk, brown sugar, syrup and cinnamon. Pour over bread. Sprinkle with the cooked bacon. Refrigerate, covered, 4 hours or overnight.
2. Remove casserole from refrigerator for 30 minutes before baking. Preheat oven to 350°. Bake, uncovered, until a knife inserted in center comes out clean, 50-60 minutes. Let stand 5-10 minutes before serving.
1 piece: 256 cal., 10g fat (3g sat. fat), 141mg chol., 426mg sod., 29g carb. (18g sugars, 1g fiber), 12g pro.

VEGGIE SAUSAGE STRATA

As a retired home economics teacher, I've made a lot of recipes. This is a favorite.
—Dorothy Erickson, Blue Eye, MO

Prep: 15 min. + chilling
Bake: 1 hour 20 min. • **Makes:** 12 servings

- 2   lbs. bulk Italian sausage
- 2   medium green peppers, coarsely chopped
- 1   medium onion, chopped
- 8   large eggs
- 2   cups whole milk
- 2   tsp. salt
- 2   tsp. white pepper
- 2   tsp. ground mustard
- 12 slices bread, cut into ½-in. pieces
- 1   pkg. (10 oz.) frozen chopped spinach, thawed and squeezed dry
- 2   cups shredded Swiss cheese
- 2   cups shredded cheddar cheese
- 1   medium zucchini, cut into ¼-in. slices

1. In a large skillet, cook the sausage, green peppers and onion over medium heat until meat is no longer pink; drain. Meanwhile, in a large bowl, whisk the eggs, milk, salt, pepper and mustard. Stir in the sausage mixture, bread, chopped spinach, cheeses and sliced zucchini.
2. Transfer mixture to a greased 13x9-in. baking dish. Cover dish and refrigerate overnight.
3. Remove from the refrigerator 30 minutes before baking. Cover and bake at 350° for 40 minutes. Uncover; bake 40-45 minutes longer or until a knife inserted in the center comes out clean.
1 piece: 501 cal., 34g fat (14g sat. fat), 204mg chol., 1236 sod., 22 carb. (5g sugars, 2g fiber), 27g pro.

GOLDEN BUTTERMILK WAFFLES

You'll hear nothing but cheering from family and friends when you stack up these golden waffles for breakfast! My gang regularly requests this morning mainstay.
—Kim Branges, Grand Canyon, AZ

Takes: 25 min. • **Makes:** 16 waffffles

1¾ cups all-purpose flour
1 tsp. baking powder
1 tsp. baking soda
½ tsp. salt
2 large eggs, room temperature
2 cups buttermilk
⅓ cup canola oil
Optional: Sliced fresh strawberries, strawberry syrup and whipped cream

1. In a large bowl, combine the flour, baking powder, baking soda and salt. In another bowl, beat the eggs; add buttermilk and oil. Stir into dry ingredients just until combined.
2. Bake in a preheated waffle iron according to manufacturer's directions until golden brown. If desired, serve with sliced fresh strawberries, syrup and whipped cream.
2 waffles: 223 cal., 11g fat (2g sat. fat), 56mg chol., 435mg sod., 24g carb. (4g sugars, 1g fiber), 6g pro.

HAM & CHEESE EGG BAKE

This make-ahead egg casserole is just the thing when entertaining in the morning. It's loaded with ham, cheese and mushrooms.
—Susan Miller, North Andover, MA

Prep: 25 min. + chilling • **Bake:** 35 min.
Makes: 10 servings

- 1½ cups shredded cheddar cheese
- 1½ cups shredded part-skim mozzarella cheese
- 2 Tbsp. butter
- ½ lb. sliced fresh mushrooms
- 1 medium sweet red pepper, chopped
- 6 green onions, chopped
- 1¾ cups cubed fully cooked ham
- 8 large eggs
- 1¾ cups 2% milk
- ¼ cup all-purpose flour
- ¼ tsp. salt
- ¼ tsp. pepper

1. Sprinkle cheeses into a greased 13x9-in. baking dish. In a large skillet, heat butter over medium-high heat; saute mushrooms, red pepper and green onions until tender. Stir in ham; spoon over cheese.
2. In a large bowl, whisk together eggs, milk, flour, salt and pepper; pour over ham mixture. Refrigerate, covered, overnight.
3. Preheat oven to 350°. Remove casserole from refrigerator while oven heats. Bake, uncovered, until a knife inserted in the center comes out clean, 35-45 minutes. Let stand 5 minutes before serving.
1 serving: 272 cal., 17g fat (9g sat. fat), 201mg chol., 678mg sod., 8g carb. (4g sugars, 1g fiber), 21g pro.

BRUNCH PUFF WITH SAUSAGE GRAVY

When company stays overnight, I make this puff with sausage gravy as a hearty breakfast treat. It's meaty, cheesy and delightful with a fresh fruit salad.
—Danielle Cochran, Grayling, MI

- -

Prep: 25 min. • **Bake:** 20 min.
Makes: 9 servings

7	**large eggs, divided use**
¼	**cup 2% milk**
¼	**tsp. salt**
¼	**tsp. plus ⅛ tsp. pepper, divided**
1	**Tbsp. butter**
1	**Tbsp. water**
1	**pkg. (17.3 oz.) frozen puff pastry, thawed**
8	**oz. sliced deli ham (¼ in. thick)**
1	**cup shredded cheddar cheese**

SAUSAGE GRAVY

¾	**lb. bulk pork sausage**
1	**envelope country gravy mix**

1. Preheat oven to 400°. In a small bowl, whisk 6 eggs, milk, salt and ¼ tsp. pepper until blended.

2. In a large nonstick skillet, heat butter over medium heat. Pour in egg mixture; cook and stir just until eggs are thickened and no liquid egg remains. Remove from heat.

3. In a small bowl, whisk remaining egg with water. On a lightly floured surface, unfold one sheet of puff pastry and roll to a 10-in. square. Transfer to a parchment-lined baking sheet. Arrange ham over pastry to within 1 in. of edges; top with scrambled eggs. Sprinkle with cheese.

4. Brush beaten egg mixture over edges of pastry. Roll remaining puff pastry to a 10-in. square; place over filling. Press edges with a fork to seal; cut slits in top. Brush top with additional egg mixture; sprinkle with the remaining pepper. Bake until golden brown, 20-25 minutes.

5. Meanwhile, in a large skillet, cook the sausage over medium heat 6-8 minutes or until no longer pink, breaking into crumbles. Remove with a slotted spoon; drain on paper towels. Discard drippings, wiping skillet clean if necessary.

6. In same pan, prepare gravy mix according to package directions. Stir in sausage. Serve with pastry.

1 piece with ¼ cup gravy: 546 cal., 35g fat (10g sat. fat), 193mg chol., 1138mg sod., 36g carb. (1g sugars, 4g fiber), 21g pro.

EGGS BENEDICT WITH HOMEMADE HOLLANDAISE

Here's my quick and easy take on an all-time brunch classic. Don't let the hollandaise sauce intimidate you. It's so much easier to make than you think!
—Barbara Pletzke, Herndon, VA

- -

Takes: 30 min. • **Makes:** 8 servings

- 4 **large egg yolks**
- 2 **Tbsp. water**
- 2 **Tbsp. lemon juice**
- ¾ **cup butter, melted**
  Dash white pepper

ASSEMBLY

- 8 **large eggs**
- 4 **English muffins, split and toasted**
- 8 **slices Canadian bacon, warmed**
  Paprika

1. For hollandaise sauce, in top of a double boiler or a metal bowl over simmering water, whisk egg yolks, water and lemon juice until blended; cook until mixture is just thick enough to coat a metal spoon and temperature reaches 160°, whisking constantly. Remove from heat. Very slowly drizzle in warm melted butter, whisking constantly. Whisk in pepper. Transfer to a small bowl if necessary. Place bowl in a larger bowl of warm water. Keep warm, stirring occasionally, until ready to serve, up to 30 minutes.

2. Place 2-3 in. of water in a large saucepan or skillet with high sides. Bring to a boil; adjust heat to maintain a gentle simmer. Break 1 egg into a small bowl; holding bowl close to surface of water, slip egg into water. Repeat with 3 more eggs.

3. Cook, uncovered, 2-4 minutes or until whites are completely set and yolks begin to thicken but are not hard. Using a slotted spoon, lift eggs out of water. Repeat with remaining 4 eggs.

4. Top each muffin half with a slice of bacon, a poached egg and 2 Tbsp. sauce; sprinkle with paprika. Serve immediately.

1 serving: 345 cal., 26g fat (14g sat. fat), 331mg chol., 522mg sod., 15g carb. (1g sugars, 1g fiber), 13g pro.

RASPBERRY BRAID

We like using blackberries as well as raspberries in this simple pastry.
—Tressa Nicholls, Sandy, OR

- -

Prep: 20 min. • **Bake:** 15 min.
Makes: 12 servings

    2   cups biscuit/baking mix
    3   oz. cream cheese, cubed
    ¼   cup cold butter, cubed
    ⅓   cup 2% milk
  1¼   cups fresh raspberries
    3   Tbsp. sugar
    ¼   cup vanilla frosting

1. Preheat oven to 425°. Place biscuit mix in a large bowl. Cut in cream cheese and butter until mixture resembles coarse crumbs. Stir in milk just until moistened. Turn onto a lightly floured surface; knead gently 8-10 times.
2. On a greased baking sheet, roll dough into an 18x12-in. rectangle. Spoon the raspberries down center third of dough; sprinkle with sugar.
3. On each long side, cut 1-in.-wide strips about 2½ in. into center. Starting at one end, fold alternating strips at an angle across raspberries; seal ends.
4. Bake until golden brown, 15-20 minutes. Remove to a wire rack to cool slightly. In a microwave-safe dish, microwave frosting on high until it reaches desired consistency, 5-10 seconds; drizzle over pastry.
1 slice: 185 cal., 10g fat (5g sat. fat), 19mg chol., 319mg sod., 22g carb. (8g sugars, 1g fiber), 2g pro.

EGGNOG FRENCH TOAST

This recipe is a longtime family favorite, not only at Christmas but any time of the year. We especially like to prepare it when we go camping.
—Robert Northrup, Las Cruces, NM

Prep: 10 min. • **Cook:** 30 min.
Makes: 8 servings

- 8 large eggs
- 2 cups eggnog
- ¼ cup sugar
- ½ tsp. vanilla or rum extract
- 24 slices English muffin bread
  Confectioners' sugar, optional
  Maple syrup

In a bowl, beat eggs, eggnog, sugar and extract; soak bread for 2 minutes per side. Cook on a greased hot griddle until golden brown on both sides and cooked through. Dust with confectioners' sugar if desired. Serve with syrup.
3 slices: 541 cal., 10g fat (4g sat. fat), 223mg chol., 832mg sod., 87g carb. (18g sugars, 6g fiber), 24g pro.

> "I served this dish to my grandkids, and now they want it all the time. We love it!"
> —BONITO, TASTEOFHOME.COM

AMISH APPLE SCRAPPLE

Just the aroma of this cooking at breakfast takes me back to my days growing up in Pennsylvania. We enjoyed this recipe at home and at church breakfasts.
—Marion Lowery, Medford, OR

Prep: 1 hour 20 min. + chilling
Cook: 10 min. • **Makes:** 8 servings

- ¾ lb. bulk pork sausage
- ½ cup finely chopped onion
- 4 Tbsp. butter, divided
- ½ cup diced apple, unpeeled
- ¾ tsp. dried thyme
- ½ tsp. ground sage
- ¼ tsp. pepper
- 3 cups water, divided
- ¾ cup cornmeal
- 1 tsp. salt
- 2 Tbsp. all-purpose flour
  Maple syrup

1. In a large skillet, cook sausage and onion over medium-high heat until sausage is no longer pink and onion is tender. Remove from skillet; set aside.
2. Discard all but 2 Tbsp. drippings. Add 2 Tbsp. butter, apple, thyme, sage and pepper to drippings; cook over low heat for 5 minutes or until apple is tender. Remove from heat; stir in sausage mixture. Set aside.
3. In a large heavy saucepan, bring 2 cups water to a boil. Combine the cornmeal, salt and remaining water; slowly pour into boiling water, stirring constantly. Return to a boil. Reduce heat; simmer, covered, for 1 hour, stirring occasionally. Stir in the sausage mixture. Pour into a greased 8x4-in. loaf pan. Refrigerate, covered, for 8 hours or overnight.
4. Slice ½ in. thick. Sprinkle flour over both sides of each slice. In a large skillet, heat remaining butter over medium heat. Add slices; cook until both sides are browned. Serve with syrup.
1 piece: 251 cal., 18g fat (7g sat. fat), 44mg chol., 667mg sod., 16g carb. (1g sugars, 1g fiber), 7g pro.

CALICO SCRAMBLED EGGS

When you're short on time and scrambling to get a meal on the table, this classic breakfast dish is "eggs-actly" what you need. There's a short ingredient list, and cooking is kept to a minimum. Plus, with green pepper and tomato, it's colorful.
—*Taste of Home* Test Kitchen

- -

Takes: 15 min. • **Makes:** 4 servings

- 8 large eggs
- ¼ cup 2% milk
- ⅛ to ¼ tsp. dill weed
- ⅛ to ¼ tsp. salt
- ⅛ to ¼ tsp. pepper
- 1 Tbsp. butter
- ½ cup chopped green pepper
- ¼ cup chopped onion
- ½ cup chopped fresh tomato

1. In a bowl, whisk the first 5 ingredients until blended. In a 12-in. nonstick skillet, heat butter over medium-high heat. Add green pepper and onion; cook and stir until tender. Remove from pan.

2. In same pan, pour in egg mixture; cook and stir over medium heat until eggs begin to thicken. Add tomato and pepper mixture; cook until heated through and no liquid egg remains, stirring gently.

1 cup: 188 cal., 13g fat (5g sat. fat), 381mg chol., 248mg sod., 4g carb. (3g sugars, 1g fiber), 14g pro. **Diabetic exchanges:** 2 medium-fat meat, ½ fat.

CHEESE GRITS & SAUSAGE BREAKFAST CASSEROLE

I can't resist this breakfast casserole. It brings all my favorites into one: creamy grits, tangy cheese, rich eggs and flavorful sausage. It's the perfect alternative to traditional breakfast casseroles.
—Mandy Rivers, Lexington, SC

- -

Prep: 30 min. • **Bake:** 40 min. + standing
Makes: 12 servings

- 2 lbs. bulk Italian sausage
- 2 cups water
- 2 cups chicken broth
- ½ tsp. salt
- 1¼ cups quick-cooking grits
- 1 lb. sharp cheddar cheese, shredded
- 1 cup 2% milk
- 1½ tsp. garlic powder
- 1 tsp. rubbed sage
- 6 large eggs, beaten
   Paprika, optional

1. In a large skillet, cook sausage over medium heat until no longer pink; drain.

2. In a large saucepan, bring the water, broth and salt to a boil. Slowly stir in grits. Reduce heat; cook and stir for 5-7 minutes or until thickened. Remove from the heat. Add the cheese, milk, garlic powder and sage, stirring until cheese is melted. Stir in sausage and eggs. Transfer to a greased 13x9-in. baking dish; sprinkle with paprika if desired.

3. Bake, uncovered, at 350° until a knife inserted in the center comes out clean, 40-45 minutes. Let casserole stand for about 10 minutes before serving.

1 piece: 496 cal., 35g fat (17g sat. fat), 201mg chol., 1173mg sod., 17g carb. (4g sugars, 1g fiber), 28g pro.

APPLE-SAGE SAUSAGE PATTIES

Apple and sausage naturally go together. Add sage, and you've got a standout patty. They're freezer-friendly, so I make them ahead and grab when needed.
—Scarlett Elrod, Newnan, GA

Prep: 35 min. + chilling • **Cook:** 10 min./batch
Makes: 16 patties

  1   large apple
  1   large egg, lightly beaten
  ½   cup chopped fresh parsley
  3   to 4 Tbsp. minced fresh sage
  2   garlic cloves, minced
1¼   tsp. salt
  ½   tsp. pepper
  ½   tsp. crushed red pepper flakes
1¼   lbs. lean ground turkey
  6   tsp. olive oil, divided

1. Peel and coarsely shred apple; place apple in a colander over a plate. Let stand 15 minutes. Squeeze and blot dry with paper towels.
2. In a large bowl, combine egg, parsley, sage, garlic, seasonings and apple. Add turkey; mix lightly but thoroughly. Shape into sixteen 2-in. patties. Place the patties on waxed paper-lined baking sheets. Refrigerate, covered, 8 hours or overnight.
3. In a large nonstick skillet, heat 2 tsp. oil over medium heat. In batches, cook patties 3-4 minutes on each side or until golden brown and a thermometer reads 165°, adding more oil as needed.
Freeze option: Place uncooked patties on waxed paper-lined baking sheets; wrap and freeze until firm. Remove from pans and transfer to a freezer container; return to freezer. To use, cook the frozen patties as directed, increasing time to 4-5 minutes on each side.
1 patty: 79 cal., 5g fat (1g sat. fat), 36mg chol., 211mg sod., 2g carb. (1g sugars, 0 fiber), 8g pro. **Diabetic exchanges:** 1 lean meat, ½ fat.

GRAN'S GRANOLA PARFAITS

When my mother-in-law has us over for brunch, I especially enjoy her yogurt parfaits. They are refreshing, light and wholesome. I made a few changes to her recipe and came up with this sweet, crunchy and nutty variation. Yum!
—Angela Keller, Newburgh, IN

Prep: 15 min. • **Bake:** 30 min. + cooling
Makes: 16 servings

  2   cups old-fashioned oats
  1   cup Wheaties
  1   cup whole almonds
  1   cup pecan halves
  1   cup sweetened shredded coconut
4½   tsp. toasted wheat germ
  1   Tbsp. sesame seeds, toasted
  1   tsp. ground cinnamon
  ¼   cup butter, melted
  2   Tbsp. maple syrup
  2   Tbsp. honey
  1   can (20 oz.) pineapple tidbits, drained
  1   can (15 oz.) mandarin oranges, drained
  1   cup halved green grapes
  2   to 3 medium firm bananas, sliced
  1   cup sliced fresh strawberries
  4   cups vanilla yogurt

1. In a bowl, combine the first 8 ingredients. Combine butter, syrup and honey; drizzle over oat mixture and stir until well coated. Pour into a greased 13x9-in. baking pan. Bake, uncovered, at 350° for 30 minutes, stirring every 10 minutes. Cool on a wire rack; crumble granola into pieces.
2. Combine the fruits in a large bowl. For each parfait, layer 2 Tbsp. yogurt, 2 Tbsp. granola and 3 rounded Tbsp. fruit in a parfait glass or dessert bowl. Repeat layers. Sprinkle with remaining granola. Serve the parfaits immediately.
1 parfait: 327 cal., 17g fat (6g sat. fat), 13mg chol., 104mg sod., 39g carb. (26g sugars, 4g fiber), 8g pro.

BLUEBERRY-ORANGE BLINTZES

Old-world blintzes are great for brunch time because I can make the crepes ahead. They taste so indulgent that guests don't know they're lower in fat and calories.
—Mary Johnson, Coloma, WI

Prep: 15 min. + chilling • **Bake:** 25 min.
Makes: 6 servings

1	**large egg**
1	**cup fat-free milk**
¾	**cup all-purpose flour**
1	**carton (15 oz.) part-skim ricotta cheese**
6	**Tbsp. orange marmalade, divided**
1	**Tbsp. sugar**
⅛	**tsp. ground cinnamon**
2	**cups fresh blueberries or raspberries, divided**
⅔	**cup reduced-fat sour cream**

1. In a large bowl, whisk egg, milk and flour until blended. Refrigerate, covered, 1 hour.

2. Preheat oven to 350°. Place a 6-in. skillet coated with cooking spray over medium heat. Stir batter; fill a ¼-cup measure halfway with batter and pour into center of pan. Quickly lift and tilt pan to coat bottom evenly. Cook until top appears dry; turn crepe over and cook 15-20 seconds longer or until bottom is cooked. Remove to a wire rack. Repeat with remaining batter.

3. In a small bowl, mix ricotta cheese, 2 Tbsp. marmalade, sugar and cinnamon. Spoon about 2 Tbsp. mixture onto each crepe; top with about 1 Tbsp. blueberries. Fold opposite sides of crepes over filling, forming a rectangular bundle.

4. Place blintzes on a 15x10x1-in. baking pan coated with cooking spray, seam side down. Bake, uncovered, 10-15 minutes or until heated through. Serve with sour cream and the remaining marmalade and blueberries.

Freeze option: Cool crepes completely. Freeze cooled crepes between layers of waxed paper in a freezer container. To use, thaw overnight in refrigerator overnight. Proceed as directed.

2 blintzes with toppings: 301 cal., 9g fat (5g sat. fat), 63mg chol., 129mg sod., 42g carb. (23g sugars, 2g fiber), 14g pro.
Diabetic exchanges: 2 starch, 2 lean meat, ½ fruit.

GOLDEN OAT PANCAKES

My husband's face lights up when I make these country-style flapjacks. Serve them for a weekend breakfast or brunch, or freeze and reheat them later.
—Raymonde Bourgeois, Swastika, ON

Takes: 25 min. • **Makes:** 10 pancakes

- 1 **cup old-fashioned oats**
- 1⅓ **cups 2% milk**
- ¾ **cup all-purpose flour**
- 4 **tsp. baking powder**
- 4 **tsp. brown sugar**
- ¼ **tsp. salt**
- 2 **large eggs, lightly beaten**
- 3 **Tbsp. canola oil**

1. In a small bowl, mix the oats and milk; let stand 5 minutes. In a large bowl, whisk flour, baking powder, brown sugar and salt.
2. Stir eggs and oil into oat mixture. Add to flour mixture; stir just until moistened.
3. Lightly grease a griddle; heat over medium heat. Pour batter by ¼ cupfuls onto griddle. Cook until bubbles on top begin to pop and bottoms are golden brown. Turn; cook until second side is golden brown.

Freeze option: Freeze cooled pancakes between layers of waxed paper in a freezer container. To use, place pancakes on an ungreased baking sheet, cover with foil and reheat in a preheated 375° oven for 5-10 minutes. Or, place 2 pancakes on a microwave-safe plate and microwave for 1-1¼ minutes or until heated through.

2 pancakes: 270 cal., 13g fat (2g sat. fat), 80mg chol., 498mg sod., 30g carb. (7g sugars, 2g fiber), 8g pro.

MAPLE BACON WALNUT COFFEE CAKE

Sleepyheads will roll out of bed when they smell this sweet and savory coffee cake baking. Nuts and bacon in the crumbly topping blend perfectly with maple syrup, nutmeg and cinnamon.
—Angela Spengler, Niceville, FL

Prep: 25 min. • **Bake:** 35 min. + cooling
Makes: 24 servings

2½ cups all-purpose flour
1 cup packed brown sugar
½ tsp. salt
⅓ cup cold butter
2 tsp. baking powder
½ tsp. baking soda
½ tsp. ground cinnamon
¼ tsp. ground nutmeg
2 large eggs, room temperature
1½ cups buttermilk
½ cup maple syrup
⅓ cup unsweetened applesauce
5 bacon strips, cooked and crumbled
½ cup chopped walnuts

1. In a large bowl, combine the flour, brown sugar and salt. Cut in butter until crumbly. Set aside ½ cup for topping. Combine the baking powder, baking soda, cinnamon and nutmeg; stir into remaining flour mixture.
2. In a small bowl, whisk the eggs, buttermilk, syrup and applesauce until well blended. Gradually stir into flour mixture until combined.
3. Spread into a 13x9-in. baking pan coated with cooking spray. Sprinkle with reserved topping, then bacon and walnuts. Bake at 350° for 35-40 minutes or until a toothpick inserted in the center comes out clean. Cool on a wire rack.

1 piece: 160 cal., 5g fat (2g sat. fat), 27mg chol., 183mg sod., 25g carb. (14g sugars, 1g fiber), 3g pro. **Diabetic exchanges:** 1½ starch, 1 fat.

HOMEMADE BISCUITS & MAPLE SAUSAGE GRAVY

I remember digging into these flaky, gravy-smothered biscuits on special occasions when I was a child. What a satisfying way to start the day!
—Jenn Tidwell, Fair Oaks, CA

- -

Prep: 30 min. • **Bake:** 15 min.
Makes: 8 servings

- 2 cups all-purpose flour
- 3 tsp. baking powder
- 1 Tbsp. sugar
- 1 tsp. salt
- ¼ tsp. pepper, optional
- 3 Tbsp. cold butter, cubed
- 1 Tbsp. shortening
- ¾ cup 2% milk

SAUSAGE GRAVY
- 1 lb. bulk maple pork sausage
- ¼ cup all-purpose flour
- 3 cups 2% milk
- 2 Tbsp. maple syrup
- ½ tsp. salt
- ¼ tsp. ground sage
- ¼ tsp. coarsely ground pepper

1. Preheat oven to 400°. In a large bowl, whisk flour, baking powder, sugar, salt and, if desired, pepper. Cut in the butter and shortening until mixture resembles coarse crumbs. Add milk; stir just until moistened. Turn onto a lightly floured surface; knead gently 8-10 times.

2. Pat or roll dough to 1-in. thickness; cut with a floured 2-in. biscuit cutter. Place 1 in. apart on an ungreased baking sheet. Bake until golden brown, 15-17 minutes.

3. Meanwhile, in a large skillet, cook sausage over medium heat until no longer pink, 6-8 minutes, breaking into crumbles. Stir in flour until blended; gradually stir in milk. Bring to a boil, stirring constantly; cook and stir until sauce is thickened, 4-6 minutes. Stir in remaining ingredients. Serve with warm biscuits.

1 biscuit with ½ cup gravy: 371 cal., 19g fat (8g sat. fat), 41mg chol., 915mg sod., 38g carb. (11g sugars, 1g fiber), 11g pro.

TEST KITCHEN TIP
Make the biscuits ahead of time and freeze them for easy preparation in the morning. Simply thaw the biscuits in the refrigerator overnight, and prepare the gravy in the morning.

CORNFLAKE-COATED BAKED FRENCH TOAST

We fed a group of hungry Air Force cadets breakfast for dinner with this baked French toast, along with eggs, sausage, bacon and fresh fruit.
—Lois Enger, Colorado Springs, CO

- -

Takes: 25 min.
Makes: 6 servings (1 cup syrup)

- 2 large eggs
- ½ cup 2% milk
- ½ tsp. salt
- ½ tsp. vanilla extract
- 1 cup cornflake crumbs
- 6 slices Texas toast
- ¼ cup butter, melted

CINNAMON SYRUP

- ⅔ cup sugar
- ⅓ cup light corn syrup
- 2 Tbsp. water
- ½ tsp. ground cinnamon
- ⅓ cup evaporated milk or 2% milk
- 1½ tsp. butter
- ¼ tsp. almond extract

1. Preheat oven to 450°. In a shallow bowl, whisk the eggs, milk, salt and vanilla until blended. Place cornflake crumbs in another shallow bowl. Dip both sides of bread in egg mixture, then in cornflake crumbs, patting to help coating adhere.
2. Place in a greased 15x10x1-in. baking pan. Drizzle with melted butter. Bake until golden brown, 10-12 minutes.
3. For syrup, in a small saucepan, combine sugar, corn syrup, water and cinnamon; bring to a boil. Cook and stir 2 minutes. Remove from heat. Stir in milk, butter and extract. Serve with French toast.
1 slice with 3 Tbsp. syrup: 419 cal., 13g fat (7g sat. fat), 91mg chol., 619mg sod., 70g carb. (43g sugars, 1g fiber), 8g pro.

CORNED BEEF HASH & EGGS

Sunday breakfasts have always been special in our house. It's fun to get in the kitchen and cook with the little ones. No matter how many new recipes we try, the kids always rate this No. 1!
—Rick Skildum, Maple Grove, MN

- -

Prep: 15 min. • **Bake:** 20 min.
Makes: 8 servings

- 1 pkg. (32 oz.) frozen cubed hash browns
- 1½ cups chopped onion
- ½ cup canola oil
- 4 to 5 cups chopped cooked corned beef
- ½ tsp. salt
- 8 large eggs
  Salt and pepper to taste
- 2 Tbsp. minced fresh parsley

1. In a large ovenproof skillet, cook hash browns and onion in oil until potatoes are browned and onion is tender. Remove from the heat; stir in corned beef and salt.
2. Make 8 wells in the hash browns. Break one egg into each well. Sprinkle with salt and pepper. Cover and bake at 325° for 20-25 minutes or until eggs reach desired doneness. Garnish with parsley.
1 serving: 442 cal., 30g fat (6g sat. fat), 242mg chol., 895mg sod., 24g carb. (3g sugars, 2g fiber), 20g pro.

TURKEY SWISS QUICHE

If you're looking to use up leftover turkey, here's your answer. My family looks forward to having this the day after Thanksgiving.
—Lois Forehand, Little River-Academy, TX

- -

Prep: 25 min.
Bake: 30 min. + standing
Makes: 6 servings

- 1 pastry shell (9 in.), unbaked
- 1½ cups finely chopped cooked turkey
- 4 large eggs
- ¾ cup half-and-half cream
- 2 cups shredded Swiss cheese
- 4 green onions, finely chopped
- 2 Tbsp. diced pimientos
- 1 tsp. dried oregano
- 1 tsp. dried parsley flakes
  Dash salt and pepper
- 3 slices (¾ oz. each) Swiss cheese, cut into thin strips

1. Preheat oven to 450°. Line unpricked crust with a double thickness of heavy-duty foil. Bake 8 minutes. Remove foil; bake until golden brown, 5-7 minutes longer. Reduce heat to 375°.
2. Sprinkle turkey into pastry shell. In a large bowl, whisk eggs and cream. Stir in the shredded Swiss cheese, onions, pimientos, oregano, parsley, salt and pepper. Pour into the crust.
3. Bake 20 minutes. Arrange Swiss cheese strips in a lattice pattern over quiche. Bake until a knife inserted in the center comes out clean, 10-15 minutes longer. Let stand 10 minutes before cutting.
1 slice: 489 cal., 31g fat (16g sat. fat), 234mg chol., 334mg sod., 21g carb. (4g sugars, 0 fiber), 30g pro.

PECAN WAFFLES

I've tried for years to duplicate a delicious waffle I sampled at a restaurant here in the South. This crisp and nutty version is what I came up with.
—Susan Elise Jansen, Smyrna, GA

- -

Takes: 30 min. • **Makes:** 10 waffles (4½ in.)

- 1¾ cups all-purpose flour
- 1 Tbsp. baking powder
- ½ tsp. salt
- 2 large eggs, room temperature, separated
- 1¾ cups milk
- ½ cup canola oil
- 1 cup chopped pecans
  Maple syrup

1. In a bowl, combine flour, baking powder and salt. Combine egg yolks, milk and oil; stir into dry ingredients. Beat egg whites until stiff; fold into batter.
2. Sprinkle hot waffle iron with 2 Tbsp. chopped pecans. Pour ¼ to ⅓ cup of batter over the pecans and bake according to the manufacturer's directions until golden brown. Repeat with remaining pecans and batter. Serve with syrup.
2 waffles: 299 cal., 22g fat (3g sat. fat), 48mg chol., 272mg sod., 20g carb. (3g sugars, 2g fiber), 6g pro.

CANADIAN BACON WITH APPLES

I'd rather spend time with family than in the kitchen, so I rely on easy-to-fix recipes like this. No one can resist Canadian bacon and apples coated with a brown sugar glaze.
—Paula Marchesi, Lenhartsville, PA

- -

Takes: 20 min. • **Makes:** 6 servings

- ½ cup packed brown sugar
- 1 Tbsp. lemon juice
- ⅛ tsp. pepper
- 1 large red apple, unpeeled
- 1 large green apple, unpeeled
- 1 lb. sliced Canadian bacon

1. In a large cast-iron or other heavy skillet, mix brown sugar, lemon juice and pepper. Cook and stir over medium heat until sugar is dissolved. Cut each apple into 16 wedges; add to brown sugar mixture. Cook over medium heat until the apples are tender, 5-7 minutes, stirring occasionally. Remove apples to a platter with a slotted spoon; keep warm.
2. Add bacon to skillet; cook over medium heat, turning once, until heated through, about 3 minutes. Transfer to platter. Pour remaining brown sugar mixture over apples and bacon.

1 serving: 199 cal., 4g fat (1g sat. fat), 28mg chol., 744mg sod., 30g carb. (27g sugars, 2g fiber), 12g pro.

EGG SALAD ENGLISH MUFFINS

These toasty breakfast muffins help you get a jump-start on mornings. I make the egg salad ahead of time, then assemble them as needed. They're also good with bacon or ham piled on top.
—Deborah Flora, Sawyer, KS

- -

Takes: 15 min. • **Makes:** 2 servings

- 3 hard-boiled large eggs, chopped
- ¼ cup mayonnaise
- ¼ tsp. prepared mustard
- 2 English muffins, split and toasted
- 4 slices Canadian bacon
- ¼ cup shredded cheddar cheese

1. In a small bowl, combine the eggs, mayonnaise and mustard. Place English muffins cut side up on an ungreased baking sheet. Top each with a slice of Canadian bacon, ¼ cup egg mixture and the shredded cheddar cheese.
2. Bake at 350° for 6-8 minutes or until cheese is melted.

1 serving: 475 cal., 26g fat (7g sat. fat), 365mg chol., 1410mg sod., 31g carb. (5g sugars, 2g fiber), 29g pro.

ORANGE MARMALADE BREAKFAST BAKE

When I host brunch, I make something that can be prepared a day ahead so I can spend time making other recipes. Grapefruit or a mixed-fruit marmalade will work just as well as the orange.
—Judy Wilson, Sun City West, AZ

Prep: 25 min. + chilling • **Bake:** 40 min.
Makes: 12 servings (1½ cups syrup)

- 3 Tbsp. butter, softened
- 24 slices French bread (½ in. thick)
- 1 jar (12 oz.) orange marmalade
- 6 large eggs
- 2¾ cups 2% milk
- ⅓ cup sugar
- 1 tsp. vanilla extract
- ¼ tsp. ground nutmeg
- ⅓ cup finely chopped walnuts

SYRUP
- 1¼ cups maple syrup
- ⅓ cup orange juice
- 2 tsp. grated orange zest

1. Spread the butter over one side of each bread slice. Arrange half of the bread slices overlapping in a greased 3-qt. or 13x9-in. baking dish, buttered side down. Spread marmalade over bread slices; top with remaining bread slices, buttered side up.
2. In a large bowl, whisk eggs, milk, sugar, vanilla and nutmeg until blended; pour over bread. Refrigerate, covered, several hours or overnight.
3. Preheat oven to 350°. Remove casserole from refrigerator while oven heats. Sprinkle with walnuts. Bake, uncovered, until golden brown and a knife inserted in the center comes out clean, 40-50 minutes.
4. Let stand 5-10 minutes before serving. In a small saucepan, combine maple syrup, orange juice and zest; heat through. Serve with casserole.
1 piece with 2 Tbsp. syrup: 356 cal., 9g fat (4g sat. fat), 105mg chol., 244mg sod., 63g carb. (49g sugars, 1g fiber), 8g pro.

WARM GRAPEFRUIT WITH GINGER SUGAR

I greet my guests sweetly with broiled grapefruit—a specialty at my Lansing, New York, bed-and-breakfast. Try it as an appetizer for breakfast or brunch, or as a light, anytime dessert.
—Stephanie Levy, Lansing, NY

Takes: 15 min. • **Makes:** 2 servings

- 1 large red grapefruit
- 2 to 3 tsp. chopped crystallized ginger
- 2 tsp. sugar

1. Preheat broiler. Cut grapefruit crosswise in half. With a small knife, cut around the membrane in the center of each half and discard. Cut around each section to loosen fruit. Place on a baking sheet, cut side up.
2. Mix ginger and sugar; sprinkle over fruit. Broil 4 in. from heat until sugar is melted, about 4 minutes.
½ grapefruit: 85 cal., 0 fat (0 sat. fat), 0 chol., 3mg sod., 22g carb. (17g sugars, 2g fiber), 1g pro. **Diabetic exchanges:** 1 fruit, ½ starch.

DELICIOUS ALMOND BRAIDS

Similar to an almond crescent, this coffee cake is light and flaky, with a rich almond center. It's so versatile you can serve it for dessert, breakfast or brunch. Its from-scratch flavor tastes like it came from a grandma's kitchen, but puff pastry dough makes it easy for today's home bakers.
—Gina Idone, Staten Island, NY

Prep: 25 min. • **Bake:** 30 min. + cooling
Makes: 2 braids (6 slices each)

- 1 pkg. (7 oz.) almond paste
- ½ cup butter
- ½ cup sugar
- 1 large egg
- 2 Tbsp. all-purpose flour
- 1 pkg. (17.3 oz.) frozen puff pastry, thawed

GLAZE
- ¾ cup plus 1 Tbsp. confectioners' sugar
- 2 Tbsp. 2% milk
- ½ tsp. almond extract
- ¼ cup sliced almonds, toasted

1. Preheat oven to 375°. Place the almond paste, butter and sugar in a food processor; cover and pulse until chopped. Add egg and flour; process until smooth.

2. Place puff pastry sheets onto a greased baking sheet. Spread half of filling mixture down the center third of 1 pastry sheet. On each side, cut 8 strips about 3½ in. into the center. Starting at 1 end, fold alternating strips at an angle across filling. Pinch ends to seal. Repeat with remaining pastry and filling. Bake until pastry is golden brown, 30-35 minutes. Remove to a wire rack.

3. Combine the confectioners' sugar, milk and almond extract. Drizzle over braids; sprinkle with sliced almonds. Cut into slices to serve.

1 slice: 430 cal., 25g fat (8g sat. fat), 38mg chol., 197mg sod., 49g carb. (22g sugars, 4g fiber), 6g pro.

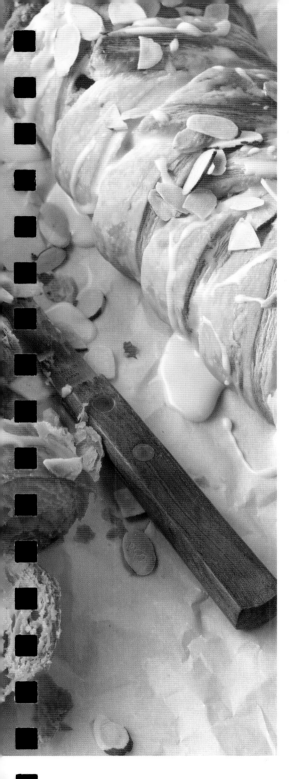

SWEDISH PUFF COFFEE CAKE

Some of my most treasured childhood memories involve waking to the heavenly scent of this almond-glazed coffee cake baking in the oven.
—Mary Shenk, DeKalb, IL

Prep: 35 min. • **Bake:** 30 min. + cooling
Makes: 12 servings

- 1   cup all-purpose flour
- ½   cup cold butter, cubed
- 2   Tbsp. ice water

TOPPING

- 1   cup water
- ½   cup butter
- 1   tsp. almond extract
- 1   cup all-purpose flour
- 3   large eggs

GLAZE

- 1   cup confectioners' sugar
- 2   Tbsp. butter, softened
- 1   Tbsp. 2% milk
- 1   tsp. almond extract
- 1   cup sweetened shredded coconut

1. Preheat oven to 375°. Place flour in a small bowl; cut in butter until crumbly. Gradually add ice water, tossing with a fork until dough holds together when pressed. On an ungreased baking sheet, press dough into a 10-in. circle.

2. For topping, in a large saucepan, bring water and butter to a rolling boil. Remove from heat; stir in extract. Add flour all at once and beat until blended. Cook over medium heat until mixture pulls away from sides of the pan and forms a ball, stirring vigorously. Remove from heat; let stand for 5 minutes.

3. Add the eggs, one at a time, beating well after each addition until smooth. Continue beating until mixture is smooth and shiny; spread over pastry.

4. Bake for 30-35 minutes or until lightly browned. Cover loosely with foil during the last 5 minutes if needed to prevent overbrowning. Remove from pan to a wire rack to cool completely.

5. For the glaze, in a small bowl, beat the confectioners' sugar, softened butter, milk and extract until smooth. Spread over top; sprinkle with coconut.

1 slice: 326 cal., 21g fat (14g sat. fat), 98mg chol., 160mg sod., 30g carb. (12g sugars, 1g fiber), 4g pro.

"Very tasty and easy to make. My guests just loved it."
—JDNJB5, TASTEOFHOME.COM

BACON-CHEESE PUFF PIE

This recipe comes from my grandma, and it's one of my family's favorites—we love the combination of bacon, tomatoes and cheese. It's great for special mornings.
—Sherry Lee, Sheridan, IN

- -

Prep: 20 min. + cooling • **Bake:** 45 min.
Makes: 6 servings

1	pastry shell (9 in.), unbaked
1	lb. sliced bacon, cooked and crumbled
1	large tomato, peeled and sliced
1	cup shredded cheddar cheese
3	large eggs, separated
¾	cup sour cream
½	cup all-purpose flour
½	tsp. salt
	Paprika

1. Line unpricked pastry shell with a double thickness of heavy-duty foil. Bake at 450° for 5 minutes. Remove foil. Bake 5 minutes longer. Cool completely.
2. Sprinkle bacon over the crust. Top with tomato and cheese. In a large bowl, beat the egg yolks, sour cream, flour and salt until smooth. In another large bowl, beat egg whites until stiff. Fold into the sour cream mixture; spread over the cheese. Sprinkle with paprika.
3. Bake at 350° until a knife inserted in the center comes out clean, about 45 minutes. Let stand 5-10 minutes before cutting.
1 piece: 518 cal., 35g fat (17g sat. fat), 176mg chol., 901mg sod., 29g carb. (4g sugars, 1g fiber), 19g pro.

BUTTERMILK PANCAKES

You just can't beat an old-fashioned pancake for a down-home hearty breakfast. Pair it with sausage and fresh fruit for a mouthwatering morning meal.
—Betty Abrey, Imperial, SK

- -

Prep: 10 min. • **Cook:** 5 min./batch
Makes: 2½ dozen

4	cups all-purpose flour
¼	cup sugar
2	tsp. baking soda
2	tsp. salt
1½	tsp. baking powder
4	large eggs, room temperature
4	cups buttermilk

1. In a large bowl, combine the flour, sugar, baking soda, salt and baking powder. In another bowl, whisk the eggs and buttermilk until blended; stir into dry ingredients just until moistened.
2. Pour batter by ¼ cupfuls onto a lightly greased hot griddle; turn when bubbles form on top. Cook until second side is golden brown.

Freeze option: Freeze cooled pancakes between layers of waxed paper in a freezer container. To use, place pancakes on an ungreased baking sheet, cover with foil and reheat in a preheated 375° oven for 6-10 minutes. Or, place a stack of 3 pancakes on a microwave-safe plate and microwave on high for 45-90 seconds or until pancakes are heated through.
3 pancakes: 270 cal., 3g fat (1g sat. fat), 89mg chol., 913mg sod., 48g carb. (11g sugars, 1g fiber), 11g pro.
Pecan Apple Pancakes: To flour mixture, stir in 1¾ tsp. ground cinnamon, ¾ tsp. ground ginger, ¾ tsp. ground mace and ¾ tsp. ground cloves. To batter, fold in 2½ cups shredded peeled apples and ¾ cup chopped pecans.
Blueberry Pancakes: Fold in 1 cup fresh or frozen blueberries.
Banana Walnut Pancakes: Fold in 2 finely chopped ripe bananas and ⅔ cups finely chopped walnuts.

UPSIDE-DOWN BANANA MONKEY BREAD

Everyone digs in to monkey bread thanks to its pull-apart shape. We add bananas and pecans in this scrumptious showpiece for family gatherings.
—Donna-Marie Ryan, Topsfield, MA

- -

Prep: 45 min. + rising • **Bake:** 25 min.
Makes: 24 servings

- 2 tsp. active dry yeast
- 1 Tbsp. plus ½ cup packed brown sugar, divided
- 1 cup warm 2% milk (110° to 115°)
- 1 cup mashed ripe bananas (about 2 large)
- 1 large egg, room temperature
- 2 Tbsp. butter, melted
- 1 tsp. salt
- 1 tsp. ground cinnamon
- 5¼ to 5¾ cups all-purpose flour
- 2 tsp. banana extract, optional

GLAZE
- ⅔ cup packed brown sugar
- ½ cup half-and-half cream
- 6 Tbsp. butter, cubed

COATING
- ¾ cup chopped pecans, toasted
- 6 Tbsp. butter, melted
- 1¼ cups sugar
- 2½ tsp. ground cinnamon
- 1 large banana, sliced

1. In a small bowl, dissolve yeast and 1 Tbsp. brown sugar in warm milk. In a large bowl, combine the bananas, egg, butter, yeast mixture, salt, cinnamon, 1½ cups flour and remaining brown sugar; if desired, add the extract. Beat on medium speed 2 minutes. Stir in enough remaining flour to form a soft dough (dough will be sticky).

2. Turn dough onto a floured surface; knead until smooth and elastic, 6-8 minutes. Place in a greased bowl, turning once to grease the top. Cover and let rise in a warm place until doubled, about 1 hour.

3. In a small saucepan, combine the glaze ingredients; bring just to a boil, stirring constantly. Reserve ¼ cup for topping. Pour remaining glaze into a greased 13x9-in. baking pan; sprinkle with pecans.

4. Pour melted butter into a shallow bowl. In another shallow bowl, mix the sugar and cinnamon. Punch down dough. Turn onto a lightly floured surface; divide and shape into 48 balls.

5. Dip dough balls in butter, roll in sugar mixture and place in prepared pan. Cover with a kitchen towel; let rise in a warm place until almost doubled, about 30 minutes. Preheat oven to 375°.

6. Bake 25-30 minutes or until golden brown. Cool in pan 5 minutes before inverting onto a serving plate. Top with sliced banana; drizzle with reserved glaze. Serve warm.

Note: To toast nuts, bake in a shallow pan in a 350° oven for 5-10 minutes or cook in a skillet over low heat until lightly browned, stirring occasionally.

2 pieces: 296 cal., 10g fat (5g sat. fat), 29mg chol., 166mg sod., 47g carb. (24g sugars, 2g fiber), 4g pro.

GRAPEFRUIT ORANGE MEDLEY

Brighten up mornings with this refreshing medley. The citrus flavors really perk up breakfast time.
—*Taste of Home* Test Kitchen

Prep: 10 min. • **Cook:** 20 min. + chilling
Makes: 5 servings

2   **Tbsp. sugar**
1   **Tbsp. cornstarch**
½   **cup lemon-lime soda**
2   **cans (11 oz. each) mandarin oranges, drained**
2   **medium grapefruit, peeled and sectioned**
1½ **cups green grapes**

1. In a small saucepan, combine sugar and cornstarch. Whisk in soda until smooth. Bring to a boil; cook and stir for 1 minute or until sauce is thickened. Cover and refrigerate until cool.
2. In a large bowl, combine the oranges, grapefruit and grapes. Add the sauce; stir to coat.
½ cup: 140 cal., 0 fat (0 sat. fat), 0 chol., 8mg sod., 36g carb. (32g sugars, 2g fiber), 1g pro.

SNACKS

There are plenty of goodies, nibbles and bites at Grandma's house! Turn here when you need a tried-and-true snack or appetizer. From casual to formal, these party favorites make any get-together a bit more special.

BACON CHEESEBURGER SLIDER BAKE

I created this dish to fill two pans because these sliders disappear fast. Just cut the recipe in half if you only want to make one batch.
—Nick Iverson, Denver, CO

- -

Prep: 20 min. • **Bake:** 25 min.
Makes: 2 dozen

- 2 pkg. (17 oz. each)
  Hawaiian sweet rolls
- 4 cups shredded cheddar
  cheese, divided
- 2 lbs. ground beef
- 1 cup chopped onion
- 1 can (14½ oz.) diced tomatoes
  with garlic and onion, drained
- 1 Tbsp. Dijon mustard
- 1 Tbsp. Worcestershire sauce
- ¾ tsp. salt
- ¾ tsp. pepper
- 24 bacon strips, cooked and crumbled

GLAZE

- 1 cup butter, cubed
- ¼ cup packed brown sugar
- 4 tsp. Worcestershire sauce
- 2 Tbsp. Dijon mustard
- 2 Tbsp. sesame seeds

1. Preheat the oven to 350°. Without separating rolls, cut each package of rolls horizontally in half; arrange bottom halves in 2 greased 13x9-in. baking pans. Sprinkle each pan of rolls with 1 cup cheese. Bake until cheese is melted, 3-5 minutes.
2. In a large skillet, cook beef and onion over medium heat until beef is no longer pink and onion is tender, breaking up beef into crumbles, 6-8 minutes; drain. Stir in the tomatoes, mustard, Worcestershire sauce, salt and pepper. Cook and stir until combined, 1-2 minutes.

3. Spoon beef mixture evenly over rolls; sprinkle with remaining cheese. Top with bacon. Replace tops. For the glaze, in a microwave-safe bowl, combine butter, brown sugar, Worcestershire sauce and mustard. Microwave, covered, on high until butter is melted, stirring occasionally. Pour over rolls; sprinkle with sesame seeds. Bake, uncovered, until golden brown and heated through, 20-25 minutes.

Freeze option: Cover and freeze unbaked sandwiches; prepare and freeze glaze. To use, partially thaw in refrigerator overnight. Remove from refrigerator 30 minutes before baking. Preheat oven to 350°. Pour glaze over buns and sprinkle with sesame seeds. Bake sandwiches as directed, increasing the baking time by 10-15 minutes or until cheese is melted and a thermometer inserted in center reads 165°.

1 slider: 380 cal., 24g fat (13g sat. fat), 86mg chol., 628mg sod., 21g carb. (9g sugars, 2g fiber), 18g pro.

TEST KITCHEN TIP
The sweet-savory flavor in these sliders has been popular for years, but if you want a more traditional burger flavor, use a package of dinner rolls in place of the Hawaiian rolls. You could also try using half of the glaze if you'd like.

EGGNOG DIP

I put together a cookbook of my grandma's recipes, and it simply had to includes this classic holiday appetizer. Serve it as a dip with fresh fruit or drizzle it over cake for dessert.
—Sharon MacDonnell, Lantzville, BC

Takes: 10 min. + chilling
Makes: about 2½ cups

- 1½ cups eggnog
- 2 Tbsp. cornstarch
- ½ cup sour cream
- ½ cup heavy whipping cream
- 1 Tbsp. sugar
- ½ tsp. rum extract, optional
  Assorted fruit and
  pound cake cubes

1. In a small saucepan, combine the eggnog and cornstarch until smooth. Bring to a boil; boil and stir for 2 minutes. Remove from the heat; stir in sour cream. Cool completely.
2. In a small bowl, beat whipping cream and sugar until stiff peaks form. Fold into the eggnog mixture, with rum extract if desired. Cover and refrigerate overnight. Serve with fruit and cake cubes.
Note: This recipe was tested with commercially prepared eggnog.
2 Tbsp.: 64 cal., 5g fat (3g sat. fat), 23mg chol., 16mg sod., 4g carb. (4g sugars, 0 fiber), 1g pro.

NUTTY SNACK MIX

This toasty mix is a little spicy, and a whole lot of tasty! It's perfect for parties or for that long car ride to Grandma's house. No matter when you serve it, it's always a hit!
—*Taste of Home* Test Kitchen

Prep: 15 min. • **Bake:** 20 min. + cooling
Makes: 7 cups

- 2 cups Multi-Bran Chex
- 2 cups Wheat Chex
- 1 cup Cheerios
- 1 cup unblanched almonds
- 1 cup pecan halves
- ¼ cup reduced-fat butter, melted
- ¼ cup Worcestershire sauce
- 2 tsp. chili powder
- 2 tsp. paprika
- ½ tsp. onion powder
- 4 to 6 drops hot pepper sauce
- ½ cup dried cranberries

1. In a large bowl, combine the cereal and nuts. Spread into 2 ungreased 15x10x1-in. baking pans. In a small bowl, combine the butter, Worcestershire sauce, chili powder, paprika, onion powder and pepper sauce; pour over cereal mixture and toss to coat.
2. Bake at 300° for 20 minutes, stirring once. Stir in cranberries. Cool completely. Store in airtight containers.
Note: This recipe was tested with Land O'Lakes light stick butter.
⅓ cup: 128 cal., 9g fat (1g sat. fat), 4mg chol., 121mg sod., 12g carb. (4g sugars, 3g fiber), 3g pro.

CRANBERRY MEATBALLS

Lots of people have asked me for this recipe, but I knew I had a real winner when my grandmother asked me for it!
—Tammy Neubauer, Ida Grove, IA

Prep: 20 min. • **Bake:** 20 min.
Makes: 6 dozen

- 2 large eggs, lightly beaten
- 1 cup cornflake crumbs
- ⅓ cup ketchup
- 2 Tbsp. dried minced onion
- 2 Tbsp. soy sauce
- 1 Tbsp. dried parsley flakes
- ½ tsp. salt
- ¼ tsp. pepper
- 2 lbs. ground pork

SAUCE
- 1 can (14 oz.) jellied cranberry sauce
- 1 cup ketchup
- 3 Tbsp. brown sugar
- 1 Tbsp. lemon juice

1. Preheat oven to 350°. Mix the first 8 ingredients. Add pork; mix lightly but thoroughly. Shape into 1-in. meatballs. Place on a greased rack in a 15x10x1-in. pan. Bake until a thermometer reads 160°, 20-25 minutes. Drain on paper towels.
2. In a large skillet, cook and stir sauce ingredients over medium heat until blended. Stir in meatballs; heat through.
1 meatball: 58 cal., 2g fat (1g sat. fat), 16mg chol., 142mg sod., 6g carb. (4g sugars, 0 fiber), 3g pro.

SWEET CEREAL TREATS

As a small child, I helped my grandma make these no-bake treats. Now my three children enjoy helping me. It doesn't take long to mix up a batch of these yummy snacks because they only require a handful of ingredients.
—Barri VanderHulst, Allegan, MI

Takes: 20 min. • **Makes:** about 5 dozen

5⅓ cups Peanut Butter
     Captain Crunch cereal
1 cup dry roasted peanuts
1 pkg. (10 to 12 oz.) white
     baking chips
1 Tbsp. butter

1. In a large bowl, combine the cereal and peanuts; set aside. In a microwave or double boiler, melt white baking chips and butter; stir until smooth.
2. Pour over the cereal mixture and stir to coat. Drop by rounded tablespoonfuls onto waxed paper-lined baking sheets. Refrigerate until firm.
2 treats: 119 cal., 7g fat (3g sat. fat), 3mg chol., 101mg sod., 13g carb. (2g sugars, 1g fiber), 2g pro.

ASPARAGUS WRAPS

Asparagus makes lovely finger food, especially when wrapped in pastry with a tasty filling. Serve this to guests, but don't forget how easy it is for weeknight noshing.
—Linda Hall, Evington, VA

Prep: 20 min. • **Bake:** 15 min./batch
Makes: 2 dozen

3 Tbsp. butter, softened
1 Tbsp. Mrs. Dash Onion &
     Herb seasoning blend
¼ tsp. garlic salt
1 pkg. (17.3 oz.) frozen
     puff pastry, thawed
1 cup crumbled feta cheese
3 oz. thinly sliced prosciutto
     or deli ham
24 thick fresh asparagus
     spears, trimmed

1. Preheat oven to 425°. Mix the butter, seasoning blend and garlic salt. Unfold puff pastry sheets onto a lightly floured surface. Spread each with 1½ Tbsp. butter mixture and sprinkle with ½ cup cheese. Top with prosciutto, pressing lightly to adhere.
2. Using a pizza cutter or sharp knife, cut each sheet into 12 strips (about ½ in. thick). Wrap each strip, filling side in, around an asparagus spear; place on parchment-lined baking sheets.
3. Bake until wraps are golden brown, about 15 minutes. Serve warm.
1 appetizer: 139 cal., 8g fat (3g sat. fat), 11mg chol., 248mg sod., 12g carb. (0 sugars, 2g fiber), 4g pro.

SPICED AMBROSIA PUNCH

I love this chai-inspired twist on basic spiced cider punch. It's so easy to make in the slow cooker, and everyone seems pleasantly surprised by the apricot and peach nectars.
—Aysha Schurman, Ammon, ID

- -

Prep: 15 min. • **Cook:** 3 hours
Makes: 10 servings (about 2 qt.)

3½ cups apple cider or juice
3 cups apricot nectar
1 cup peach nectar or additional apricot nectar
¼ cup water
3 Tbsp. lemon juice
½ tsp. ground cardamom
½ tsp. ground nutmeg
2 cinnamon sticks (3 in.)
1 tsp. finely chopped fresh gingerroot
1 tsp. grated orange zest
8 whole cloves
   Optional: Orange slices and lemon zest strips

1. In a 3- or 4-qt. slow cooker, combine first 7 ingredients. Place the cinnamon sticks, ginger, orange zest and cloves on a double thickness of cheesecloth. Gather corners of cloth to enclose seasonings; tie securely with string. Add to slow cooker.
2. Cook, covered, on low until flavors are blended, 3-4 hours. Discard the spice bag. Serve warm. If desired, garnish with orange slices and lemon zest strips.

¾ cup: 115 cal., 0 fat (0 sat. fat), 0 chol., 14mg sod., 29g carb. (26g sugars, 1g fiber), 0 pro.

RICOTTA SAUSAGE TRIANGLES

Stuffed with ricotta cheese, sausage and seasonings, these pockets are hard to put down! They freeze well, so go ahead and make a big batch for future parties.
—Virginia Anthony, Jacksonville, FL

- -

Prep: 1 hour • **Bake:** 15 min./batch
Makes: 12 dozen

- 1 carton (15 oz.) part-skim ricotta cheese
- 1 pkg. (10 oz.) frozen chopped spinach, thawed and squeezed dry
- 1 jar (8 oz.) roasted sweet red peppers, drained and chopped
- ⅓ cup grated Parmesan cheese
- 3 Tbsp. chopped ripe olives
- 1 large egg
- 1 Tbsp. minced fresh basil or 1 tsp. dried basil
- 1 tsp. Italian seasoning
- ¼ tsp. salt
- ¼ tsp. pepper
- 1 lb. bulk Italian sausage
- 1 medium onion, chopped
- 96 sheets phyllo dough (14x9-in. size) Olive oil-flavored cooking spray Warm marinara sauce, optional

1. In a large bowl, combine the first 10 ingredients. In a large skillet, cook the sausage and onion over medium heat until the meat is no longer pink; drain. Stir into the cheese mixture.

2. Place 1 sheet of phyllo dough on a work surface with a short end facing you; spray with cooking spray. Top with a second sheet of phyllo; spray again with cooking spray. (Keep remaining phyllo covered with a damp towel to prevent it from drying out.) Cut layered sheets into three 14x3-in. strips.

3. Place a rounded teaspoonful of filling on lower corner of each strip. Fold dough over filling, forming a triangle. Fold triangle up, then fold triangle over, forming another triangle. Continue folding, like a flag, until you come to the end of the strip.

4. Spritz end of dough with spray and press onto triangle to seal. Turn triangle and spritz top with spray. Repeat with the remaining phyllo and filling.

5. Place triangles on baking sheets coated with cooking spray. Bake at 375° until golden brown, 15-20 minutes. Serve warm and, if desired, with marinara sauce.

Freeze option: Freeze unbaked triangles in freezer containers, separating layers with waxed paper. To use, bake the triangles as directed, increasing time as necessary until golden and heated through.

1 appetizer: 42 cal., 2g fat (0 sat. fat), 4mg chol., 64mg sod., 5g carb. (0 sugars, 0 fiber), 2g pro.

THREE-CHEESE FONDUE

This easy recipe is our go-to fondue. I make it often for family get-togethers.
—Betty Mangas, Toledo, OH

Takes: 30 min. • **Makes:** 4 cups

- ½ lb. each Emmenthaler, Gruyere and Jarlsberg cheeses, shredded
- 2 Tbsp. cornstarch, divided
- 4 tsp. cherry brandy
- 2 cups dry white wine
- ⅛ tsp. ground nutmeg
- ⅛ tsp. paprika
  Dash cayenne pepper
  Cubed French bread baguette, boiled red potatoes and/or tiny whole pickles

1. In a large bowl, combine the cheeses and 1 Tbsp. cornstarch. In a small bowl, combine remaining cornstarch and brandy; set aside. In a large saucepan, heat wine over medium heat until bubbles form around sides of pan.

2. Reduce heat to medium-low; add a handful of cheese mixture. Stir constantly, using a figure-8 motion, until the cheese is almost completely melted. Continue adding the cheese mixture, one handful at a time, allowing cheese to almost completely melt between additions.

3. Stir brandy mixture; gradually stir into cheese mixture. Add spices; cook and stir until mixture is thickened and smooth.

4. Transfer to a fondue pot and keep warm. Serve with French bread cubes, potatoes and/or pickles.

¼ cup: 191 cal., 12g fat (7g sat. fat), 37mg chol., 151mg sod., 3g carb. (1g sugars, 0 fiber), 12g pro.

ROAST BEEF FINGER SANDWICHES

These simple tea sandwiches are ideal for a bridal shower, brunch or high tea, when the menu is a bit more substantial. I think the mustard adds a nice kick without being overly spicy.
—Anndrea Bailey, Huntington Beach, CA

Takes: 15 min. • **Makes:** 1½ dozen

- ½ cup butter, softened
- ½ cup chopped pitted Greek olives
- ¼ cup spicy brown mustard
- ¼ tsp. pepper
- 6 slices whole wheat bread, crusts removed
- 6 oz. thinly sliced deli roast beef
- 6 slices white bread, crusts removed

Place butter, olives, mustard and pepper in a food processor; pulse until chopped. Spread butter mixture over wheat bread; top with roast beef and white bread. Cut each sandwich crosswise into thirds.

1 tea sandwich: 98 cal., 7g fat (4g sat. fat), 19mg chol., 240mg sod., 5g carb. (1g sugars, 1g fiber), 3g pro.

OYSTER CHEESE APPETIZER LOG

I make lots of cheese logs and freeze them for when I'm expecting company or need to take a dish to pass to a party. This blend of smoked oysters, chili powder, nuts and cream cheese tastes so good. Even those who say they don't like oysters seem to enjoy this interesting appetizer.
—William Tracy, Jerseyville, IL

- -

Takes: 20 min. • **Makes:** 2 logs

- 3 **pkg. (8 oz. each) cream cheese, softened**
- 2 **Tbsp. steak sauce**
- ¼ **cup Miracle Whip**
- 1 **garlic clove, peeled and minced, or 1 tsp. garlic powder**
- 1 **small onion, finely chopped**
- 2 **cans (3¾ oz. each) smoked oysters, well-drained and chopped**
- 3 **cups chopped pecans, divided**
- 3 **Tbsp. chili powder**
   Minced fresh parsley

In mixer bowl, combine the cheese, steak sauce, Miracle Whip, garlic and onion. Stir in oysters and 1 cup of pecans. Shape into two 9-in. logs. Roll logs in mixture of chili powder, remaining pecans and parsley.
2 Tbsp.: 117 cal., 12g fat (2g sat. fat), 10mg chol., 62mg sod., 3g carb. (1g sugars, 1g fiber), 2g pro.

LEMON-HERB SALMON TOASTS

Quick, light and tasty, my salmon toasts make irresistible finger food.
—Christie Wells, Lake Villa, IL

- -

Takes: 20 min. • **Makes:** 2 dozen

- 1 **pkg. (8 oz.) cream cheese, softened**
- 4 **green onions, chopped**
- 2 **Tbsp. snipped fresh dill or 2 tsp. dill weed**
- ¾ **tsp. sea salt**
- ½ **tsp. pepper**
- ¼ **tsp. cayenne pepper**
- ¼ **tsp. grated lemon zest**
- 2 **tsp. lemon juice**
- 24 **slices snack rye bread**
- 8 **oz. smoked salmon or lox**
   Optional toppings: Grated lemon zest, coarsely ground pepper and fresh dill sprigs

Preheat broiler. In a small bowl, beat the first 8 ingredients. Place bread slices on baking sheets. Broil 4-5 in. from heat until lightly toasted, 1-2 minutes on each side. Spread with cream cheese mixture; top with lox. Serve with toppings as desired.
2 Tbsp.: 117 cal., 12g fat (2g sat. fat), 10mg chol., 62mg sod., 3g carb. (1g sugars, 1g fiber), 2g pro.

HAM & CHEESE BISCUIT STACKS

These finger sandwiches are a pretty addition to any spread, yet filling enough to satisfy hearty appetites. I've served them at holidays, showers and tailgate parties.
—Kelly Williams, Forked River, NJ

Prep: 1 hour • **Bake:** 10 min. + cooling
Makes: 40 appetizers

- 4 tubes (6 oz. each) small refrigerated flaky biscuits (5 count each)
- ¼ cup stone-ground mustard

ASSEMBLY

- ½ cup butter, softened
- ¼ cup chopped green onions
- ½ cup stone-ground mustard
- ¼ cup mayonnaise
- ¼ cup honey
- 10 thick slices deli ham, quartered
- 10 slices Swiss cheese, quartered
- 2½ cups shredded romaine
- 20 pitted ripe olives, drained and patted dry
- 20 pimiento-stuffed olives, drained and patted dry
- 40 frilled toothpicks

1. Preheat oven to 400°. Cut biscuits in half to make half-circles; place 2 in. apart on ungreased baking sheets. Spread mustard over tops. Bake 8-10 minutes or until golden brown. Cool completely on wire racks.
2. Mix butter and green onions. In another bowl, mix mustard, mayonnaise and honey. Split each biscuit into 2 layers.
3. Spread biscuit bottoms with the butter mixture; top with ham, cheese, romaine and biscuit tops. Spoon mustard mixture over tops. Thread 1 olive onto each toothpick; insert into stacks. Serve immediately.
1 appetizer: 121 cal., 7g fat (3g sat. fat), 16mg chol., 412mg sod., 11g carb. (2g sugars, 0 fiber), 4g pro.

CHICKEN & BACON ROLL-UPS

My children liked these so much that they asked for them every day for lunch during the summer. What a great, tasty and easy way to use up any leftover chicken or turkey breast.
—Patricia Nieh, Portola Valley, CA

Prep: 20 min. + chilling • **Makes:** 4 dozen

- 1 can (9¾ oz.) chunk white chicken, drained
- 1 carton (8 oz.) spreadable garden vegetable cream cheese
- 1 cup salsa, divided
- 4 pieces ready-to-serve fully cooked bacon, crumbled
- 6 flour tortillas (8 in.), room temperature

Mix chicken, cream cheese, ½ cup salsa and bacon; spread over tortillas. Roll up tightly; wrap in plastic. Refrigerate at least 1 hour. Just before serving, unwrap and cut the tortillas into 1-in. slices. Serve with the remaining salsa.
1 roll-up: 43 cal., 2g fat (1g sat. fat), 4mg chol., 100mg sod., 4g carb. (0 sugars, 0 fiber), 3g pro.

TATER-DIPPED VEGGIES

Deep-fried vegetables are terrific, but it's not always convenient to prepare them for company. Here's a recipe that produces the same deliciously crisp results in the oven. Serve with your favorite ranch-style dressing as a dip.
—Earleen Lillegard, Prescott, AZ

- -

Prep: 15 min. • **Bake:** 20 min.
Makes: 6 servings

- 1 cup instant potato flakes
- ⅓ cup grated Parmesan cheese
- ½ tsp. celery salt
- ¼ tsp. garlic powder
- ¼ cup butter, melted and cooled
- 2 large eggs
- 4 to 5 cups raw bite-sized vegetables (mushrooms, peppers, broccoli, cauliflower, zucchini and/or parboiled carrots)
  Prepared ranch salad dressing or dip, optional

1. In a small bowl, combine potato flakes, Parmesan cheese, celery salt, garlic powder and butter. In another bowl, beat eggs. Dip each vegetable piece into egg, then into potato mixture; coat well.
2. Place on an ungreased baking sheet. Bake at 400° for 20-25 minutes. Serve with dressing or dip if desired.
1 serving: 159 cal., 11g fat (6g sat. fat), 86mg chol., 282mg sod., 11g carb. (1g sugars, 2g fiber), 6g pro.

SWEET & SAVORY CHEESE PIE

Layer ruby red preserves on a savory appetizer spread as the crowning touch to any buffet.
—Annette Whitmarsh, Lincoln, NE

- -

Prep: 15 min. + chilling • **Makes:** 32 servings

- 1 cup chopped pecans
- 1 pkg. (8 oz.) cream cheese, softened
- ½ cup mayonnaise
- 4 cups shredded sharp cheddar cheese
- 6 green onions, chopped
- ½ lb. bacon strips, cooked and crumbled
- 1 jar (10 oz.) seedless raspberry or strawberry preserves
  Sliced green onions, optional
  Assorted crackers

1. Spread pecans evenly over bottom of a greased 9-in. springform pan. In a large bowl, beat cream cheese and mayonnaise until smooth. Stir in cheddar cheese, green onions and bacon. Carefully spread over pecans. Refrigerate, covered, overnight.
2. Loosen sides from pan with a knife; remove rim from pan. Spread preserves over top. If desired, top with sliced onions. Serve with crackers.
2 Tbsp.: 161 cal., 13g fat (5g sat. fat), 27mg chol., 170mg sod., 7g carb. (6g sugars, 0 fiber), 5g pro.

GRANDMA'S DIVINITY

Every Christmas my grandmother and I made divinity—just the two of us. I still make it every year in her memory.
—Anne Clayborne, Walland, TN

Prep: 5 min. • **Cook:** 40 min. + standing
Makes: 1½ lbs. (60 pieces)

2 large egg whites
3 cups sugar
⅔ cup water
½ cup light corn syrup
1 tsp. vanilla extract
1 cup chopped pecans

1. Place egg whites in the bowl of a stand mixer; let stand at room temperature for 30 minutes. Meanwhile, line three 15x10x1-in. pans with waxed paper.
2. In a large heavy saucepan, combine the sugar, water and corn syrup; bring to a boil, stirring constantly to dissolve sugar. Cook, without stirring, over medium heat until a candy thermometer reads 252° (hard-ball stage). Just before the temperature is reached, beat egg whites on medium speed until stiff peaks form.
3. Slowly add hot sugar mixture in a thin stream over egg whites, beating constantly and scraping sides of bowl occasionally. Add the vanilla. Beat until candy holds its shape, 5-6 minutes. (Do not overmix or the candy will get stiff and crumbly.) Immediately fold in pecans.
4. Quickly drop by heaping teaspoonfuls onto prepared pans. Let stand at room temperature until dry to the touch. Store between waxed paper in an airtight container at room temperature.
Note: We recommend that you test your candy thermometer before each use by bringing water to a boil; the thermometer should read 212°. Adjust your recipe temperature up or down based on your test.
1 piece: 61 cal., 1g fat (0 sat. fat), 0 chol., 4mg sod., 13g carb. (12g sugars, 0 fiber), 0 pro.

PINK PARTY PUNCH

Here's a punch that will be the highlight of any party. The fruity flavors blend perfectly together, making it impossible to have just one glass.
—Carol Garnett, Bellevue, WA

Takes: 10 min. • **Makes:** 32 servings (6 qt.)

2 bottles (46 oz. each) white grape juice, chilled
1 bottle (48 oz.) cranberry juice, chilled
2 cans (12 oz. each) frozen lemonade concentrate, thawed
1 bottle (1 liter) club soda, chilled
2 cups lemon sherbet or sorbet

1. In 2 pitchers, combine bottled juices and lemonade concentrate; refrigerate until serving.
2. Just before serving, stir in club soda and top with scoops of sherbet.
¾ cup: 127 cal., 0 fat (0 sat. fat), 0 chol., 16mg sod., 31g carb. (30g sugars, 0 fiber), 1g pro.

CHEDDAR BACON BEER DIP

My tangy, smoky dip won the top prize in a recipe contest. Use whatever beer you like, but steer clear of dark varieties. Best of all, it uses an all-in-one cooker.
—Ashley Lecker, Green Bay, WI

Prep: 15 min. • **Cook:** 10 min.
Makes: 4½ cups

- 18 oz. cream cheese, softened
- ¼ cup sour cream
- 1½ Tbsp. Dijon mustard
- 1 tsp. garlic powder
- 1 cup beer or nonalcoholic beer
- 1 lb. bacon strips, cooked and crumbled
- 2 cups shredded cheddar cheese
- ¼ cup heavy whipping cream
- 1 green onion, thinly sliced
   Soft pretzel bites

1. In a greased 6-qt. electric pressure cooker, combine cream cheese, sour cream, mustard and garlic powder until smooth. Stir in beer; add bacon, reserving 2 Tbsp. Lock lid; close pressure-release valve. Adjust to pressure-cook on high for 5 minutes. Quick-release pressure.
2. Select saute setting and adjust for normal heat. Stir in cheese and heavy cream. Cook and stir until the mixture has thickened, 3-4 minutes. Transfer to serving dish. Sprinkle with onion and reserved bacon. Serve with pretzel bites.

¼ cup: 213 cal., 19g fat (10g sat. fat), 60mg chol., 378mg sod., 2g carb. (1g sugars, 0 fiber), 8g pro.

TEST KITCHEN TIP
To lighten up this popular dip, use reduced-fat cream cheese, light sour cream, half-and-half and reduced-fat shredded cheese. Serve with fresh celery and carrot sticks.

PARTY CRAB PUFFS

I received this recipe years ago from my grandmother, who taught me to have fun being creative and experimenting in the kitchen. My friends request these little puffs at every gathering.
—Jean Bevilacqua, Rhododendron, OR

- -

Prep: 45 min. • **Bake:** 20 min./batch
Makes: 8 dozen

- 1 **cup water**
- ½ **cup butter, cubed**
- ¼ **tsp. salt**
- 1 **cup all-purpose flour**
- 4 **large eggs**

FILLING
- 4 **hard-boiled large eggs, finely chopped**
- 1 **can (6 oz.) lump crabmeat, drained**
- 4 **oz. cream cheese, softened**
- ¼ **cup mayonnaise**
- 2 **Tbsp. finely chopped onion**
- 2 **Tbsp. prepared horseradish, drained Minced fresh parsley, optional**

1. Preheat oven to 400°. In a large saucepan, bring water, butter and salt to a boil. Add flour all at once and stir until a smooth ball forms. Remove from heat; let stand 5 minutes. Add 1 egg at a time, beating well after each addition. Continue beating until mixture is smooth and shiny.
2. Drop by teaspoonfuls 2 in. apart onto greased baking sheets. Bake 18-22 minutes or until golden brown. Remove to a wire rack. Immediately split puffs open; remove tops and set aside. Discard soft dough from inside. Cool puffs.
3. In a large bowl, combine the filling ingredients. Just before serving, spoon 1 teaspoonful filling into each puff; sprinkle with parsley if desired. Replace tops.

1 puff: 30 cal., 2g fat (1g sat. fat), 23mg chol., 32mg sod., 1g carb. (0 sugars, 0 fiber), 1g pro.

VANILLA ALMOND HOT COCOA

Treat family and friends to this rich homemade cocoa. It will warm even the coldest winter's chill!
—Vicki Holloway, Joelton, TN

- -

Takes: 15 min. • **Makes:** 10 servings (2½ qt.)

- 1 **cup sugar**
- ⅔ **cup baking cocoa**
- ¼ **tsp. salt**
- 8 **cups 2% milk**
- ⅔ **cup water**
- 2 **tsp. vanilla extract**
- ½ **tsp. almond extract**
  Miniature marshmallows, optional

In a large saucepan, combine the sugar, cocoa and salt. Stir in milk and water. Cook and stir over medium heat until heated through. Remove from the heat; stir in extracts. Serve in mugs with marshmallows if desired.

1 cup: 195 cal., 4g fat (2g sat. fat), 16mg chol., 151mg sod., 33g carb. (30g sugars, 1g fiber), 8g pro.

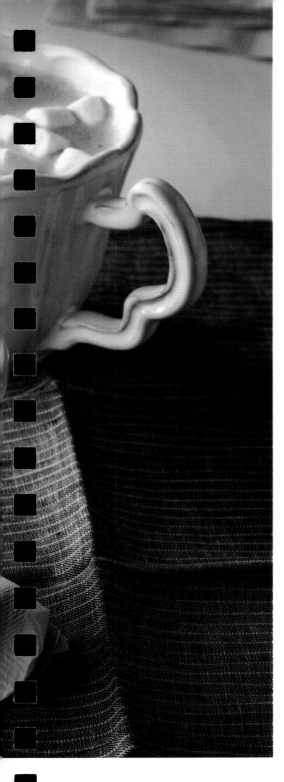

BEEF WELLINGTON APPETIZERS

Flaky puff pastry, savory beef tenderloin and tangy horseradish cream easily come together for an impressive hors d'oeuvre.
—Joan Cooper, Sussex, WI

- -

Prep: 45 min. • **Bake:** 15 min.
Makes: 16 appetizers (1½ cups sauce)

- 2 beef tenderloin steaks (8 oz. each), cut into ½-in. cubes
- 2 Tbsp. olive oil, divided
- 1¼ cups chopped fresh mushrooms
- 2 shallots, chopped
- 2 garlic cloves, minced
- ⅓ cup sherry or chicken broth
- ⅓ cup heavy whipping cream
- ½ tsp. salt
- ⅛ tsp. pepper
- 1 Tbsp. minced fresh parsley
- 1 pkg. (17.3 oz.) frozen puff pastry, thawed
- 1 large egg, beaten

HORSERADISH CREAM

- 1 cup sour cream
- ½ cup mayonnaise
- 2 Tbsp. prepared horseradish
- 1 Tbsp. minced chives
- ¼ tsp. pepper
- Additional minced chives, optional

1. In a large skillet, brown beef in 1 Tbsp. oil. Remove and keep warm.

2. In same skillet, saute mushrooms and shallots in remaining oil until tender. Add garlic; cook 1 minute longer. Add sherry, stirring to loosen browned bits from pan. Stir in cream, salt and pepper. Bring to a boil; cook until liquid is almost evaporated, about 7 minutes. Stir in beef and parsley; set aside and keep warm.

3. Preheat oven to 400°. On a lightly floured surface, unfold the puff pastry. Roll each sheet into a 12-in. square. Cut each into 16 squares.

4. Place 2 tablespoonfuls of beef mixture in center of half of squares. Top with the remaining squares; press edges with a fork to seal. Place on parchment-lined baking sheets. Cut slits in top; brush with beaten egg. Bake until golden brown, 14-16 minutes.

5. In a small bowl, combine horseradish cream ingredients; serve with appetizers. Garnish with additional chives if desired.

Freeze option: Freeze unbaked pastries on baking sheets until firm, then wrap and store in the freezer for up to 2 months. When ready to use, bake frozen appetizers at 400° for 16-18 minutes or until golden brown.

1 appetizer: 315 cal., 22g fat (6g sat. fat), 45mg chol., 231mg sod., 19g carb. (1g sugars, 2g fiber), 10g pro.

MAKE-AHEAD SAUSAGE PINWHEELS

Filled with sausage, sweet pepper and cream cheese, these roll-ups are excellent for unexpected visitors, a cocktail party or a halftime snack. Besides being easy to make, they can be done way ahead and kept in the freezer.
—Cindy Nerat, Menominee, MI

- -

Prep: 30 min. + freezing • **Bake:** 15 min.
Makes: about 6½ dozen

- 1 **lb. bulk regular or spicy pork sausage**
- ½ **cup diced sweet red pepper**
- 1 **green onion, chopped**
- 1 **pkg. (8 oz.) cream cheese, cubed**
- 2 **tubes (8 oz. each) refrigerated crescent rolls**

1. Preheat oven to 350°. In a large skillet, cook and crumble sausage over medium-high heat until no longer pink, 5-7 minutes; drain. Add pepper and green onion; cook and stir 2 minutes. Transfer to a bowl; cool 10 minutes. Stir in cream cheese until blended; cool completely.
2. Unroll 1 can of crescent dough. Separate into 4 rectangles; pinch perforations to seal. Press each rectangle to 6x4½ in.; spread each with ⅓ cup filling to within ¼ in. of edges. Roll up jelly-roll style, starting with a short side; pinch seam to seal. Roll gently to make logs smooth. Place on a waxed paper-lined baking sheet, seam side down. Repeat with remaining crescent dough. Freeze, covered, until firm, about 1 hour.
3. Cut each log into 10 slices. Bake on parchment-lined baking sheets until golden brown, 15-18 minutes. Serve warm.
Freeze option: Freeze pinwheels in freezer containers, separating layers with waxed paper. To use, bake frozen pinwheels as directed, increasing time by 3-5 minutes.
1 appetizer: 46 cal., 3g fat (1g sat. fat), 6mg chol., 89mg sod., 2g carb. (1g sugars, 0 fiber), 1g pro.

CHEWY CARAMEL-COATED POPCORN

When I was a kid, my mom often made this recipe. I've adapted it to make a more chewy, gooey version. I get requests to make this for every event that I host. Packed into pretty decorative bags, it makes a welcome hostess gift, too.
—Shannon Dobos, Calgary, AB

- -

Takes: 25 min. • **Makes:** about 6 qt.

- 1½ **cups butter, cubed**
- 2⅔ **cups packed light brown sugar**
- 1 **cup golden syrup**
- 1 **tsp. vanilla extract**
- 24 **cups popped popcorn**

1. Line two 15x10x1-in. baking pans with parchment. In a large heavy saucepan, melt butter over medium-high heat. Add brown sugar and syrup, stirring to dissolve brown sugar. Bring to a full rolling boil. Boil and stir 1 minute. Remove from heat and quickly stir in vanilla.
2. Pour caramel mixture over popcorn; stir lightly to coat. Using a rubber spatula, press the caramel popcorn into prepared pans. Cool. Pull apart into pieces. Store in airtight containers.
Note: This recipe was tested with Lyle's Golden Syrup.
1 cup: 303 cal., 16g fat (8g sat. fat), 31mg chol., 216mg sod., 40g carb. (35g sugars, 1g fiber), 1g pro.

FOCACCIA BARESE

This focaccia has been in my mom's family for several generations. It is one of my most requested recipes. Whenever I am invited to a party—I am not allowed to attend unless I bring it!
—Dora Travaglio, Mount Prospect, IL

Prep: 30 min. + rising • **Bake:** 30 min.
Makes: 8 servings

- 1⅛ tsp. active dry yeast
- ¾ cup warm water (110° to 115°), divided
- ½ tsp. sugar
- ⅓ cup mashed potato flakes
- 1½ tsp. plus 2 Tbsp. olive oil, divided
- ¼ tsp. salt
- 1¾ cups bread flour

TOPPING
- 2 medium tomatoes, thinly sliced
- ¼ cup pitted Greek olives, halved
- 1½ tsp. minced fresh or dried oregano
- ½ tsp. coarse salt

1. In a large bowl, dissolve yeast in ½ cup warm water. Add sugar; let stand about 5 minutes. Add the potato flakes, 1½ tsp. oil, salt, 1 cup flour and remaining water. Beat until smooth. Stir in enough remaining flour to form a soft dough.

2. Turn onto a floured surface; knead until smooth and elastic, 6-8 minutes. Place in a greased bowl, turning once to grease the top. Cover and let rise in a warm place until doubled, about 1 hour. Punch dough down. Cover and let rest for 10 minutes.

3. Place 1 Tbsp. olive oil in a 10-in. cast-iron or other ovenproof skillet; tilt pan to evenly coat. Add dough; shape to fit pan. Cover and let rise until doubled, about 30 minutes.

4. With fingertips, make several dimples over top of dough. Brush with remaining oil. Blot tomato slices with paper towels. Arrange tomato slices and olives over dough; sprinkle with oregano and salt.

5. Bake at 375° for 30-35 minutes or until golden brown.

1 slice: 142 cal., 4g fat (0 sat. fat), 0 chol., 269mg sod., 24g carb. (1g sugars, 1g fiber), 4g pro. **Diabetic exchanges:** 1½ starch, ½ fat.

GRANDMA'S BUTTERSCOTCH CANDY

The recipe for this buttery candy was handed down from my grandma. My brothers, sisters and I love it now as much as we did when we were little—and so do our families! It's become a cherished tradition with all of us.
—Catherine Rothermel, Columbus, OH

Prep: 5 min. • **Cook:** 30 min. + cooling
Makes: about ¾ lb.

- 2 cups sugar
- ⅔ cup water
- ¼ tsp. cream of tartar
- 2 Tbsp. butter
- 1 tsp. vanilla extract

1. Butter a 13x9-in. pan; set aside. In a heavy saucepan, combine the sugar, water and cream of tartar. Bring to a boil, without stirring, over medium heat until a candy thermometer reads 300° (hard-crack stage). Syrup will turn a golden color.
2. Remove from the heat; stir in butter and vanilla. Return to heat. Cook and stir until thermometer returns to 300°. Pour into prepared pan. Cool. Break into pieces.
Note: We recommend that you test your candy thermometer before each use by bringing water to a boil; the thermometer should read 212°. Adjust your recipe temperature up or down based on your test.
½ oz. serving: 73 cal., 1g fat (1g sat. fat), 3mg chol., 10mg sod., 17g carb. (16g sugars, 0 fiber), 0 pro.

ANTIPASTO BAKE

Stuffed with savory meats and cheeses, this hearty dish comes together quickly and bakes in under an hour, making it the perfect potluck bring-along. Salami, Swiss, pepperoni, Colby-Monterey Jack, and even prosciutto and provolone are all found under the crisp topping.
—Brea Barclay, Green Bay, WI

- -

Prep: 20 min. • **Bake:** 45 min. + standing
Makes: 20 servings

- 2 **tubes (8 oz. each) refrigerated crescent rolls**
- ¼ **lb. thinly sliced hard salami**
- ¼ **lb. thinly sliced Swiss cheese**
- ¼ **lb. thinly sliced pepperoni**
- ¼ **lb. thinly sliced Colby-Monterey Jack cheese**
- ¼ **lb. thinly sliced prosciutto**
- ¼ **lb. thinly sliced provolone cheese**
- 2 **large eggs**
- ½ **tsp. garlic powder**
- ½ **tsp. pepper**
- 1 **jar (12 oz.) roasted sweet red peppers, drained**
- 1 **large egg yolk, beaten**

1. Preheat oven to 350°. Unroll 1 tube of crescent dough into a long rectangle and press perforations to seal. Press onto bottom and up sides of an ungreased 11x7-in. baking dish.
2. Layer meats and cheeses on dough in the order listed. Whisk eggs and seasonings until well blended; pour into dish. Top with roasted pepper.
3. Unroll remaining tube of dough into a long rectangle; press perforations to seal. Place over filling; pinch seams tight. Brush with beaten egg yolk; cover with foil. Bake 30 minutes; remove foil. Bake until golden brown, 15-20 minutes. Let stand roughly 20 minutes.

1 piece: 229 cal., 15g fat (7g sat. fat), 58mg chol., 662mg sod., 10g carb. (2g sugars, 0 fiber), 11g pro.

SLOW-COOKER SPICED MIXED NUTS

What slow cookers do for soups and stews, they do for mixed nuts, too. The scent of the spices is delightful, and the nuts are simply delicious.
—Stephanie Loaiza, Layton, UT

- -

Prep: 15 min.
Cook: 1 hour 50 min. + cooling
Makes: 6 cups

- 1 **large egg white**
- 2 **tsp. vanilla extract**
- 1 **cup unblanched almonds**
- 1 **cup pecan halves**
- 1 **cup shelled walnuts**
- 1 **cup unsalted cashews**
- 1 **cup sugar**
- 1 **cup packed brown sugar**
- 4 **tsp. ground cinnamon**
- 2 **tsp. ground ginger**
- 1 **tsp. ground nutmeg**
- ½ **tsp. ground cloves**
- ⅛ **tsp. salt**
- 2 **Tbsp. water**

1. In a large bowl, whisk egg white and vanilla until blended; stir in nuts. In a small bowl, mix sugars, spices and salt. Add to nut mixture and toss to coat.
2. Transfer to a greased 3-qt. slow cooker. Cook, covered, on high 1½ hours, stirring every 15 minutes. Gradually stir in water. Cook, covered, on low 20 minutes.
3. Carefully spread onto waxed paper; cool completely. Store in airtight containers up to 1 week.

⅓ cup: 261 cal., 15g fat (2g sat. fat), 0 chol., 26mg sod., 30g carb. (24g sugars, 2g fiber), 5g pro.

9-LAYER GREEK DIP

Instead of the same taco dip at every family event or potluck, try this cool, refreshing alternative. It's a light and lively change of pace.
—Shawn Barto, Winter Garden, FL

Takes: 20 min. • **Makes:** 5 ½ cups

- 1 carton (10 oz.) hummus
- 1 cup refrigerated tzatziki sauce
- ½ cup chopped green pepper
- ½ cup chopped sweet red pepper
- ½ cup chopped peeled cucumber
- ½ cup chopped water-packed artichoke hearts, drained
- ½ cup chopped pitted Greek olives, optional
- ¼ cup chopped pepperoncini
- 1 cup crumbled feta cheese
  Baked pita chips

In a 9-in. deep-dish pie plate, layer first 6 ingredients; top with olives, if desired, and pepperoncini. Sprinkle with feta cheese. Refrigerate until serving. Serve with pita chips.

¼ cup: 60 cal., 4g fat (1g sat. fat), 5mg chol., 210mg sod., 4g carb. (1g sugars, 1g fiber), 3g pro. **Diabetic exchanges:** ½ starch, ½ fat.

LITTLE PIGS IN A HAMMOCK

Pigs in a blanket aren't just for kids! Dijon and Camembert transform this children's favorite into a version that's perfect for grown-ups.
—Crystal Schlueter, Northglenn, CO

Takes: 30 min. • **Makes:** 1½ dozen

- 1 pkg. (17.3 oz.) frozen puff pastry, thawed
- 3 Tbsp. seedless raspberry jam
- 1 Tbsp. Dijon mustard
- 1 round (8 oz.) Camembert cheese
- 18 miniature smoked sausages
- 1 large egg
- 1 Tbsp. water

1. Preheat oven to 425°. Unfold pastry. Cut each pastry into 9 squares. Cut each square into 2 triangles. In a small bowl, mix jam and mustard; spread over triangles. Cut cheese in half crosswise; cut each half into 9 wedges.

2. Top each triangle with a cheese piece and a sausage. Fold pastry over sausage and cheese; press to seal. Place on a parchment-lined baking sheet. In a small bowl, whisk egg with water. Brush over pastries. Bake 15-17 minutes or until golden brown.

1 appetizer: 211 cal., 13g fat (5g sat. fat), 25mg chol., 312mg sod., 18g carb. (2g sugars, 2g fiber), 6g pro.

TEST KITCHEN TIP
For fresh-from-Grandma's-kitchen taste, make your own tzatziki sauce. Combine ½ cup peeled, seeded and finely chopped cucumber with ½ cup plain Greek yogurt, 4 tsp. lemon juice, 1 Tbsp. chopped dill, 1 minced garlic clove, and salt and pepper to taste. Refrigerate.

NO-FUSS FILLING

Save time when filling deviled eggs, especially when making big batches. Simply spoon the prepared filling into a pastry bag and pipe the filling into the egg white halves.

GARLIC-DILL DEVILED EGGS

In my family, a party isn't complete without deviled eggs. Fresh dill and garlic perk up the flavor of these irresistible appetizers you'll want to eat at every occasion.
—Kami Horch, Calais, ME

- -

Prep: 20 min. + chilling • **Makes:** 2 dozen

- 12 **hard-boiled large eggs**
- ⅔ **cup mayonnaise**
- 4 **tsp. dill pickle relish**
- 2 **tsp. snipped fresh dill**
- 2 **tsp. Dijon mustard**
- 1 **tsp. coarsely ground pepper**
- ¼ **tsp. garlic powder**
- ⅛ **tsp. paprika or cayenne pepper**

1. Cut eggs lengthwise in half. Remove the yolks, reserving whites. In a bowl, mash the yolks. Stir in all remaining ingredients except paprika. Spoon or pipe into egg whites.
2. Refrigerate, covered, at least 30 minutes before serving. Sprinkle with paprika.

1 stuffed egg half: 81 cal., 7g fat (1g sat. fat), 94mg chol., 81mg sod., 1g carb. (0 sugars, 0 fiber), 3g pro.

GARDEN-FRESH SEAFOOD COCKTAIL

For something cool on a hot day, we mix shrimp and crabmeat with crunchy veggies straight from the garden. Look for adobo seasoning in your grocery's international section. It jazzes up this longtime favorite.
—Teri Rasey, Cadillac, MI

- -

Prep: 15 min. + chilling • **Makes:** 6 cups

- ¾ lb. peeled and deveined cooked shrimp (31-40 per lb.), thawed
- 1 container (8 oz.) refrigerated jumbo lump crabmeat, drained
- 3 celery ribs, chopped
- 1 medium cucumber, peeled, seeded and chopped
- 1 medium sweet orange pepper, chopped
- 2 plum tomatoes, seeded and chopped
- ½ cup red onion, finely chopped
- 1 to 2 jalapeno peppers, seeded and finely chopped
- ¼ cup minced fresh cilantro
- 3 Tbsp. lime juice
- 1 Tbsp. olive oil
- 2¼ tsp. adobo seasoning

Combine first 9 ingredients. Whisk together lime juice, oil and adobo seasoning; drizzle over shrimp mixture and toss gently to coat. Refrigerate at least 1 hour, tossing gently every 20 minutes. Place shrimp mixture in cocktail glasses.
¾ cup: 103 cal., 3g fat (0 sat. fat), 92mg chol., 619mg sod., 5g carb. (2g sugars, 1g fiber), 15g pro.

HEIRLOOM TOMATO GALETTE WITH PECORINO

I found beautiful heirloom tomatoes and had to show them off. Here, the tomatoes are tangy and the crust is beyond buttery.
—Jessica Chang, Playa Vista, CA

- -

Prep: 10 min. + chilling
Bake: 25 min. + cooling
Makes: 6 servings

- 1 cup all-purpose flour
- 1 tsp. baking powder
- ¾ tsp. kosher salt, divided
- ½ cup cold unsalted butter, cubed
- ½ cup sour cream
- 2 cups cherry tomatoes, halved
- 3 oz. Pecorino Romano cheese, thinly sliced

1. Whisk flour, baking powder and ½ tsp. salt; cut in butter until mixture resembles coarse crumbs. Stir in the sour cream until dough forms a ball. Shape into a disk; wrap and refrigerate until firm enough to roll, about 2 hours.
2. Place tomatoes in a colander; toss with remaining salt. Let stand 15 minutes.
3. Preheat oven to 425°. On a floured sheet of parchment, roll dough into a 12-in. circle. Transfer to a baking sheet.
4. Place cheese slices over pastry to within 2 in. of edge; arrange the tomatoes over the cheese. Gently fold pastry edges over filling, pleating as you go and leaving the center uncovered. Bake until crust is golden brown and cheese is bubbly, about 25 minutes. Cool 10 minutes before slicing.
1 slice: 317 cal., 23g fat (15g sat. fat), 68mg chol., 559mg sod., 19g carb. (2g sugars, 1g fiber), 9g pro.

TUSCAN SAUSAGE & BEAN DIP

This stick-to-your-ribs appetizer is a hearty change of pace from taco dips. Take it to your next get-together. I'll bet you no one else will bring anything like it!
—Mandy Rivers, Lexington, SC

- -

Prep: 25 min. • **Bake:** 20 min.
Makes: 16 servings

- 1 lb. bulk hot Italian sausage
- 1 medium onion, finely chopped
- 4 garlic cloves, minced
- ½ cup dry white wine or chicken broth
- ½ tsp. dried oregano
- ¼ tsp. salt
- ¼ tsp. dried thyme
- 1 pkg. (8 oz.) cream cheese, softened
- 1 pkg. (6 oz.) fresh baby spinach, coarsely chopped
- 1 can (15 oz.) cannellini beans, rinsed and drained
- 1 cup chopped seeded tomatoes
- 1 cup shredded part-skim mozzarella cheese
- ½ cup shredded Parmesan cheese
  Assorted crackers or toasted French bread baguette slices

1. Preheat oven to 375°. In a large skillet, cook the sausage, onion and garlic over medium heat until sausage is no longer pink, breaking up sausage into crumbles; drain. Stir in the wine, oregano, salt and thyme. Bring to a boil; cook until liquid is almost evaporated.
2. Add cream cheese; stir until melted. Stir in spinach, beans and tomatoes; cook and stir until spinach is wilted. Transfer to a greased 8-in. square baking dish; if using an ovenproof skillet, leave in skillet. Sprinkle with cheeses.
3. Bake until bubbly, 20-25 minutes. Serve with crackers.

¼ cup: 200 cal., 14g fat (7g sat. fat), 41mg chol., 434mg sod., 7g carb. (2g sugars, 2g fiber), 10g pro.

FRESH FROM THE GARDEN WRAPS

This is a delicious way to use homegrown herbs, eat light, and keep things refreshing and unique. They're wonderful for simple lunches, too.
—Chris Bugher, Asheville, NC

- -

Prep: 20 min. + standing • **Makes:** 8 servings

- 1 medium ear sweet corn
- 1 medium cucumber, chopped
- 1 cup shredded cabbage
- 1 medium tomato, chopped
- 1 small red onion, chopped
- 1 jalapeno pepper, seeded and minced
- 1 Tbsp. minced fresh basil
- 1 Tbsp. minced fresh cilantro
- 1 Tbsp. minced fresh mint
- ⅓ cup Thai chili sauce
- 3 Tbsp. rice vinegar
- 2 tsp. reduced-sodium soy sauce
- 2 tsp. creamy peanut butter
- 8 Bibb or Boston lettuce leaves

1. Cut corn from cob and place in a large bowl. Add cucumber, cabbage, tomato, onion, jalapeno and herbs.
2. Whisk together chili sauce, vinegar, soy sauce and peanut butter. Pour over the vegetable mixture; toss to coat. Let stand 20 minutes.
3. Using a slotted spoon, place ½ cup salad in each lettuce leaf. Fold lettuce over filling.
Note: Wear disposable gloves when cutting hot peppers; the oils can burn skin. Avoid touching your face.
1 filled lettuce wrap: 64 cal., 1g fat (0 sat. fat), 0 chol., 319mg sod., 13g carb. (10g sugars, 2g fiber), 2g pro. **Diabetic exchanges:** 1 vegetable, ½ starch.

CHOCOLATY FRUIT DIP

My grandma helped me experiment with chocolate and yogurt combinations to create this fruit dip for a tea party we had. Our guests said it was yummy!
—Abigail Sims, Terrell, TX

- -

Prep: 10 min. + chilling
Cook: 5 min. + cooling
Makes: 1 cup

 1½ **cups plain yogurt**
  2 **Tbsp. fat-free milk**
 10 **miniature marshmallows**
  2 **Tbsp. semisweet chocolate chips**
     Assorted fresh fruit

1. Line a strainer with 4 layers cheesecloth or 1 coffee filter and place over a bowl. Place plain yogurt in prepared strainer; cover yogurt with edges of cheesecloth. Refrigerate for 8 hours or overnight.
2. In a small heavy saucepan, combine the milk, marshmallows and chocolate chips. Cook and stir until chips are melted and mixture is smooth. Transfer to a small bowl; cool to room temperature.
3. Remove yogurt from cheesecloth and discard liquid from bowl. Gradually stir yogurt into milk mixture. Refrigerate until serving. Serve with fruit.
¼ cup: 88 cal., 5g fat (3g sat. fat), 12mg chol., 47mg sod., 9g carb. (8g sugars, 0 fiber), 4g pro. **Diabetic exchanges:** 1 fat, ½ starch.

MUSTARD PRETZEL NUGGETS

This quick and fun snack is similar to the mustard pretzels you can buy at the store, but you can make these for a fraction of the cost. It's a killer recipe for all kinds of parties and football gatherings.
—Sarah Mathews, Ava, MO

- -

Prep: 10 min. • **Bake:** 15 min. + cooling
Makes: 6 cups

  6 **cups sourdough pretzel nuggets**
 ⅓ **cup prepared mustard**
  2 **Tbsp. honey**
  1 **Tbsp. cider vinegar**
 ½ **tsp. onion powder**
 ½ **tsp. garlic powder**
 ½ **tsp. ground mustard**

1. Preheat oven to 350°. Place pretzels in a bowl. In another bowl, mix the remaining ingredients. Drizzle over the pretzels; toss to coat.
2. Spread seasoned pretzels on a greased 15x10-in. pan. Bake until lightly browned and crisp, 15-20 minutes, stirring every 5 minutes. Cool completely in pan on a wire rack. Store in an airtight container.
¾ cup: 204 cal., 0 fat (0 sat. fat), 0 chol., 411mg sod., 43g carb. (6g sugars, 2g fiber), 5g pro.

HOMEMADE EGGNOG

After just one sip, folks will know this homemade holiday treat came from the kitchen, not from the store.
—Pat Waymire, Yellow Springs, OH

Prep: 15 min. • **Cook:** 30 min. + chilling
Makes: 12 servings (about 3 qt.)

    12 large eggs
    1½ cups sugar
    ½   tsp. salt
    8   cups whole milk, divided
    2   Tbsp. vanilla extract
    1   tsp. ground nutmeg
    2   cups heavy whipping cream
        Additional nutmeg, optional

1. In a heavy saucepan, whisk together eggs, sugar and salt. Gradually add 4 cups milk; cook and stir mixture over low heat until a thermometer reads 160°-170°, 30-35 minutes. Do not allow to boil. Immediately transfer to a large bowl.
2. Stir in vanilla, nutmeg and remaining milk. Place bowl in an ice-water bath, stirring until the milk mixture is cool. (If mixture separates, process in a blender until smooth.)
3. Refrigerate, covered, until cold, at least 3 hours.
4. To serve, beat cream until soft peaks form. Whisk gently into the cooled milk mixture. If desired, sprinkle with additional nutmeg before serving.
1 cup: 411 cal., 25g fat (14g sat. fat), 247mg chol., 251mg sod., 35g carb. (35g sugars, 0 fiber), 13g pro.

HONEY HORSERADISH DIP

Our family loves having appetizers on Friday night instead of a meal, and during the summer we enjoy cooler foods. This has just the right amount of zing.
—Ann Marie Eberhart, Gig Harbor, WA

Prep: 10 min. + chilling • **Makes:** 1 cup

    ½   cup fat-free plain Greek yogurt
    ¼   cup stone-ground mustard
    ¼   cup honey
    2   Tbsp. prepared horseradish
    1   lb. cold peeled and deveined cooked shrimp (16-20 per lb.), optional
    ½   lb. cold fresh sugar snap peas, optional

Combine yogurt, mustard, honey and horseradish; refrigerate 1 hour. If desired, serve with cold cooked shrimp and sugar snap peas.
2 Tbsp.: 54 cal., 1g fat (0 sat. fat), 0 chol., 177mg sod., 11g carb. (10g sugars, 0 fiber), 2g pro. **Diabetic exchanges:** 1 starch.

INSIDE-OUT VEGGIE DIP

Cherry tomatoes and cucumber slices convert to savory, bite-sized treats ideal for any gathering.
—Judie Thurstenson, Colcord, OK

Prep: 35 min. + chilling • **Makes:** 3½ dozen

- 2 **large cucumbers**
- 16 **cherry tomatoes**
- 1 **pkg. (8 oz.) cream cheese, softened**
- ¼ **cup finely chopped sweet red pepper**
- 2 **Tbsp. finely chopped celery**
- 2 **Tbsp. finely chopped green onion**
- 1 **Tbsp. finely chopped carrot**
- 1 **tsp. garlic powder**
- ½ **tsp. salt**
- ½ **tsp. onion powder**

1. Peel strips from cucumbers to create decorative edges if desired; cut into ½-in. slices. Finely chop 2 slices; set aside. With a small spoon, scoop some of the seeds from the remaining slices.

2. Cut a thin slice from the bottoms of tomatoes to allow them to rest flat. Cut a thin slice from tops of tomatoes; scoop out pulp, leaving a ¼-in. shell. Invert onto paper towels to drain.

3. In a large bowl, combine the cream cheese, red pepper, celery, onion, carrot, seasonings and chopped cucumber.

4. Fill tomatoes and cucumber slices with cream cheese mixture, about 1 tsp. in each. Refrigerate for at least 1 hour.

1 piece: 23 cal., 2g fat (1g sat. fat), 6mg chol., 45mg sod., 1g carb. (1g sugars, 0 fiber), 1g pro.

LEFTOVER TURKEY TURNOVERS

I created this dish in 1993 while putting together a booklet called *Totally Turkey* for leftover turkey recipes. The little ones in my family gobble them up in no time.
—Renee Murby, Johnston, RI

- -

Prep: 40 min. + chilling • **Cook:** 5 min./batch
Makes: 1 dozen

- 1¼ cups all-purpose flour
- ¼ tsp. salt
- ½ cup shortening
- 1 large egg
- 2 Tbsp. ice water, divided

FILLING
- 2 Tbsp. canola oil
- ⅓ cup finely chopped onion
- ¼ tsp. ground turmeric
- ¼ tsp. ground cinnamon
- 1 garlic clove, minced
- 1 cup finely chopped cooked turkey
- ¼ cup raisins
- ¼ tsp. salt
- ⅛ tsp. pepper
   Oil for frying

1. In a large bowl, mix flour and salt; cut in shortening until crumbly. Whisk egg and 1 Tbsp. ice water; gradually add to flour with remaining water as needed, tossing with a fork until dough holds together when pressed. Turn onto a lightly floured surface; knead gently 6-8 times. Shape into a disk; wrap and refrigerate 1 hour or overnight.

2. In a skillet, heat oil over medium-high heat. Add onion, turmeric and cinnamon; cook and stir 1-2 minutes or until tender. Add garlic; cook 30 seconds longer. Stir in turkey, raisins, salt and pepper.

3. On a lightly floured surface, roll dough to ⅛-in. thickness. Cut with a floured 4-in. round cookie cutter. Place a heaping tablespoon of filling in center of each circle. Moisten edges with water; fold in half and press edges with a fork to seal. Repeat with remaining dough and filling.

4. In a deep skillet or electric skillet, heat ½ in. oil to 375°. Fry turnovers, a few at a time, 2-3 minutes on each side or until golden brown. Drain on paper towels.

1 turnover: 212 cal., 15g fat (3g sat. fat), 27mg chol., 117mg sod., 13g carb. (2g sugars, 1g fiber), 5g pro.

TEST KITCHEN TIP
The flaky homemade turnovers are an appetizing way to use up all sort of leftovers. Try the recipe with cooked ham or chicken. Use last night's taco meat for the filling and swap out the herbs, seasonings and raisins with shredded cheese and diced peppers.

BARBECUE SAUSAGE BITES

This slow-cooked appetizer pairs tangy pineapple with sweet barbecue sauce and three kinds of sausage. It'll tide over even the biggest appetites until dinner.
—Rebekah Randolph, Greer, SC

- -

Prep: 10 min. • **Cook:** 2½ hours
Makes: 14 servings

- 1 pkg. (16 oz.) miniature smoked sausages
- ¾ lb. fully cooked bratwurst links, cut into ½-in. slices
- ¾ lb. smoked kielbasa or Polish sausage, cut into ½-in. slices
- 1 bottle (18 oz.) barbecue sauce
- ⅔ cup orange marmalade
- ½ tsp. ground mustard
- ⅛ tsp. ground allspice
- 1 can (20 oz.) pineapple chunks, drained

1. In a 3-qt. slow cooker, combine the sausages. In a small bowl, whisk the barbecue sauce, marmalade, mustard and allspice. Pour over sausage mixture; stir to coat.
2. Cover and cook on high until heated through, 2½-3 hours. Stir in pineapple. Serve with toothpicks.
1 serving: 327 cal., 22g fat (8g sat. fat), 53mg chol., 980mg sod., 20g carb. (19g sugars, 1g fiber), 11g pro.

TANGY PICKLED MUSHROOMS

Home-canned pickled mushrooms are a handy addition to your pantry. They are ideal for appetizers, salads, relish trays and even cocktails.
—Jill Hihn, West Grove, PA

- -

Prep: 50 min. • **Process:** 20 min./batch
Makes: 8 pints

- 5 lbs. small fresh mushrooms
- 2 large onions, halved and sliced
- 2 cups white vinegar
- 1½ cups canola oil
- ¼ cup sugar
- 2 Tbsp. canning salt
- 3 garlic cloves, minced
- 1½ tsp. pepper
- ¼ tsp. dried tarragon

1. Place all ingredients in a stockpot. Bring to a boil. Reduce heat; simmer, uncovered, 10 minutes. Carefully ladle the hot mixture into 8 hot 1-pint jars, leaving ½-in. headspace.
2. Remove air bubbles and adjust headspace, if necessary, by adding hot mixture. Wipe rims. Center lids on jars; screw on bands until fingertip tight. Place jars into canner, ensuring that they are completely covered with water. Bring to a boil. Process for 20 minutes. Remove jars and cool.
Note: The processing time listed is for altitudes of 1,000 feet or less. For altitudes up to 3,000 feet, add 5 minutes; 6,000 feet, add 10 minutes; 8,000 feet, add 15 minutes; 10,000 feet, add 20 minutes.
¼ cup: 18 cal., 1g fat (0 sat. fat), 0 chol., 35mg sod., 2g carb. (1g sugars, 1g fiber), 1g pro.

BAKED CRAB DIP

We enjoyed this exquisite dip at my grandson's wedding reception. It looks fancy but is easy to make. You can even fill the bread bowl early in the day and chill it until serving. Just remove it from the refrigerator 30 minutes before baking.
—Marie Shelley, Exeter, MO

- -

Prep: 15 min. • **Bake:** 45 min.
Makes: 5 cups

- 1 pkg. (8 oz.) cream cheese, softened
- 2 cups sour cream
- 2 cans (6 oz. each) crabmeat, drained, flaked and cartilage removed or 2 cups flaked imitation crabmeat
- 2 cups shredded cheddar cheese
- 4 green onions, thinly sliced
- 2 round loaves (1 lb. each) unsliced sourdough or Italian bread
-   Additional sliced green onions, optional
    Fresh vegetables, crackers and/or toasted bread cubes.

1. In a bowl, beat cream cheese until smooth. Add sour cream; mix well. Fold in crab, cheese and onions. Cut the top third off each loaf of bread; carefully hollow out bottoms, leaving 1-in. shells. Cube the removed bread and tops; set aside. Spoon crab mixture into bread bowls. Place on baking sheets. Place reserved bread cubes in a single layer around bread bowls.
2. Bake, uncovered, at 350° until the dip is heated through, 45-50 minutes or. Garnish with green onions if desired. Serve with assorted fresh vegetables, crackers or toasted bread cubes.
2 Tbsp.: 100 cal., 6g fat (4g sat. fat), 24mg chol., 140mg sod., 7g carb. (1g sugars, 0 fiber), 4g pro.

RISOTTO BALLS (ARANCINI)

My Italian grandma made these for me. I still ask for them when I visit her, and so do my children. They freeze well, so I make them ahead of time.
—Gretchen Whelan, San Francisco, CA

- -

Prep: 35 min. • **Bake:** 25 min.
Makes: about 3 dozen

- 1½ cups water
- 1 cup uncooked arborio rice
- 1 tsp. salt
- 2 large eggs, lightly beaten
- ⅔ cup sun-dried tomato pesto
- 2 cups panko (Japanese) bread crumbs, divided
    Marinara sauce, warmed

1. Preheat oven to 375°. In a large saucepan, combine water, rice and salt; bring to a boil. Reduce heat; simmer, covered, until liquid is absorbed and rice is tender, 18-20 minutes. Let stand, covered, 10 minutes. Transfer to a large bowl; cool slightly. Add eggs and pesto; stir in 1 cup bread crumbs.
2. Place the remaining bread crumbs in a shallow bowl. Shape rice mixture into 1¼-in. balls. Roll in bread crumbs, patting to help coating adhere.
3. Place rice balls on greased 15x10x1-in. baking pans. Bake until golden brown, 25-30 minutes. Serve with marinara sauce.
1 appetizer: 42 cal., 1g fat (0 sat. fat), 10mg chol., 125mg sod., 7g carb. (1g sugars, 0 fiber), 1g pro. **Diabetic exchanges:** ½ starch.

CHICKEN FRIES

Kid-friendly and quick, these crunchy oven-baked chicken fries are coated with a mixture of crushed potato chips, panko bread crumbs and Parmesan cheese. Dip them in ranch dressing, barbecue sauce or honey-mustard.
—Nick Iverson, Denver, CO

- -

Prep: 20 min. • **Bake:** 15 min.
Makes: 4 servings

- 2 large eggs, lightly beaten
- ½ tsp. salt
- ½ tsp. garlic powder
- ¼ to ½ tsp. cayenne pepper
- 2 cups finely crushed ridged potato chips
- 1 cup panko (Japanese) bread crumbs
- ½ cup grated Parmesan cheese
- 2 boneless skinless chicken breasts (6 oz. each), cut into ¼-in.-thick strips

Preheat oven to 400°. In a shallow bowl, whisk eggs, salt, garlic powder and cayenne. In a separate shallow bowl, combine chips, bread crumbs and cheese. Dip chicken in egg mixture, then in potato chip mixture, patting to help coating adhere. Transfer to a greased wire rack in a foil-lined rimmed baking sheet. Bake until golden brown, 12-15 minutes.

1 serving: 376 cal., 17g fat (6g sat. fat), 149mg chol., 761mg sod., 27g carb. (1g sugars, 2g fiber), 27g pro.

TEST KITCHEN TIP
Replace the potato chips with finely crushed taco or pita chips. Or pulse pretzels in a food processor for an extra savory coating.

MARINATED MOZZARELLA

I come home with an empty container when I bring these cheese cubes to a party. They can be made ahead to free up time later. I serve them with pretty party picks for a festive look.
—Peggy Cairo, Kenosha, WI

- -

Prep: 15 min. + marinating
Makes: 10 servings

- ⅓ cup olive oil
- 1 Tbsp. chopped oil-packed sun-dried tomatoes
- 1 Tbsp. minced fresh parsley
- 1 tsp. crushed red pepper flakes
- 1 tsp. dried basil
- 1 tsp. minced chives
- ¼ tsp. garlic powder
- 1 lb. cubed part-skim mozzarella cheese

In a large bowl, combine first 7 ingredients; add cheese cubes. Stir to coat. Cover and refrigerate at least 30 minutes.

¼ cup: 203 cal., 16g fat (7g sat. fat), 24mg chol., 242mg sod., 2g carb. (trace sugars, trace fiber), 12g pro.

BREADS, BISCUITS & MORE

Dinner rolls and doughnuts...French bread and fruitcake...
let the aroma of these freshly baked delights usher in
heartwarming memories of Grandma's kitchen today.

SOUR CREAM LOAVES WITH WALNUT FILLING

When I was little, my grandmother taught me how to make these rolls. I felt so special.
—Nadine Mesch, Mount Healthy, OH

Prep: 1 hour + rising • **Bake:** 20 min.
Makes: 8 loaves (6 servings each)

- 4 cups ground walnuts (about 14 oz.)
- 1 cup sugar
- ¾ cup butter, melted
- ½ cup 2% milk
- ⅓ cup honey

DOUGH

- 2 pkg. (¼ oz. each) active dry yeast
- 1 tsp. plus ⅓ cup sugar, divided
- ½ cup warm 2% milk (110° to 115°)
- 1 cup butter, melted
- 1 cup sour cream
- 4 large eggs, room temperature, divided use
- 1 tsp. salt
- 5¼ to 5¾ cups all-purpose flour

1. In a large bowl, mix the first 5 ingredients until blended. In a small bowl, dissolve yeast and 1 tsp. sugar in warm milk; let stand for 15 minutes. In a large bowl, combine melted butter, sour cream, 3 eggs, salt, remaining sugar, yeast mixture and 2 cups flour; beat on medium speed 3 minutes. Stir in enough remaining flour to form a soft dough (the dough will be sticky).

2. Turn dough onto a floured surface; knead until smooth and elastic, 6-8 minutes. Place in a greased bowl, turning once to grease the top. Cover and let rise in a warm place until doubled, about 1 hour.

3. Punch down dough. Turn onto a lightly floured surface; divide dough and shape into 8 portions. Roll each into a 12x8-in. rectangle (dough will be very thin). Spread each with ½ cup walnut mixture to within ¾ in. of edges. Carefully roll up jelly-roll style, starting with a long side; pinch seam and ends to seal.

4. Place rolls 2 in. apart on parchment-lined baking sheets, seam side down. Prick tops with a fork. Cover; let rise in a warm place until almost doubled, about 1 hour. Preheat oven to 350°.

5. Lightly beat remaining egg; brush over rolls. Bake 20-25 minutes or until golden brown, switching position of pans halfway through baking (filling may leak during baking). Remove loaves to wire racks to cool. To serve, cut into slices.

1 serving: 201 cal., 13g fat (5g sat. fat), 37mg chol., 113mg sod., 20g carb. (8g sugars, 1g fiber), 3g pro.

"This is a great recipe. My grandmother, who was born in Yugoslavia, used this same recipe, and now I do. I try to make it every year at Easter, and everyone loves it."
—FMMSLKL, TASTEOFHOME.COM

BACON DATE BREAD

There is a joke between friends that whenever I'm asked to bring a dish to a party, it always contains bacon. This recipe has the sweet and salty flavors of date-nut bread and bacon-wrapped dates.
—Terrie Gammon, Eden Prairie, MN

Prep: 25 min. • **Bake:** 45 min. + cooling
Makes: 1 loaf (16 slices)

- 8 **bacon strips, chopped**
- 8 **green onions, thinly sliced**
- 2 **cups all-purpose flour**
- 3 **tsp. baking powder**
- 1 **tsp. sugar**
- ¼ **tsp. salt**
- ⅛ **tsp. cayenne pepper**
- 2 **large eggs, room temperature**
- 1 **cup sour cream**
- ¼ **cup butter, melted**
- 1½ **cups shredded Asiago cheese, divided**
- ⅔ **cup pitted dates, chopped**

1. Preheat oven to 350°. In a skillet, cook bacon over medium heat until crisp, stirring occasionally. Remove with a slotted spoon; drain on paper towels. Discard drippings, reserving 2 Tbsp. in pan.
2. Add the green onions to drippings; cook and stir over medium-high heat until tender, 1-2 minutes. Cool slightly.
3. In a large bowl, whisk the flour, baking powder, sugar, salt and cayenne. In another bowl, whisk eggs, sour cream and melted butter until blended. Add to flour mixture; stir just until moistened. Fold in 1 cup cheese, dates, bacon and green onions (batter will be thick).
4. Transfer to a greased 9x5-in. loaf pan; sprinkle with the remaining cheese. Bake until a toothpick inserted in center comes out clean, 45-50 minutes. Cool in pan for 10 minutes before removing to a wire rack. Serve warm.

1 slice: 211 cal., 13g fat (7g sat. fat), 49mg chol., 267mg sod., 17g carb. (4g sugars, 1g fiber), 7g pro.

FLAKY CHEDDAR-CHIVE BISCUITS

These buttery biscuits will complement just about any dinner. Speckled with cheese and chives, they look wonderful—and taste even better!
—Elizabeth King, Duluth, MN

- -

Takes: 25 min. • **Makes:** 10 biscuits

2¼ cups all-purpose flour
2½ tsp. baking powder
 2   tsp. sugar
 ½   tsp. baking soda
 ½   tsp. salt
 ½   cup cold butter, cubed
 1   cup shredded cheddar cheese
 3   Tbsp. minced fresh chives
 1   cup buttermilk

1. Preheat oven to 425°. In a large bowl, whisk the first 5 ingredients. Cut in butter until mixture resembles coarse crumbs; stir in cheese and chives. Add the buttermilk; stir just until moistened. Turn onto a lightly floured surface; knead gently 8-10 times.
2. Pat or roll dough to ¾-in. thickness; cut with a floured 2½-in. biscuit cutter. Place 2 in. apart on a greased baking sheet. Bake 10-12 minutes or until golden brown. Serve biscuits warm.

1 biscuit: 236 cal., 13g fat (8g sat. fat), 37mg chol., 440mg sod., 24g carb. (3g sugars, 1g fiber), 6g pro.

BUTTERY HERB LOAVES

This is one of my family's favorite bread recipes. They love it with a warm bowl of soup when there's a chill in the air.
—Lillian Hatcher, Plainfield, IL

- -

Prep: 45 min. + rising
Bake: 20 min. + cooling
Makes: 2 loaves (16 slices each)

- 4 to 5 cups all-purpose flour
- 1 pkg. (¼ oz.) active dry yeast
- ¼ cup sugar
- 1 tsp. salt
- 1¼ cups 2% milk
- ⅓ cup butter, cubed
- 2 large eggs, room temperature

FILLING

- ½ cup butter, softened
- 1 garlic clove, minced
- ½ tsp. dried minced onion
- ½ tsp. dried basil
- ½ tsp. caraway seeds
- ¼ tsp. dried oregano
- ⅛ tsp. cayenne pepper

1. In a large bowl, combine 2 cups flour, yeast, sugar and salt. In a small saucepan, heat milk and butter to 120°-130°. Add to dry ingredients; beat just until moistened. Add eggs; beat until smooth. Stir in enough remaining flour to form a soft dough.

2. Turn onto a floured surface; knead until smooth and elastic, 6-8 minutes. Place in a greased bowl, turning once to grease top. Cover and let rise in a warm place until doubled, about 1 hour.

3. In a small bowl, combine the filling ingredients; set aside. Punch down dough; divide in half. Turn onto a lightly floured surface. Roll each portion into a 15x9-in. rectangle. Spread filling over each to within ½ in. of edges. Roll up rectangles jelly-roll style, starting with a short side; pinch seams to seal and tuck ends under.

4. Place seam side down in 2 greased 9x5-in. loaf pans. Cover and let rise in a warm place until doubled, about 30 minutes.

5. Bake at 350° for 20-25 minutes or until golden brown. Cool loaves for 10 minutes before removing from pans to wire racks to cool completely.

1 slice: 109 cal., 5g fat (3g sat. fat), 27mg chol., 116mg sod., 13g carb. (2g sugars, 0 fiber), 3g pro. **Diabetic exchanges:** 1 starch, 1 fat.

OVEN-FRIED CORNBREAD

This is an old family recipe that has been passed down through generations. Few things says good southern cooking like crisp cornbread baked in a cast-iron skillet.
—Emory Doty, Jasper, GA

- -

Prep: 20 min. • **Bake:** 15 min.
Makes: 8 servings

    4   Tbsp. canola oil, divided
 1½   cups finely ground white cornmeal
    ¼   cup sugar
    2   tsp. baking powder
    1   tsp. baking soda
    1   tsp. salt
    2   large eggs, room temperature
    2   cups buttermilk

1. Place 2 Tbsp. oil in a 10-in. cast-iron skillet; place in oven. Preheat oven to 450°. Whisk together cornmeal, sugar, baking powder, baking soda and salt. In another bowl, whisk together eggs, buttermilk and remaining oil. Add to cornmeal mixture; stir just until moistened.
2. Carefully remove hot skillet from oven. Add batter; bake until golden brown and a toothpick inserted in center comes out clean, 15-20 minutes. Cut into wedges; serve warm.
1 wedge: 238 cal., 9g fat (1g sat. fat), 49mg chol., 709mg sod., 33g carb. (10g sugars, 1g fiber), 6g pro.

CELERY-ONION POPOVERS

I found this handwritten recipe in an old cookbook I received from my mom. With onion and celery, these pleasing popovers taste a little like stuffing.
—Barbara Carlucci, Orange Park, FL

- -

Prep: 15 min. • **Bake:** 40 min.
Makes: 9 servings

    2   cups all-purpose flour
    1   tsp. onion salt
    ⅛   tsp. celery salt
    4   large eggs, room temperature
    2   cups whole milk
    ¼   cup grated onion
    ¼   cup grated celery
    3   Tbsp. butter, melted

1. In a large bowl, combine the flour, onion salt and celery salt. Combine the eggs, milk, onion, celery and butter; whisk into the dry ingredients just until blended. Grease and flour the bottom and sides of 9 popover cups; fill two-thirds full with batter.
2. Bake at 450° for 15 minutes. Reduce heat to 350° (do not open oven door). Bake until deep golden brown (do not underbake), about 25 minutes longer. Immediately cut a slit in the top of each popover to allow steam to escape.
1 popover: 202 cal., 8g fat (4g sat. fat), 98mg chol., 306mg sod., 25g carb. (3g sugars, 1g fiber), 7g pro.

GRANDMA'S POPOVERS

My grandmother made these for our Sunday dinners. The recipe could not be simpler. Warm from the oven, popovers are always a fun accompaniment to a homey meal.
—Debbie Terenzini, Lusby, MD

Prep: 10 min. • **Bake:** 30 min.
Makes: 6 popovers

- 1 cup all-purpose flour
- ⅛ tsp. salt
- 3 large eggs, room temperature
- 1 cup 2% milk

1. In a large bowl, combine flour and salt. Beat the eggs and milk; whisk into the dry ingredients just until combined. Cover the mixture and let stand at room temperature for 45 minutes. Grease cups of a popover pan well with butter or oil; fill the cups two-thirds full with batter.
2. Bake at 450° for 15 minutes. Reduce heat to 350° (do not open oven door). Bake until deep golden brown (do not underbake), about 15 minutes longer.
3. Run a table knife or small metal spatula round edges of cups to loosen if necessary. Immediately remove popovers from pan; prick with a small sharp knife to allow steam to escape. Serve immediately.
Note: You may use greased muffin tins instead of a popover pan. Fill every other cup two-thirds full with batter to avoid crowding the popovers; fill remaining cups with water. Bake at 450° for 15 minutes and 350° for 10 minutes.
1 popover: 132 cal., 3g fat (1g sat. fat), 109mg chol., 105mg sod., 18g carb. (2g sugars, 1g fiber), 7g pro.

JELLY DOUGHNUTS

There's no need to run to the bakery for old-fashioned jelly doughnuts! These sweet treats are lighter than air. I've been fixing them for my family for many years.
—Kathy Westendorf, Westgate, IA

Prep: 30 min. • **Cook:** 10 min.
Makes: 16 doughnuts

- 2 pkg. (¼ oz. each) active dry yeast
- ½ cup warm water (110° to 115°)
- ½ cup warm 2% milk (110° to 115°)
- ⅓ cup butter, softened
- 1⅓ cups sugar, divided
- 3 large egg yolks, room temperature
- 1 tsp. salt
- 3 to 3¾ cups all-purpose flour
- 3 Tbsp. jelly or jam
- 1 large egg white, lightly beaten
  Oil for deep-fat frying

1. In a small bowl, dissolve yeast in warm water. In a large bowl, combine milk, butter, ⅓ cup sugar, egg yolks, salt, yeast mixture and 3 cups flour; beat until smooth. Stir in enough remaining flour to form a soft dough (do not knead).
2. Place in a greased bowl, turning once to grease top. Cover and let rise in a warm place until doubled, about 45 minutes.
3. Punch dough down. Turn onto a lightly floured surface; knead about 10 times. Divide dough in half.
4. Roll each portion to ¼-in. thickness; cut with a floured 2½-in. round cutter. Place about ½ tsp. jelly in the center of half of the circles; brush the edges with egg white. Top with the remaining circles; press edges to seal tightly.
5. Place on greased baking sheet. Cover and let rise until doubled, about 45 minutes.
6. In an electric skillet or deep-fat fryer, heat oil to 375°. Fry doughnuts, a few at a time, 1-2 minutes on each side or until golden brown. Drain on paper towels. Roll warm doughnuts in remaining sugar.
1 doughnut: 232 cal., 5 fat (3 sat. fat), 49 chol.,183mg sod., 42g carb. (20g sugars, 1g fiber), 4g pro.

BABA'S ROSEMARY DINNER ROLLS

My grandma (I called her Baba) made these in her coal oven. How she regulated the temperature is beyond me! My mom and aunts would always deliver a few extra formed rolls to the neighbors to bake in their own ovens.
—Charlotte Hendershot, Hudson, PA

- -

Prep: 35 min. + rising • **Bake:** 20 min.
Makes: 1 dozen

1	pkg. (¼ oz.) active dry yeast
¼	cup warm water (110° to 115°)
3	cups bread flour
2	Tbsp. sugar

1	Tbsp. minced fresh rosemary, divided
¾	tsp. salt
⅔	cup warm 2% milk (110° to 115°)
1	large egg, room temperature
¼	to ⅓ cup canola oil

EGG WASH

1	large egg yolk
2	Tbsp. 2% milk

1. In a small bowl, dissolve yeast in warm water. Place the flour, sugar, 2 tsp. rosemary and salt in a food processor; pulse until blended. Add the warm milk, egg and yeast mixture; cover and pulse 10 times or until almost blended.

2. While processing, gradually add oil just until dough pulls away from sides and begins to form a ball. Process 2 minutes longer to knead dough (the dough will be very soft).

3. Transfer the dough to a greased bowl, turning once to grease the top. Cover and let rise in a warm place until doubled, about 1 hour.

4. Punch down dough. Turn onto a lightly floured surface; divide and shape into 12 balls. Roll each into a 15-in. rope. Starting at 1 end, loosely wrap dough around itself to form a coil. Tuck end under; pinch to seal.

5. Place 2 in. apart on greased baking sheets. Cover and let rise until doubled, about 30 minutes.

6. For egg wash, in a small bowl, whisk egg yolk and milk; brush over rolls. Sprinkle with the remaining rosemary. Bake at 350° until golden brown, 18-22 minutes. Remove from pans to wire racks; serve warm.

1 roll: 194 cal., 6g fat (1g sat. fat), 32mg chol., 163mg sod., 28g carb. (3g sugars, 1g fiber), 6g pro.

"When I saw these, I immediately thought of my own Baba's rolls! She used this same recipe. The smell in her kitchen was heaven! Thanks for such a wonderful memory."
—TAMI, TASTEOFHOME.COM

GOLDEN HONEY PAN ROLLS

A cousin in North Carolina gave me the recipe for these delicious honey-glazed rolls. Using my bread machine to make the dough saves me about 2 hours compared to the traditional method. The rolls' rich buttery taste is so popular with family and friends that I usually make two batches so I have enough!
—Sara Wing, Philadelphia, PA

Prep: 35 min. + rising • **Bake:** 20 min.
Makes: 2 dozen

- 1 cup warm 2% milk (70° to 80°)
- 1 large egg, room temperature
- 1 large egg yolk, room temperature
- ½ cup canola oil
- 2 Tbsp. honey
- 1½ tsp. salt
- 3½ cups bread flour
- 2¼ tsp. active dry yeast

GLAZE

- ⅓ cup sugar
- 2 Tbsp. butter, melted
- 1 Tbsp. honey
- 1 large egg white
  Additional honey, optional

1. In bread machine pan, place the first 8 ingredients in order suggested by the manufacturer. Select dough setting (check dough after 5 minutes of mixing; add 1 to 2 Tbsp. of water or flour if needed.)

2. When cycle is completed, turn dough onto a lightly floured surface. Punch down; cover and let rest for 10 minutes. Divide into 24 pieces; shape each piece into a ball. Place 12 balls each in 2 greased 8-in. square baking pans. Cover and let rise in a warm place until doubled, about 30 minutes.

3. For glaze, combine the sugar, butter, honey and egg white; drizzle over dough. Bake at 350° for 20-25 minutes or until golden brown. Brush with additional honey if desired.

Note: We recommend you do not use a bread machine's time-delay feature for this recipe.

1 roll: 139 cal., 6g fat (2g sat. fat), 22mg chol., 168mg sod., 18g carb. (5g sugars, 1g fiber), 3g pro.

NO BREAD MACHINE? NO PROBLEM!

Grandma didn't always have a bread machine. Simply follow these directions to make Golden Honey Pan Rolls without the help of a bread machine.

Dissolve yeast in warm milk. In another bowl, combine egg, egg yolk, oil, honey, salt, yeast mixture and 2 cups flour; beat on medium speed until smooth. Stir in enough remaining flour to form a soft dough (dough will be sticky).

Turn onto a floured surface; knead until smooth and elastic, 6-8 minutes. Place in a greased bowl, turning once to grease top. Cover and let rise in a warm place until dough is doubled, about 1 hour. Punch down the dough; cover and let rest for 10 minutes.

Turn onto a lightly floured surface. Divide and shape into 24 balls; place 12 each in 2 greased 8x8-in. baking pans. Cover and let rise in a warm place until doubled, about 30 minutes. Preheat oven to 350°; glaze and bake as directed.

GRANDMA'S MOLASSES FRUITCAKE

This was my grandmother's recipe. The flavor gets better as it sits in the fridge.
—Debbie Harmon, Lavina, MT

- -

Prep: 25 min. + chilling
Bake: 1¼ hours + cooling
Makes: 3 loaves (16 slices each)

- 3¼ cups dried currants
- 2⅔ cups raisins
- 1 cup chopped walnuts
- ⅔ cup chopped candied citron or candied lemon peel
- 4 cups all-purpose flour, divided
- 1 cup butter, softened
- 2 cups packed brown sugar
- 4 large eggs, room temperature
- 1 cup molasses
- 1 tsp. baking soda
- 1 tsp. each ground cinnamon, nutmeg and cloves
- 1 cup strong brewed coffee

1. Preheat oven to 300°. Grease and flour three 9x5-in. loaf pans. Line bottoms with waxed paper; grease and flour the paper. Combine currants, raisins, walnuts, candied citron and ¼ cup flour. Toss to coat.
2. Cream butter and brown sugar until light and fluffy. Add 1 egg at a time, beating well after each addition. Beat in molasses. In another bowl, whisk baking soda, cinnamon, nutmeg, cloves and remaining flour; add to creamed mixture alternately with coffee. Stir into currant mixture and mix well.
3. Transfer to prepared pans. Bake until a toothpick inserted in the center comes out clean, 1¼-1½ hours. Cool in pans 10 minutes before removing loaves to wire racks to cool completely. Wrap tightly and store in the refrigerator at least 2 days to blend the flavors. Bring to room temperature before serving. Refrigerate leftovers.
1 slice: 210 cal., 6g fat (3g sat. fat), 26mg chol., 79mg sod., 39g carb. (28g sugars, 2g fiber), 3g pro.

GRANNY'S BISCUITS

My grandmother makes these homemade biscuits to go with her seafood chowder, but they taste great with almost any dish.
—Melissa Obernesser, Utica, NY

- -

Takes: 25 min. • **Makes:** 10 biscuits

- 2 cups all-purpose flour
- 3 tsp. baking powder
- 1 tsp. salt
- ⅓ cup shortening
- ⅔ cup 2% milk
- 1 large egg, lightly beaten

1. Preheat oven to 450°. In a large bowl, whisk flour, baking powder and salt. Cut in shortening until mixture resembles coarse crumbs. Add milk; stir just until moistened.
2. Turn onto a lightly floured surface; knead gently 8-10 times. Pat dough into a 10x4-in. rectangle. Cut rectangle lengthwise in half; cut crosswise to make 10 squares.
3. Place 1 in. apart on an ungreased baking sheet; brush tops with egg. Bake until golden brown, 8-10 minutes. Serve warm.
1 biscuit: 165 cal., 7g fat (2g sat. fat), 20mg chol., 371mg sod., 20g carb. (1g sugars, 1g fiber), 4g pro.

APPLE CIDER DOUGHNUTS

When we were kids, we always stopped at a drugstore that sold doughnuts like these before camping in the Badlands. Share a batch with someone you know who appreciates the old-fashioned taste of fresh doughnuts.
—Melissa Hansen, Ellison Bay, WI

- -

Prep: 40 min. + chilling • **Cook:** 5 min./batch
Makes: 1 dozen doughnuts plus doughnut holes

- 2 **cups apple cider**
- 3 **cups all-purpose flour**
- ½ **cup whole wheat flour**
- ⅔ **cup packed brown sugar**
- 2 **tsp. baking powder**
- ¾ **tsp. salt**
- ½ **tsp. baking soda**
- ¼ **tsp. each ground cardamom, nutmeg, cinnamon and allspice**
- 2 **large eggs, room temperature**
- 6 **Tbsp. butter, melted and cooled**
   Oil for deep-fat frying
   Ginger-Sugar, optional

1. In a small saucepan, bring cider to a rapid boil; cook over high heat until reduced by half, about 12 minutes. Cool completely.
2. Whisk together flours, brown sugar, baking powder, salt, baking soda and spices. In a separate bowl, whisk eggs, melted butter and cooled cider; stir into the dry ingredients just until moistened (dough will be sticky). Refrigerate, covered, until firm enough to shape, about 1 hour.
3. Divide the dough in half. On a floured surface, pat each portion to ½-in. thickness; cut with a floured 3-in. doughnut cutter.
4. In an electric skillet or deep fryer, heat oil to 325°. Fry doughnuts, a few at a time, until golden brown, 2-3 minutes on each side. Fry doughnut holes, a few at time, until golden brown and cooked through, about 1 minute on each side. Drain on paper towels; cool slightly. If desired, toss doughnuts with Ginger-Sugar (recipe below).

1 doughnut: 335 cal., 15g fat (5g sat. fat), 46mg chol., 338mg sod., 45g carb. (16g sugars, 1g fiber), 5g pro.
Ginger-Sugar: In a shallow bowl, mix ¾ cup sugar and 2-3 Tbsp. ground ginger.

SHAPING DOUGHNUTS
All you need to flatten this dough are your hands. Pat it down, then cut with a doughnut cutter. To keep the dough from sticking, wiggle your cutter in a little flour between cuts.

SWEET ITALIAN HOLIDAY BREAD

This is authentic ciambellotto, a sweet loaf my great-grandmother used to bake in Italy. I still use her traditional recipe.
—Denise Perrin, Vancouver, WA

Prep: 15 min. • **Bake:** 45 min.
Makes: 1 loaf (20 slices)

- 4 **cups all-purpose flour**
- 1 **cup sugar**
- 2 **Tbsp. grated orange zest**
- 3 **tsp. baking powder**
- 3 **large eggs, room temperature**
- ½ **cup 2% milk**
- ½ **cup olive oil**
- 1 **large egg yolk**
- 1 **Tbsp. coarse sugar**

1. Preheat oven to 350°. In a large bowl, whisk flour, sugar, orange zest and baking powder. In another bowl, whisk eggs, milk and oil until blended. Add to flour mixture; stir just until moistened.

2. Shape into a 6-in. round loaf on a greased baking sheet. Brush top with the egg yolk; sprinkle with coarse sugar. Bake until a toothpick inserted in center comes out clean, 45-50 minutes. Cover top loosely with foil during the last 10 minutes if needed to prevent overbrowning. Remove from pan to a wire rack; serve warm.

1 slice: 197 cal., 7g fat (1g sat. fat), 38mg chol., 87mg sod., 30g carb. (11g sugars, 1g fiber), 4g pro.

AMISH ONION CAKE

This rich, moist bread with an onion-poppy seed topping is a wonderful break from your everyday bread routine. You can serve it with any meat, soup or salad. I've made it many times and have often been asked to share the recipe.
—Mitzi Sentiff, Annapolis, MD

- -

Prep: 25 min. • **Bake:** 35 min.
Makes: 12 servings

- 3   to 4 medium onions, chopped
- 2   cups cold butter, divided
- 1   Tbsp. poppy seeds
- 1½ tsp. salt
- 1½ tsp. paprika
- 1   tsp. coarsely ground pepper
- 4   cups all-purpose flour
- ½   cup cornstarch
- 1   Tbsp. baking powder
- 1   Tbsp. sugar
- 1   Tbsp. brown sugar
- 5   large eggs, room temperature
- ¾   cup 2% milk
- ¾   cup sour cream

1. In a large skillet, cook onions in ½ cup butter over low heat for 10 minutes. Stir in the poppy seeds, salt, paprika and pepper; cook until onions are golden brown, stirring occasionally. Remove from the heat; set the mixture aside.

2. In a large bowl, combine the flour, cornstarch, baking powder and sugars. Cut in 1¼ cups butter until mixture resembles coarse crumbs. Melt the remaining butter. In a small bowl, whisk the eggs, milk, sour cream and melted butter. Make a well in dry ingredients; stir in the egg mixture just until moistened.

3. Spread into a greased 10-in. cast-iron skillet or springform pan. Spoon onion mixture over the batter. Place pan on a baking sheet. Bake at 350° until a toothpick inserted in the center comes out clean, 35-40 minutes. Serve warm.

1 slice: 539 cal., 36g fat (22g sat. fat), 182mg chol., 748mg sod., 44g carb. (7g sugars, 2g fiber), 9g pro.

PASSOVER POPOVERS

Popovers have an important role at the table, substituting for bread. When puffed and golden brown, they're ready to share.
—Gloria Mezikofsky, Wakefield, MA

- -

Prep: 25 min. • **Bake:** 20 min. + standing
Makes: 1 dozen

- 1   cup water
- ½   cup safflower oil
- ⅛   to ¼ tsp. salt
- 1   cup matzo cake meal
- 7   large eggs, room temperature

1. Preheat oven to 450°. Generously grease 12 muffin cups. In a large saucepan, bring water, oil and salt to a rolling boil. Add cake meal all at once and beat until blended. Remove from heat; let stand 5 minutes.

2. Transfer the mixture to a blender. Add 2 eggs; process, covered, until blended. Continue adding 1 egg at a time and process until incorporated. Process until mixture is smooth, about 2 minutes longer.

3. Fill prepared muffin cups three-fourths full. Bake until puffed, very firm and golden brown, 18-22 minutes. Turn off oven (do not open oven door); leave the popovers in oven 10 minutes. Immediately remove from pan to a wire rack. Serve hot.

Note: This recipe was tested with Manischewitz cake meal. Look for it in the baking aisle or kosher foods section.

1 popover: 174 cal., 12g fat (2g sat. fat), 109mg chol., 66mg sod., 11g carb. (0 sugars, 0 fiber), 5g pro.

GARDEN VEGETABLE BREAD

When I was a kid, my parents would make cornbread for my siblings and me. We would slather butter and maple syrup over the warm bread—it was delicious. Today, I experiment a lot with recipes, just like my grandma and mom did, and that's how my healthier version of their easy cornbread recipe was born!
—Kim Moyes, Kenosha, WI

Prep: 20 min. • **Bake:** 20 min.
Makes: 9 servings

- 1 cup yellow cornmeal
- ¾ cup whole wheat flour
- 2½ tsp. baking powder
- 2 tsp. minced fresh chives
- ¾ tsp. salt
- 2 large eggs, room temperature
- 1 cup 2% milk
- 2 Tbsp. honey
- ¾ cup shredded carrots (about 1½ carrots)
- ¼ cup finely chopped sweet red pepper
- ¼ cup finely chopped fresh poblano pepper, seeded

1. Preheat oven to 400°. Whisk together the first 5 ingredients. In another bowl, whisk eggs, milk and honey until blended. Add to cornmeal mixture; stir just until moistened. Fold in carrots and peppers.

2. Transfer to a greased 8-in. square baking pan. Bake until a toothpick inserted in the center comes out clean, 20-25 minutes. Serve warm.

1 piece: 149 cal., 2g fat (1g sat. fat), 44mg chol., 367mg sod., 28g carb. (6g sugars, 2g fiber), 5g pro. **Diabetic exchanges:** 2 starch.

GRANDMA'S FAVORITE HOT CROSS BUNS

My husband's grandma used to make these every year for Good Friday, and I carry on the tradition with my own version of her recipe. I make 6 dozen every year, and they all disappear.

—Jill Evely, Wilmore, KY

- -

Prep: 45 min. + rising • **Bake:** 15 min./batch
Makes: 6 dozen

- 4 pkg. (¼ oz. each) active dry yeast
- 3 cups warm 2% milk (110° to 115°)
- 2 cups canola oil
- 8 large eggs, room temperature
- 4 large eggs, room temperature, separated
- 1⅓ cups sugar
- 4 tsp. ground cinnamon
- 3 tsp. salt
- 2 tsp. ground cardamom
- 13 to 15 cups all-purpose flour
- 2⅔ cups raisins
- 2 tsp. water

ICING

- 3 cups confectioners' sugar
- 2 Tbsp. butter, melted
- 4 to 5 Tbsp. 2% milk

1. In a very large bowl, dissolve yeast in warm milk. Add oil, eggs, egg yolks, sugar, cinnamon, salt, cardamom, yeast mixture and 10 cups flour. Beat until smooth. Stir in enough remaining flour to form a firm dough. Stir in raisins.

2. Turn onto a floured surface; knead until smooth and elastic, 6-8 minutes. Place in a greased bowl, turning once to grease the top. Cover and let rise in a warm place until doubled, about 1¼ hours.

3. Punch dough down. Turn onto a lightly floured surface. Cover and let rest 10 minutes. Divide into 72 pieces; shape each into a ball. Place balls 2 in. apart in 4 greased 15x10x1-in. baking pans. Cover and let rise in a warm place until balls are doubled, about 40 minutes.

4. Preheat oven to 375°. Combine egg whites and water; brush over tops. Bake 12-15 minutes or until golden brown. Remove from pans to wire racks to cool. For icing, combine confectioners' sugar, butter and enough milk to achieve desired consistency. Pipe a cross on the top of each bun.

1 bun: 219 cal., 8g fat (1g sat. fat), 37mg chol., 120mg sod., 32g carb. (12g sugars, 2g fiber), 5g pro.

GRANDMA'S APPLE BREAD

The heartwarming aroma of cinnamon, apples and nuts baking in this bread will make anyone's mouth water.
—Sheila Bradshaw, Powell, OH

Prep: 20 min. • **Bake:** 35 min. + cooling
Makes: 2 loaves (12 slices each)

- 1⅓ cups all-purpose flour
- ⅔ cup rye flour
- ½ cup sugar
- 2 tsp. baking powder
- 1½ tsp. ground cinnamon
- ½ tsp. baking soda
- ½ tsp. salt
- 1 large egg, room temperature
- ¾ cup unsweetened apple juice
- ¾ cup sweetened applesauce
- ⅓ cup canola oil
- ½ cup chopped pecans

1. In a large bowl, combine the flours, sugar, baking powder, cinnamon, baking soda and salt. In another bowl, whisk the egg, apple juice, applesauce and oil until smooth. Stir into dry ingredients just until moistened. Fold in pecans.

2. Pour into 2 greased 8x4-in. loaf pans. Bake at 350° for 35-40 minutes or until a toothpick inserted in the center comes out clean. Cool for 10 minutes before removing from pans to wire racks.

1 slice: 108 cal., 5g fat (1g sat. fat), 9mg chol., 112mg sod., 15g carb. (7g sugars, 1g fiber), 1g pro.

CORNMEAL PARKER HOUSE ROLLS

My mom made this recipe a cherished family tradition. These sweet, tender rolls have been on every holiday table at her house for as long as I can remember.
—Lisa Brenner, Harrisburg, NE

Prep: 40 min. + rising • **Bake:** 15 min.
Makes: 2½ dozen

- ½ cup butter, cubed
- ½ cup sugar
- ⅓ cup cornmeal
- 1 tsp. salt
- 2 cups 2% milk
- 1 pkg. (¼ oz.) active dry yeast
- ½ cup warm water (110° to 115°)
- 2 large eggs, room temperature
- 4½ to 5½ cups all-purpose flour
- 3 Tbsp. butter, melted
  Optional: Olive oil and balsamic vinegar

1. In a small saucepan, melt butter. Stir in the sugar, cornmeal and salt. Gradually add milk. Bring to a boil over medium-high heat, stirring constantly. Reduce heat; cook and stir for 5-10 minutes or until thickened. Cool to 110°-115°.

2. In a large bowl, dissolve yeast in warm water. Add eggs and cornmeal mixture. Beat in enough flour to form a soft dough. Turn onto a floured surface; knead until smooth and elastic, 6-8 minutes. Place in a greased bowl, turning once to grease top. Cover and let rise in a warm place until doubled, about 1 hour.

3. Punch dough down. Turn onto a lightly floured surface; roll out to ½-in. thickness. Cut with a floured 2½-in. biscuit cutter. Brush with melted butter.

4. Using the dull edge of a table knife, make an off-center crease in each roll. Fold along crease so the large half is on top; press along folded edge. Place 2 in. apart on greased baking sheets. Cover and let rise until nearly doubled, about 30 minutes.

5. Bake at 375° for 15-20 minutes or until golden brown. Brush with melted butter. Remove from pans to wire racks. If desired, serve with olive oil and balsamic vinegar.

1 roll: 137 cal., 5g fat (3g sat. fat), 26mg chol., 122mg sod., 20g carb. (4g sugar, 1g fiber), 3g pro. **Diabetic exchanges:** 1 starch, 1 fat.

EASY YEAST ROLLS

These tender rolls always disappear in no time. If you have never made homemade yeast bread, this simple dough is the perfect place to start. You can easily cut the recipe in half.

—Wilma Harter, Witten, SD

- -

Prep: 45 min. + rising • **Bake:** 15 min.
Makes: 4 dozen

- 2 **pkg. (¼ oz. each) active dry yeast**
- 2 **cups warm water (110° to 115°)**
- ½ **cup sugar**
- 1 **large egg, room temperature**
- ¼ **cup canola oil**
- 2 **tsp. salt**
- 6 **to 6½ cups all-purpose flour**

1. In a small bowl, dissolve yeast in warm water. In a large bowl, combine the sugar, egg, oil, salt, yeast mixture and 4 cups all-purpose flour; beat on medium speed until smooth. Stir in enough remaining flour to form a stiff dough.

2. Turn dough onto a floured surface; knead until smooth and elastic, 6-8 minutes. Place in a greased bowl, turning once to grease the top. Cover and let rise in a warm place until doubled, about 1 hour.

3. Punch down dough. Turn onto a lightly floured surface; divide into 4 portions. Divide and shape each portion into 12 balls. Roll each ball into an 8-in. rope; tie into a loose knot. Tuck ends under. Place 2 in. apart on greased baking sheets. Cover; let rise in a warm place until doubled, about 30 minutes. Preheat oven to 350°.

4. Bake 15-20 minutes or until golden brown. Remove from pans to wire racks.

1 roll: 78 cal., 1g fat (0 sat. fat), 4mg chol., 100mg sod., 14g carb. (2g sugars, 0 fiber), 2g pro. **Diabetic exchanges:** 1 starch.

GRANDMA'S SWEET POTATO BISCUITS

The recipe for these mild-tasting biscuits was my grandmother's. They are truly a fast family favorite.

—Nancy Daugherty, Cortland, OH

- -

Takes: 30 min. • **Makes:** 1½ dozen

- 2½ **cups all-purpose flour**
- 1 **Tbsp. baking powder**
- 1 **tsp. salt**
- ⅓ **cup shortening**
- 1 **can (15¾ oz.) sweet potatoes, drained**
- ¾ **cup whole milk**

1. In a large bowl, combine the flour, baking powder and salt. Cut in the shortening until the mixture resembles coarse crumbs. In another bowl, mash the sweet potatoes and milk. Add to the crumb mixture just until combined.

2. Turn dough onto a floured surface; knead 8-10 times. Roll to ½-in. thickness; cut with a 2½-in. biscuit cutter. Place on ungreased baking sheets.

3. Bake at 425° 8-10 minutes or until golden brown. Remove to wire racks. Serve warm.

1 biscuit: 124 cal., 4g fat (1g sat. fat), 1mg chol., 214mg sod., 19g carb. (4g sugars, 1g fiber), 2g pro.

TENDER WHOLE WHEAT ROLLS

Even though these are whole wheat rolls, they have a light texture and are soft and tender. This recipe reminds me of lots of happy meals with my family.
—Wilma Orlano, Carroll, IA

Prep: 40 min. + rising • **Bake:** 10 min.
Makes: 2 dozen

1½	cups boiling water
⅓	cup wheat bran
3	Tbsp. ground flaxseed
1½	tsp. salt
1	tsp. ground cinnamon
⅓	cup honey
¼	cup canola oil
2	pkg. (¼ oz. each) active dry yeast
¼	cup warm water (110° to 115°)
2	tsp. sugar
1½	cups whole wheat flour
2½	to 3 cups bread flour

1. In a small bowl, pour boiling water over wheat bran, flaxseed, salt and cinnamon. Add the honey and oil. Let stand until mixture cools to 110°-115°, stirring occasionally.
2. In a large bowl, dissolve yeast in warm water. Add the sugar, whole wheat flour and wheat bran mixture. Beat on medium speed for 3 minutes. Stir in enough bread flour to form a firm dough.
3. Turn onto a floured surface; knead until smooth and elastic, 6-8 minutes. Place in a greased bowl, turning once to grease the top. Cover and let rise in a warm place until doubled, about 1 hour. Punch dough down.
4. Turn onto a lightly floured surface; divide into 24 pieces. Shape each into a roll. Place 2 in. apart on greased baking sheets. Cover and let rise until doubled, about 30 minutes.
5. Bake at 375° for 10-15 minutes or until golden brown. Carefully remove from pans to wire racks.

1 roll: 120 cal., 3g fat (0 sat. fat), 0 chol., 149mg sod., 22g carb. (4g sugars, 2g fiber), 4g pro. **Diabetic exchanges:** 1½ starch, ½ fat.

BUTTERMILK BRAN MUFFINS

For proof that good-for-you bran muffins need not be dry and bland, give this recipe a try. Even after I altered it to reduce sugar and fat, these moist muffins are still a hit.
—Anita Kay Brown, Greenbush, MI

- -

Prep: 20 min. • **Bake:** 15 min./batch
Makes: 22 muffins

- 1 cup All-Bran
- 2 cups buttermilk, divided
- 1½ cups raisin bran
- 2¾ cups all-purpose flour
- ¾ cup sugar
- ½ cup sugar blend
- ¼ cup packed brown sugar
- 1 tsp. baking powder
- ½ tsp. baking soda
- ½ tsp. salt
- 1 large egg, room temperature
- 2 large egg whites, room temperature
- ½ cup unsweetened applesauce
- ¼ cup canola oil

1. In a bowl, combine All-Bran and 1 cup buttermilk; let stand for 5 minutes. Stir in raisin bran; let stand 5 minutes longer.
2. Meanwhile, in a large bowl, combine the flour, sugar, sugar blend, brown sugar, baking powder, baking soda and salt. In another bowl, combine the egg, egg whites, applesauce, oil and remaining buttermilk. Stir into the dry ingredients just until moistened. Stir in bran mixture.
3. Coat muffin cups with cooking spray; fill three-fourths full with batter. Bake at 375° for 15-20 minutes or until a toothpick inserted in the center comes out clean. Cool for 5 minutes before removing from pans to wire racks.
Note: This recipe was tested with Splenda sugar blend.
1 muffin: 169 cal., 3g fat (0 sat. fat), 11mg chol., 165mg sod., 33g carb. (17g sugars, 2g fiber), 4g pro. **Diabetic exchanges:** 2 starch, ½ fat.

NO-KNEAD KNOT ROLLS

My mom loved to serve these light, pretty rolls when I was growing up on our Iowa farm. They're extra nice since they require no kneading. The dough rises in the refrigerator overnight, so there's little last-minute fuss to serve fresh hot rolls with any meal.
—Toni Hilscher, Omaha, NE

- -

Prep: 25 min. + rising • **Bake:** 10 min.
Makes: 4 dozen

- 2 pkg. (¼ oz. each) active dry yeast
- 2 cups warm water (110° to 115°)
- ½ cup sugar
- 2 tsp. salt
- 6 to 6½ cups all-purpose flour
- 1 large egg, room temperature
- ½ cup shortening
- ½ cup butter, softened

1. In a large bowl, dissolve yeast in warm water. Add the sugar, salt and 2 cups flour. Beat on medium speed for 2 minutes. Beat in the egg and shortening. Stir in enough of the remaining flour to form a soft dough (do not knead). Cover the dough and refrigerate overnight.
2. Punch the dough down and divide into 4 portions; roll each portion into a 14x12-in. rectangle. Spread 2 Tbsp. butter over the dough. Fold in half lengthwise; cut into 12 strips. Tie each strip into a knot; tuck and pinch the ends under. Place 2 in. apart on greased baking sheets. Repeat with the remaining dough.
3. Cover and let rise until doubled, about 1 hour. Bake at 400° until golden brown, 10-12 minutes. Remove to wire rack to cool.
1 roll: 102 cal., 4g fat (2g sat. fat), 10mg chol., 119mg sod., 14g carb. (2g sugars, 0 fiber), 2g pro.

DOUBLE CHOCOLATE BANANA MUFFINS

Combining two favorite flavors like rich chocolate and soft banana makes these muffins doubly good.
—Donna Brockett, Kingfisher, OK

- -

Prep: 15 min. • **Bake:** 20 min.
Makes: about 1 dozen

- 1½ cups all-purpose flour
- 1 cup sugar
- ¼ cup baking cocoa
- 1 tsp. baking soda
- ½ tsp. salt
- ¼ tsp. baking powder
- 1⅓ cups mashed ripe bananas (about 3 medium)
- ⅓ cup canola oil
- 1 large egg, room temperature
- 1 cup (6 oz.) miniature semisweet chocolate chips

1. Preheat oven to 350°. Whisk together the first 6 ingredients. In a separate bowl, whisk bananas, oil and egg until blended. Add to flour mixture; stir just until moistened. Fold in chocolate chips.
2. Fill greased or paper-lined muffin cups three-fourths full. Bake 20-25 minutes or until a toothpick inserted in center comes out clean. Cool 5 minutes before removing from pan to a wire rack. Serve warm.
1 muffin: 278 cal., 11g fat (3g sat. fat), 16mg chol., 220mg sod., 45g carb. (28g sugars, 2g fiber), 3g pro.

OLD-FASHIONED CARDAMOM BRAID BREAD

I came across this recipe in 1983, and I have been making it ever since.
—Rita Bergman, Olympia, WA

- -

Prep: 30 min. + rising
Bake: 20 min. + cooling
Makes: 2 loaves (20 slices each)

- 6 cups all-purpose flour
- 2 pkg. (¼ oz. each) active dry yeast
- 1½ tsp. ground cardamom
- 1 tsp. salt
- 1½ cups plus 2 Tbsp. whole milk, divided
- ½ cup butter, cubed
- ½ cup honey
- 2 large eggs, room temperature
- 2 Tbsp. sugar

1. In a large bowl, combine 2 cups flour, yeast, cardamom and salt. In a small saucepan, heat 1½ cups milk, butter and honey to 120°-130°. Add to dry ingredients; beat just until moistened. Add eggs; beat until smooth. Stir in enough remaining flour to form a firm dough (dough will be sticky).
2. Turn onto a floured surface; knead until smooth and elastic, 6-8 minutes. Place in a greased bowl, turning once to grease top. Cover and let rise in a warm place until doubled, about 45 minutes.
3. Punch dough down. Turn onto a lightly floured surface; divide in half. Divide each portion into thirds. Shape each into a 14-in. rope. Place the 3 ropes on a greased baking sheet and braid; pinch ends to seal and tuck under. Repeat with remaining dough. Cover and let rise until doubled, about 30 minutes.
4. Brush with remaining milk and sprinkle with sugar. Bake at 375° for 20-25 minutes or until golden brown. Remove from pans to wire racks to cool.

1 slice: 114 cal., 3g fat (2g sat. fat), 18mg chol., 91mg sod., 19g carb. (5g sugars, 1g fiber), 3g pro.

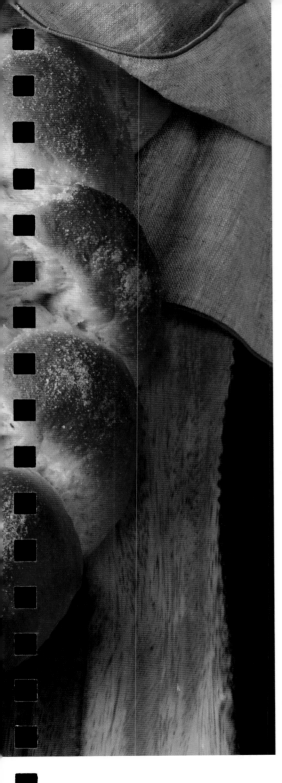

ICEBOX POTATO ROLLS

These tender rolls are a family favorite, and we sometimes have more than 20 people around the table. Make the dough in advance and bake when you're ready.
—Barb Linnerud, Boiling Springs, SC

- -

Prep: 1 hour + rising • **Bake:** 15 min.
Makes: about 2½ dozen

- 1¼ lbs. potatoes, peeled and cubed (about 3½ cups)
- ¾ cup sugar
- 2 tsp. salt
- 1 pkg. (¼ oz.) active dry yeast
- 5½ to 6 cups bread flour
- 1 cup 2% milk
- ½ cup water
- ½ cup shortening
- 3 large eggs, room temperature
- ⅓ cup butter, melted

1. Place potatoes in a saucepan; add water to cover. Bring to a boil. Reduce heat; cook, uncovered, until tender, 10-15 minutes. Drain; return to pan. Mash potatoes (you should have about 2 cups). Cool slightly.
2. In a large bowl, mix sugar, salt, yeast and 2 cups flour. In a small saucepan, heat milk, water and shortening to 120°-130°. Add to the dry ingredients; beat on medium speed 2 minutes. Add eggs and potatoes; beat on high 2 minutes. Stir in enough remaining flour to form a soft dough (dough will be very sticky).

3. Do not knead. Place dough in a large greased bowl, turning once to grease top. Cover; refrigerate overnight.
4. Punch down dough. Using a tablespoon dipped in melted butter, drop 3 spoonfuls of dough into a greased muffin cup. Repeat, re-dipping spoon in butter.
5. Cover dough; let rise in a warm place until almost doubled, about 45 minutes. Preheat oven to 375°.
6. Brush tops with remaining melted butter. Bake until golden brown, 12-15 minutes. Cool in pans 5 minutes. Remove to wire racks; serve warm.
Note: Dough can be made up to 3 days before baking. Prepare dough as directed, refrigerating dough for 1-3 days and punching down dough every 24 hours. Shape and bake rolls as directed.
1 roll: 181 cal., 6g fat (2g sat. fat), 25mg chol., 187mg sod., 26g carb. (6g sugars, 1g fiber), 4g pro.

CAPE COD BAY BROWN BREAD

This reminds me of the brown bread my grandmother made whenever we went out East to visit. The aroma evokes fond memories of her New England home during the peak of fall. I use blackstrap molasses and agave nectar to make mine a little different without sacrificing any of the flavor.

—Kellie Foglio, Salem, WI

- -

Prep: 40 min. + rising
Bake: 30 min. + cooling
Makes: 2 loaves (12 slices each)

2 pkg. (¼ oz. each) active dry yeast
3 Tbsp. molasses
2 tsp. agave nectar or honey
2⅔ cups warm water (110° to 115°)
½ cup dried cranberries
2 Tbsp. wheat bran
1 tsp. salt
6 to 7 cups whole wheat flour
TOPPING
1 Tbsp. 2% milk
1 Tbsp. old-fashioned oats

1. In a small bowl, dissolve yeast, molasses and agave nectar in ⅔ cup warm water. In a large bowl, combine cranberries, wheat bran, salt, yeast mixture, 4 cups flour and remaining water; beat on medium speed 3 minutes until smooth. Stir in enough remaining flour to form a soft dough (dough will be sticky).
2. Turn dough onto a floured surface; knead until smooth and elastic, 6-8 minutes. Place in a greased bowl, turning once to grease the top. Cover and let rise in a warm place until doubled, about 1 hour.
3. Turn onto a lightly floured surface; divide in half. Shape into loaves. Place in 2 greased 8x4-in. loaf pans. Cover; let rise in a warm place until nearly doubled, about 1 hour. Preheat oven to 400°.
4. Brush tops with milk. Sprinkle with oats. Bake until golden brown, 30-40 minutes. Remove loaves from pans to wire racks; cool completely.

1 slice: 125 cal., 1g fat (0 sat. fat), 0 chol., 101mg sod., 27g carb. (5g sugars, 4g fiber), 4g pro.

TEST KITCHEN TIP
While cranberries add a lovely touch to this brown bread, feel free to swap them with raisins or simply leave the cranberries out altogether.

PRALINE-TOPPED APPLE BREAD

Apples and candied pecans make this bread so much tastier than the usual coffee cakes you see at brunches.
—Sonja Blow, Nixa, MO

- -

Prep: 30 min. • **Bake:** 50 min. + cooling
Makes: 1 loaf (16 slices)

    2   cups all-purpose flour
    2   tsp. baking powder
    ½   tsp. baking soda
    ½   tsp. salt
    1   cup sugar
    1   cup sour cream
    2   large eggs, room temperature
    3   tsp. vanilla extract
    1½ cups chopped peeled
        Granny Smith apples
    1¼ cups chopped pecans,
        toasted, divided
    ½   cup butter, cubed
    ½   cup packed brown sugar

1. Preheat oven to 350°. In a large bowl, mix flour, baking powder, baking soda and salt. In another bowl, beat the sugar, sour cream, eggs and vanilla until well blended. Stir into flour mixture just until moistened. Fold in apples and 1 cup pecans.

2. Transfer to a greased 9x5-in. loaf pan. Bake 50-55 minutes or until a toothpick inserted in center comes out clean. Cool in pan 10 minutes. Remove to a wire rack to cool completely.

3. In a small saucepan, combine the butter and brown sugar. Bring to a boil, stirring constantly to dissolve sugar; boil 1 minute. Spoon over bread. Sprinkle with remaining pecans; let stand until set.

Note: To toast nuts, bake in a shallow pan in a 350° oven for 5-10 minutes or cook in a skillet over low heat until lightly browned, stirring occasionally.

1 slice: 288 cal., 16g fat (6g sat. fat), 42mg chol., 235mg sod., 34g carb. (21g sugars, 1g fiber), 4g pro.

SUGAR PLUM BREAD

I grew up with my Grandma Mitchell's irresistible plum bread. We slathered it with butter and ate it with cottage cheese and fresh fruit for a simple breakfast.
—Emily Tyra, Traverse City, MI

Prep: 15 min. + standing
Bake: 40 min. + cooling
Makes: 1 loaf (12 slices)

- 1 cup pitted dried plums, coarsely chopped
- ¾ cup water
- 2 Tbsp. plus ¾ cup sugar, divided
- 2 Tbsp. shortening
- 1 large egg, room temperature
- 2 cups all-purpose flour
- 2 tsp. baking powder
- 1 tsp. baking soda
- ½ tsp. salt
- 2 Tbsp. coarse sugar

1. Preheat oven to 350°. In a small saucepan, combine dried plums, water and 2 Tbsp. sugar. Bring to a simmer over medium heat for 1 minute. Remove from the heat; let stand until plumped, about 10 minutes. Drain plums, reserving fruit and liquid. Measure liquid, adding enough water to yield ½ cup.
2. Cream shortening and remaining sugar until light and fluffy, about 4 minutes. Beat in egg. In another bowl, whisk together flour, baking powder, baking soda and salt. Add to creamed mixture alternately with cooking liquid; fold in cooled dried plums (batter will be thick).
3. Transfer batter to a greased 8x4-in. loaf pan. Sprinkle with coarse sugar. Bake until a toothpick inserted in center comes out with moist crumbs, 40-45 minutes. Cool in pan 10 minutes before removing to a wire rack to cool completely.

1 slice: 202 cal., 3g fat (1g sat. fat), 16mg chol., 291mg sod., 41g carb. (21g sugars, 1g fiber), 3g pro.

NO-FUSS ROLLS

These 4-ingredient rolls are ready in no time. And they're fantastic with herb butter or jam.
—Glenda Trail, Manchester, TN

Takes: 25 min. • **Makes:** 6 rolls

- 1 cup self-rising flour
- ½ cup 2% milk
- 2 Tbsp. mayonnaise
- ½ tsp. sugar

In a small bowl, combine all ingredients. Spoon mixture into 6 muffin cups coated with cooking spray. Bake at 450° until a toothpick comes out clean, 12-14 minutes. Cool for 5 minutes before removing from pan to a wire rack. Serve rolls warm.
Note: As a substitute for 1 cup of self-rising flour, place 1½ tsp. baking powder and ½ tsp. salt in a measuring cup. Add all-purpose flour to measure 1 cup.
1 roll: 111 cal., 4g fat (1g sat. fat), 3mg chol., 275mg sod., 16g carb. (1g sugars, 0 fiber), 3g pro. **Diabetic exchanges:** 1 starch, 1 fat.

GRANDMA'S OATMEAL BREAD

The aroma from this old-fashioned oat bread will draw your family to the kitchen to enjoy it fresh from the oven.
—Marcia Hostetter, Canton, NY

- -

Prep: 20 min. + rising • **Bake:** 35 min.
Makes: 2 loaves (8 slices each)

1½	cups boiling water
1	Tbsp. butter
2	tsp. salt
½	cup sugar
1	cup old-fashioned oats
2	pkg. (¼ oz. each) active dry yeast
¾	cup warm water (110° to 115°)
¼	cup molasses
¼	cup packed brown sugar
6	to 6½ cups all-purpose flour, divided

1. In a small bowl, combine the boiling water, butter, salt and sugar. Stir in oats; cool to lukewarm. In a large bowl, dissolve yeast in warm water. Stir in the molasses, brown sugar and 1 cup flour. Beat until smooth. Stir in oat mixture and enough remaining flour to make a stiff dough.

2. Turn out onto a floured surface; knead until smooth and elastic, 6-8 minutes. Place in a greased bowl, turning once to grease top. Cover and let rise in a warm place until doubled, about 1½ hours.

3. Punch dough down. Turn onto a lightly floured surface; divide in half. Shape each portion into a ball. Cover and let rest for 10 minutes; Shape into loaves. Place in 2 greased 9x5-in. loaf pans. Cover and let rise until nearly doubled, about 1 hour.

4. Bake at 375° for 30-35 minutes (cover loosely with foil if top browns too quickly). Remove from pans to wire racks to cool.

1 slice: 247 cal., 2g fat (1g sat. fat), 2mg chol., 307mg sod., 52g carb. (13g sugars, 2g fiber), 6g pro.

CHOCOLATE CHIP CINNAMON ROLLS

I started adding chocolate chips to my cinnamon rolls because several children in my family didn't like raisins. The chocolate and cinnamon are a fun flavor combination. My family loves them, and so does my Sunday school class.
—Patty Wynn, Pardeeville, WI

Prep: 45 min. + rising • **Bake:** 25 min./batch
Makes: 4 dozen

- 4 pkg. (¼ oz. each) active dry yeast
- 2½ cups warm water (110° to 115°)
- 3 cups warm 2% milk (110° to 115°)
- ½ cup butter, softened
- 2 large eggs, room temperature
- ¾ cup honey
- 4 tsp. salt
- 14 cups all-purpose flour

FILLING
- 6 Tbsp. butter, softened
- 2¼ cups packed brown sugar
- 1 pkg. (12 oz.) miniature semisweet chocolate chips
- 3 tsp. ground cinnamon

GLAZE
- 3 cups confectioners' sugar
- 6 Tbsp. butter, softened
- 1 tsp. vanilla extract
- 6 to 8 Tbsp. whole milk

1. In a large bowl, dissolve yeast in warm water; let stand 5 minutes. Add the milk, butter, eggs, honey, salt and 3 cups flour; beat on low for 3 minutes. Stir in enough remaining flour to form a soft dough.

2. Turn onto a floured surface; knead until smooth and elastic, 6-8 minutes. Place in a large greased bowl, turning once. Cover and let rise in a warm place until doubled, about 1 hour.

3. Punch dough down. Turn onto a floured surface; divide into 4 pieces. Roll each into a 14x8-in. rectangle; spread with butter. Combine the brown sugar, chips and cinnamon; sprinkle over dough to within ½ in. of edges and press into dough.

4. Roll up jelly-roll style, starting with a long side; pinch the seam to seal. Cut each into 12 slices. Place cut side down in 4 greased 13x9-in. baking dishes. Cover and let rise until doubled, about 30 minutes.

5. Bake at 350° for 25-30 minutes or until golden brown. Cool for 5 minutes; remove from pans to wire racks.

6. For glaze, in a large bowl, combine the confectioners' sugar, butter, vanilla and enough milk to reach desired consistency; drizzle over warm rolls.

Note: This recipe can be halved to fit into a mixing bowl.

1 roll: 308 cal., 8g fat (5g sat. fat), 22mg chol., 251mg sod., 56g carb. (27g sugars, 1g fiber), 5g pro.

"Amazing flavor served hot! Gooey goodness from an easy-to-follow recipe."
—T2GETCOOKING, TASTEOFHOME.COM

EVELYN'S SOUR CREAM TWISTS

Evelyn is my mother-in-law who always keeps some of these terrific flaky twists in her freezer to serve in a pinch.
—Linda Welch, North Platte, NE

- -

Prep: 40 min. + chilling • **Bake:** 15 min.
Makes: 4 dozen

- 1 pkg. (¼ oz.) active dry yeast
- ¼ cup warm water (110° to 115°)
- 3 cups all-purpose flour
- 1½ tsp. salt
- ½ cup cold butter
- ½ cup shortening
- 2 large eggs, room temperature
- ½ cup sour cream
- 3 tsp. vanilla extract, divided
- 1½ cups sugar

1. In a small bowl, dissolve yeast in water. In a bowl, combine flour and salt. Cut in butter and shortening until the mixture resembles coarse crumbs. Stir in eggs, sour cream, 1 tsp. vanilla and the yeast mixture; mix thoroughly. Cover and refrigerate the dough overnight.
2. Combine sugar and remaining vanilla; lightly sprinkle ½ cup over a pastry cloth or countertop surface. On the sugared surface, roll half the dough into a 12x8-in. rectangle; refrigerate remaining dough. Sprinkle rolled dough with about 1 Tbsp. of the sugar mixture. Fold the rectangle into thirds.
3. Give dough a quarter turn and repeat rolling, sugaring and folding 2 more times. Roll into a 12x8-in. rectangle. Cut into 4x1-in. strips; twist each strip 2 or 3 times. Place on chilled ungreased baking sheets. Repeat with the remaining sugar mixture and dough.
4. Bake at 375° 12-14 minutes or until lightly browned. Immediately remove from pan and cool on wire racks.
1 twist: 97 cal., 5g fat (2g sat. fat), 16mg chol., 97mg sod., 12g carb. (6g sugars, 0 fiber), 1g pro.

CRANBERRY SWEET POTATO BREAD

This bread is moist and so flavorful. I often make two loaves and give one as a gift.
—Janice Christofferson, Eagle River, WI

- -

Prep: 30 min. • **Bake:** 50 min. + cooling
Makes: 1 loaf (12 slices)

- ½ cup dried cranberries
- ½ cup all-purpose flour, divided
- 1 cup whole wheat flour
- ½ cup packed brown sugar
- 1 tsp. baking powder
- ½ tsp. salt
- ½ tsp. each ground cinnamon, nutmeg and allspice
- ¼ tsp. baking soda
- 1 can (15¾ oz.) sweet potatoes, drained and mashed
- 2 large eggs, room temperature, lightly beaten
- ¼ cup canola oil
- 1 tsp. vanilla extract
- ½ tsp. orange extract

1. Toss cranberries with 1 Tbsp. all-purpose flour; set aside. In a large bowl, combine the whole wheat flour, brown sugar, baking powder, salt, spices, baking soda and the remaining all-purpose flour. In another bowl, combine the sweet potatoes, eggs, oil and extracts. Stir into dry ingredients just until moistened. Fold in cranberries.
2. Transfer to an 8x4-in. loaf pan coated with cooking spray. Bake at 350° until a toothpick inserted in the center comes out clean, 50-60 minutes. Cool for 10 minutes before removing from pan to a wire rack to cool completely.
1 slice: 192 cal., 6g fat (1g sat. fat), 35mg chol., 189mg sod., 32g carb. (18g sugars, 3g fiber), 3g pro. **Diabetic exchanges:** 2 starch, 1 fat.

HUNGARIAN NUT ROLLS

It isn't officially Christmas until I've made this treasured recipe from my husband's grandmother. The apple-walnut filling has the most amazing flavor.
—Donna Bardocz, Howell, MI

Prep: 40 min. + rising
Bake: 30 min. + cooling
Makes: 4 loaves (12 slices each)

- 2 pkg. (¼ oz. each) active dry yeast
- ½ cup warm 2% milk (110° to 115°)
- ¼ cup plus 2 Tbsp. sugar
- ¾ tsp. salt
- 1 cup butter, softened
- 1 cup sour cream
- 3 large eggs, room temperature, lightly beaten
- 6 to 6½ cups all-purpose flour

FILLING
- 1¼ cups sugar
- ½ cup butter, cubed
- 1 large egg
- ½ tsp. ground cinnamon
- 4½ cups ground walnuts
- 1 large apple, peeled and grated

ICING
- 2 cups confectioners' sugar
- 2 to 3 Tbsp. 2% milk

1. In a large bowl, dissolve yeast in warm milk. Add sugar, salt, butter, sour cream, eggs and 3 cups flour. Beat on medium speed for 3 minutes. Beat until smooth. Stir in enough remaining flour to form a soft dough (dough will be sticky).

2. Turn onto a floured surface; knead until smooth and elastic, 6-8 minutes. Place in a greased bowl, turning once to grease top. Cover and let rise in a warm place until doubled, about 1 hour.

3. Meanwhile, in a large saucepan, combine the sugar, butter, egg and cinnamon. Cook and stir over medium heat until mixture is thick enough to coat the back of a spoon. Remove from the heat; gently stir in walnuts and apple. Cool completely.

4. Punch dough down. Turn onto a lightly floured surface; divide into 4 portions. Roll each portion into a 12x10-in. rectangle. Spread the filling to within ½ in. of edges. Roll up jelly-roll style, starting with a long side; pinch seams to seal. Place seam side down on greased baking sheets. Cover and let rise until doubled, about 30 minutes.

5. Bake at 350° for 30-40 minutes or until lightly browned. Remove from pans to wire racks to cool. Combine icing ingredients; drizzle over loaves.

1 slice: 222 cal., 12g fat (5g sat. fat), 36mg chol., 87mg sod., 26g carb. (13g sugars, 1g fiber), 4g pro.

CRUSTY FRENCH BREAD

I love to treat my guests to these crusty loaves. Don't hesitate to try this recipe even if you are not an accomplished bread baker. It's so easy because there's no kneading required!
—Christy Freeman, Central Point, OR

- -

Prep: 30 min. + rising
Bake: 20 min. + cooling
Makes: 2 loaves (10 slices each)

1 pkg. (¼ oz.) active dry yeast
1½ cups warm water (110°
   to 115°), divided
1 Tbsp. sugar
2 tsp. salt
1 Tbsp. shortening, melted
4 to 5 cups all-purpose flour
   Cornmeal

1. In a large bowl, dissolve yeast in ½ cup water. Add the sugar, salt, shortening, remaining water and 3½ cups flour. Beat until smooth. Stir in enough remaining flour to form a soft dough. Do not knead. Cover and let rise in a warm place for 1 hour or until doubled.
2. Turn onto a floured surface. Divide in half; let rest for 10 minutes. Roll each half into a 10x8-in. rectangle. Roll up from a long side; pinch to seal. Place seam side down on greased baking sheets sprinkled with the cornmeal. Sprinkle the tops with cornmeal. Cover and let rise until doubled, about 45 minutes.
3. With a very sharp knife, make 5 diagonal cuts across the top of each loaf. Bake at 400° for 20-30 minutes or until lightly browned. Remove loaves from pans to wire rack to cool.
1 slice: 100 cal., 1g fat (0 sat. fat), 0 chol., 233mg sod., 20g carb. (0 sugars, 0 fiber), 3g pro. **Diabetic exchanges:** 1½ starch.

OLD-WORLD RYE BREAD

Rye and caraway lend to this bread's wonderful flavor, while the surprise ingredient of baking cocoa gives it a rich, dark color. For a variation, stir in a cup each of raisins and walnuts.
—Perlene Hoekema, Lynden, WA

Prep: 25 min. + rising
Bake: 35 min. + cooling
Makes: 2 loaves (12 slices each)

    2 pkg. (¼ oz. each) active dry yeast
1½ cups warm water (110° to 115°)
    ½ cup molasses
    6 Tbsp. butter, softened
    2 cups rye flour
    ¼ cup baking cocoa
    2 Tbsp. caraway seeds
    2 tsp. salt
3½ to 4 cups all-purpose flour
       Cornmeal

1. In a large bowl, dissolve yeast in warm water. Beat in the molasses, butter, rye flour, cocoa, caraway seeds, salt and 2 cups all-purpose flour until smooth. Stir in enough remaining all-purpose flour to form a stiff dough.
2. Turn onto a floured surface; knead until smooth and elastic, 6-8 minutes. Place in a greased bowl, turning once to grease top. Cover and let rise in a warm place until doubled, about 1½ hours.
3. Punch dough down. Turn onto a lightly floured surface; divide in half. Shape each piece into a loaf about 10 in. long. Grease 2 baking sheets and sprinkle with cornmeal. Place loaves on prepared pans. Cover and let rise until doubled, about 1 hour.
4. Bake at 350° for 35-40 minutes or until bread sounds hollow when tapped. Remove from pans to wire racks to cool.
1 slice: 146 cal., 3g fat (2g sat. fat), 8mg chol., 229mg sod., 26g carb. (5g sugars, 2g fiber), 3g pro.

YOGURT YEAST ROLLS

Bring these fluffy, golden rolls to a potluck and people will snap them up in a hurry. They make a nice contribution because rolls are easy to transport and one batch goes a long way.
—Carol Forcum, Marion, IL

Prep: 30 min. + rising • **Bake:** 15 min.
Makes: 2 dozen

1½ cups whole wheat flour
3¼ cups all-purpose flour, divided
    2 pkg. (¼ oz. each) active dry yeast
    2 tsp. salt
    ½ tsp. baking soda
1½ cups plain yogurt
    ½ cup water
    3 Tbsp. butter
    2 Tbsp. honey
       Additional melted butter, optional

1. In a large bowl, combine whole wheat flour, ½ cup all-purpose flour, yeast, salt and baking soda. In a saucepan over low heat, heat yogurt, water, butter and honey to 120°-130°. Pour over dry ingredients; blend well. Beat on medium speed for 3 minutes. Add enough of the remaining all-purpose flour to form a soft dough.
2. Turn onto a floured surface; knead until smooth and elastic, 6-8 minutes. Place in a greased bowl, turning once to grease top. Cover and let rise in a warm place until doubled, about 1 hour.
3. Punch dough down. Turn onto a lightly floured surface; divide into 24 portions. Roll each into a 10-in. rope. Shape rope into an "S," then coil each end until it touches the center. Place 3 in. apart on greased baking sheets. Cover and let rise until doubled, about 30 minutes. Preheat oven to 400°.
4. Bake until rolls are golden brown, about 15 minutes. If desired, brush tops with additional butter while warm. Remove from pans to wire racks to cool.
1 roll: 115 cal., 2g fat (1g sat. fat), 6mg chol., 245mg sod., 21g carb. (3g sugars, 1g fiber), 3g pro. **Diabetic exchanges:** 1½ starch, ½ fat.

GRANDMA'S FAVORITE

SOUPS & STEWS

- -

Grandma's savory chicken soup, potato chowder and hearty beef stew deliver comforting goodness like few foods can. These satisfying dishes always guarantee a smile, so turn the page and ladle out a bit of love today.

STOVETOP GOULASH

I created this after trying an old-fashioned goulash at a local restaurant. The blend of spices gives it great flavor, and it's so easy on a weeknight.
—Karen Schelert, Portland, OR

Takes: 25 min. • **Makes:** 4 servings

- 1 lb. ground beef
- 1 pkg. (16 oz.) frozen mixed vegetables, thawed
- 2 cans (10¾ oz. each) condensed tomato soup, undiluted
- 1 cup water
- 1 small onion, chopped
- 2 tsp. Worcestershire sauce
- 1 tsp. garlic salt
- 1 tsp. chili powder
- ½ tsp. dried oregano
- ½ tsp. paprika
- ⅛ tsp. ground cinnamon
- ⅛ tsp. pepper
- 1 pkg. (24 oz.) refrigerated mashed potatoes

1. Cook beef in a large skillet over medium heat until no longer pink; drain. Add the mixed vegetables, soup, water, onion, Worcestershire sauce and seasonings; bring to a boil. Reduce heat; simmer, uncovered, until slightly thickened, 10 minutes.
2. Meanwhile, heat potatoes according to package directions. Serve with goulash.
1½ cups goulash with 1 cup potatoes: 605 cal., 22g fat (9g sat. fat), 92mg chol., 1425mg sod., 58g carb. (18g sugars, 8g fiber), 28g pro.

GRANDMA'S PEA SOUP

My grandma's pea soup was a family favorite. What makes it different from any other pea soups I've tried is the addition of whole peas, spaetzle-like dumplings and sausage. Try it once and you'll be hooked.
—Carole Talcott, Dahinda, IL

- -

Prep: 15 min. + soaking • **Cook:** 2¾ hours
Makes: 16 servings (4 qt.)

- ½ lb. dried whole peas
- ½ lb. dried green split peas
- 1 meaty ham bone
- 3 qt. water
- 1 large onion, chopped
- 1 medium carrot, chopped
- 2 celery ribs, chopped
- ½ cup chopped celery leaves
- 1 tsp. bouquet garni (mixed herbs)
- 1 Tbsp. minced fresh parsley
- 1 bay leaf
- 1 tsp. salt
- ¼ tsp. pepper
- ½ lb. smoked sausage, chopped, optional

SPAETZLE DUMPLINGS

- 1 cup all-purpose flour
- 1 large egg, beaten
- ⅓ cup water

1. Cover the peas with water and soak overnight. Drain, rinse and place in a Dutch oven.
2. Add ham bone, water and remaining soup ingredients except sausage and dumplings. Bring to a boil. Reduce heat; cover and simmer 2 to 2½ hours.
3. Remove ham bone and skim fat. Remove meat from bone; dice. Add the ham and, if desired, sausage to pan.
4. For dumplings, place flour in a small bowl. Make a depression in the center of the flour; add egg and water and stir until smooth.
5. Place a colander with ³⁄₁₆-in.-diameter holes over simmering soup; transfer dough to the colander and press through with a wooden spoon. Cook, uncovered, about 10-15 minutes. Discard bay leaf.

1 cup: 155 cal., 2g fat (1g sat. fat), 20mg chol., 171mg sod., 26g carb. (2g sugars, 6g fiber), 9g pro.

TEST KITCHEN TIP
If cooking for two, prepare soup without dumplings and freeze in serving-size portions to enjoy for months to come.

LEMONY TURKEY RICE SOUP

While growing up in Texas, I spent a lot of time helping my grandma cook. Lemon and cilantro add a deliciously different twist to this turkey soup.
—Margarita Cuellar, East Chicago, IN

- -

Takes: 30 min. • **Makes:** 8 servings (2 qt.)

- 2 **cups diced cooked turkey**
- 2 **cups cooked long grain rice**
- 1 **can (10¾ oz.) condensed cream of chicken soup, undiluted**
- ¼ **tsp. pepper**
- 6 **cups chicken broth, divided**
- 2 **Tbsp. cornstarch**
- ¼ **to ⅓ cup lemon juice**
- ¼ **to ½ cup minced fresh cilantro**

1. In a large saucepan, combine the first 4 ingredients and 5½ cups broth. Bring to a boil; cook 3 minutes.
2. In a small bowl, mix the cornstarch and remaining broth until smooth; gradually stir into soup. Bring to a boil; cook and stir until thickened, 1-2 minutes. Remove from heat; stir in lemon juice and cilantro.

1 cup: 166 cal., 4g fat (1g sat. fat), 42mg chol., 1047mg sod., 17g carb. (1g sugars, 1g fiber), 13g pro.

"I made this soup exactly according to the recipe, and it was very tasty! My friend and her mother were also fans. It's very comforting on a chilly evening, and I'll be making it again."

—VETZLER, TASTEOFHOME.COM

WEEKDAY BEEF STEW

Beef stew capped with flaky puff pastry adds old-fashioned comfort to your weeknight menu. Make a salad and call everyone to the table.
—Daniel Anderson, Kenosha, WI

- -

Takes: 30 min. • **Makes:** 4 servings

- 1 **sheet frozen puff pastry, thawed**
- 1 **pkg. (15 oz.) refrigerated beef roast au jus**
- 2 **cans (14½ oz. each) diced tomatoes, undrained**
- 1 **pkg. (16 oz.) frozen vegetables for stew**
- ¾ **tsp. pepper**
- 2 **Tbsp. cornstarch**
- 1¼ **cups water**

1. Preheat oven to 400°. Unfold puff pastry. Using a 4-in. round cookie cutter, cut out 4 circles. Place 2 in. apart on a greased baking sheet. Bake until golden brown, for 14-16 minutes.
2. Meanwhile, shred beef with 2 forks; transfer to a large saucepan. Add tomatoes, vegetables and pepper; bring to a boil. In a small bowl, mix cornstarch and water until smooth; stir into beef mixture. Return to a boil, stirring constantly; cook and stir until thickened, 1-2 minutes.
3. Ladle stew into 4 bowls; top each with a pastry round.

1½ cups with 1 pastry round: 604 cal., 25g fat (8g sat. fat), 73mg chol., 960mg sod., 65g carb. (10g sugars, 9g fiber), 32g pro.

HAM & WHITE BEAN SOUP

Here's a modern take on a classic soup recipe. The slow cooker makes it easy, and convenience items make it fast. It's a full-flavored staple at my house.
—Stacey Cornell, Saratoga Springs, NY

Prep: 20 min. • **Cook:** 6 hours
Makes: 12 servings (3 qt.)

- 1 carton (32 oz.) chicken broth
- 1 can (28 oz.) diced tomatoes, undrained
- 1 can (15 to 15½ oz.) cannellini beans, rinsed and drained
- 1 pkg. (10 to 12 oz.) frozen cooked winter squash, thawed
- 1 pkg. (10 oz.) frozen leaf spinach, thawed and squeezed dry
- 1¾ cups cubed fully cooked ham
- 3 medium carrots, peeled, chopped
- 1 large onion, chopped
- 3 garlic cloves, minced
- 1 tsp. reduced-sodium seafood seasoning
- ¼ tsp. pepper
  Grated Parmesan cheese, optional

In a 5- or 6-qt. slow cooker, combine all ingredients. Cook, covered, on low for 6-8 hours. If desired, sprinkle servings with Parmesan cheese.

1 cup: 102 cal., 1g fat (0 sat. fat), 14mg chol., 808mg sod., 15g carb. (4g sugars, 4g fiber), 8g pro.

TEST KITCHEN TIP
To make pasta e fagioli, add ditalini or elbow pasta to this soup. For a spicy twist, stir in a dash of hot sauce.

ROASTED CAULIFLOWER & RED PEPPER SOUP

When cooler weather comes, soup is one of our favorite meals. I created this as a healthier version of all the cream-based soups out there. After a bit of trial and error, my husband and I decided that this version is a real keeper.
—Elizabeth Bramkamp, Gig Harbor, WA

- -

Prep: 50 min. + standing • **Cook:** 25 min.
Makes: 6 servings

- 2 **medium sweet red peppers, halved and seeded**
- 1 **large head cauliflower, broken into florets (about 7 cups)**
- 4 **Tbsp. olive oil, divided**
- 1 **cup chopped sweet onion**
- 2 **garlic cloves, minced**
- 2½ **tsp. minced fresh rosemary or ¾ tsp. dried rosemary, crushed**
- ½ **tsp. paprika**
- ¼ **cup all-purpose flour**
- 4 **cups chicken stock**
- 1 **cup 2% milk**
- ½ **tsp. salt**
- ¼ **tsp. pepper**
- ⅛ **to ¼ tsp. cayenne pepper Shredded Parmesan cheese, optional**

1. Preheat broiler. Place peppers on a foil-lined baking sheet, skin side up. Broil 4 in. from heat until skins are blistered, about 5 minutes. Transfer to a bowl; let stand, covered, 20 minutes. Change oven setting to bake; preheat oven to 400°.
2. Toss cauliflower with 2 Tbsp. oil; spread in a 15x10x1-in. pan. Roast until tender, 25-30 minutes, stirring pieces occasionally. Remove skin and seeds from the peppers; chop peppers.
3. In a 6-qt. stockpot, heat remaining oil over medium heat. Add onion; cook until golden and softened, 6-8 minutes, stirring occasionally. Add the garlic, rosemary and paprika; cook and stir 1 minute. Stir in flour until blended; cook and stir for 1 minute. Gradually stir in stock. Bring mixture to a boil, stirring constantly; cook and stir until sauce is thickened.
4. Stir in cauliflower and peppers. Puree soup using an immersion blender. Or, cool slightly and puree the soup in batches in a blender; return to pot. Stir in the milk and remaining seasonings; heat through. If desired, serve with cheese.

Freeze option: Freeze the cooled soup in freezer containers. To use, partially thaw in refrigerator overnight. Heat through in a saucepan, stirring occasionally and adding a little stock or milk if necessary.

1 cup: 193 cal., 10g fat (2g sat. fat), 3mg chol., 601mg sod., 19g carb. (8g sugars, 4g fiber), 8g pro. **Diabetic exchanges:** 2 vegetable, 2 fat, ½ starch.

CURRY CHICKEN STEW

My grandma Inky grew up in India and passed down this recipe to my mother, who then passed it down to me. I tweaked the ingredients a bit to fit my toddler's taste buds, but it's just as scrumptious as the original. This recipe brings back fond memories of my family happily gathered around the table.
—Teresa Flowers, Sacramento, CA

Prep: 15 min. • **Cook:** 4 hours
Makes: 6 servings

- 2 cans (14½ oz. each) chicken broth
- 1 can (10¾ oz.) condensed cream of chicken soup, undiluted
- 1 tub Knorr concentrated chicken stock (4.66 oz.)
- 4 garlic cloves, minced
- 1 Tbsp. curry powder
- ¼ tsp. salt
- ¼ tsp. cayenne pepper
- ¼ tsp. pepper
- 6 boneless skinless chicken breasts (6 oz. each)
- 1 medium green pepper, cut into thin strips
- 1 medium onion, thinly sliced
  Hot cooked rice
  Chopped fresh cilantro and chutney, optional

1. In a large bowl, combine the first 8 ingredients. Place chicken, green pepper and onion in a 5- or 6-qt. slow cooker; pour broth mixture over top. Cook, covered, on low until the chicken and vegetables are tender, 4-5 hours.
2. Remove chicken and cool slightly. Cut or shred meat into bite-size pieces and return to slow cooker; heat through. Serve stew with rice. If desired, top with fresh cilantro and chutney.
1¾ cups: 266 cal., 8g fat (2g sat. fat), 101mg chol., 1604mg sod., 9g carb. (2g sugars, 2g fiber), 36g pro.

ITALIAN CABBAGE SOUP

After doing yard work on a windy day, we love to come in for an old-fashioned soup like this one. It's brimming with cabbage, veggies and white beans. The slow cooker makes it a snap.
—Jennifer Stowell, Deep River, IA

Prep: 15 min. • **Cook:** 6 hours
Makes: 8 servings (2 qt.)

- 4 cups chicken stock
- 1 can (6 oz.) tomato paste
- 1 small head cabbage (about 1½ lbs.), shredded
- 4 celery ribs, chopped
- 2 large carrots, chopped
- 1 small onion, chopped
- 1 can (15½ oz.) great northern beans, rinsed and drained
- 2 garlic cloves, minced
- 2 fresh thyme sprigs
- 1 bay leaf
- ½ tsp. salt
  Shredded Parmesan cheese, optional

1. In a 5- or 6-qt. slow cooker, whisk together stock and tomato paste. Stir in vegetables, beans, garlic and seasonings. Cook, covered, on low until vegetables are tender, 6-8 hours.
2. Remove thyme sprigs and bay leaf. If desired, serve with cheese.
1 cup: 111 cal., 0 fat (0 sat. fat), 0 chol., 537mg sod., 21g carb. (7g sugars, 6g fiber), 8g pro. **Diabetic exchanges:** 1½ starch.

CHEESY CHICKEN CHOWDER

I like to serve this hearty chowder with garlic bread and a salad. It's a wonderful dish to prepare for any occasion because the rich, mild flavor of the tender chicken and vegetables appeals even to picky eaters—and children.
—Hazel Fritchie, Palestine, IL

Prep: 10 min. • **Cook:** 25 min.
Makes: 8 servings

- 3 cups chicken broth
- 2 cups diced peeled potatoes
- 1 cup diced carrots
- 1 cup diced celery
- ½ cup diced onion
- 1½ tsp. salt
- ¼ tsp. pepper
- ¼ cup butter, cubed
- ⅓ cup all-purpose flour
- 2 cups whole milk
- 2 cups shredded cheddar cheese
- 2 cups diced cooked chicken

1. In a 4-qt. saucepan, bring chicken broth to a boil. Reduce heat; add the potatoes, carrots, celery, onion, salt and pepper. Cover and simmer until the vegetables are tender, 12-15 minutes.
2. Meanwhile, melt the butter in a medium saucepan; stir in the flour until smooth. Gradually stir in milk. Bring to a boil over medium heat; cook and stir until thickened, 2 minutes. Reduce heat; add cheese, stirring until melted; add to broth along with the chicken. Cook and stir until heated through.
1 cup: 322 cal., 19g fat (12g sat. fat), 85mg chol., 1100mg sod., 18g carb. (6g sugars, 2g fiber), 21g pro.

CLASSIC SLOW-COOKER STEW

Start this warming one-pot meal before you head out for the day. By the time you get home, the mouthwatering dish will be seasoned and cooked to perfection.
—Stephanie Rabbitt-Schapp, Cincinnati, OH

Prep: 20 min. • **Cook:** 7½ hours
Makes: 5 servings

- 1 lb. beef stew meat
- 2 medium potatoes, peeled and cubed
- 1 can (14½ oz.) beef broth
- 1 can (11½ oz.) V8 juice
- 2 celery ribs, chopped
- 2 medium carrots, chopped
- 1 medium sweet onion, chopped
- 3 bay leaves
- ½ tsp. salt
- ½ tsp. dried thyme
- ½ tsp. chili powder
- ¼ tsp. pepper
- 2 Tbsp. cornstarch
- 1 Tbsp. cold water
- ½ cup frozen corn
- ½ cup frozen peas

1. In a 3-qt. slow cooker, combine the first 12 ingredients. Cover and cook on low until meat is tender, about 7-8 hours. Discard the bay leaves.
2. In a small bowl, combine cornstarch and water until smooth; stir into stew. Add corn and peas. Cover and cook stew on high until thickened, 30 minutes.
1⅓ cups: 273 cal., 7g fat (2g sat. fat), 56mg chol., 865mg sod., 31g carb. (9g sugars, 4g fiber), 22g pro. **Diabetic exchanges:** 3 lean meat, 2 vegetable, 1 starch.

HAM, POTATO & PEPPER CHOWDER

I've served this chowder for years. When I'm feeding family members who don't eat dairy, I simply substitute oil for the butter and use either coconut milk or soy creamer instead of heavy cream. The versatile soup still turns out great!
—Eileen Stefanski, Wales, WI

- -

Prep: 20 min. • **Cook:** 30 min.
Makes: 6 servings (2 qt.)

1½ **lbs. potatoes (about 2 large), peeled and cut into 1-in. cubes**

1 **carton (32 oz.) chicken broth, divided**
2 **Tbsp. butter**
1 **large sweet red pepper, coarsely chopped**
1 **large green pepper, coarsely chopped**
1 **large onion, finely chopped**
1 **large carrot, chopped**
1½ **cups cubed fully cooked ham (about 8 oz.)**
2 **Tbsp. chopped seeded jalapeno pepper**
¼ **tsp. white pepper**
¼ **tsp. cayenne pepper**
1 **large egg yolk**
¼ **cup heavy whipping cream**
Optional toppings: Shredded cheddar cheese, cooked and crumbled bacon, minced fresh chives and sour cream

1. Place potatoes and 2 cups broth in a Dutch oven; bring to a boil. Reduce heat; simmer, covered, until potatoes are tender, 10-15 minutes. Cool slightly. Transfer the mixture to a food processor; cover and process until smooth.
2. In same pan, heat butter over medium heat; saute red and green peppers, onion and carrot until carrot is tender, for about 8-10 minutes. Add the ham, jalapeno and seasonings; cook and stir 1 minute.
3. Stir in pureed potatoes and remaining broth; bring just to a boil. In a small bowl, whisk a small amount of hot soup into egg yolk and cream; return all to the pan, whisking constantly. Bring to a gentle boil; cook and stir until thickened, 1-2 minutes. Serve with toppings as desired.

1⅓ cups: 226 cal., 10g fat (6g sat. fat), 76mg chol., 1124mg sod., 23g carb. (6g sugars, 3g fiber), 11g pro.

> **TEST KITCHEN TIP**
> Concerned about the spice level? Just omit the jalapeno and cayenne if you'd like.

PESTO BEAN SOUP

This is one of my favorite vegetarian recipes, especially on those cold winter evenings. I make large batches and freeze it. Homemade pesto is tasty, but you can use store-bought to make the soup really simple. Serve warm bowlfuls with garlic toast and a green salad.
—Liz Bellville, Tonasket, WA

Prep: 10 min. • **Cook:** 4 hours
Makes: 8 servings

- 1 carton (32 oz.) reduced-sodium vegetable broth
- 1 large white onion, chopped
- 4 garlic cloves, minced
- 2½ cups sliced baby portobello mushrooms
- 3 cans (15 to 15½ oz. each) cannellini beans, rinsed and drained
- ¾ cup prepared pesto, divided
- ¼ cup grated Parmigiano Reggiano cheese

In a 4-qt. slow cooker, combine the first 5 ingredients. Stir in ½ cup pesto. Cook, covered, on low until vegetables are tender, 4-6 hours. Before serving, stir in reserved pesto and cheese. If desired, serve with additional cheese and pesto.
1¼ cups: 244 cal., 9g fat (2g sat. fat), 2mg chol., 586mg sod., 30g carb. (3g sugars, 8g fiber), 9g pro. **Diabetic exchanges:** 2 starch, 1½ fat, 1 lean meat.

TEST KITCHEN TIP
Mash half the beans before adding to give soup a thick, velvety texture. Garnish with lemon wedges, cracked black pepper and fresh basil.

ITALIAN BEEF TORTELLINI STEW

This hearty recipe is a real keeper! I hope you enjoy this rich stew full of veggies, tender beef, and with a splash of wine.
—Tammy Munyon, Wichita, KS

Prep: 25 min. • **Cook:** 1¾ hours
Makes: 6 servings (2¼ qt.)

- ⅓ cup all-purpose flour
- 1 tsp. pepper, divided
- 1 lb. beef stew meat, cut into 1-in. cubes
- 3 Tbsp. olive oil, divided
- 2 medium zucchini, cut into ½-in. pieces
- 1 large onion, chopped
- 2 celery ribs, sliced
- 3 small carrots, sliced
- 3 garlic cloves, minced
- 1½ tsp. each dried oregano, basil and marjoram
- ½ cup dry red wine or reduced-sodium beef broth
- 1 can (28 oz.) crushed tomatoes
- 3 cups reduced-sodium beef broth
- 1 tsp. sugar
- 1 pkg. (9 oz.) refrigerated cheese tortellini
- 1 pkg. (6 oz.) fresh baby spinach

1. In a shallow dish, combine the flour and ½ tsp. pepper. Add beef, a few pieces at a time, and turn to coat. Shake off excess flour; remove.
2. In a Dutch oven, brown beef in 2 Tbsp. oil; drain. Remove and set aside. In the same pan, saute the zucchini, onion, celery and carrots in remaining oil until tender. Add the garlic, oregano, basil and marjoram; cook 1 minute longer.
3. Add wine, stirring to loosen browned bits from pan. Return beef to the pan; add the tomatoes, broth, sugar and remaining pepper. Bring to a boil. Reduce heat; cover and simmer until beef is tender, 1½ hours. Add tortellini and spinach. Return to a boil. Cook, uncovered, until tortellini are tender, for 7-9 minutes.
1½ cups: 416 cal., 16g fat (5g sat. fat), 68mg chol., 642mg sod., 43g carb. (6g sugars, 7g fiber), 26g pro. **Diabetic exchanges:** 3 starch, 2 lean meat, 1½ fat.

SUNDAY CHICKEN STEW

We have this dish on Sunday, so I too can have a day off. I prepare the veggies the night before and, in the morning, brown the chicken and assemble everything in a slow cooker before I go to church. Be sure to see the stovetop directions, too, if that cooking method fits your schedule better.
—Diane Halferty, Corpus Christi, TX

- -

Prep: 30 min. • **Cook:** 6½ hours
Makes: 6 servings

- ½   **cup all-purpose flour**
- 1   **tsp. salt**
- ½   **tsp. white pepper**
- 1   **broiler/fryer chicken (3 lbs.), cut up and skin removed**
- 2   **Tbsp. canola oil**
- 3   **cups chicken broth**
- 6   **large carrots, cut into 1-in. pieces**
- 2   **celery ribs, cut into ½-in. pieces**
- 1   **large sweet onion, thinly sliced**
- 1   **tsp. dried rosemary, crushed**
- 1½   **cups frozen peas**

DUMPLINGS

- 1   **cup all-purpose flour**
- 2   **tsp. baking powder**
- ½   **tsp. salt**
- ½   **tsp. dried rosemary, crushed**
- 1   **large egg, lightly beaten**
- ½   **cup 2% milk**

1. In a large shallow dish, combine the flour, salt and pepper; add chicken, a few pieces at a time, and turn to coat. In a large skillet, brown the chicken in oil; remove and keep warm. Gradually add broth to the skillet; bring to a boil.

2. In a 5-qt. slow cooker, layer the carrots, celery and onion; sprinkle with rosemary. Add chicken and hot broth. Cover and cook on low until the chicken and vegetables are tender and stew is bubbling, for 6-8 hours.

3. Remove chicken; when cool enough to handle, remove meat from the bones and discard bones. Cut the meat into bite-size pieces and return to the slow cooker. Stir in the peas.

4. For dumplings, in a small bowl, combine the flour, baking powder, salt and rosemary. Combine the egg and milk; stir into dry ingredients. Drop by heaping teaspoonfuls onto simmering chicken mixture. Cover and cook on high (do not lift cover while stew is simmering) 25-30 minutes until a toothpick inserted in a dumpling comes out clean.

1 serving: 420 cal., 13g fat (3g sat. fat), 113mg chol., 1403mg sod., 42g carb. (10g sugars, 5g fiber), 33g pro.

Stovetop Sunday Chicken Stew: In a Dutch oven, brown chicken as directed; add broth to the pan. Add rosemary. Cover and simmer for 1 hour. Add the vegetables; cover and simmer 30 minutes longer. Cut chicken and prepare dumplings as directed. Cover and simmer (do not lift cover while simmering) about 20 minutes until a toothpick inserted in a dumpling comes out clean.

CHEDDAR PEAR SOUP

Pears and sharp cheddar have always been one of my favorite flavor combos. This recipe brings the two together in a creamy, delicious soup. I like to serve it with a warm baguette and fresh fruit.
—Trisha Kruse, Eagle, ID

Prep: 15 min. • **Cook:** 35 min.
Makes: 8 servings (2 qt.)

- ¼ cup butter, cubed
- 1 large onion, chopped
- 2 garlic cloves, minced
- ⅓ cup all-purpose flour
- 2 tsp. smoked paprika
- 5 cups chicken broth
- 3 medium ripe pears, peeled and chopped
- 3 cups sharp cheddar cheese, shredded
- ¼ tsp. freshly ground pepper
  Fresh pear slices, optional

1. In a Dutch oven, heat the butter over medium-high heat; saute onion and garlic until tender, 7-9 minutes. Stir in flour and paprika until blended; cook and stir for 2 minutes. Gradually stir in broth. Add chopped pears; bring to a boil. Reduce heat; simmer, covered, until pears are tender, about 15 minutes, stirring occasionally.
2. Puree soup using an immersion blender or cool slightly and puree soup in batches in a blender; return to pan. Add cheese and pepper; cook and stir over low heat until cheese is melted, 3-5 minutes. If desired, top with pear slices.

1 cup: 299 cal., 20g fat (12g sat. fat), 60mg chol., 938mg sod., 18g carb. (8g sugars, 3g fiber), 12g pro.

CHUNKY CHICKEN NOODLE SOUP

This hearty, old-fashioned soup is just like Grandma used to make—full of veggies and rich flavor. When winter holds me in its icy grip, I can always rely on chicken soup to warm me right down to my toes.
—Sharon Skildum, Maple Grove, MN

Takes: 25 min. • **Makes:** 2 servings

- ¼ cup diced carrot
- 2 Tbsp. diced celery
- 2 Tbsp. chopped onion
- 1 tsp. butter
- 2½ cups reduced-sodium chicken broth
- ⅔ cup diced cooked chicken
- ¼ tsp. salt
- ¼ tsp. dried marjoram
- ¼ tsp. dried thyme
- Dash pepper
- ½ cup uncooked medium egg noodles
- 1 tsp. minced fresh parsley

In a large saucepan, saute the carrot, celery and onion in butter until tender. Stir in the broth, chicken and seasonings; bring to a boil. Reduce heat. Add the noodles; cook until tender, 10 minutes. Sprinkle with the minced parsley.

1¾ cups: 167 cal., 6g fat (2g sat. fat), 55mg chol., 511mg sod., 12g carb. (3g sugars, 1g fiber), 16g pro.

SQUASH & LENTIL LAMB STEW

My family lived in New Zealand many years ago. Every Sunday my mother made a lamb stew—it was Dad's favorite. I changed the recipe to suit my family's more modern palates, but it seems just as exotic, special and delicious as it did then.
—Nancy Heishman, Las Vegas, NV

- -

Prep: 30 min. • **Cook:** 6 hours
Makes: 8 servings (2½ qt.)

- 1   can (13.66 oz.) coconut milk
- ½   cup creamy peanut butter
- 2   Tbsp. red curry paste
- 1   Tbsp. hoisin sauce
- 1   tsp. salt
- ½   tsp. pepper
- 1   can (14½ oz.) chicken broth
- 3   tsp. olive oil, divided
- 1   lb. lamb or beef stew meat (1 to 1½ in.)
- 2   small onions, chopped
- 1   Tbsp. minced fresh gingerroot
- 3   garlic cloves, minced
- 1   cup dried brown lentils, rinsed
- 4   cups cubed peeled butternut squash (about 1 lb.)
- 2   cups chopped fresh spinach
- ¼   cup minced fresh cilantro
- ¼   cup lime juice

1. In a 5- or 6-qt slow cooker, whisk together the first 7 ingredients. In a large skillet, heat 2 tsp. oil over medium heat; brown lamb in batches. Add to slow cooker.
2. In the same skillet, saute onions in the remaining oil over medium heat until tender, 4-5 minutes. Add ginger and garlic; cook and stir 1 minute. Add to slow cooker. Stir in lentils and squash.
3. Cook, covered, on low until meat and lentils are tender, 6-8 hours. Stir in spinach until wilted. Stir in cilantro and lime juice.
Freeze option: Freeze cooled stew in freezer containers. To use, partially thaw in refrigerator overnight. Heat through in a saucepan, stirring occasionally and adding a little broth if necessary.
1¼ cups: 411 cal., 21g fat (11g sat. fat), 38mg chol., 777mg sod., 34g carb. (7g sugars, 6g fiber), 23g pro.

TEST KITCHEN TIP
No peeking! Opening the slow cooker allows steam to escape, causing the temperature to drop. So you may need to add 20-30 minutes to the cook time for each time you lift the lid.

VEGETABLE ORZO SOUP

Grandma always found the perfect dish to warm up chilly nights. This rustic-style soup is heavy on the veggies but light on the prep work. Protein-rich beans and a handful of orzo fortify against the cold.
—*Taste of Home* Test Kitchen

- -

Prep: 15 min. • **Cook:** 25 min.
Makes: 6 servings (2 qt.)

- 1 medium sweet yellow pepper, chopped
- 1 medium onion, chopped
- 2 tsp. olive oil
- 3 garlic cloves, minced
- 1 jar (24 oz.) garden-style spaghetti sauce
- 1 pkg. (16 oz.) frozen Italian vegetables
- 1 can (15 oz.) cannellini beans, rinsed and drained
- 1 can (14½ oz.) chicken broth
- ½ lb. small red potatoes, quartered
- 1 cup water
- ⅓ cup uncooked orzo pasta
- ½ tsp. dried marjoram
- ½ tsp. dried thyme

Saute pepper and onion in oil in a Dutch oven until tender. Add garlic; cook 1 minute longer. Stir in the remaining ingredients. Bring to a boil. Reduce the heat; cover and simmer until potatoes and pasta are tender, 15-20 minutes.

1⅓ cups: 254 cal., 4g fat (0 sat. fat), 2mg chol., 841mg sod., 45g carb. (12g sugars, 8g fiber), 8g pro.

QUICK CHICKEN & DUMPLINGS

Oh, the things you can make with frozen biscuit dough. Here's chicken-dumpling soup with old-time flavor and hardly any extra work at all.
—Lakeya Astwood, Schenectady, NY

- -

Takes: 30 min. • **Makes:** 6 servings

- 6 individually frozen biscuits
- ¼ cup chopped onion
- ¼ cup chopped green pepper
- 1 Tbsp. olive oil
- 4 cups shredded rotisserie chicken
- 3 cans (14½ oz. each) reduced-sodium chicken broth
- 1 can (4 oz.) mushroom stems and pieces, drained
- 1 tsp. chicken bouillon granules
- 1 tsp. minced fresh parsley
- ½ tsp. dried sage leaves
- ¼ tsp. dried rosemary, crushed
- ¼ tsp. pepper

1. Cut each biscuit into fourths; set aside. In a large saucepan, saute onion and green pepper in oil until tender. Stir in the chicken, broth, mushrooms, bouillon granules, parsley, sage, rosemary and pepper.
2. Bring to a boil. Reduce heat; add biscuits for dumplings. Cover and simmer (do not lift cover while simmering) 10 minutes or until a toothpick inserted in the center of a dumpling comes out clean.

1½ cups: 420 cal., 20g fat (5g sat. fat), 83mg chol., 1443mg sod., 26g carb. (6g sugars, 1g fiber), 34g pro.

1. In a Dutch oven, cook the bacon over medium heat until crisp; stir occasionally. Remove with a slotted spoon; drain on paper towels. Cook and stir carrots and onions in bacon drippings, adding olive oil if necessary, until crisp-tender, 3-4 minutes. Add the tomato paste, garlic, thyme and pepper; cook 1 minute longer.

2. Add the stock and wine; increase the heat to medium-high. Cook 2 minutes, stirring to loosen browned bits from pan. Stir in butter beans, lentils and bacon. Bring mixture to a boil. Reduce the heat; simmer, covered, for 5 minutes. Uncover; continue simmering until vegetables are tender, 15-20 minutes. Serve with thyme sprigs.

1 cup: 271 cal., 6g fat (2g sat. fat), 9mg chol., 672mg sod., 41g carb. (7g sugars, 13g fiber), 18g pro. **Diabetic exchanges:** 3 starch, 1 medium-fat meat.

LIFESAVING LENTILS
Perhaps "lifesaving" is a bit strong, but lentils can truly save the day when it comes to that last-minute dinner prep.

High in protein and fiber but low in fat, the tiny beans make great additions to soups and stews. Dried lentils cook up in 20-30 minutes, but canned ones decrease prep time even further. You'll find dried lentils in different varieties—brown, green and orange—but they can be used interchangeably in most recipes.

LENTIL, BACON & BEAN SOUP
This easy soup feels extra cozy with lots of lentils and a touch of smoky, bacony goodness. You just might want to cook up extra—it's even better the next day.
—Janie Zirbser, Mullica Hill, NJ

Prep: 15 min. • **Cook:** 30 min.
Makes: 8 servings (2 qt.)

- 4 bacon strips, chopped
- 6 medium carrots, chopped
- 2 small onions, diced
- Olive oil, optional
- 2 Tbsp. tomato paste
- 2 garlic cloves, minced
- 1 tsp. minced fresh thyme
- ½ tsp. pepper
- 5 cups chicken stock
- 1 cup dry white wine or additional chicken stock
- 2 cans (15 to 16 oz. each) butter beans, rinsed and drained
- 2 cans (15 oz. each) cooked lentils, rinsed and drained
- 6 fresh thyme sprigs

BUTTERNUT SQUASH CHILI

Add butternut squash to chili for a tasty, filling, energy-packed dish your whole family will love. Mine does!
—Jeanne Larson,
Rancho Santa Margarita, CA

- -

Prep: 20 min. • **Cook:** 30 min.
Makes: 8 servings (2 qt.)

- 1 lb. ground beef or turkey
- ¾ cup chopped red onion
- 5 garlic cloves, minced
- 3 Tbsp. tomato paste
- 1 Tbsp. chili powder
- 1 tsp. ground cumin
- ½ to 1 tsp. salt
- 1¾ to 2 cups water
- 1 can (15 oz.) black beans, rinsed and drained
- 1 can (15 oz.) pinto beans, rinsed and drained
- 1 can (14½ oz.) diced tomatoes
- 1 can (14½ to 15 oz.) tomato sauce
- 3 cups cubed peeled butternut squash, (½-in. cubes)
- 2 Tbsp. cider vinegar
  Optional: Chopped avocado, plain Greek yogurt and shredded mozzarella cheese

1. In a Dutch oven over medium heat, cook beef and onion, crumbling meat, until beef is no longer pink and onion is tender, about 6-8 minutes.
2. Add next 5 ingredients; cook 1 minute longer. Stir in water, both types of beans, diced tomatoes and tomato sauce. Bring to a boil; reduce heat. Stir in squash; simmer, covered, until the squash is tender, about 20-25 minutes. Stir in vinegar.
3. If desired, serve with chopped avocado, yogurt and shredded mozzarella cheese.
1 cup: 261 cal., 8g fat (3g sat. fat), 35mg chol., 704mg sod., 32g carb. (6g sugars, 8g fiber), 18g pro. **Diabetic exchanges:** 2 starch, 2 lean meat.

TEST KITCHEN TIP
Unexpected company? Ladle chili over macaroni or other pasta to stretch the servings. Don't let your guests know that your secret ingredient is vinegar! Added just before serving, it helps brighten and gives a surprising punch to many dishes.

CREAMY CARROT SOUP

Delight guests with the bright orange color and deliciously different flavor of this soup. A hint of rosemary adds a nice spark to the slightly sweet taste.

—Grace Yaskovic, Lake Hiawatha, NJ

- -

Prep: 15 min. + cooling • **Cook:** 40 min.
Makes: 10 servings (2½ qt.)

- 1 cup chopped onion
- ¼ cup butter, cubed
- 4½ cups sliced fresh carrots
- 1 large potato, peeled and cubed
- 2 cans (14½ oz. each) chicken broth
- 1 tsp. ground ginger
- 2 cups heavy whipping cream
- 1 tsp. dried rosemary, crushed
- ½ tsp. salt
- ⅛ tsp. pepper

1. In a Dutch oven, saute onion in butter until tender. Add the carrots, potato, broth and ginger. Cover and cook over medium heat until vegetables are tender, for about 30 minutes. Cool 15 minutes.

2. In a blender, cover and puree in batches. Return all to the pan; stir in the cream, rosemary, salt and pepper. Cook over low heat until heated through.

1 cup: 267 cal., 22g fat (14g sat. fat), 77mg chol., 367mg sod., 15g carb. (7g sugars, 3g fiber), 3g pro.

SPINACH & WHITE BEAN SOUP

For me, soup is love, comfort, happiness and memories. With all its veggies and beans, this one especially appeals to my kitchen-sink style of cooking.
—Annette Palermo, Beach Haven, NJ

Takes: 30 min. • **Makes:** 6 servings

- 2 tsp. olive oil
- 3 garlic cloves, minced
- 3 cans (15 oz. each) cannellini beans, rinsed and drained, divided use
- ¼ tsp. pepper
- 1 carton (32 oz.) vegetable or reduced-sodium chicken broth
- 4 cups chopped fresh spinach (about 3 oz.)
- ¼ cup thinly sliced fresh basil Shredded Parmesan cheese, optional

1. In a large saucepan, heat the oil over medium heat. Add garlic; cook and stir until tender, 30-45 seconds. Stir in two cans of beans, pepper and broth.
2. Puree the mixture using an immersion blender or puree in a blender and return to pan. Stir in remaining can of beans; bring to a boil. Reduce the heat; simmer, covered, 15 minutes, stirring occasionally.
3. Stir in spinach and basil; cook, uncovered, until the spinach is wilted, for 2-4 minutes. If desired, serve with cheese.

Note: Reduced-sodium vegetable broth isn't widely available, but organic versions of big-brand vegetable broths are typically lower in sodium than conventional broths.
1¼ cups: 192 cal., 2g fat (0 sat. fat), 0 chol., 886mg sod., 33g carb. (1g sugars, 9g fiber), 9g pro.

COMFORTING BEEF STEW

The aroma of slow-simmered stew that's loaded with root vegetables just says fall comfort food to me. Even toddlers love to gobble up this stew!
—Courtney Percy, Brooksville, FL

Prep: 20 min. • **Cook:** 2½ hours
Makes: 6 servings

- 2 lbs. beef stew meat
- 1 tsp. salt
- ¾ tsp. pepper
- 3 Tbsp. canola oil
- 1 Tbsp. butter
- 1 medium onion, chopped
- 2 garlic cloves, minced
- ¼ cup tomato paste
- 4 cups beef broth
- 3 Tbsp. all-purpose flour
- 3 Tbsp. water
- 5 medium carrots, cut into ½-in. pieces
- 3 medium turnips, peeled and cubed
- 2 Tbsp. minced fresh parsley

1. Sprinkle beef with salt and pepper. In a Dutch oven, heat oil over medium-high heat. Brown beef in batches. Remove with a slotted spoon.
2. In same pan, heat butter over medium heat. Add onion; cook and stir until tender, 2-3 minutes. Add the garlic; cook 1 minute longer. Stir in tomato paste. Gradually stir in broth until blended. Return beef to the pan; bring to a boil. Reduce the heat; simmer, covered, 1½ hours.
3. In a small bowl, mix flour and water until smooth; gradually stir into stew. Add the carrots and turnips; cook, covered, until stew is thickened and beef and vegetables are tender, about 30-40 minutes longer. Stir in the parsley.
Freeze option: Freeze the cooled stew in freezer containers. To use, partially thaw stew in the refrigerator overnight. Heat through in a saucepan, stirring occasionally and adding a little broth if necessary.
1½ cups: 375 cal., 20g fat (6g sat. fat), 99mg chol., 1142mg sod., 15g carb. (6g sugars, 3g fiber), 33g pro.

GRANDMA'S HARVEST SOUP

I have fond memories of eating soup Grandma made when I was a child. Now I make it myself as a treat for my wife. It always tastes just like home.
—Ronald Desjardins, St. Andrews West, ON

- -

Prep: 20 min. • **Cook:** 2½ hours
Makes: 18 servings (4¼ qt.)

- 3 smoked ham hocks (about 1½ lbs.)
- 3 qt. water
- 1 Tbsp. beef bouillon granules
- 6 medium potatoes, peeled and chopped
- 6 medium carrots, sliced
- 2 medium onions, chopped
- ½ medium head cabbage, chopped
- 1 small turnip, diced
- 1½ tsp. salt
- ¼ tsp. pepper

1. Place ham hocks, water and bouillon in a Dutch oven or soup kettle; bring to a boil. Reduce the heat; cover and simmer for 1½ hours. Remove hocks; allow to cool.
2. Add potatoes, carrots, onions, cabbage and turnip to broth; cover and simmer until the vegetables are tender, 1 hour. Using a potato masher, coarsely mash vegetables.
3. Remove meat from bones; cut into bite-size pieces and add to soup. Stir in salt and pepper; heat through.
1 cup: 189 cal., 9g fat (3g sat. fat), 41mg chol., 377mg sod., 15g carb. (4g sugars, 2g fiber), 12g pro.

SLOW-SIMMERED BURGUNDY BEEF STEW

My mother-in-law shared this recipe with me almost 25 years ago. Ever since then, it's been a go-to whenever I need a hearty dinner without a lot of last-minute bother.
—Mary Lou Timpson, CO City, AZ

- -

Prep: 30 min. • **Bake:** 1¾ hours
Makes: 4 servings

- 1½ lbs. beef stew meat (1¼-in. pieces)
- 3 Tbsp. all-purpose flour
- ¾ tsp. salt
- 2 to 4 tsp. canola oil, divided
- 2 tsp. beef bouillon granules
- 2 tsp. dried parsley flakes
- 1½ tsp. Italian seasoning
- 2 cups water
- 1 cup Burgundy wine or beef stock
- 3 medium potatoes (about 1⅓ lbs.), peeled and quartered
- 1 cup fresh mushrooms, halved
- 1 medium onion, cut into 8 wedges
- 2 medium carrots, cut into 1-in. pieces
- 2 celery ribs, cut into ½-in. pieces
  Additional water, optional

1. Preheat oven to 350°. Toss beef with flour and salt to coat lightly; shake off excess. In an ovenproof Dutch oven, heat 2 tsp. oil over medium heat. Brown beef in batches, adding additional oil as needed. Remove from pan.
2. Add bouillon, herbs, 2 cups water and wine to same pan; bring to a boil, stirring to loosen browned bits from pan. Add beef; return to a boil. Transfer to the oven; bake, covered, 1 hour.
3. Stir in vegetables and, if desired, thin with additional water. Bake, covered, until beef and vegetables are tender, 45-60 minutes.
1½ cups: 419 cal., 15g fat (5g sat. fat), 106mg chol., 949mg sod., 33g carb. (5g sugars, 4g fiber), 37g pro.

CARROT SOUP WITH ORANGE & TARRAGON

A pretty orange color, delicious hint of citrus and garden-fresh flavor make this soup a requested dish at our celebrations. Try sprinkling individual bowls with fresh tarragon before serving.
—Phyllis Schmalz, Kansas City, KS

- -

Prep: 20 min. • **Cook:** 20 min.
Makes: 8 servings (2 qt.)

- 2 lbs. fresh carrots, sliced
- 2 medium onions, chopped
- 2 Tbsp. butter
- 6 cups reduced-sodium chicken broth
- 1 cup orange juice
- 2 Tbsp. brandy
- 4 tsp. minced fresh tarragon or ½ tsp. dried tarragon
- 1 tsp. salt
- 1 tsp. pepper
- 8 tarragon sprigs

1. In a Dutch oven, saute carrots and onion in butter until the onion is tender, about 8-10 minutes. Add the broth; bring to a boil. Reduce heat; simmer, uncovered, until the carrots are very tender, 10-12 minutes. Cool soup slightly.
2. In a blender, process soup in batches until smooth. Return all to pan; stir in the orange juice, brandy and minced tarragon. Bring to a boil. Reduce heat; simmer, uncovered, for 5 minutes to allow flavors to blend. Season with salt and pepper. Garnish with tarragon sprigs before serving.
1 cup: 117 cal., 3g fat (2g sat. fat), 8mg chol., 823mg sod., 18g carb. (10g sugars, 4g fiber), 4g pro.

GRANDMA'S SEAFOOD CHOWDER

My grandmother makes this recipe every year for Christmas morning—the only time I've ever had it. Why wait, though, when you can enjoy this satisfying chowder anytime of year?
—Melissa Obernesser, Utica, NY

- -

Prep: 15 min. • **Cook:** 25 min.
Makes: 10 servings (3¼ qt.)

- 3 Tbsp. plus ¼ cup butter, divided
- 1 lb. sliced fresh mushrooms
- ⅓ cup all-purpose flour
- 1 tsp. salt
- ⅛ tsp. pepper
- 4 cups half-and-half cream
- 1½ cups 2% milk
- 1 lb. haddock fillets, skin removed, cut into 1-in. pieces
- 1 lb. uncooked medium shrimp, peeled and deveined
- 2 cups frozen peas (about 10 oz.)
- ¾ cup shredded cheddar cheese
- 1 cup lump crabmeat (about 5 oz.), drained
- 1 jar (4 oz.) diced pimientos, drained
- 1 tsp. paprika

1. In a 6-qt. stockpot, heat 3 Tbsp. butter over medium-high heat. Add mushrooms; cook and stir until tender, for 8-10 minutes. Remove from pot.
2. In same pot, heat remaining butter over medium heat. Stir in flour, salt and pepper until smooth; gradually whisk in cream and milk. Bring to a boil, stirring constantly; cook and stir until thickened, 2-3 minutes.
3. Stir in haddock, shrimp, peas and sauteed mushrooms; cook until fish just begins to flake easily with a fork and shrimp turn pink, 5-7 minutes. Add the cheese, crab and pimientos; stir gently until cheese is melted. If desired, sprinkle servings with paprika.
1¼ cups: 390 cal., 23g fat (14g sat. fat), 176mg chol., 596mg sod., 14g carb. (8g sugars, 2g fiber), 28g pro.

LOUISIANA RED BEANS & RICE

Smoked turkey sausage and red pepper flakes add zip to this slow-cooked version of the New Orleans classic. For extra heat, add red pepper sauce.
—Julia Bushree, Menifee, CA

Prep: 20 min. • **Cook:** 3 hours
Makes: 8 servings

- 4 cans (16 oz. each) kidney beans, rinsed and drained
- 1 can (14½ oz.) diced tomatoes, undrained
- 1 pkg. (14 oz.) smoked turkey sausage, sliced
- 3 celery ribs, chopped
- 1 large onion, chopped
- 1 cup chicken broth
- 1 medium green pepper, chopped
- 1 small sweet red pepper, chopped
- 6 garlic cloves, minced
- 1 bay leaf
- ½ tsp. crushed red pepper flakes
- 2 green onions, chopped
  Hot cooked rice

1. In a 4- or 5-qt. slow cooker, combine the first 11 ingredients. Cook, covered, on low until vegetables are tender, 3-4 hours.
2. Stir before serving. Remove bay leaf. Serve with green onions and rice.
Freeze option: Discard bay leaf and freeze cooled bean mixture in freezer containers. To use, partially thaw in the refrigerator overnight. Heat through in a saucepan, stirring occasionally and adding a little broth or water if necessary. Serve as directed.
1 cup: 291 cal., 3g fat (1g sat. fat), 32mg chol., 1070mg sod., 44g carb. (8g sugars, 13g fiber), 24g pro.

EGG DROP SOUP

I got this recipe from my grandma's old cookbook, and we continue to start stir-fry meals with it. The easy soup cooks in just minutes, and we like how the addition of cornstarch thickens it.
—Amy Beth Corlew-Sherlock, Lapeer, MI

Takes: 15 min. • **Makes:** 4 servings

- 3 cups chicken broth
- 1 Tbsp. cornstarch
- 2 Tbsp. cold water
- 1 large egg, lightly beaten
- 1 green onion, sliced

1. In a large saucepan, bring broth to a boil over medium heat. Combine cornstarch and water until smooth; gradually stir into broth. Bring to a boil; cook and stir until thickened, 2 minutes.
2. Reduce heat. Drizzle beaten egg into hot broth, stirring constantly. Remove from the heat; stir in onion.
¾ cup: 39 cal., 2g fat (0 sat. fat), 53mg chol., 714mg sod., 3g carb. (1g sugars, 0 fiber), 3g pro.

ROOT VEGETABLE BISQUE

I like cozy comfort soups that seem creamy but don't actually contain all of that heavy cream. This one's full of good stuff such as rutabagas, leeks and fresh herbs.
—Merry Graham, Newhall, CA

Prep: 25 min. • **Cook:** 50 min.
Makes: 12 servings (3½ qt.)

- ¼ cup dairy-free spreadable margarine
- 2 tsp. minced fresh chives
- 2 tsp. minced fresh parsley
- ½ tsp. grated lemon zest

BISQUE

- 2 Tbsp. olive oil
- 2 large rutabagas, peeled and cubed (about 9 cups)
- 1 large celery root, peeled and cubed (about 3 cups)
- 3 medium leeks (white portion only), chopped (about 2 cups)
- 1 large carrot, cubed (about ⅔ cup)
- 3 garlic cloves, minced
- 7 cups vegetable stock
- 2 tsp. minced fresh thyme
- 1½ tsp. minced fresh rosemary
- 1 tsp. salt
- ½ tsp. coarsely ground pepper
- 2 cups almond milk
- 2 Tbsp. minced fresh chives

1. Mix first 4 ingredients. Using a melon baller or 1-tsp. measuring spoon, shape mixture into 12 balls. Freeze on a waxed paper-lined baking sheet until firm. Transfer the balls to a freezer container; freeze up to 2 months.

2. In a 6-qt. stock pot, heat oil over medium heat; saute rutabagas, celery root, leeks and carrot 8 minutes. Add the garlic; cook, stirring, 2 minutes. Stir in stock, herbs, salt and pepper; bring to a boil. Reduce heat; simmer, covered, until the vegetables are tender, 30-35 minutes.

3. Puree soup using an immersion blender, or cool slightly and puree in batches in a blender; return to pan. Stir in the milk; heat through. Top servings with chives and balls of herbed margarine.

1 cup: 146 cal., 7g fat (2g sat. fat), 0 chol., 672mg sod., 20g carb. (9g sugars, 5g fiber), 3g pro. **Diabetic exchanges:** 1 starch, 1 fat.

PUMPKIN HARVEST BEEF STEW

By the time the stew is done simmering and a batch of bread finishes baking, the house smells absolutely wonderful.
—Marcia O'Neil, Cedar Crest, NM

Prep: 25 min. • **Cook:** 6½ hours
Makes: 6 servings

- 1 Tbsp. canola oil
- 1 beef top round steak (1½ lbs.), cut into 1-in. cubes
- 1½ cups cubed peeled pie pumpkin or sweet potatoes
- 3 small red potatoes, peeled and cubed
- 1 cup cubed acorn squash
- 1 medium onion, chopped
- 2 cans (14½ oz. each) reduced-sodium beef broth
- 1 can (14½ oz.) diced tomatoes, undrained
- 2 bay leaves
- 2 garlic cloves, minced
- 2 tsp. reduced-sodium beef bouillon granules
- ½ tsp. chili powder
- ½ tsp. pepper
- ¼ tsp. ground allspice
- ¼ tsp. ground cloves
- ¼ cup water
- 3 Tbsp. all-purpose flour

1. In a large skillet, heat oil over medium-high heat. Brown beef in batches; remove with a slotted spoon to a 4- or 5-qt. slow cooker. Add the pumpkin, potatoes, squash and onion. Stir in the broth, tomatoes and seasonings. Cover and cook on low until meat is tender, 6-8 hours.

2. Remove bay leaves. In a small bowl, mix water and flour until smooth; gradually stir into the stew. Cover and cook on high until liquid is thickened, 30 minutes.

1⅔ cups: 258 cal., 6g fat (1g sat. fat), 67mg chol., 479mg sod., 21g carb. (6g sugars, 4g fiber), 29g pro. **Diabetic exchanges:** 3 lean meat, 1 starch, 1 vegetable, ½ fat.

HEIRLOOM TOMATO SOUP

During the late summer months I make this soup nearly every week. Even my son, who normally does not like tomatoes, enjoys them in this dish.
—Kimberly Danek Pinkson, San Anselmo, CA

- -

Prep: 30 min. • **Cook:** 20 min.
Makes: 20 servings (5 qt.)

1	large sweet onion, halved and thinly sliced
¼	cup extra virgin olive oil
6	garlic cloves, minced
12	medium heirloom tomatoes, quartered (about 8 lbs.)
1	large carrot, chopped
1	cup fresh corn
¼	cup loosely packed basil leaves
2	tsp. sea salt
5½	cups reduced-sodium chicken broth
⅓	cup heavy whipping cream

1. In a stockpot, saute onion in oil until tender. Add garlic; cook 1 minute longer. Add the tomatoes, carrot, corn, basil and salt. Stir in broth. Bring to a boil. Reduce heat; cover and simmer until the tomatoes are softened, for15-20 minutes, stirring occasionally. Cool slightly.

2. In a food processor, process soup in batches until smooth. Return all to pan and heat through. Ladle into bowls; drizzle each with ¾ tsp. cream.

1 cup: 73 cal., 4g fat (1g sat. fat), 5mg chol., 356mg sod., 7g carb. (4g sugars, 2g fiber), 2g pro. **Diabetic exchanges:** 1 vegetable, 1 fat.

SPICY PORK & GREEN CHILI VERDE

My pork chili is brimming with poblanos for a hearty kick and sweet red peppers. Serve it with sour cream, Monterey Jack cheese and tortilla chips.
—Anthony Bolton, Bellevue, NE

Prep: 40 min. + standing • **Cook:** 25 min.
Makes: 6 servings

- 6 poblano peppers
- 2 Tbsp. butter
- 1½ lbs. pork tenderloin, cut into 1-in. pieces
- 2 medium sweet red or yellow peppers, coarsely chopped
- 1 large sweet onion, coarsely chopped
- 1 jalapeno pepper, seeded and finely chopped
- 2 Tbsp. chili powder
- 2 garlic cloves, minced
- 1 tsp. salt
- ¼ tsp. ground nutmeg
- 2 cups chicken broth
  Optional toppings: Sour cream, shredded Monterey Jack cheese, crumbled tortilla chips and lime wedges

1. Place poblano peppers on a foil-lined baking sheet. Broil 4 in. from heat until skins blister, about 5 minutes. With tongs, rotate peppers a quarter turn. Broil and rotate until all sides are blistered and blackened. Immediately place peppers in a large bowl; let stand, covered, 10 minutes.

2. Peel off and discard charred skin. Remove and discard stems and seeds. Finely chop the peppers.

3. In a 6-qt. stockpot, heat the butter over medium heat. Brown the pork in batches. Remove with a slotted spoon.

4. In same pan, add red peppers, onion and jalapeno; cook, covered, over medium heat until tender, 8-10 minutes, stirring mixture occasionally. Stir in chili powder, garlic, salt and nutmeg. Add broth, roasted peppers and pork; bring to a boil. Reduce the heat; simmer, uncovered, until the pork is tender, 10-15 minutes. Serve; top as desired.

1 cup: 235 cal., 9g fat (4g sat. fat), 75mg chol., 913mg sod., 14g carb. (8g sugars, 4g fiber), 25g pro.

"I'm so grateful for this delicious recipe. I can't wait to make it again. It had the perfect heat and incredible flavor from the spices."
—SUMMY, TASTEOFHOME.COM

MOMMA'S TURKEY & DUMPLINGS

My mother used to make turkey stew every year with our Thanksgiving leftovers. It's simple and really celebrates the natural flavors of good, simple ingredients. To this day it's one of my favorite meals.
—Stephanie Rabbitt-Schapp, Cincinnati, OH

- -

Prep: 20 min. • **Cook:** 6½ hours
Makes: 6 servings

- 3 cups shredded cooked turkey
- 1 large sweet onion, chopped
- 1 large potato, peeled and cubed
- 2 large carrots, chopped
- 2 celery ribs, chopped
- 2 bay leaves
- 1 tsp. salt
- ½ tsp. poultry seasoning
- ½ tsp. dried thyme
- ¼ tsp. pepper
- 1 carton (32 oz.) chicken broth
- ⅓ cup cold water
- 3 Tbsp. cornstarch
- ½ cup frozen corn, thawed
- ½ cup frozen peas, thawed
- 1 cup biscuit/baking mix
- ⅓ cup 2% milk

1. In a 6-qt. slow cooker, combine the first 10 ingredients; stir in broth. Cover and cook on low for 6-7 hours.
2. Remove bay leaves. In a small bowl, mix water and cornstarch until smooth; stir into turkey mixture. Add corn and peas. Cover and cook on high until the mixture reaches a simmer.
3. Meanwhile, in a small bowl, mix baking mix and milk just until moistened. Carefully drop by rounded tablespoonfuls on top of simmering liquid. Reduce heat to low; cover and cook until a toothpick inserted in a dumpling comes out clean, 20-25 minutes.
1 serving: 287 cal., 6g fat (2g sat. fat), 74mg chol., 1410mg sod., 33g carb. (6g sugars, 3g fiber), 25g pro.

STUFFED PEPPER SOUP

Some of us cooks at the restaurant where I work were talking about stuffed peppers. We decided to stir up similar ingredients for an old-fashioned soup. The customer response was overwhelming!
—Krista Muddiman, Meadville, PA

- -

Prep: 15 min. • **Cook:** 45 min.
Makes: 8 servings (2 qt.)

- 2 lbs. ground beef
- 6 cups water
- 1 can (28 oz.) tomato sauce
- 1 can (28 oz.) diced tomatoes, undrained
- 2 cups chopped green peppers
- ¼ cup packed brown sugar
- 2 tsp. salt
- 2 tsp. beef bouillon granules
- 1 tsp. pepper
- 2 cups cooked long grain rice
  Chopped fresh parsley, optional

1. In a Dutch oven over medium heat, cook and stir beef until no longer pink; drain. Stir in next 8 ingredients; bring to a boil. Reduce heat; simmer, uncovered, until peppers are tender, about 30 minutes.
2. Add the cooked rice; simmer, uncovered, 10 minutes longer. If desired, sprinkle with chopped fresh parsley.
1 cup: 337 cal., 14g fat (5g sat. fat), 70mg chol., 1466mg sod., 30g carb. (13g sugars, 4g fiber), 24g pro.

HEARTY MINESTRONE SOUP

Packed with sausage and veggies, this soup is not only nutritious, it's also a great way to use up your garden bounty.
—Donna Smith, Fairport, NY

Prep: 25 min. • **Cook:** 30 min.
Makes: 9 servings

1	lb. bulk Italian sausage
2	cups sliced celery
1	cup chopped onion
6	cups chopped zucchini
1	can (28 oz.) diced tomatoes, undrained
1½	cups chopped green pepper
1½	tsp. Italian seasoning
1½	tsp. salt
1	tsp. dried oregano
1	tsp. sugar
½	tsp. dried basil
¼	tsp. garlic powder

In a large saucepan, cook the sausage until no longer pink. Remove with a slotted spoon to paper towel to drain, reserving 1 Tbsp. of drippings. Saute celery and onion in drippings for 5 minutes. Add sausage and the remaining ingredients; bring to a boil. Reduce heat; cover and simmer until the vegetables are tender, 20-30 minutes.

1 cup: 224 cal., 16g fat (6g sat. fat), 38mg chol., 901mg sod., 12g carb. (7g sugars, 4g fiber), 10g pro.

LAMB STEW

My grandmother used to make this stew for Sunday dinners. It's a memorable treat from Ireland. If you like your stew thick and rich, you've got to try this.
—Vickie Desourdy, Washington, NC

Prep: 40 min. • **Bake:** 1½ hours
Makes: 8 servings (2½ qt.)

2	lbs. lamb stew meat, cut into 1-in. cubes
1	Tbsp. butter
1	Tbsp. olive oil
1	lb. carrots, sliced
2	medium onions, thinly sliced
2	garlic cloves, minced
1½	cups reduced-sodium chicken broth
1	bottle (12 oz.) Guinness stout or additional reduced-sodium chicken broth
6	medium red potatoes, peeled and cut into 1-in. cubes
4	bay leaves
2	fresh thyme sprigs
2	fresh rosemary sprigs
2	tsp. salt
1½	tsp. pepper
¼	cup heavy whipping cream

1. Preheat oven to 325°. In an ovenproof Dutch oven, brown lamb in butter and oil in batches. Remove and keep warm. In the same pan, saute carrots and onions in drippings until crisp-tender. Add garlic; cook 1 minute. Gradually add broth and beer. Stir in the lamb, potatoes, bay leaves, thyme, rosemary, salt and pepper.
2. Cover and bake until meat and vegetables are tender, about 1½ -2 hours, stirring every 30 minutes. Discard bay leaves, thyme and rosemary. Stir in cream; heat through.

Freeze option: Place individual portions of stew in freezer containers and freeze up to 3 months. To use, partially thaw in refrigerator overnight. Heat stew through in a saucepan, stirring occasionally and adding a little water if necessary.

1¼ cups: 311 cal., 12g fat (5g sat. fat), 88mg chol., 829mg sod., 23g carb. (6g sugars, 4g fiber), 26g pro. **Diabetic exchanges:** 3 lean meat, 2 vegetable, 1 starch, 1 fat.

GARLICKY CHEDDAR CHEESE BISQUE

I came up with a cheddar cheese soup a while ago and decided to give it a boost with a variety of root vegetables. Crushed pita chips and fresh parsley make fun and pretty garnishes to the hearty bisque.
—Patricia Harmon, Baden, PA

- -

Prep: 30 min. • **Cook:** 40 min.
Makes: 6 servings

- 1   Tbsp. butter
- 1   Tbsp. canola oil
- 1   medium leek
     (white portion only), sliced
- ½   cup chopped carrot
- ½   cup chopped celery
- ½   cup chopped peeled parsnip
- 1   tsp. salt
- ½   tsp. pepper
- 6   garlic cloves, minced
- 2   cans (14½ oz. each) chicken broth
- ⅔   cup dry white wine
- 2   Tbsp. cornstarch
- ¼   cup cold water
- 1   can (12 oz.) evaporated milk
- 2   cups shredded sharp
     white cheddar cheese
     Crushed baked pita chips
     Minced fresh parsley

1. In a large saucepan, heat butter and oil over medium heat. Add vegetables, salt and pepper; cook and stir until vegetables are crisp-tender, 7-8 minutes. Add garlic; cook 1-2 minutes longer.

2. Stir in broth and wine; bring to a boil. Reduce heat; simmer, uncovered, until the vegetables are tender, for 15-20 minutes. Remove from heat; cool slightly. Meanwhile, in a small bowl, mix cornstarch and water until smooth.

3. Process the soup in batches in a food processor until smooth. Return all to pan. Stir in evaporated milk and cornstarch mixture; bring to a boil. Reduce heat; simmer, uncovered, until thickened and bubbly, stirring frequently. Add cheese; cook and stir until cheese is blended. Top individual servings with crushed pita chips and parsley.

1 cup: 320 cal., 19g fat (12g sat. fat), 68mg chol., 1307mg sod., 18g carb. (9g sugars, 1g fiber), 13g pro.

RED FLANNEL STEW

When I was child, every Saturday night was red flannel night. Grandpa and I wore our red flannel underwear to supper while Grandma, the cook, dressed in a long calico dress and sunbonnet. We'd eat this red flannel stew spooned over fluffy southern-style biscuits. Grandma had learned to make the stew from earlier generations.
—Kathy Padgett, Diamond City, AR

Prep: 25 min. • **Cook:** 1½ hours
Makes: 5 servings

2   whole fresh beets, washed, trimmed and halved
6   cups water, divided
1   lb. corned beef brisket, trimmed and cut into 1-in. pieces
4   small carrots, sliced
1   large potato, cubed
1   small turnip, peeled and cubed
1   small onion, chopped
1   tsp. each dried parsley flakes, basil and thyme
¼   tsp. salt
⅛   tsp. pepper

1. In a large saucepan, bring the beets and 4 cups water to a boil. Reduce heat; simmer, uncovered, until tender, for 20-25 minutes. Drain, reserving 2 cups cooking liquid. Peel and dice beets; set aside.
2. In the same pan, combine corned beef, carrots, potato, turnip, onion, seasonings, remaining water and reserved cooking liquid. Bring to a boil. Reduce heat; cover and simmer until meat and vegetables are tender, 1¼ -1½ hours. Stir in diced beets; heat through.
1⅓ cups: 209 cal., 9g fat (3g sat. fat), 31mg chol., 881mg sod., 22g carb. (6g sugars, 3g fiber), 11g pro.

FROGMORE STEW

This picnic-style medley of shrimp, smoked kielbasa, corn and spuds has been a South Carolina cuisine specialty for generations. It's commonly dubbed Frogmore Stew or Beaufort Stew in recognition of both of the low country communities that lay claim to its origin. No matter what you call it, this one-pot wonder won't disappoint!
—*Taste of Home* Test Kitchen

Prep: 10 min. • **Cook:** 35 min.
Makes: 8 servings

16 cups water
1 large sweet onion, quartered
3 Tbsp. seafood seasoning
2 medium lemons, halved, optional
1 lb. small red potatoes
1 lb. smoked kielbasa or fully cooked hot links, cut into 1-in. pieces
4 medium ears sweet corn, cut into thirds
2 lbs. uncooked medium shrimp, peeled and deveined
   Seafood cocktail sauce
   Melted butter
   Additional seafood seasoning

1. In a stockpot, combine water, onion, seafood seasoning and, if desired, lemons; bring to a boil. Add the potatoes; cook, uncovered, 10 minutes. Add kielbasa and corn; return to a boil. Reduce heat; simmer, uncovered, until potatoes are tender, for 10-12 minutes. Add shrimp; cook until pink, 2-3 minutes longer.

2. Drain; transfer to a bowl. Serve stew with cocktail sauce, melted butter and additional seafood seasoning.

1 serving: 369 cal., 18g fat (6g sat. fat), 175mg chol., 751mg sod., 24g carb. (7g sugars, 2g fiber), 28g pro.

SWEET POTATO BISQUE

I love to serve this bright orange bisque for special occasions with my large family in fall and winter. The recipe includes a minted chili oil to drizzle on top: It's well worth the few extra minutes it takes to make it.
—Lily Julow, Lawrenceville, GA

- -

Prep: 30 min. • **Cook:** 40 min.
Makes: 8 servings (2 qt.)

- 8 bacon strips, finely chopped
- 6 medium carrots, chopped (2 cups)
- 1 medium onion, chopped (1 cup)
- 3 garlic cloves, minced
- 3 cups water
- 1¾ lbs. sweet potatoes (about 4 medium), peeled and cubed
- 3 bay leaves
- 2½ tsp. curry powder
- ¾ tsp. salt
- ½ tsp. ground cinnamon
- ½ tsp. smoked paprika
- ½ tsp. pepper
- 1½ cups heavy whipping cream
- 1 cup sour cream

MINTED CHILI OIL

- 18 mint sprigs, chopped
- 3 Tbsp. olive oil
- ¼ tsp. sugar
- ¼ tsp. salt
- ¼ tsp. crushed red pepper flakes
- ¼ tsp. pepper

1. In a large saucepan, cook bacon over medium heat until crisp; stir occasionally. Remove with a slotted spoon; drain on paper towels. Discard drippings, reserving 2 Tbsp. in pan.

2. Add carrots and onion to drippings; cook and stir over medium-high heat until tender. Add garlic; cook 1 minute longer.

3. Stir in water, sweet potatoes, bay leaves, curry, salt, cinnamon, paprika and pepper. Bring to a boil. Reduce the heat; simmer, covered, until vegetables are tender, 10-15 minutes. Discard bay leaves. Stir in cream and sour cream just until blended. Cool.

4. Meanwhile, in a small bowl, combine mint, oil, sugar, salt, pepper flakes and pepper. Let stand 5-10 minutes.

5. Process bisque in batches in a blender until smooth; return all to the pan. Heat through (do not boil). Ladle bisque into bowls; drizzle with minted chili oil.

1 cup with 1½ tsp. minted chili oil: 413 cal., 32g fat (16g sat. fat), 90mg chol., 512mg sod., 24g carb. (10g sugars, 4g fiber), 6g pro.

CHEESEBURGER SOUP

A local restaurant serves a similar soup but wouldn't share its recipe with me. So I developed my own, modifying a recipe for potato soup. I was really pleased with the way this all-American soup turned out.
—Joanie Shawhan, Madison, WI

Prep: 45 min. • **Cook:** 10 min.
Makes: 8 servings (2¼ qt.)

- ½ lb. ground beef
- 4 Tbsp. butter, divided
- ¾ cup chopped onion
- ¾ cup shredded carrots
- ¾ cup diced celery
- 1 tsp. dried basil
- 1 tsp. dried parsley flakes
- 1¾ lbs. (about 4 cups) cubed peeled potatoes
- 3 cups chicken broth
- ¼ cup all-purpose flour
- 2 to 4 cups shredded Velveeta process cheese
- 1½ cups whole milk
- ¾ tsp. salt
- ¼ to ½ tsp. pepper
- ¼ cup sour cream

1. In a large saucepan over medium heat, cook and crumble beef until no longer pink; drain and set aside. In same saucepan, melt 1 Tbsp. butter over medium heat. Saute onion, carrots, celery, basil and parsley until vegetables are tender, about 10 minutes. Add potatoes, ground beef and broth; bring to a boil. Reduce the heat; simmer, covered, until potatoes are tender, 10-12 minutes.
2. Meanwhile, in a small skillet, melt the remaining butter. Add flour; cook and stir until bubbly, 3-5 minutes. Add to the soup; bring to a boil. Cook and stir for 2 minutes. Reduce the heat to low. Stir in cheese, milk, salt and pepper; cook until cheese melts. Remove from heat; blend in sour cream.
1 cup: 450 cal., 27g fat (15g sat. fat), 100mg chol., 1421mg sod., 33g carb. (8g sugars, 3g fiber), 19g pro.

BRATWURST SOUP

I came up with this recipe one day when I had some leftover bratwurst. It's been a favorite of my husband's ever since.
—Anna Miller, Churdan, IA

Prep: 10 min. • **Cook:** 25 min.
Makes: 8 servings (2 qt.)

- 1 lb. uncooked bratwurst links, casings removed
- ½ cup chopped onion
- 1 medium carrot, chopped
- 2 cans (15½ oz. each) navy beans, rinsed and drained
- ¼ cup pickled jalapeno slices, chopped
- ½ tsp. pepper
- 2 cups reduced-sodium chicken broth
- ¼ cup all-purpose flour
- 1½ cups 2% milk, divided
- 12 slices process American cheese

1. In a Dutch oven, cook and crumble the bratwurst with onion and carrot over medium heat until meat is no longer pink, 5-7 minutes; drain.
2. Stir in beans, jalapeno, pepper and broth; bring to a boil. Whisk together flour and ½ cup milk until smooth; stir into the soup. Bring to a boil, stirring constantly; cook and stir until thickened, 5 minutes. Gradually stir in the remaining milk. Add cheese; cook and stir over low heat until melted.
1 cup: 468 cal., 25g fat (11g sat. fat), 53mg chol., 1322mg sod., 33g carb. (5g sugars, 6g fiber), 25g pro.

GRANDMA'S FAVORITE
SIDE DISHES

When struggling to round out a menu, look no further than
Grandma's apron strings. Indulge in these longtime staples
that turn any meal into a special occasion.

MALLOW-TOPPED SWEET POTATOES

My grandmother always served this sweet potato casserole at Thanksgiving. A puffy marshmallow topping gives the dish festive flair, and spices enhance the autumnal flavor of the potatoes.
—Edna Hoffman, Hebron, IN

- -

Prep: 40 min. • **Bake:** 45 min.
Makes: 12 servings

4 lbs. sweet potatoes (about 5 large), peeled and cut into 1-in. pieces
1 cup 2% milk
6 Tbsp. butter, softened
½ cup packed brown sugar
1 large egg
1½ tsp. ground cinnamon
1½ tsp. vanilla extract
¾ tsp. ground allspice
½ tsp. salt
¼ tsp. ground nutmeg
10 large marshmallows, halved lengthwise

1. Preheat oven to 350°. Place the sweet potatoes in a 6-qt. stockpot; add water to cover. Bring to a boil. Reduce heat; cook, uncovered, until tender, 15-20 minutes. Drain potatoes; place in a large bowl.
2. Beat potatoes until smooth. Add the next 9 ingredients; beat until blended.
3. Spread into a greased shallow 2½-qt. baking dish. Bake, uncovered, until heated through, 40-45 minutes. Increase oven setting to 425°.
4. Top casserole with marshmallows. Bake until marshmallows are lightly browned, 3-4 minutes.

⅔ cup: 312 cal., 7g fat (4g sat. fat), 36mg chol., 201mg sod., 59g carb. (35g sugars, 3g fiber), 4g pro.

TEST KITCHEN TIP
Light brown sugar has a delicate flavor while dark brown sugar has a stronger molasses flavor. Use them interchangeably as you'd like.

GRANDMA'S FRUIT SALAD

I can't believe how easy this pretty salad is to make. The colorful blend of bananas, pineapple, pears, peaches and grapes is tossed with a creamy pudding sauce. People of all ages enjoy it.
—Carolyn Tomatz, Jackson, WI

- -

Prep: 25 min. + chilling
Makes: 12 servings

- 1 **can (20 oz.) unsweetened pineapple chunks**
- 1 **can (15 oz.) reduced-sugar sliced pears, drained**
- 1 **can (15 oz.) sliced peaches in juice, drained**
- 1½ **cups seedless red grapes**
- 1 **pkg. (3 oz.) cook-and-serve vanilla pudding mix**
- 2 **medium firm bananas**
- 3 **Tbsp. lemon juice**
- 1 **jar (10 oz.) maraschino cherries, well drained**

1. Drain pineapple chunks, reserving juice in a 1-cup measuring cup. In a large bowl, combine the pineapple, pears, peaches and grapes. Cover and refrigerate.
2. Add enough water to pineapple juice to measure 1 cup. Pour into a small saucepan. Whisk in pudding mix. Bring to a boil over medium heat, stirring constantly. Remove from the heat; set mixture aside to cool to room temperature.
3. Slice bananas into a small bowl. Drizzle with lemon juice; gently toss to coast. Let stand for 5 minutes; drain. Add bananas and cherries to chilled fruit. Add cooled pudding; toss fruit salad gently to combine. Refrigerate until serving. Refrigerate leftover salad.

½ cup: 140 cal., 0 fat (0 sat. fat), 0 chol., 53mg sod., 37g carb. (33g sugars, 2g fiber), 0 pro. **Diabetic exchanges:** 2 fruit.

GERMAN NOODLE BAKE

This is a recipe I serve each year for my holiday open house. Store-bought noodles can always be substituted, but I prefer homemade noodles...and so does everyone else.
—Kathleen Meineke, Cologne, NJ

Prep: 45 min. + standing • **Bake:** 30 min.
Makes: 8 servings

- 1 cup all-purpose flour
- ½ tsp. salt
- 2 large eggs, lightly beaten
- 2 qt. water

CHEESE SAUCE
- 3 Tbsp. butter
- 3 Tbsp. all-purpose flour
- ½ tsp. salt
- ½ tsp. paprika
- 1½ cups whole milk
- 8 oz. Swiss cheese, diced
- 2 large eggs, well beaten

1. In a small bowl, combine flour and salt. Make a well in the center; add eggs. Stir together, forming a dough.
2. Turn dough onto a floured surface; knead 5-6 minutes. Divide dough in half. Roll each portion into a 12x9-in. rectangle. Dust both sides of dough with flour; roll up, jelly-roll style. Cut into ¼-in. slices. Unroll noodles on paper towels; let dry for up to 2 hours.
3. Preheat oven to 350°. In a Dutch oven, bring water to a rapid boil. Add noodles; cook 7-9 minutes or until tender.
4. Meanwhile, in a small saucepan, melt butter. Stir in flour, salt and paprika until smooth; gradually add milk. Bring to a boil; cook and stir 2 minutes or until thickened. Remove from heat; stir in the cheese until melted. Stir in eggs.
5. Drain the noodles; transfer to a greased 11x7-in. baking dish. Top with cheese sauce. Cover and bake 20 minutes. Uncover; bake 10-15 minutes longer or until bubbly.
⅔ cup: 275 cal., 16g fat (9g sat. fat), 148mg chol., 453mg sod., 17g carb. (4g sugars, 1g fiber), 15g pro.

CRANBERRY ROASTED SQUASH

I created this recipe one day when I wanted a warm, fragrant side dish. The aroma of the squash and cranberries cooking in the oven is just as heavenly as the flavor.
—Jamillah Almutawakil, Superior, CO

Prep: 15 min. • **Bake:** 45 min.
Makes: 12 servings

- 1 medium butternut squash (5 to 6 lbs.), peeled and cut into 1-in. cubes
- 1 medium acorn squash (1½ lbs.), peeled and cut into 1-in. cubes
- ⅔ cup chopped fresh or frozen cranberries
- ¼ cup sugar
- 2 Tbsp. olive oil
- 1 Tbsp. butter, melted
- 1 Tbsp. molasses
- 2 garlic cloves, minced
- 1½ tsp. rubbed sage
- 1 tsp. salt
- ½ tsp. pepper

Preheat oven to 400°. In a large bowl, combine all ingredients. Transfer to two 15x10x1-in. baking pans. Roast until tender, stirring and rotating pans halfway through cooking, 45-55 minutes.
¾ cup: 161 cal., 3g fat (1g sat. fat), 3mg chol., 214mg sod., 35g carb. (12g sugars, 8g fiber), 2g pro. **Diabetic exchanges:** 2 starch, ½ fat.

BLUE CHEESE & GRAPE COLESLAW

Dishes like coleslaw beg for a fresh approach. I updated mine with almonds, grapes, blue cheese and bacon for a grand bowl of color and crunch.
—Jeannine Bunge, Hartley, IA

Prep: 20 min. + chilling • **Makes:** 8 servings

- 1 pkg. (14 oz.) coleslaw mix
- ¾ cup sliced almonds, toasted
- ¾ cup quartered green grapes
- ¾ cup quartered seedless red grapes
- ½ cup crumbled blue cheese
- 3 bacon strips, cooked and crumbled
- ¼ tsp. pepper
- ¾ cup coleslaw salad dressing

Combine first 7 ingredients. Pour dressing over salad; toss to coat. Refrigerate 1 hour.
Note: To toast nuts, bake in a shallow pan in a 350° oven for 5-10 minutes or cook in a skillet over low heat until lightly browned, stirring occasionally.
¾ cup: 212 cal., 15g fat (3g sat. fat), 17mg chol., 339mg sod., 16g carb. (12g sugars, 3g fiber), 5g pro.

LEMON-PEPPER ROASTED BROCCOLI

Fresh green broccoli turns tangy and tasty when roasted with lemon juice and pepper. A sprinkle of almonds adds crunch.
—Liz Bellville, Tonasket, WA

Takes: 25 min. • **Makes:** 8 servings

- 1½ lbs. fresh broccoli florets (about 12 cups)
- 2 Tbsp. olive oil
- ½ tsp. lemon juice
- ¼ tsp. salt
- ¼ tsp. coarsely ground pepper, divided
- ¼ cup chopped almonds
- 2 tsp. grated lemon zest

1. Preheat oven to 450°. Place broccoli in a large bowl. Whisk oil, lemon juice, salt and ⅛ tsp. pepper until blended; drizzle over broccoli and toss to coat. Transfer to a 15x10x1-in. baking pan.
2. Roast 10-15 minutes or until tender. Transfer to a serving dish. Sprinkle with almonds, lemon zest and remaining pepper; toss to combine.
1 cup: 84 cal., 6g fat (1g sat. fat), 0 chol., 103mg sod., 7g carb. (0 sugars, 4g fiber), 4g pro. **Diabetic exchanges:** 1 vegetable, 1 fat.

ASPARAGUS, SQUASH & RED PEPPER SAUTE

Made in a cast-iron skillet, my veggie trio is enlivened by a wine-scented saute. Yum!
—Deirdre Cox, Kansas City, MO

Takes: 30 min. • **Makes:** 4 servings

- 2 medium sweet red peppers, julienned
- 2 medium yellow summer squash, halved lengthwise and cut into ¼-in. slices
- 6 oz. fresh asparagus, trimmed and cut into 1½-in. pieces
- ¼ cup white wine or ¼ cup vegetable broth
- 4½ tsp. olive oil
- ¼ tsp. salt
- ¼ tsp. pepper

In a large cast-iron or other heavy skillet, saute the peppers, squash and asparagus in wine and oil until crisp-tender. Sprinkle with salt and pepper.

¾ cup: 90 cal., 5g fat (1g sat. fat), 0 chol., 163mg sod., 8g carb. (5g sugars, 3g fiber), 2g pro. **Diabetic exchanges:** 1 vegetable, 1 fat.

TEST KITCHEN TIP

This recipe is very adaptable, so you can use whatever is in season. Substitute zucchini, different colors of peppers, or even some fresh green beans.

ROASTED CABBAGE & ONIONS

I roast veggies to bring out their sweetness, and it works wonders with onions and cabbage. The piquant vinegar-mustard sauce makes this dish similar to a slaw.
—Ann Sheehy, Lawrence, MA

Prep: 10 min. • **Cook:** 30 min. + standing
Makes: 6 servings

- 1   medium head cabbage (about 2 lbs.), coarsely chopped
- 2   large onions, chopped
- ¼   cup olive oil
- ¾   tsp. salt
- ¾   tsp. pepper
- 3   Tbsp. minced fresh chives
- 3   Tbsp. minced fresh tarragon

DRESSING
- 2   Tbsp. white balsamic vinegar or white wine vinegar
- 2   Tbsp. olive oil
- 2   Tbsp. Dijon mustard
- 1   Tbsp. lemon juice
- ½   tsp. salt
- ½   tsp. pepper

1. Preheat oven to 450°. Place the cabbage and onions in a large bowl. Drizzle with oil; sprinkle with salt and pepper and toss to coat. Transfer to a shallow roasting pan, spreading evenly. Roast until vegetables are tender and lightly browned, stirring halfway, 30-35 minutes.

2. Transfer cabbage mixture to a large bowl. Add chives and tarragon; toss to combine. In a small bowl, whisk dressing ingredients until blended. Drizzle over cabbage mixture; toss to coat. Let stand about 10 minutes to allow flavors to blend. Serve warm or at room temperature.

¾ cups: 183 cal., 14g fat (2g sat. fat), 0 chol., 636mg sod., 15g carb. (7g sugars, 4g fiber), 2g pro.

MASHED POTATOES WITH GARLIC-OLIVE OIL

Garlic mashed potatoes are high on our family's list. To intensify the flavor, I combine garlic and olive oil in the food processor and drizzle it on top.
—Emory Doty, Jasper, GA

Takes: 30 min. • **Makes:** 12 servings

- 4   lbs. red potatoes, quartered
- ½   cup olive oil
- 2   garlic cloves
- ⅔   cup heavy whipping cream
- ¼   cup butter, softened
- 2   tsp. salt
- ½   tsp. pepper
- ⅔   to ¾ cup whole milk
- 3   green onions, chopped
- ¾   cup grated Parmesan cheese, optional

1. Place the potatoes in a Dutch oven; add water to cover. Bring to a boil. Reduce heat; cook, uncovered, until potatoes are tender, 15-20 minutes. Meanwhile, place oil and garlic in a small food processor; process until well blended.
2. Drain potatoes; return to pan. Mash potatoes, gradually adding cream, butter, salt, pepper and enough milk to reach desired consistency. Stir in green onions. Serve with the garlic olive oil and, if desired, Parmesan cheese.
Note: For food safety purposes, prepare garlic olive oil just before serving; do not store leftover oil mixture.
¾ cup mashed potatoes with 1 Tbsp. cheese and about 2 tsp. oil mixture: 299 cal., 20g fat (8g sat. fat), 31mg chol., 533mg sod., 26g carb. (3g sugars, 3g fiber), 5g pro.

GRANDMA'S SPINACH SALAD

With all its fresh ingredients, this pretty salad was my grandma's favorite. Even my little ones like it. Just don't tell them spinach is good for them!
—Shelley Riebel, Armada, MI

Takes: 20 min. • **Makes:** 8 servings

- ½   cup sugar
- ½   cup canola oil
- ¼   cup white vinegar
- ½   tsp. celery seed
- 10   oz. fresh baby spinach (about 13 cups)
- 1   small red onion, thinly sliced
- ½   lb. sliced fresh mushrooms
- 5   hard-boiled large eggs, sliced
- 8   bacon strips, cooked and crumbled

1. Whisk the first 4 ingredients until the sugar is dissolved.
2. In a 13x9-in. dish, layer half of each of the following: spinach, onion, mushrooms and eggs. Repeat layers. Drizzle with dressing; top with bacon.
1¼ cups: 280 cal., 21g fat (3g sat. fat), 125mg chol., 214mg sod., 16g carb. (14g sugars, 1g fiber), 9g pro.

SAUERKRAUT LATKES

Sauerkraut in potato pancakes might seem like an unusual combination, but it's one worth trying. The apples mellow the tang for an wonderfully pleasant flavor.
—Aysha Schurman, Ammon, ID

- -

Prep: 20 min. • **Cook:** 5 min./batch
Makes: 2½ dozen

3	lbs. russet potatoes, peeled and shredded
1½	cups shredded peeled apples
1½	cups sauerkraut, rinsed and well drained
6	large eggs, lightly beaten
6	Tbsp. all-purpose flour
2	tsp. salt
1½	tsp. pepper
¾	cup canola oil
	Optional: Sour cream and chopped green onions

1. In a large bowl, combine the potatoes, apples, sauerkraut and eggs. Combine the flour, salt and pepper; stir into the potato mixture.
2. Heat 2 Tbsp. oil in a large nonstick skillet over medium heat. Drop the batter by ¼ cupfuls into oil; press lightly to flatten. Fry in batches until golden brown on both sides, using remaining oil as needed. Drain on paper towels. Top with sour cream and green onions if desired.

3 latkes: 306 cal., 20g fat (2g sat. fat), 127mg chol., 658mg sod., 27g carb. (5g sugars, 3g fiber), 6g pro.

EMILY'S HONEY LIME COLESLAW

Here's a refreshing take on slaw with a honey-lime vinaigrette rather than the traditional mayo. It's a great take-along for summer picnics.
—Emily Tyra, Traverse City, MI

- -

Prep: 20 min. + chilling • **Makes:** 8 servings

1½	tsp. grated lime zest
¼	cup lime juice
2	Tbsp. honey
1	garlic clove, minced
½	tsp. salt
¼	tsp. pepper
¼	tsp. crushed red pepper flakes
3	Tbsp. canola oil
1	small head red cabbage (about ¾ lb.), shredded
1	cup shredded carrots (about 2 medium carrots)
2	green onions, thinly sliced
½	cup fresh cilantro leaves

Whisk together the first 7 ingredients until smooth. Gradually whisk in oil until blended. Combine the cabbage, carrots and green onions; toss with the lime mixture to lightly coat. Refrigerate, covered, 2 hours. Sprinkle with cilantro.

½ cup: 86 cal., 5g fat (0 sat. fat), 0 chol., 170mg sod., 10g carb. (7g sugars, 2g fiber), 1g pro. **Diabetic exchanges:** 1 vegetable, 1 fat.

SPINACH & BACON SALAD WITH PEACHES

Peaches and bacon? Oh, yeah! This is a favorite of my family. I make it for all sorts of warm-weather parties by prepping the parts separately, then tossing them all together right before chow time.
—Megan Riofski, Frankfort, IL

- -

Takes: 25 min.
Makes: 8 servings (1½ cups dressing)

- 1 cup olive oil
- ⅓ cup cider vinegar
- ¼ cup sugar
- 1 tsp. celery seed
- 1 tsp. ground mustard
- ½ tsp. salt

SALAD

- 6 cups fresh baby spinach (about 6 oz.)
- 2 medium peaches, sliced
- 1¾ cups sliced fresh mushrooms
- 3 large hard-boiled large eggs, halved and sliced
- ½ lb. bacon strips, cooked and crumbled
- 1 small red onion, halved and thinly sliced
- ¼ cup sliced almonds, toasted
  Grated Parmesan cheese

Place the first 6 ingredients in a blender; cover and process until blended. In a large bowl, combine the spinach, peaches, mushrooms, eggs, bacon, onion and almonds. Serve with dressing and cheese.
Note: To toast nuts, bake in a shallow pan in a 350° oven for 5-10 minutes or cook in a skillet over low heat until lightly browned, stirring occasionally.
1½ cups salad with 3 Tbsp. dressing: 391 cal., 35g fat (6g sat. fat), 80mg chol., 372mg sod., 13g carb. (10g sugars, 2g fiber), 8g pro.

GRANDMA'S FAST POTATO DUMPLINGS

Don't be surprised if you make too many mashed potatoes on purpose. Day-old rolls and leftover spuds are scrumptious the second time around when you turn them into 30-minute potato dumplings.
—Wendy Stenman, Germantown, WI

- -

Takes: 25 min. • **Makes:** 4 servings

- 2 day-old hard rolls
- ½ cup water
- 2 tsp. canola oil
- ½ cup leftover mashed potatoes
- 1 large egg, lightly beaten
  Dash ground nutmeg
- 1 to 2 Tbsp. all-purpose flour
- ¼ cup butter, cubed

1. Tear the rolls into ½-in. pieces; place in a 15x10x1-in. baking pan. Drizzle with water and squeeze dry.
2. In a large skillet, heat oil over medium-high heat. Add torn rolls; cook and stir until lightly toasted, 1-2 minutes.
3. In a small bowl, combine potatoes, egg, nutmeg and bread. Add enough flour to achieve a shaping consistency. With floured hands, shape mixture into 3-in. balls.
4. Fill a Dutch oven two-thirds full with water; bring to a boil. Carefully add the dumplings. Reduce the heat; simmer, uncovered, until a toothpick inserted in center of dumplings comes out clean, 8-10 minutes. Meanwhile, in a small heavy saucepan, melt butter over medium heat. Heat until golden brown, 4-6 minutes.
5. Serve warm dumplings with butter.
1 dumpling with 1 Tbsp. butter: 255 cal., 17g fat (8g sat. fat), 84mg chol., 322mg sod., 22g carb. (1g sugars, 1g fiber), 5g pro.

MOLDED CRANBERRY-ORANGE SALAD

I take this old-time dish to potlucks, and people always "ooh" and "aah" at how beautiful it is. Feel free to top with whipped cream for added appeal.
—Carol Mead, Los Alamos, NM

Prep: 20 min. + chilling • **Makes:** 12 servings

- 1 tsp. unflavored gelatin
- 1 Tbsp. plus 1 cup cold water, divided
- 1 cup boiling water
- 1 pkg. (3 oz.) raspberry gelatin
- 3 cups (12 oz.) fresh or thawed frozen cranberries, divided
- 2 medium apples, cut into wedges
- 1 medium navel orange, peeled
- 1 cup sugar
- ½ cup chopped walnuts
- ½ cup finely chopped celery

1. Sprinkle unflavored gelatin over 1 Tbsp. cold water; let stand 1 minute. Add boiling water and raspberry gelatin; stir until gelatin is dissolved, about 2 minutes. Stir in the remaining cold water. Refrigerate until thickened, about 45 minutes.
2. Pulse 2⅓ cups cranberries, apples and orange in a food processor until chopped. Transfer to a small bowl; stir in sugar. Stir fruit mixture into thickened gelatin. Fold in the walnuts, celery and remaining whole cranberries.
3. Coat a 10-in. fluted tube pan, an 8-cup ring mold or two 4-cup molds with cooking spray; pour in gelatin mixture. Cover and refrigerate overnight or until firm. Unmold onto a platter.
½ cup: 154 cal., 3g fat (0 sat. fat), 0 chol., 21mg sod., 32g carb. (28g sugars, 2g fiber), 2g pro.

MOIST POULTRY DRESSING

Tasty mushrooms and onions complement the big herb flavor in this amazing stuffing. This dressing stays so moist because it's made in the slow cooker.
—Ruth Ann Stelfox, Raymond, AB

Prep: 20 min. • **Cook:** 4 hours
Makes: 16 servings

- 2 jars (4½ oz. each) sliced mushrooms, drained
- 4 celery ribs, chopped
- 2 medium onions, chopped
- ¼ cup minced fresh parsley
- ¾ cup butter, cubed
- 1½ lbs. day-old bread, crusts removed and cubed (about 13 cups)
- 1½ tsp. salt
- 1½ tsp. rubbed sage
- 1 tsp. poultry seasoning
- 1 tsp. dried thyme
- ½ tsp. pepper
- 2 large eggs
- 1 can (14½ oz.) chicken broth or 14½ oz. vegetable broth

1. In a large skillet, saute the mushrooms, celery, onions and parsley in butter until the vegetables are tender. In a large bowl, toss the bread cubes with salt, sage, poultry seasoning, thyme and pepper. Add the mushroom mixture. Combine eggs and broth; add to the bread mixture and toss.
2. Transfer to 5-qt. slow cooker. Cover and cook on low until a thermometer reads 160°, 4-5 hours.
¾ cup: 212 cal., 11g fat (6g sat. fat), 50mg chol., 694mg sod., 24g carb. (3g sugars, 2g fiber), 5g pro.

GRANDMA'S GELATIN FRUIT SALAD

Whenever I'm hosting a family dinner, my grandchildren ask me to make this fruit salad. Its popularity doesn't just run in my family—the salad is a hit at charity potluck gatherings, too!
—Wilma McLean, Medford, OR

- -

Prep: 25 min. + chilling
Makes: 15 servings

- 2   cups boiling water, divided
- 1   pkg. (3 oz.) lemon gelatin
- 2   cups ice cubes, divided
- 1   can (20 oz.) crushed pineapple, liquid drained and reserved
- 1   pkg. (3 oz.) orange gelatin
- 2   cups miniature marshmallows
- ½   cup sugar
- 2   Tbsp. cornstarch
- 1   cup reserved pineapple juice
- 1   large egg, lightly beaten
- 1   Tbsp. butter
- 3   large bananas, sliced
- 1   cup whipped topping
- ½   cup finely shredded cheddar cheese

1. In a large bowl, combine 1 cup boiling water and lemon gelatin. Add 1 cup ice cubes, stirring until melted. Stir in the pineapple. Pour into a 13x9-in. dish coated with cooking spray; refrigerate until set but not firm.

2. Repeat with the orange gelatin, remaining water and ice. Stir in marshmallows. Pour over lemon layer; refrigerate until firm.

3. Meanwhile, in a small saucepan, combine sugar and cornstarch. Stir in the reserved pineapple juice until smooth. Cook and stir over medium-high heat until thickened and bubbly. Reduce heat; cook and stir 2 minutes longer. Remove from the heat.

4. Stir a small amount of hot filling into egg; return all to the pan, stirring constantly. Bring to a gentle boil; cook and stir for 2 minutes longer. Remove from the heat; stir in butter. Cool to room temperature without stirring. Refrigerate for 1 hour or until chilled.

5. Arrange bananas over gelatin. Stir whipped topping into dressing. Spread over the bananas. Sprinkle with cheese.

1 piece: 194 cal., 3g fat (2g sat. fat), 20mg chol., 64mg sod., 40g carb. (35g sugars, 1g fiber), 3g pro.

CANDIED ACORN SQUASH RINGS

This 3-ingredient acorn squash recipe was passed down to me from my grandma, who always made it in autumn. Now I prepare it whenever I am feeling nostalgic.
—Rita Addicks, Weimar, TX

- -

Prep: 15 min. • **Bake:** 40 min.
Makes: 6 servings

- 2 **medium acorn squash**
- ⅔ **cup packed brown sugar**
- ½ **cup butter, softened**

1. Preheat oven to 350°; cut squash in half lengthwise; remove and discard seeds. Cut each half crosswise into ½-in. slices; discard ends. Arrange squash in a shallow baking pan; cover with foil. Bake until just tender, 25-30 minutes.
2. Combine sugar and butter; spread over squash. Bake, uncovered, 15-20 minutes longer, basting occasionally.
1 serving: 287 cal., 15g fat (9g sat. fat), 41mg chol., 168mg sod., 40g carb. (27g sugars, 2g fiber), 1g pro.

LEMON MUSHROOM ORZO

Sometimes I serve this side dish chilled; sometimes I serve it hot. I think it has a lovely appearance, and it really goes well with any entree.
—Shelly Nelson, Akeley, MN

Takes: 25 min. • **Makes:** 12 servings

    1   pkg. (16 oz.) orzo pasta
    3   Tbsp. olive oil, divided
    ¾   lb. sliced fresh mushrooms
    ¾   cup chopped pecans, toasted
    ½   cup minced fresh parsley
    1   tsp. grated lemon zest
    3   Tbsp. lemon juice
    1   tsp. salt
    ½   tsp. pepper

1. Cook orzo according to the package directions. Meanwhile, in a large skillet, heat 2 Tbsp. oil over medium-high heat. Add the mushrooms; cook and stir until tender and lightly browned. Drain orzo.
2. In a large bowl, place orzo, mushroom mixture, pecans, parsley, lemon zest, lemon juice, salt, pepper and remaining oil; gently toss to combine.
¾ cup: 225 cal., 9g fat (1g sat. fat), 0 chol., 202mg sod., 31g carb. (2g sugars, 2g fiber), 6g pro. **Diabetic exchanges:** 2 starch, 1½ fat.

SUPER SIMPLE SCALLOPED POTATOES

I've made all sorts of scalloped potatoes but I always come back to this rich, creamy, foolproof recipe. The dish gets scraped clean every time I make it.
—Kallee Krong-McCreery, Escondido, CA

Prep: 20 min. • **Bake:** 45 min. + standing
Makes: 10 servings

    3   cups heavy whipping cream
    1½   tsp. salt
    ½   tsp. pepper
    1   tsp. minced fresh thyme, optional
    3   lbs. russet potatoes, thinly
         sliced (about 10 cups)

1. Preheat oven to 350°. In a large bowl, combine cream, salt, pepper and, if desired, thyme. Arrange the potatoes in a greased 13x9-in. baking dish. Pour cream mixture over top.
2. Bake, uncovered, until the potatoes are tender and top is lightly browned, 45-55 minutes. Let stand 10 minutes before serving.
¾ cup: 353 cal., 27g fat (17g sat. fat), 99mg chol., 390mg sod., 26g carb. (3g sugars, 3g fiber), 4g pro.

GRANDMA'S COLLARD GREENS

My grandmother made the best collard greens in the world! Eating them with a slice of buttermilk cornbread is pure bliss.
—Sherri Williams, Crestview, FL

- -

Prep: 30 min. • **Cook:** 2 hours
Makes: 6 servings

- 3 Tbsp. lard or shortening, divided
- 1 large onion, chopped
- 6 garlic cloves, minced
- 1½ lbs. smoked ham hocks
- 6 cups water
- 2 tsp. seasoned salt
- 1 to 3 tsp. crushed red pepper flakes
- 1 large bunch collard greens (about 2 lbs.), coarsely chopped
- 1½ cups white wine
- ¼ tsp. sugar

1. In a 6-qt. stockpot, heat 1 Tbsp. lard over medium heat. Add onion and garlic; cook and stir until tender. Add ham hocks, water, seasoned salt and pepper flakes. Bring to a boil. Reduce heat; simmer, uncovered, 55-60 minutes or until meat is tender.
2. Add the collard greens, wine, sugar and remaining lard. Return to a boil. Reduce heat; simmer, uncovered, 55-60 minutes or until greens are very tender. Remove meat from bones; finely chop and return to pan. Discard bones. Serve with a slotted spoon.
1 cup: 204 cal., 9g fat (3g sat. fat), 19mg chol., 849mg sod., 13g carb. (3g sugars, 7g fiber), 110 pro.

ORANGE-GLAZED BEETS

Beets were a popular vegetable in our house when I was growing up, and this recipe is a real favorite of ours. It's very easy to make, and the orange gives it a delightful citrus flavor.
—Susan Punzal, Orchard Park, NY

- -

Takes: 25 min. • **Makes:** 8 servings

- ¾ cup orange marmalade
- 6 Tbsp. orange juice
- ⅓ cup butter, cubed
- ¼ tsp. salt
- ¼ tsp. pepper
- 3 cans (14½ oz. each) sliced beets, drained

In a large skillet, combine first 5 ingredients. Bring to a boil; cook and stir until mixture is thickened, 3-4 minutes. Add the beets; cook and stir until most of the liquid is absorbed, 6-8 minutes longer.
½ cup: 194 cal., 8g fat (5g sat. fat), 20mg chol., 443mg sod., 32g carb. (27g sugars, 3g fiber), 2g pro.

CREAMY CRANBERRY SALAD

One of my piano students taught me the perfect lesson—for salad. The keys are cranberries, pineapple, marshmallows and chopped walnuts.
—Alexandra Lypecky, Dearborn, MI

Prep: 15 min. + chilling • **Makes:** 16 servings

- 3 cups fresh or thawed frozen cranberries, chopped
- 1 can (20 oz.) unsweetened crushed pineapple, drained
- 2 cups miniature marshmallows
- 1 medium apple, chopped
- ⅔ cup sugar
- ⅛ tsp. salt
- 2 cups heavy whipping cream
- ¼ cup chopped walnuts

1. In a large bowl, mix the first 6 ingredients. Refrigerate, covered, overnight.
2. To serve, beat cream until stiff peaks form. Fold whipped cream and walnuts into cranberry mixture.

½ cup: 200 cal., 12g fat (7g sat. fat), 34mg chol., 32mg sod., 23g carb. (20g sugars, 1g fiber), 1g pro.

TEST KITCHEN TIP
Make it easy on yourself: Pulse the cranberries in a food processor to chop them.

LAYERED SALAD FOR A CROWD

This salad is a hit with my sons. I even took it to a luncheon honoring our school's food service manager, and she asked for the recipe! I like to make the dressing the day before so the flavors blend together.
—Linda Ashley, Leesburg, GA

Takes: 20 min. • **Makes:** 20 servings

- 1 cup mayonnaise
- ¼ cup whole milk
- 2 tsp. dill weed
- ½ tsp. seasoning blend
- 1 bunch romaine, torn
- 2 medium carrots, grated
- 1 cup chopped red onion
- 1 medium cucumber, sliced
- 1 pkg. (10 oz.) frozen peas, thawed
- 1½ cups shredded cheddar cheese
- 8 bacon strips, cooked and crumbled

1. For dressing, in a small bowl, whisk the mayonnaise, milk, dill and seasoning blend. In a 4-qt. clear glass serving bowl, layer the romaine, carrots, onion and cucumber (do not toss). Pour the dressing over the top; sprinkle with peas, cheese and bacon. Cover and refrigerate until serving.

Note: This recipe was tested with Nature's Seasons seasoning blend by Morton. Look for it in the spice aisle.

⅔ cup: 151 cal., 13g fat (4g sat. fat), 16mg chol., 216mg sod., 5g carb. (2g sugars, 1g fiber), 4g pro.

GRANDMOTHER'S CORN PUDDING

My grandmother always served this pudding for family reunions and other big gatherings. Corn pudding is an especially popular side dish on Maryland's Eastern Shore, but I'm sure it will be a big hit in your town as well!
—Susan Brown Langenstein, Salisbury, MD

Prep: 10 min. • **Bake:** 50 min.
Makes: 9 servings

- 4 large eggs
- 1 cup whole milk
- 1 can (15 oz.) cream-style corn
- ½ cup sugar
- 5 slices day-old bread, crusts removed
- 1 Tbsp. butter, softened

In a bowl, beat eggs and milk. Add corn and sugar; mix well. Cut bread into ½-in. cubes and place in a greased 9-in. square baking dish. Pour egg mixture over bread. Dot with butter. Bake, uncovered, at 350° until a knife inserted in the center comes out clean, 50-60 minutes.

1 serving: 175 cal., 5g fat (2g sat. fat), 102mg chol., 264mg sod., 28g carb. (14g sugars, 1g fiber), 6g pro.

GRANDMA'S POTATO SALAD

Our Fourth of July feast wouldn't be complete without this cool, old-fashioned potato salad. The red potatoes hold their shape and texture even after they are boiled. It's Grandma's treasured recipe.
—Sue Gronholz, Beaver Dam, WI

- -

Prep: 45 min. + cooling
Cook: 15 min. + chilling
Makes: 24 servings

6   **lbs. medium red potatoes**
    Water
DRESSING
1   **cup water**
½   **cup butter, cubed**
¼   **cup white vinegar**
2   **large eggs**
½   **cup sugar**
4½   **tsp. cornstarch**
¾   **cup heavy whipping cream**
¾   **cup Miracle Whip**
SALAD
1   **small onion, finely chopped**
2   **green onions, sliced**
1   **tsp. salt**
½   **tsp. pepper**
3   **hard-boiled large eggs, sliced**
    Paprika

1. Place potatoes in a stockpot and cover with water. Bring to a boil. Reduce heat; cover and cook for 15-20 minutes or until tender. Drain. When cool enough to handle, peel and slice potatoes; cool completely.
2. For the dressing, in the top of a double boiler or metal bowl over barely simmering water, heat water, butter and vinegar until butter is melted. In a small bowl, beat eggs; add sugar and cornstarch. Add to butter mixture; cook and stir for 5-7 minutes or until thickened. Transfer to a large bowl; cool completely.
3. In a small bowl, beat cream until stiff peaks form. Stir Miracle Whip into cooled dressing mixture; fold in whipped cream. Stir in onion, green onions, salt and pepper. Add potatoes; toss lightly to combine. Refrigerate, covered, until chilled.
4. To serve, top with hard-boiled eggs; sprinkle with paprika.
¾ cup: 197 cal., 10g fat (5g sat. fat), 58mg chol., 202mg sod., 24g carb. (6g sugars, 2g fiber), 4g pro.

CHOP, CHOP
Instead of slicing the hard-boiled eggs for this salad, use a grid-style cooling rack to "chop" them. It's faster (and less slippery) than using a knife. Set the rack on top of a bowl and "smoosh" the peeled egg through.

GRANDMA'S CORNBREAD DRESSING

Growing up, we didn't have turkey during holidays. We had chicken, chopped and baked in this, my grandmother's dressing. Now we leave out the chicken and keep the cornbread dressing!
—Suzanne Mohme, Bastrop, TX

- -

Prep: 40 min. + cooling • **Bake:** 45 min.
Makes: 12 servings

- 1 **cup all-purpose flour**
- 1 **cup cornmeal**
- 2 **tsp. baking powder**
- 1 **tsp. salt**
- 2 **large eggs**
- 1 **cup buttermilk**
- ¼ **cup canola oil**

DRESSING
- 1 **Tbsp. canola oil**
- 1 **medium onion, chopped**
- 2 **celery ribs, chopped**
- 3 **large eggs**
- 2 **cans (10¾ oz. each) condensed cream of chicken soup, undiluted**
- 3 **tsp. poultry seasoning**
- 1 **tsp. pepper**
- ½ **tsp. salt**
- 2 **cups chicken broth**

1. Preheat oven to 400°. In a large bowl, whisk flour, cornmeal, baking powder and salt. In another bowl, whisk eggs and buttermilk. Pour oil into an 8-in. ovenproof skillet; place skillet in oven 4 minutes.
2. Meanwhile, add buttermilk mixture to flour mixture; stir just until moistened.
3. Carefully tilt and rotate skillet to coat bottom with oil; add batter. Bake until a toothpick inserted in center comes out clean, 20-25 minutes. Cool completely in pan on a wire rack.
4. Reduce oven setting to 350°. For the dressing, in a large skillet, heat oil over medium-high heat. Add onion and celery; cook and stir 4-6 minutes or until tender. Remove from heat. Coarsely crumble cornbread into skillet; toss to combine. In a small bowl, whisk eggs, condensed soup and seasonings; stir into bread mixture. Stir in broth.
5. Transfer to a greased 13x9-in. baking dish. Bake 45-55 minutes or until dressing is lightly browned.

⅔ cup: 236 cal., 12g fat (2g sat. fat), 83mg chol., 969mg sod., 25g carb. (2g sugars, 2g fiber), 7g pro.

CREAMED PEAS

I can still taste these wonderful peas in Mama's delicious white sauce. Our food was pretty plain during the week, so I thought this white sauce made the peas "extra fancy" and fitting for a Sunday meal.
—Imogene Hutton, Brownwood, TX

- -

Takes: 15 min. • **Makes:** 4 servings

- 1   **pkg. (10 oz.) frozen peas**
- 1   **Tbsp. butter**
- 1   **Tbsp. all-purpose flour**
- ¼   **tsp. salt**
- ⅛   **tsp. pepper**
- ½   **cup whole milk**
- 1   **tsp. sugar**

Cook peas according to package directions. Meanwhile, in a small saucepan, melt the butter. Stir in the flour, salt and pepper until blended; gradually add milk and sugar. Bring to a boil; cook and stir for 1-2 minutes or until thickened. Drain peas; stir into the sauce and heat through.

½ cup: 110 cal., 4g fat (2g sat. fat), 12mg chol., 271mg sod., 14g carb. (6g sugars, 3g fiber), 5g pro.

CAULIFLOWER-BROCCOLI CHEESE BAKE

One of the first dishes my mom taught me is this tasty pairing of broccoli and cauliflower in a thick cheese sauce.
—Devin Mulertt, Cedarburg, WI

Prep: 15 min. • **Bake:** 50 min. + standing
Makes: 9 servings

- 2 Tbsp. butter
- 1 small onion, chopped
- 2 Tbsp. all-purpose flour
- ½ cup 2% milk
- 1 pkg. (8 oz.) process cheese (Velveeta), cubed
- ¼ tsp. salt
- 3 large eggs, lightly beaten
- 2 pkg. (12 oz. each) frozen broccoli-cauliflower blend, thawed

1. Preheat oven to 325°. In a Dutch oven, heat butter over medium-high heat. Add onion; cook and stir for 2-3 minutes or until tender. Stir in flour until blended; gradually whisk in the milk. Bring to a boil, stirring constantly; cook and stir until thickened, 1-2 minutes. Stir in cheese and salt until cheese is melted.
2. Remove from heat. Gradually whisk in eggs. Stir in vegetable blend. Transfer to a greased 8-in. square baking dish. Bake, uncovered, until set, 50-60 minutes. Let stand 10 minutes before serving.
1 piece: 170 cal., 11g fat (6g sat. fat), 95mg chol., 461mg sod., 8g carb. (2g sugars, 1g fiber), 8g pro.

> ### TEST KITCHEN TIP
> Try this casserole as a side dish with dinner, or pop it on your brunch buffet. Feel free to use all broccoli or cauliflower if you're not a fan of one of them.

HONEY GARLIC GREEN BEANS

Green beans are great, but they can seem ordinary on their own. Here, a couple of extra ingredients give them sweet-salty flair that's tough to beat.
—Shannon Dobos, Calgary, AB

Takes: 20 min. • **Makes:** 8 servings

- 4 Tbsp. honey
- 2 Tbsp. reduced-sodium soy sauce
- 4 garlic cloves, minced
- ¼ tsp. salt
- ¼ tsp. crushed red pepper flakes
- 2 lbs. fresh green beans, trimmed

1. Whisk together first 5 ingredients; set aside. In a 6-qt. stockpot, bring 10 cups water to a boil. Add beans in batches; cook, uncovered, just until crisp-tender, 2-3 minutes. Remove beans and immediately drop into ice water. Drain and pat dry.
2. Coat stockpot with cooking spray. Add beans; cook, stirring constantly, over high heat until slightly blistered, 2-3 minutes. Add sauce; continue stirring until beans are coated and sauce starts to evaporate slightly, 2-3 minutes. Remove from heat.
¾ cup: 72 cal., 0 fat (0 sat. fat), 0 chol., 225mg sod., 18g carb. (12g sugars, 4g fiber), 2g pro. **Diabetic exchanges:** 1 vegetable, ½ starch.

GRANDMA'S STUFFED YELLOW SQUASH

My grandma, who raised me, was an awesome cook. This is a recipe she fixed in summer when our garden overflowed with yellow squash. My family still enjoys it.
—Janie McGraw, Sallisaw, OK

- -

Prep: 25 min. • **Bake:** 25 min.
Makes: 2 servings

- 1 medium yellow summer squash
- ¼ cup egg substitute
- 2 Tbsp. finely chopped onion
- ¼ tsp. salt
- ⅛ tsp. pepper
- 2 slices bread, toasted and diced

1. Place squash in a large saucepan; cover with water. Bring to a boil; cover and cook for 7-9 minutes or until crisp-tender. Drain.
2. When cool enough to handle, cut squash in half lengthwise; scoop out and reserve pulp, leaving a ⅜-in. shell. Invert shells on paper towel.
3. In a small bowl, combine the egg substitute, onion, salt and pepper. Stir in toasted bread cubes and squash pulp. Spoon into squash shells.
4. Place in an 8-in. square baking dish coated with cooking spray. Cover and bake at 375° for 20 minutes. Uncover; bake until lightly browned, 5-10 minutes longer.
½ each: 103 cal., 1g fat (0 sat. fat), 0 chol., 490mg sod., 18g carb. (4g sugars, 3g fiber), 6g pro. **Diabetic exchanges:** 1 starch, 1 vegetable.

CLASSIC COBB SALAD

Making this salad is a lot like putting in a garden. I plant everything in nice, neat sections, just as I do with seedlings.
—Patricia Kile, Elizabethtown, PA

- -

Takes: 20 min. • **Makes:** 4 servings

- 6 cups torn iceberg lettuce
- 2 medium tomatoes, chopped
- 1 medium ripe avocado, peeled and chopped
- ¾ cup diced fully cooked ham
- 2 hard-boiled large eggs, chopped
- ¾ cup diced cooked turkey
- 1¼ cups sliced fresh mushrooms
- ½ cup crumbled blue cheese
  Salad dressing of choice
  Optional: Sliced ripe olives and lemon wedges

Place lettuce on a platter or in a large serving bowl. Arrange the remaining ingredients in rows or sections as desired. Serve with salad dressing of choice; if desired, serve with sliced ripe olives and lemon wedges.
1 serving: 260 cal., 15g fat (5g sat. fat), 148mg chol., 586mg sod., 10g carb. (5g sugars, 4g fiber), 23g pro. **Diabetic exchanges:** 3 lean meat, 2 vegetable, 2 fat.

PERFECT WINTER SALAD

This is my most-requested salad recipe. It is delicious as a side salad, or add grilled chicken breast for an easy main dish. I think it's so good, I sometimes eat it at the end of the meal, instead of dessert!
—DeNae Shewmake, Burnsville, MN

Takes: 20 min.
Makes: 12 servings

- ¼ cup reduced-fat mayonnaise
- ¼ cup maple syrup
- 3 Tbsp. white wine vinegar
- 2 Tbsp. minced shallot
- 2 tsp. sugar
- ½ cup canola oil
- 2 pkg. (5 oz. each) spring mix salad greens
- 2 medium tart apples, thinly sliced
- 1 cup dried cherries
- 1 cup pecan halves
- ¼ cup thinly sliced red onion

1. In a small bowl, mix first 5 ingredients; gradually whisk in canola oil until blended. Refrigerate, covered, until serving.
2. To serve, place remaining ingredients in a large bowl; toss with dressing.

1 cup: 235 cal., 18g fat (1g sat. fat), 2mg chol., 47mg sod., 20g carb. (15g sugars, 2g fiber), 2g pro.

BRANDY-GLAZED CARROTS

Once these carrots are glazed, they are not just delicious, but they look pretty, too. I found this recipe about 10 years ago in an old cookbook that I brought from a thrift store. I changed the sugar to honey.
—Tammy Landry, Saucier, MS

Takes: 30 min.
Makes: 12 servings

- 3 lbs. fresh baby carrots
- ½ cup butter, cubed
- ½ cup honey
- ¼ cup brandy
- ¼ cup minced fresh parsley
- ½ tsp. salt
- ¼ tsp. pepper

In a large skillet, bring ½ in. of water to a boil. Add carrots. Cover and cook until crisp-tender, 5-9 minutes. Drain and set aside. In the same skillet, cook butter and honey over medium heat until butter is melted. Remove from heat; stir in brandy. Bring to a boil; cook until liquid is reduced to about ½ cup. Add the carrots, parsley, salt and pepper; heat through.

¾ cup: 153 cal., 8g fat (5g sat. fat), 20mg chol., 242mg sod., 21g carb. (17g sugars, 2g fiber), 1g pro.

GRANDMA'S CRANBERRY STUFF

What could taste better than turkey and cranberry on Thanksgiving Day? My grandmother's classic recipe makes the best "cranberry stuff" to share with your family and friends.
—Catherine Cassidy, Milwaukee, WI

Start to Finish: 10 min. • **Makes:** 3 cups

1   medium navel orange
1   pkg. (12 oz.) fresh or frozen cranberries, thawed
1   cup sugar
1   cup chopped walnuts, toasted

Cut the unpeeled orange into wedges, removing any seeds, and place in a food processor. Add cranberries and sugar; pulse until chopped. Add the walnuts; pulse just until combined.

Note: To toast nuts, bake in a shallow pan in a 350° oven for 5-10 minutes or cook in a skillet over low heat until lightly browned, stirring occasionally.

¼ cup: 148 cal., 6g fat (1g sat. fat), 0 chol., 1mg sod., 23g carb. (19g sugars, 2g fiber), 2g pro.

LAST-MINUTE RICE

My family has enjoyed this delicious rice dish for many years. With chopped red and green peppers, it's both fresh-tasting and festive-looking. It's the perfect light side dish for a big meal.
—Chere Bell, Colorado Springs, CO

- -

Takes: 20 min. • **Makes:** 6 servings

½   cup finely chopped onion
3   celery ribs, finely chopped
½   medium sweet red
    pepper, chopped
½   medium green pepper, chopped
1   Tbsp. butter
2   cups chicken broth
2   cups uncooked instant rice
¼   tsp. pepper
½   tsp. salt, optional

1. In a skillet, saute the onion, celery and peppers in butter over medium heat for 2 minutes or until crisp-tender. Remove from the heat; set aside.

2. In a saucepan, bring broth to a full boil. Remove from the heat. Quickly stir in rice, celery mixture, pepper, and, if desired, salt. Cover and let stand for 6-7 minutes. Stir before serving.

½ cup: 156 cal., 2g fat (1g sat. fat), 7mg chol., 362mg sod., 29g carb. (2g sugars, 2g fiber), 3g pro. **Diabetic exchanges:** 1½ starch, 1 vegetable, ½ fat.

TEST KITCHEN TIP

Freezing peppers and onions is a great way to enjoy garden produce when summer days are long gone. A medium green pepper, chopped, will yield about 1 cup. A large green pepper, chopped, will yield about 1⅓ to 1½ cups. A medium onion, chopped, will equal about ½ cup; a large onion will yield about 1 cup. Store both green peppers and onions in heavy-duty resealable plastic bags. Green peppers can be frozen for up to 6 months, and onions can be frozen for up to 1 year.

CREAMY MAKE-AHEAD MASHED POTATOES

Creamy make-ahead mashed potatoes get even better when topped with a savory trio of cheese, onions and bacon.
—JoAnn Koerkenmeier, Damiansville, IL

Prep: 35 min. + chilling • **Bake:** 40 min.
Makes: 10 servings

- 3 lbs. potatoes (about 9 medium), peeled and cubed
- 6 bacon strips, chopped
- 8 oz. cream cheese, softened
- ½ cup sour cream
- ½ cup butter, cubed
- ¼ cup 2% milk
- 1½ tsp. onion powder
- 1 tsp. salt
- 1 tsp. garlic powder
- ½ tsp. pepper
- 1 cup shredded cheddar cheese
- 3 green onions, chopped

1. Place potatoes in a Dutch oven; add water to cover. Bring to a boil. Reduce heat; cook, uncovered, 10-15 minutes or until potatoes are tender.
2. Meanwhile, in a skillet, cook bacon over medium heat until crisp. Remove to paper towels with a slotted spoon; drain.
3. Drain potatoes; return to pan. Mash the potatoes, gradually adding cream cheese, sour cream and butter. Stir in the milk and seasonings. Transfer to a greased 13x9-in. baking dish; sprinkle with cheese, green onions and bacon. Refrigerate, covered, up to 1 day.
4. Preheat oven to 350°. Remove potatoes from refrigerator and let stand while oven heats. Bake, covered, about 30 minutes. Uncover; bake 10 minutes longer or until heated through.

¾ cup: 419 cal., 24g fat (15g sat. fat), 74mg chol., 544mg sod., 41g carb. (4g sugars, 4g fiber), 11g pro.

TEST KITCHEN TIP
For this recipe, we recommend using fluffy russets, creamy Yukon Golds or a mix of both.

RED, WHITE & BLUE SALAD

Our striking flag salad drew plenty of attention at our Independence Day party. I use gelatin to help create the layers of shimmering stripes.
—Laurie Neverman, Denmark, WI

- -

Prep: 30 min. + chilling • **Makes:** 16 servings

- 1   **pkg. (3 oz.) berry blue gelatin**
- 2   **cups boiling water, divided**
- 2½ **cups cold water, divided**
- 1   **cup fresh blueberries**
- 1   **envelope unflavored gelatin**
- 1   **cup heavy whipping cream**
- 6   **Tbsp. sugar**
- 2   **cups sour cream**
- 1   **tsp. vanilla extract**
- 1   **pkg. (3 oz.) raspberry gelatin**
- 1   **cup fresh raspberries**
       Optional: Whipped topping and additional berries

1. Dissolve the berry blue gelatin in 1 cup boiling water; stir in 1 cup cold water. Add blueberries. Pour into a 3-qt. serving bowl. Refrigerate until firm, about 1 hour.
2. In a saucepan, sprinkle the unflavored gelatin over ½ cup cold water; let stand for 1 minute. Add cream and sugar; cook and stir over low heat until dissolved. Cool to room temperature. Whisk in sour cream and vanilla. Spoon over the blue layer. Refrigerate until firm.
3. Dissolve raspberry gelatin in remaining hot water; stir in remaining cold water. Add raspberries. Spoon over cream layer. Chill until set. Top with whipped topping and berries if desired.
1 serving: 179 cal., 11g fat (7g sat. fat), 40mg chol., 46mg sod., 18g carb. (16g sugars, 1g fiber), 3g pro.

SUMMER'S BEST BAKED BEANS

We always choose this family recipe for any picnic because it's a meaty twist on regular baked beans, and it has a nice sweetness that you don't expect.
—Wendy Hodorowski, Bellaire, OH

- -

Prep: 10 min. • **Bake:** 55 min.
Makes: 8 servings

- ½ lb. ground beef
- 1 large onion, finely chopped
- ½ cup sugar
- ½ cup packed brown sugar
- ½ cup ketchup
- ½ cup barbecue sauce
- 2 Tbsp. yellow mustard
- 2 Tbsp. molasses
- ½ tsp. chili powder
- 2 cans (13.7 oz. each) beans with tomato sauce
- ½ lb. bacon strips, cooked and crumbled

1. Preheat oven to 350°. In a large skillet, cook beef and onion over medium heat 6-8 minutes or until beef is no longer pink, breaking up beef into crumbles; drain. Stir in the sugars, ketchup, barbecue sauce, mustard, molasses and chili powder. Add beans and bacon.
2. Transfer to a greased 13x9-in. baking dish. Bake, covered, 45 minutes. Bake, uncovered, 10-15 minutes longer or until heated through.
¾ cup: 323 cal., 8g fat (3g sat. fat), 28mg chol., 970mg sod., 51g carb. (41g sugars, 4g fiber), 14g pro.

CHEESY CHEDDAR BROCCOLI CASSEROLE

People who don't even like broccoli beg me to make this comforting side dish. It is similar to a classic green bean casserole, but the melted cheese puts it over the top.
—Elaine Hubbard, Pocono Lake, PA

- -

Prep: 15 min. • **Bake:** 35 min.
Makes: 8 servings

- 1 can (10¾ oz.) condensed cream of mushroom soup, undiluted
- 1 cup sour cream
- 1½ cups shredded sharp cheddar cheese, divided
- 1 can (6 oz.) french-fried onions, divided
- 2 pkg. (16 oz. each) frozen broccoli florets, thawed

1. Preheat oven to 325°. In a large saucepan, combine soup, sour cream, 1 cup cheese and 1¼ cups onions; heat through over medium heat for 4-5 minutes, stirring until blended. Stir in the broccoli. Transfer to a greased 2-qt. baking dish.
2. Bake, uncovered, 25-30 minutes or until bubbly. Sprinkle with the remaining cheese and onions. Bake until cheese is melted, 10-15 minutes.
¾ cup: 359 cal., 26g fat (11g sat. fat), 30mg chol., 641mg sod., 19g carb. (4g sugars, 3g fiber), 8g pro.

POTLUCK GERMAN POTATO SALAD

This is a big hit at church potlucks. One man says he only comes so he can eat this warm potato salad.
—Kathleen Rabe, Kiel, WI

Prep: 20 min. • **Cook:** 25 min.
Makes: 12 servings

- 3 lbs. small Yukon Gold potatoes, unpeeled (about 10)
- 2 celery ribs, chopped
- 1 small onion, chopped
- 1 cup water
- ½ cup white vinegar
- ¾ cup sugar
- 1 Tbsp. cornstarch
- ¼ tsp. salt
- ¼ tsp. pepper
- ½ lb. bacon strips, cooked and crumbled

1. Place potatoes in a large saucepan; add water to cover. Bring to a boil. Reduce heat; simmer, uncovered, 12-15 minutes or just until tender. Add celery and onion; continue cooking until vegetables are tender, about 5 minutes longer. Drain; set aside.
2. Meanwhile, in a small saucepan, whisk together next 6 ingredients. Bring to a boil; cook until thickened, about 2 minutes.
3. When cool enough to handle, slice potatoes; return to large saucepan with celery and onions. Add vinegar mixture, tossing to combine. Add bacon. Simmer mixture for 10-12 minutes or until heated through. Serve warm.
⅔ cup: 194 cal., 3g fat (1g sat. fat), 7mg chol., 181mg sod., 39g carb. (15g sugars, 2g fiber), 5g pro.

GARLIC ROASTED BRUSSELS SPROUTS

My roommate and I used to make garlicky Brussels sprouts at least twice a week. Now I make them as a healthy side for all sorts of occasions. What a great way to eat right!
—Katherine Moore-Colasurd, Cincinnati, OH

Prep/Total: 30 min.
Makes: 12 servings

- 2 lbs. fresh Brussels sprouts, trimmed and halved
- 2 medium red onions, cut into 1-in. pieces
- 3 Tbsp. olive oil
- 7 garlic cloves, finely chopped
- 1 tsp. salt
- ½ tsp. pepper

1. Preheat oven to 425°. Divide Brussels sprouts and onions between 2 foil-lined 15x10x1-in. baking pans.
2. In a small bowl, mix oil, garlic, salt and pepper; drizzle half of the mixture over each pan and toss to coat. Roast 20-25 minutes or until tender, stirring occasionally and switching position of pans halfway.
½ cup: 69 cal., 4g fat (1g sat. fat), 0 chol., 215mg sod., 8g carb. (2g sugars, 3g fiber), 3g pro. **Diabetic exchanges:** 1 vegetable, ½ fat.

ORANGE-GLAZED CARROTS, ONIONS & RADISHES

Carrots and radishes give color and crunch to this sweet, spicy side. We never have leftovers. If you make it ahead, reheat it and add the walnuts just before serving.
—Thomas Faglon, Somerset, NJ

- -

Prep: 15 min. • **Cook:** 20 min.
Makes: 8 servings

  1 lb. fresh pearl onions
  ¼ cup butter, cubed
  2 lbs. medium carrots, thinly sliced
  12 radishes, thinly sliced
  ½ cup dark brown sugar
  4 tsp. grated orange zest
  ½ cup orange juice
  1 cup chopped walnuts, toasted

1. In a large saucepan, bring 4 cups water to a boil. Add pearl onions; boil 3 minutes. Drain and rinse with cold water. Peel.
2. In a large skillet, heat butter over medium heat. Add carrots, pearl onions, radishes, brown sugar, orange zest and juice; cook, covered, until the vegetables are tender, stirring occasionally, 10-15 minutes. Cook, uncovered, 5-7 minutes longer or until slightly thickened. Sprinkle with walnuts.
Note: To toast nuts, bake in a shallow pan in a 350° oven for 5-10 minutes or cook in a skillet over low heat until lightly browned, stirring occasionally.
¾ cup: 277 cal., 16g fat (5g sat. fat), 15mg chol., 141mg sod., 34g carb. (23g sugars, 5g fiber), 4g pro.

CREAMY PINEAPPLE FLUFF SALAD

Guests of all ages will gravitate to this traditional fluff salad, loaded with cherry bits, pineapple and marshmallows.
—Janice Hensley, Owingsville, KY

- -

Takes: 25 min. • **Makes:** 16 servings

  1 pkg. (8 oz.) cream cheese, softened
  1 can (14 oz.) sweetened condensed milk
  ¼ cup lemon juice
  2 cans (20 oz.) pineapple tidbits, drained
  1½ cups multicolored miniature marshmallows, divided
  1 carton (8 oz.) frozen whipped topping, thawed
  ½ cup chopped nuts
  ⅓ cup maraschino cherries, chopped

In a large bowl, beat the cream cheese, milk and lemon juice until smooth. Add the pineapple and 1 cup marshmallows; fold in whipped topping. Sprinkle with the nuts, cherries and remaining marshmallows. Refrigerate leftovers.
½ cup: 161 cal., 10g fat (6g sat. fat), 16mg chol., 50mg sod., 17g carb. (12g sugars, 1g fiber), 2g pro.

GRANDMA'S POULTRY DRESSING

Every family seems to have its own favorite dressing recipe that becomes the standard, and this is ours. It came from Grandma, who passed it down to my mother. Now our children have carried it on in their very own kitchens.
—Norma Howland, Joliet, IL

- -

Prep: 20 min. • **Bake:** 40 min.
Makes: 6 cups

1   lb. bulk pork sausage
1   cup whole milk
7   cups coarse dry bread crumbs
1   cup diced celery
2   large eggs
2   to 3 Tbsp. minced fresh parsley
2   Tbsp. diced onion
½   tsp. salt or salt to taste

1. Preheat oven to 350°. In a large skillet, brown sausage. Drain sausage, discarding drippings. Meanwhile, in a small saucepan, heat milk over medium heat until bubbles form around sides of pan. In a large bowl, combine the sausage, heated milk and remaining ingredients.
2. Transfer to a greased 2-qt. baking dish. Cover and bake until lightly browned, about 40 minutes.
½ cup: 352 cal., 12g fat (4g sat. fat), 52mg chol., 826mg sod., 48g carb. (3g sugars, 2g fiber), 12g pro.

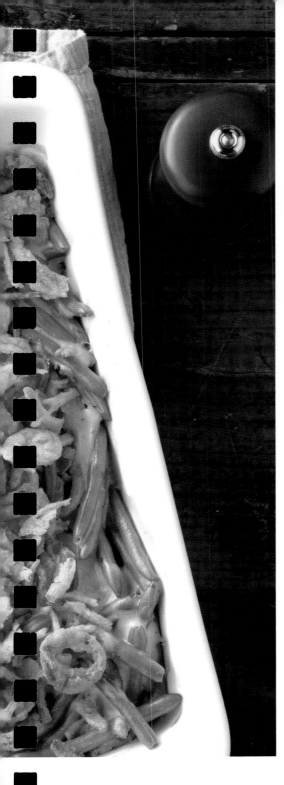

GREEN BEAN CASSEROLE

This green bean casserole has always been one of my favorite dishes—it's so easy to put together! You can make it before any guests arrive and keep it refrigerated it until baking time.
—Anna Baker, Blaine, WA

Prep: 15 min. • **Bake:** 35 min.
Makes: 10 servings

- 2 cans (10¾ oz. each) condensed cream of mushroom soup, undiluted
- 1 cup whole milk
- 2 tsp. soy sauce
- ⅛ tsp. pepper
- 2 pkg. (16 oz. each) frozen green beans, cooked and drained
- 1 can (6 oz.) french-fried onions, divided

1. In a bowl, combine soup, milk, soy sauce and pepper. Gently stir in the green beans. Spoon half of the mixture into a 13x9-in. baking dish. Sprinkle with half of the onions. Spoon the remaining bean mixture over the top. Sprinkle with remaining onions.
2. Bake at 350° until heated through and onions are brown and crispy, 30-35 minutes.

1 cup: 163 cal., 11g fat (3g sat. fat), 5mg chol., 485mg sod., 14g carb. (2g sugars, 1g fiber), 2g pro

TEST KITCHEN TIP

For a little flavor twist, experiment with different types of cream soups—cream of mushroom with roasted garlic or cream of celery are just a few examples.

GRANDMA'S EGG NOODLES

You just can't beat the down-home goodness of from-scratch noodles.
—Mary Stout, Topeka, IN

- -

Prep: 45 min. • **Cook:** 5 min.
Makes: 5 servings

2	cups all-purpose flour
½	tsp. salt
2	large egg yolks
1	large egg
⅓	cup water
1	Tbsp. olive oil
6	cups chicken broth

1. In a small bowl, combine the flour and salt. Make a well in the center. In another bowl, beat the egg yolks, egg, water and oil; pour into well. Stir to form a stiff dough.
2. Turn dough onto a well-floured surface; knead 8-10 times. Divide into thirds. Roll each portion to ⅛-in. thickness. Cut noodles into ¼-in. strips; cut the strips into 2-in. lengths. Cook immediately in boiling broth for 5-7 minutes or until tender; drain.
¾ cup: 245 cal., 6g fat (1g sat. fat), 128mg chol., 287mg sod., 38g carb. (1g sugars, 1g fiber), 8g pro.

"These were very tasty, and they reminded me of Grandma's noodles. Surprisingly easy and straightforward—and well worth the trouble."
—CRASHDOGSMOM, TASTEOFHOME.COM

HONEY-LEMON ASPARAGUS

Everyone who tastes my glazed asparagus takes more, so I double the recipe. For another option, try root veggies like turnips or parsnips in this honeyed side.
—Lorraine Caland, Shuniah, ON

- -

Takes: 15 min. • **Makes:** 8 servings

2	lbs. fresh asparagus, trimmed
¼	cup honey
2	Tbsp. butter
2	Tbsp. lemon juice
1	tsp. sea salt
1	tsp. balsamic vinegar
1	tsp. Worcestershire sauce

1. In a large saucepan, bring 8 cups water to a boil. Add asparagus in batches; cook, uncovered, for 1-2 minutes or just until crisp-tender. Drain and pat dry.
2. Meanwhile, in a small saucepan, combine the remaining ingredients. Bring to a boil. Reduce heat; simmer, uncovered, 2 minutes or until slightly thickened.
3. Transfer the asparagus to a large bowl; drizzle with glaze and toss gently to coat. If desired, sprinkle with additional sea salt.
1 serving: 73 cal., 3g fat (2g sat. fat), 8mg chol., 276mg sod., 12g carb. (10g sugars, 1g fiber), 2g pro. **Diabetic exchanges:** 1 vegetable, ½ starch, ½ fat.

OLD-FASHIONED SCALLOPED PINEAPPLE

My deliciously different dressing goes well with ham. It's also good for dessert with a little cream poured over the top.
—Nancy Brown, Dahinda, IL

- -

Prep: 10 min. • **Bake:** 30 min. + standing
Makes: 6 servings

- 3 large eggs, beaten
- 2 cups sugar
- 1 can (8 oz.) crushed pineapple, undrained
- ½ cup butter, melted
- ¼ cup whole milk
- 4 cups cubed bread

Preheat oven to 350°. Combine eggs, sugar, pineapple, butter and milk; add bread cubes and toss to coat. Transfer to a greased 8-in. square baking dish. Bake, uncovered, until a thermometer reads 160°, 30-35 minutes. Let stand 10 minutes before serving. Refrigerate leftovers.

⅔ cup: 529 cal., 19g fat (11g sat. fat), 135mg chol., 277mg sod., 87g carb. (75g sugars, 1g fiber), 6g pro.

SPINACH SOUFFLE

You just cannot prepare an easier, more delicious side dish than this. It's great with beef, pork and lamb, and I especially like serving it during special meals.
—Bette Duffy, Kenmore, WA

- -

Prep: 20 min. • **Bake:** 35 min.
Makes: 6 servings

- 2 pkg. (10 oz. each) frozen chopped spinach, thawed and squeezed dry
- 1 pkg. (8 oz.) cream cheese, cubed
- 1½ cups shredded Monterey Jack cheese
- 4 large eggs, lightly beaten
- ¼ cup butter, melted
- 1 garlic clove, minced
- ½ tsp. salt

In a large bowl, combine all ingredients. Transfer to a greased 1½-qt. baking dish. Bake at 350° until edges are lightly browned, 35-40 minutes.

½ cup: 375 cal., 33g fat (20g sat. fat), 228mg chol., 630mg sod., 5g carb. (0 sugars, 3g fiber), 17g pro.

MAIN COURSES

Pull up a chair and get ready for a mouthwatering meal that stars one of Grandma's longtime favorites. Featuring the savory goodness you've come to expect, these entrees offer today's cooks the convenience they need with the flavors they love.

BEEF TENDERLOIN WITH SAUTEED VEGETABLES

This is the most elegant, tender beef. It's made the classic French way—so easy!
—Cleo Gonske, Redding, CA

Prep: 20 min. • **Bake:** 50 min. + standing
Makes: 12 servings

- 1 beef tenderloin (5 lbs.), trimmed
- 2 tsp. salt
- ½ tsp. pepper

VEGETABLES
- ¼ cup butter, cubed
- 8 medium carrots, julienned
- 6 celery ribs, julienned
- ¼ tsp. salt
- ¼ tsp. pepper
- 3 cans (14 oz. each) water-packed artichoke hearts, drained and quartered

HOLLANDAISE SAUCE
- 3 large egg yolks
- 3 Tbsp. heavy whipping cream
- 2 tsp. Dijon mustard
- ¼ tsp. cayenne pepper
- 1 cup butter, melted
- 1 Tbsp. lemon juice

1. Preheat oven to 425°. Tuck thin tail end of tenderloin under; tie the beef at 2-in. intervals with kitchen string. Sprinkle with salt and pepper.

2. Place tenderloin on a rack in a shallow roasting pan. Roast 50-60 minutes or until the meat reaches desired doneness (for medium-rare, a thermometer should read 135°; medium, 140°; medium-well, 145°). Remove tenderloin from oven; tent with foil. Let stand 15 minutes before slicing.

3. In a large skillet, heat the butter over medium-high heat. Add carrots; cook and stir 5 minutes. Add celery, salt and pepper; cook and stir 5-7 minutes longer or until vegetables are crisp-tender. Stir in the artichoke hearts.

4. In top of a double boiler or a metal bowl over simmering water, whisk the egg yolks, cream, mustard and cayenne until blended; cook until mixture is just thick enough to coat a metal spoon and the temperature reaches 160°, whisking constantly. Remove from heat. Very slowly drizzle in warm melted butter, whisking constantly. Whisk in lemon juice.

5. Transfer sauce to a small bowl if necessary. Place the bowl in a larger bowl of warm water. Keep warm, stirring occasionally, until ready to serve, up to 30 minutes. Serve with beef and vegetables.

5 oz. cooked beef with ½ cup vegetables and about 1 Tbsp. sauce: 526 cal., 33g fat (18g sat. fat), 184mg chol., 910mg sod., 11g carb. (2g sugars, 2g fiber), 44g pro.

PIZZA MACARONI & CHEESE

My grandma made this for us once during a visit, and I never forgot just how good it was. Since my children love anything with pepperoni and cheese, I bake it so they can enjoy it as much as I did.
—Juli Meyers, Hinesville, GA

Prep: 30 min. • **Bake:** 25 min.
Makes: 12 servings

2 pkg. (14 oz. each) deluxe macaroni and cheese dinner mix
½ cup sour cream
1 can (14½ oz.) petite diced tomatoes, drained
1 can (15 oz.) pizza sauce
1 small green pepper, chopped
1 small sweet red pepper, chopped
2 cups shredded Italian cheese blend
2 oz. sliced pepperoni

1. Preheat oven to 350°. Cook macaroni according to the package directions for al dente. Drain; return to pan. Stir in the contents of cheese packets and sour cream. Transfer to a greased 13x9-in. baking dish.
2. In a small bowl, combine tomatoes and pizza sauce; drop by spoonfuls over the macaroni. Top with peppers, cheese and pepperoni. Bake, uncovered, until bubbly, 25-30 minutes.
1 cup: 340 cal., 14g fat (7g sat. fat), 37mg chol., 927mg sod., 37g carb. (5g sugars, 3g fiber), 14g pro.

GRANDMA'S RICE DISH

My grandmother often made this casserole when I was young. I forgot about it until I found myself adding the same ingredients to leftover rice one day. The memories came flooding back.
—Lorna Moore, Glendora, CA

Prep: 20 min. • **Bake:** 15 min.
Makes: 4 servings

- 1 lb. ground beef
- ⅓ cup chopped onion
- ½ cup chopped green pepper
- 2 cups cooked long grain rice
- 1 can (14½ oz.) diced tomatoes, undrained
- 1 can (11 oz.) whole kernel corn, drained
- 1 can (2¼ oz.) sliced ripe olives, drained
- 6 bacon strips, cooked and crumbled
- 2 tsp. chili powder
- 1 tsp. garlic powder
- ½ tsp. salt
- 1½ cups shredded cheddar cheese, divided
- ½ cup dry bread crumbs
- 1 Tbsp. butter, melted

1. Preheat oven to 350°. In a large skillet, cook the beef, onion and green pepper over medium heat until the meat is no longer pink; drain.

2. Stir in rice, tomatoes, corn, olives, bacon and seasonings; heat through. Stir in 1 cup cheese until melted.

3. Transfer to a greased 11x7-in. baking dish. Sprinkle with remaining cheese. Toss bread crumbs with butter; sprinkle over top.

4. Bake, uncovered, 15-20 minutes or until cheese is melted.

1½ cups: 719 cal., 37g fat (18g sat. fat), 136mg chol., 1397mg sod., 52g carb. (9g sugars, 5g fiber), 41g pro.

OLD-COUNTRY SAUERBRATEN

This recipe has been a well-guarded secret in my family for generations but I decided to share it because it is so yummy! It is sure to be a hit in your family as well.
—Inge Perreault, Oxford, NJ

- -

Prep: 20 min. + marinating • **Cook:** 1½ hours
Makes: 10 servings

    2   bay leaves
    4   whole cloves
    4   cups water
    4   cups white vinegar
    4   medium onions, sliced
    4   garlic cloves, minced
    2   tsp. salt
    1   tsp. pepper
    1   beef sirloin tip roast (3 to 4 lbs.)
    3   Tbsp. butter
    ¼   cup sugar
    2   Tbsp. molasses
    1   to 2 Tbsp. cornstarch
    2   Tbsp. cold water
    5   to 6 gingersnap cookies, crushed
        Hot cooked spaetzle

1. Place bay leaves and cloves on a double thickness of cheesecloth; bring up corners of cloth and tie with kitchen string to form a bag. In a large saucepan, combine the water, vinegar, onions, garlic, salt and pepper. Add spice bag. Bring to a boil. Remove from the heat; cool completely.

2. Place the roast in a 2-gallon resealable plastic bag. Add half of the marinade. Seal the bag and turn to coat; refrigerate for 3 days, turning once each day. Cover and refrigerate remaining marinade.

3. Remove meat from marinade; discard marinade, onions and spice bag. In a Dutch oven, brown the roast in butter on all sides. Sprinkle with sugar. Add reserved marinade. Bring to a boil. Stir in molasses. Reduce heat; cover and simmer for 1¼-1½ hours or until meat is tender.

4. Remove roast to a cutting board. Cut into thin slices; set aside. Skim fat from cooking juices. In a small bowl, combine cornstarch and cold water until smooth; gradually stir into juices. Add the gingersnaps. Bring to a boil; cook and stir for 2 minutes or until thickened. Return meat to gravy; heat through. Serve with spaetzle.

1 cup: 290 cal., 10g fat (4g sat. fat), 96mg chol., 656mg sod., 21g carb. (12g sugars, 2g fiber), 28g. pro.

ROAST PORK WITH APPLES & ONIONS

Here, the sweetness of apples and onions really complements the flavor of roast pork. This quickly became a melt-in-your-mouth favorite with my family.
—Lily Julow, Lawrenceville, GA

Prep: 30 min. • **Bake:** 45 min. + standing
Makes: 8 servings

- 1 boneless pork loin roast (2 lbs.)
- ¼ tsp. salt
- ¼ tsp. pepper
- 1 Tbsp. olive oil
- 3 large Golden Delicious apples, cut into 1-in. wedges
- 2 large onions, cut into ¾-in. wedges
- 5 garlic cloves, peeled
- 1 Tbsp. minced fresh rosemary or 1 tsp. dried rosemary, crushed

1. Preheat oven to 350°. Sprinkle roast with salt and pepper. In a large nonstick skillet, heat oil over medium heat; brown roast on all sides. Transfer to a roasting pan coated with cooking spray. Place apples, onions and garlic around roast; sprinkle with rosemary.
2. Roast until a thermometer inserted in pork reads 145°, 45-55 minutes, turning apples, onion and garlic once. Remove from oven; tent with foil. Let stand 10 minutes before slicing roast. Serve roast with the apple mixture.
1 serving: 210 cal., 7g fat (2g sat. fat), 57mg chol., 109mg sod., 14g carb. (9g sugars, 2g fiber), 23g pro. **Diabetic exchanges:** 3 lean meat, 1 starch, ½ fat.

SAUSAGE & KRAUT BUNS

This recipe has become a regular at our church potlucks. Let's just say I'm in trouble if I show up at a get-together and they don't appear! For a fun dinner spin, simply serve the sausages over mashed potatoes.
—Patsy Unruh, Perryton, TX

Prep: 20 min. • **Cook:** 4 hours
Makes: 12 servings

- 2 cans (14½ oz. each) no-salt-added diced tomatoes, drained
- 2 cans (14 oz. each) sauerkraut, rinsed and drained
- ½ lb. sliced fresh mushrooms
- 1 large sweet pepper, thinly sliced
- 1 large onion, halved and thinly sliced
- 2 Tbsp. brown sugar
- ½ tsp. pepper
- 2 pkg. (14 oz. each) smoked sausage, sliced
- 12 pretzel sausage buns, warmed and split partway

1. In a 5- or 6-qt. slow cooker, combine the first 7 ingredients. In a large skillet, saute the sausage over medium-high heat until lightly browned. Stir into tomato mixture.
2. Cook, covered, on low until vegetables are tender, 4-5 hours. Serve in buns.
1 sandwich: 468 cal., 23g fat (8g sat. fat), 44mg chol., 1491mg sod., 51g carb. (12g sugars, 4g fiber), 17g pro.

GRANDMA'S CAJUN CHICKEN & SPAGHETTI

I'm originally from Louisiana, where my grandma spoke Cajun French while teaching me to make this spicy dish on an old wood stove.
—Brenda Melancon, McComb, MS

Prep: 15 min. • **Cook:** 1¼ hours
Makes: 10 servings

- 1 broiler/fryer chicken (3 to 4 lbs.), cut up
- 1 to 1½ tsp. cayenne pepper
- ¾ tsp. salt
- 3 Tbsp. canola oil
- 1 pkg. (14 oz.) smoked sausage, sliced
- 1 large sweet onion, chopped
- 1 medium green pepper, chopped
- 1 celery rib, chopped
- 2 garlic cloves, minced
- 2 cans (14½ oz. each) diced tomatoes, undrained
- 1 can (14½ oz.) diced tomatoes with mild green chiles, undrained
- 1 pkg. (16 oz.) spaghetti

1. Sprinkle chicken with cayenne and salt. In a Dutch oven, heat oil over medium-high heat. Brown chicken in batches. Remove from pan.
2. Add the sausage, onion, green pepper and celery to same pan; cook and stir over medium heat 3 minutes. Add garlic; cook 1 minute longer. Stir in tomatoes. Return chicken to pan; bring to a boil. Reduce heat; simmer, covered, until chicken juices run clear, about 1 hour.
3. Cook spaghetti according to package directions. Remove the chicken from pan. When cool enough to handle, remove meat from bones; discard skin and bones. Shred meat with 2 forks; return to pan. Bring to boil. Reduce heat; simmer, uncovered, until slightly thickened, 8-10 minutes. Skim fat. Drain spaghetti; serve with chicken mixture.

¾ cup chicken mixture with ¾ cup spaghetti: 550 cal., 26g fat (8g sat. fat), 89mg chol., 917mg sod., 45g carb. (8g sugars, 4g fiber), 33g pro.

SLOW-COOKED CHICKEN A LA KING

When I know I'll be having a busy day with little time to prepare a meal, I use my slow cooker to make classic chicken a la king. It smells so good while it's cooking.
—Eleanor Mielke, Snohomish, WA

- -

Prep: 10 min. • **Cook:** 7½ hours
Makes: 6 servings

- 1 can (10¾ oz.) reduced-fat reduced-sodium condensed cream of chicken soup, undiluted
- 3 Tbsp. all-purpose flour
- ¼ tsp. pepper
  Dash cayenne pepper
- 1 lb. boneless skinless chicken breasts, cubed
- 1 celery rib, chopped
- ½ cup chopped green pepper
- ¼ cup chopped onion
- 1 pkg. (10 oz.) frozen peas, thawed
- 2 Tbsp. diced pimientos, drained
  Hot cooked rice

In a 3-qt. slow cooker, combine soup, flour, pepper and cayenne until smooth. Stir in chicken, celery, green pepper and onion. Cover and cook on low for 7-8 hours or until meat is no longer pink. Stir in the peas and pimientos. Cook 30 minutes longer or until heated through. Serve with rice.

1 cup chicken mixture: 174 cal., 3g fat (1g sat. fat), 44mg chol., 268mg sod., 16g carb. (6g sugars, 3g fiber), 19g pro. **Diabetic exchanges:** 2 lean meat, 1 starch.

OVEN SWISS STEAK

There's no need to brown the steak first, so you can get this main course into the oven in short order. The fork-tender results are sure to remind you of the Swiss steak that Grandma used to make, with lots of sauce left over for dipping.
—Sue Call, Beech Grove, IN

- -

Prep: 10 min. • **Bake:** 1½ hours
Makes: 8 servings

- 2 lbs. boneless beef round steak (½ in. thick)
- ¼ tsp. pepper
- 1 medium onion, thinly sliced
- 1 can (4 oz.) mushroom stems and pieces, drained
- 1 can (8 oz.) no-salt-added tomato sauce
  Hot cooked noodles

Trim beef; cut into serving-size pieces. Place in a greased 13x9-in. baking dish. Sprinkle with pepper. Top with onion, mushrooms and tomato sauce. Cover and bake at 325° for 1¾-2 hours or until meat is tender. Serve over noodles.

1 serving: 209 cal., 10g fat (0 sat. fat), 68mg chol., 112mg sod., 4g carb. (0 sugars, 0 fiber), 26g pro. **Diabetic exchanges:** 3 lean meat, 1 vegetable.

SLOW-COOKER TUNA NOODLE CASSEROLE

We tweaked this family-friendly classic to work in the slow cooker. It's easy, wholesome and totally homemade.
—*Taste of Home* Test Kitchen

Prep: 25 min. • **Cook:** 4 hours + standing
Makes: 10 servings

- ¼ cup butter, cubed
- ½ lb. sliced fresh mushrooms
- 1 medium onion, chopped
- 1 medium sweet pepper, chopped
- 1 tsp. salt, divided
- 1 tsp. pepper, divided
- 2 garlic cloves, minced
- ¼ cup all-purpose flour
- 2 cups reduced-sodium chicken broth
- 2 cups half-and-half cream
- 4 cups uncooked egg noodles (about 6 oz.)
- 3 cans (5 oz. each) light tuna in water, drained
- 2 Tbsp. lemon juice
- 2 cups shredded Monterey Jack cheese
- 2 cups frozen peas, thawed
- 2 cups crushed potato chips

1. In a large skillet, melt butter over medium-high heat. Add the mushrooms, onion, sweet pepper, ½ tsp. salt and ½ tsp. pepper; cook and stir 6-8 minutes or until tender. Add garlic; cook 1 minute longer. Stir in flour until blended. Gradually whisk in broth. Bring to a boil, stirring constantly; cook and stir until thickened, 1-2 minutes.
2. Transfer to a 5-qt. slow cooker. Stir in the cream and noodles. Cook, covered, on low until the noodles are tender, 4-5 hours. Meanwhile, in a small bowl, combine tuna, lemon juice and remaining salt and pepper.
3. Remove the insert from slow cooker. Stir cheese, tuna mixture and peas into noodle mixture. Let stand, uncovered, 20 minutes. Just before serving, sprinkle with crushed potato chips.

1 cup: 393 cal., 21g fat (12g sat. fat), 84mg chol., 752mg sod., 28g carb. (5g sugars, 3g fiber), 22g pro.

TEST KITCHEN TIP
Mix things up a bit by replacing the frozen peas with an equal amount of a frozen peas-and-carrots combo.

PRESSURE-COOKER WINE-BRAISED BEEF SHANKS

Served over egg noodles or rice, this dish has flavors that remind me of Grandma's house. I updated the method, however, to simmer in my one-pot cooker.
—Helen Nelander, Boulder Creek, CA

Prep: 30 min. • **Cook:** 40 min. + releasing
Makes: 6 servings

- 3 beef shanks (14 oz. each)
- 1 tsp. salt
- 1 tsp. canola oil
- 1 small onion, chopped
- 1 medium carrot, chopped
- 1 medium green pepper, chopped
- 1 cup dry red wine or beef broth
- 1 cup beef broth
- 1 lemon slice
- 1 Tbsp. cornstarch
- 1 Tbsp. water

1. Sprinkle beef with salt. Select saute or browning setting on a 6-qt. electric pressure cooker. Adjust for medium heat; add oil. When oil is hot, brown the beef in batches. Press cancel. Return all to pressure cooker. Add onion, carrot, green pepper, wine, broth and lemon.
2. Lock the lid; close the pressure-release valve. Adjust to pressure-cook on high for 40 minutes. Allow pressure to naturally release for 10 minutes, then quick-release any remaining pressure. Press cancel. Remove meat and vegetables from pressure cooker; keep warm. Discard lemon.
3. Skim fat from cooking juices. Select saute setting and adjust for low heat. In a small bowl, mix the cornstarch and water until smooth; stir into cooking juices. Simmer, stirring constantly, 1-2 minutes or until thickened. Serve with beef and vegetables.
3 ounces cooked beef with ½ cup sauce: 172 cal., 5g fat (2g sat. fat), 51mg chol., 592mg sod., 5g carbo. (2g sugars, 1g fiber), 23g protein. **Diabetic exchanges:** 3 lean meat.

CLASSIC CABBAGE ROLLS

I've always enjoyed cabbage rolls but never made them because most recipes seemed too complicated. This one is on the simpler side and is the best I've ever tasted.
—Beverly Zehner, McMinnville, OR

Prep: 30 min. • **Cook:** 1½ hours
Makes: 4 servings

- 1 medium head cabbage
- 1½ cups chopped onion, divided
- 1 Tbsp. butter
- 2 cans (14½ oz. each) Italian stewed tomatoes
- 4 garlic cloves, minced
- 2 Tbsp. brown sugar
- 1½ tsp. salt, divided
- 1 cup cooked rice
- ¼ cup ketchup
- 2 Tbsp. Worcestershire sauce
- ¼ tsp. pepper
- 1 lb. lean ground beef (90% lean)
- ¼ lb. bulk Italian sausage
- ½ cup V8 juice, optional

1. In a Dutch oven, cook cabbage in boiling water for 10 minutes or until outer leaves are tender; drain. Rinse in cold water; drain. Remove 8 large outer leaves (refrigerate remaining cabbage for another use); set leaves aside.
2. In a large saucepan, saute 1 cup onion in butter until tender. Add the tomatoes, garlic, brown sugar and ½ tsp. salt. Simmer for 15 minutes, stirring occasionally.
3. Meanwhile, in a large bowl, combine the rice, ketchup, Worcestershire sauce, pepper and remaining onion and salt. Crumble beef and sausage over mixture and mix well.
4. Remove thick vein from cabbage leaves for easier rolling. Place about ½ cup meat mixture on each leaf; fold in sides. Starting at an unfolded edge, roll up cabbage leaf to completely enclose filling. Place seam side down in a skillet. Top with the sauce.
5. Cover and cook over medium-low heat for 1 hour. Add V8 juice if desired. Reduce heat to low; cook 20 minutes longer or until rolls are heated through and a thermometer inserted in the filling reads 160°.
2 rolls: 499 cal., 21 g fat (8 g sat. fat), 85 mg chol., 1,845 mg sod., 49 g carb., 8 g fiber, 32 g pro.

WHITE SEAFOOD LASAGNA

We make lasagna with shrimp and scallops as part of the traditional Italian Feast of the Seven Fishes. Every bite delivers a tasty jewel from the sea.
—Joe Colamonico, North Charleston, SC

- -

Prep: 1 hour • **Bake:** 40 min. + standing
Makes: 12 servings

- 9   uncooked lasagna noodles
- 1   Tbsp. butter
- 1   lb. uncooked shrimp (31 to 40 per lb.), peeled and deveined
- 1   lb. bay scallops
- 5   garlic cloves, minced
- ¼   cup white wine
- 1   Tbsp. lemon juice
- 1   lb. fresh crabmeat

CHEESE SAUCE

- ¼   cup butter, cubed
- ¼   cup all-purpose flour
- 3   cups 2% milk
- 1   cup shredded part-skim mozzarella cheese
- ½   cup grated Parmesan cheese
- ½   tsp. salt
- ¼   tsp. pepper
      Dash ground nutmeg

RICOTTA MIXTURE

- 1   carton (15 oz.) part-skim ricotta cheese
- 1   pkg. (10 oz.) frozen chopped spinach, thawed and squeezed dry
- 1   cup shredded part-skim mozzarella cheese
- ½   cup grated Parmesan cheese
- ½   cup seasoned bread crumbs
- 1   large egg, lightly beaten

TOPPING

- 1   cup shredded part-skim mozzarella cheese
- ¼   cup grated Parmesan cheese
      Minced fresh parsley

1. Preheat oven to 350°. Cook lasagna noodles according to package directions; drain noodles.

2. Meanwhile, in a large skillet, heat butter over medium heat. Add shrimp and scallops in batches; cook 2-4 minutes or until shrimp turn pink and scallops are firm and opaque. Remove from pan.

3. Add garlic to same pan; cook 1 minute. Add wine and lemon juice, stirring to loosen browned bits from pan. Bring to a boil; cook 1-2 minutes or until liquid is reduced by half. Add crab; heat through. Stir in the shrimp and scallops.

4. For the cheese sauce, melt butter over medium heat in a large saucepan. Stir in flour until smooth; gradually whisk in milk. Bring to a boil, stirring constantly; cook and stir 1-2 minutes or until thickened. Remove from heat; stir in remaining cheese sauce ingredients. In a large bowl, combine the ricotta mixture ingredients; stir in 1 cup cheese sauce.

5. Spread ½ cup cheese sauce into a greased 13x9-in. baking dish. Layer with 3 noodles, half of the ricotta mixture, half of the seafood mixture and ⅔ cup cheese sauce. Repeat layers. Top with remaining noodles and cheese sauce. Sprinkle top with 1 cup mozzarella cheese and ¼ cup Parmesan cheese.

6. Bake, uncovered, 40-50 minutes or until bubbly and top is golden brown. Let stand 10 minutes before serving. Sprinkle with minced parsley.

1 piece: 448 cal., 19g fat (11g sat. fat), 158mg chol., 957mg sod., 29g carb. (5g sugars, 2g fiber), 39g pro.

OLD-WORLD CORNED BEEF & VEGETABLES

This traditional corned beef dinner is a winner with my husband, family and friends. It's a nice meal-in-one dish.
—Ruth Burrus, Zionsville, IN

- -

Prep: 25 min. • **Cook:** 8 hours
Makes: 8 servings

2½ lbs. red potatoes, quartered
2 cups fresh baby carrots
1 pkg. (10 oz.) frozen pearl onions
1 corned beef brisket with
    spice packet (3 to 3½ lbs.)
½ cup water
1 Tbsp. marinade for chicken
⅛ tsp. pepper
3 Tbsp. cornstarch
¼ cup cold water

1. In a 5-qt. slow cooker, combine the potatoes, carrots and onions. Add beef; discard spice packet from corned beef or save for another use. Combine the water, marinade for chicken and pepper; pour over meat. Cover and cook on low for 8-10 hours or until meat and vegetables are tender.
2. Remove meat and vegetables to a serving platter; keep warm. Skim fat from cooking juices; transfer to a small saucepan. Bring liquid to a boil. Combine cornstarch and cold water until smooth. Gradually stir into the pan. Bring to a boil; cook and stir for 1-2 minutes or until thickened. Serve with meat and vegetables.
Note: This recipe was tested with Lea & Perrins Marinade for Chicken.
1 serving: 446 cal., 23g fat (8g sat. fat), 117mg chol., 1419mg sod., 34g carb. (5g sugars, 3g fiber), 25g pro.

HEARTY RUMP ROAST

I enjoy a good pot roast, and cooking this beef in a horseradish sauce gives it a tangy flavor. Even my little ones love this roast with its tender veggies and gravy.
—Mimi Walker, Palmyra, PA

Prep: 10 min. • **Cook:** 8 hours
Makes: 8 servings

- 1 beef rump roast or bottom round roast (3 to 3½ lbs.)
- 2 Tbsp. canola oil
- 4 medium carrots, halved lengthwise and cut into 2-in. pieces
- 3 medium potatoes, peeled and cut into chunks
- 2 small onions, sliced
- ½ cup water
- 6 to 8 Tbsp. horseradish sauce
- ¼ cup red wine vinegar
- ¼ cup Worcestershire sauce
- 2 garlic cloves, minced
- 1½ to 2 tsp. celery salt
- 3 Tbsp. cornstarch
- ⅓ cup cold water

1. Cut roast in half. In a large skillet, brown meat on all sides in oil over medium-high heat; drain. Place carrots and potatoes in a 5-qt. slow cooker. Top with meat and onions. Combine the water, horseradish sauce, vinegar, Worcestershire sauce, garlic and celery salt. Pour over meat. Cover and cook on low until meat and vegetables are tender, about 8 hours.

2. Combine cornstarch and cold water until smooth; stir into slow cooker. Cover and cook on high until gravy is thickened, about 30 minutes.

1 serving: 378 cal., 15g fat (3g sat. fat), 113mg chol., 507mg sod., 23g carb. (6g sugars, 2g fiber), 35g pro. **Diabetic exchanges:** 4 lean meat, 1½ starch, 1 fat.

STUFFED PORK TENDERLOIN WITH SHIITAKE MUSHROOM SAUCE

Pork tenderloin is a versatile cut that's ideal for hurried cooks because it roasts so quickly. Filled with a stuffing of fresh herbs, sausage, porcini and shiitake mushrooms, it makes a full-flavored entree.
—*Taste of Home* Test Kitchen

- -

Prep: 40 min. + standing • **Bake:** 35 min.
Makes: 8 servings (2 cups sauce)

- 1 **cup water**
- 1 **oz. dried porcini mushrooms**
- ½ **lb. bulk pork sausage**
- 2 **small onions, chopped**
- 5 **cups coarsely chopped fresh shiitake mushrooms (about ¾ lb.), divided**
- 1½ **tsp. minced fresh rosemary or ½ tsp. dried rosemary, crushed**
- 1 **tsp. minced fresh sage or ¼ tsp. rubbed sage**
- 5 **cups soft bread crumbs**
- 3 **Tbsp. minced fresh parsley, divided**
- 2 **pork tenderloins (about 1¼ lb. each)**
- 1¼ **tsp. salt, divided**
- ¾ **tsp. pepper, divided**
- 2 **Tbsp. butter**
- 3 **Tbsp. all-purpose flour**
- 1½ **cups chicken broth**

1. In a small saucepan, bring water and porcini mushrooms to a boil. Remove from the heat; let stand 20-30 minutes or until mushrooms are softened. Using a slotted spoon, remove mushrooms; finely chop and set aside. Strain soaking liquid through a fine mesh strainer, reserving ⅔ cup.

2. In a large skillet, cook sausage and onion over medium heat until sausage is no longer pink. Remove with a slotted spoon. Remove drippings, reserving 2 Tbsp. Saute 4 cups shiitake mushrooms in reserved drippings until tender.

3. Add rosemary, sage, porcini mushrooms and ⅓ cup mushroom soaking liquid; cook 2 minutes longer, stirring occasionally. Remove from the heat; stir in the bread crumbs, 2 Tbsp. parsley and sausage.

4. Preheat oven to 425°. Make a lengthwise slit down the center of each tenderloin to within ½ in. of bottom. Open so meat lies flat. Cover with plastic wrap; flatten to ¼-in. to ½-in. thickness. Remove plastic wrap.

5. Spoon half of the stuffing down center of each tenderloin. Close roasts; tie several times with kitchen string and secure ends with toothpicks. Sprinkle each roast with ½ tsp. salt and ¼ tsp. pepper.

6. Place tenderloins on a rack in a shallow roasting pan. Bake, uncovered, until a thermometer inserted in center of pork reads 145°, 35-45 minutes. Let stand for 5 minutes before slicing.

7. Meanwhile, in a small saucepan, saute remaining shiitake mushrooms in butter until tender. Sprinkle with flour; stir until blended. Gradually add broth and remaining ⅓ cup mushroom soaking liquid. Bring to a boil; cook and stir 2 minutes or until thickened. Stir in remaining parsley, salt and pepper. Serve with pork.

Note: To make soft bread crumbs, tear bread into pieces and place in a food processor or blender. Cover and pulse until crumbs form. One slice of bread yields ½ to ¾ cup crumbs.

2 slices stuffed pork with ¼ cup sauce: 367 cal., 14g fat (6g sat. fat), 98mg chol., 938mg sod., 23g carb. (3g sugars, 3g fiber), 35g pro.

TURKEY CLUB ROULADES

Weeknights turn elegant when these short-prep roulades are on the menu. Not a fan of turkey? Substitute lightly pounded chicken breasts.
—*Taste of Home* Test Kitchen

Prep: 20 min. • **Cook:** 15 min.
Makes: 8 servings

- ¾ lb. fresh asparagus, trimmed
- 8 turkey breast cutlets (about 1 lb.)
- 1 Tbsp. Dijon-mayonnaise blend
- 8 slices deli ham
- 8 slices provolone cheese
- ½ tsp. poultry seasoning
- ½ tsp. pepper
- 8 bacon strips

SAUCE
- ⅔ cup Dijon-mayonnaise blend
- 4 tsp. 2% milk
- ¼ tsp. poultry seasoning

1. Bring 4 cups water to a boil in a large saucepan. Add asparagus; cook, uncovered, for 3 minutes or until crisp-tender. Drain and immediately place asparagus in ice water. Drain and pat dry. Set aside.
2. Spread the turkey cutlets with Dijon-mayonnaise. Layer with ham, cheese and asparagus. Sprinkle with poultry seasoning and pepper. Roll up tightly and wrap with bacon strips.
3. Cook the roulades in a large skillet over medium-high heat until the bacon is crisp and turkey is no longer pink, 12-15 minutes, turning occasionally. Combine the sauce ingredients; serve with roulades.

1 roulade with 1 Tbsp. sauce: 224 cal., 11g fat (5g sat. fat), 64mg chol., 1075mg sod., 2g carb. (1g sugars, 0 fiber), 25g pro.

CHICKEN AMANDINE

With colorful green beans and pimientos, this attractive casserole is terrific for family dinners and special occasions alike. This is true comfort food at its finest.
—Kat Woolbright, Wichita Falls, TX

Prep: 35 min. • **Bake:** 30 min.
Makes: 8 servings

- ¼ cup chopped onion
- 1 Tbsp. butter
- 1 pkg. (6 oz.) long grain and wild rice
- 2¼ cups chicken broth
- 3 cups cubed cooked chicken
- 2 cups frozen french-style green beans, thawed
- 1 can (10¾ oz.) condensed cream of chicken soup, undiluted
- ¾ cup sliced almonds, divided
- 1 jar (4 oz.) diced pimientos, drained
- 1 tsp. pepper
- ½ tsp. garlic powder
- 1 bacon strip, cooked and crumbled

1. In a large saucepan, saute onion in butter until tender. Add the rice with contents of seasoning packet and broth. Bring to a boil. Reduce heat; cover and simmer 25 minutes or until the liquid is absorbed. Uncover; set aside to cool.
2. In a large bowl, combine the chicken, green beans, soup, ½ cup of almonds, pimientos, pepper and garlic powder. Stir in the rice mixture.
3. Transfer to a greased 2½-qt. baking dish. Sprinkle with bacon and remaining almonds. Cover and bake at 350° for 30-35 minutes or until heated through.

1 cup: 297 cal., 13g fat (3g sat. fat), 54mg chol., 912mg sod., 24g carb. (3g sugars, 3g fiber), 22g pro.

GERMAN BRAT SEAFOOD BOIL

The grilled bratwurst and onion add a smoky flavor to corn, potatoes and fish for a hearty meal that's always a hit.
—Trisha Kruse, Eagle, ID

Prep: 25 min. • **Cook:** 30 min.
Makes: 6 servings

- 1 pkg. (19 oz.) uncooked bratwurst links
- 1 medium onion, quartered
- 2 qt. water
- 2 bottles (12 oz. each) beer or 3 cups reduced-sodium chicken broth
- ½ cup seafood seasoning
- 5 medium ears sweet corn, cut into 2-in. pieces
- 2 lbs. small red potatoes
- 1 medium lemon, halved
- 1 lb. cod fillet, cut into 1-in. pieces
  Coarsely ground pepper

1. Grill bratwurst, covered, over medium heat, turning frequently, until meat is no longer pink, 15-20 minutes. Grill onion, covered, until lightly browned, 3-4 minutes on each side. Cut the bratwurst links into 2-in. pieces.
2. In a stockpot, combine water, beer and seafood seasoning; add corn, potatoes, lemon, bratwurst and onion. Bring to a boil. Reduce heat; simmer, uncovered, until the potatoes are tender, 15-20 minutes. Stir in cod; cook until fish flakes easily with a fork, 4-6 minutes. Drain; transfer to a large serving bowl. Sprinkle with pepper.
1 serving: 553 cal., 28g fat (9g sat. fat), 95mg chol., 1620mg sod., 46g carb. (8g sugars, 5g fiber), 30g pro.

CHICKEN WITH CHERRY WINE SAUCE

My dad's a chef, and I learned to cook at an early age. This saucy chicken was the first dish I made by myself.
—Ben Diaz, Azusa, CA

Takes: 30 min. • **Makes:** 4 servings

- 4 boneless skinless chicken breast halves (8 oz. each)
- ¼ tsp. salt
- ¼ tsp. pepper
- 7 Tbsp. butter, divided
- ⅔ cup dry red wine
- 1 Tbsp. sugar
- ½ cup fresh or frozen pitted dark sweet cherries, thawed

1. Preheat oven to 350°. Sprinkle chicken with salt and pepper. In a large cast-iron or other ovenproof skillet, heat 2 Tbsp. butter over medium-high heat. Brown chicken on both sides. Bake until a thermometer reads 165°, 12-15 minutes.
2. Meanwhile, in a small saucepan, combine the wine and sugar. Bring to a boil; cook, uncovered, until liquid is reduced by half, 4-5 minutes. Reduce heat to low; whisk in remaining butter, 1 Tbsp. at a time, until blended. Stir in cherries; serve with chicken.
1 chicken breast half with 3 Tbsp. sauce: 480 cal., 25g fat (14g sat. fat), 179mg chol., 418mg sod., 8g carb. (5g sugars, 0 fiber), 46g pro.

GLAZED CORNISH HENS WITH PECAN-RICE STUFFING

Cornish hens bake up with a lovely golden brown shine when they are basted with my sweet and tangy glaze. The traditional rice stuffing has some added interest with crunchy pecans and sweet golden raisins.
—Agnes Ward, Stratford, ON

Prep: 1 hour
Bake: 1 hour 25 min. + standing
Makes: 8 servings

- 8 **Cornish game hens (20 to 24 oz. each)**
- ¼ **cup butter, softened**
- ½ **tsp. salt**
- ½ **tsp. pepper**
- 2 **cups unsweetened apple juice**
- 1 **Tbsp. honey**
- 1 **Tbsp. Dijon mustard**

PECAN RICE
- 2 **Tbsp. butter**
- 1½ **cups uncooked long grain rice**
- 2 **tsp. ground cumin**
- 1 **tsp. curry powder**
- 4 **cups reduced-sodium chicken broth**
- 1 **cup chopped pecans, toasted**
- 3 **green onions, thinly sliced**
- ½ **cup golden raisins**

1. Tuck wings under hens; tie drumsticks together. Rub skin with butter; sprinkle with salt and pepper. Place hens breast side up in a shallow roasting pan.
2. Bake, uncovered, at 350° for 1 hour. Meanwhile, place the apple juice in a small saucepan. Bring to a boil; cook until reduced by half. Remove from heat. Stir in honey and mustard. Set aside ½ cup for serving.
3. Brush the hens with apple juice mixture. Bake, basting occasionally with the pan drippings, 25-35 minutes longer or until a thermometer reads 180°. Cover hens loosely with foil if they brown too quickly.
4. For pecan rice, heat butter in a large saucepan over medium heat. Add rice, cumin and curry; cook and stir until rice is lightly browned, 2-3 minutes. Stir in broth. Bring to a boil. Reduce heat; simmer, covered, until rice is tender, 15-20 minutes. Stir in pecans, onions and raisins.
5. Cover hens; let stand 10 minutes before serving. Serve with rice and reserved sauce.
1 hen with 1 Tbsp. sauce: 1075 cal., 68g fat (20g sat. fat), 371mg chol., 905mg sod., 48g carb. (16g sugars, 3g fiber), 65g pro.

TEST KITCHEN TIP
If all 8 hens won't fit in your shallow roasting pan, you can bake them on two 15x10x1-in. baking pans with wire racks. Rotate the baking pans occasionally to make sure the hens cook evenly.

STUFFED ZUCCHINI

An abundance of squash from my garden inspired me to make up this recipe, which is now a favorite.
—Marjorie Roberts, West Chazy, NY

- -

Prep: 25 min. • **Bake:** 45 min.
Makes: 8 servings

1½ lbs. lean ground beef (90% lean)
1 large onion, chopped
1 large green pepper, chopped
1 jalapeno pepper, minced
1¼ cups soft bread crumbs
1 large egg, beaten
1 Tbsp. dried parsley flakes
1 tsp. dried basil
1 tsp. Italian seasoning
1 tsp. salt
⅛ tsp. pepper
2 cans (8 oz. each) tomato sauce, divided
2 medium tomatoes, coarsely chopped
4 medium zucchini
2 cups shredded mozzarella cheese

1. In a large bowl, combine the first 11 ingredients and 1 can of the tomato sauce; mix well. Stir in tomatoes. Halve zucchini lengthwise; scoop out seeds. Fill with meat mixture; place in two 13x9-in. baking dishes. Spoon remaining tomato sauce over each.

2. Bake, uncovered, at 375° until the zucchini is tender, about 45 minutes. Sprinkle with cheese during the last few minutes of baking.

Note: Wear disposable gloves when cutting hot peppers; the oils can burn skin. Avoid touching your face.

1 serving: 221 cal., 11g fat (5g sat. fat), 72mg chol., 511mg sod., 11g carb. (4g sugars, 2g fiber), 20g pro.

OLD-WORLD KIELBASA

I've been making this recipe for most of my life. No one can resist this hearty old-fashioned fare.
—Ethel Harrison, North Fort Myers, FL

Prep: 5 min. • **Cook:** 30 min.
Makes: 10 servings

- 1 medium onion, sliced
- 2 Tbsp. butter
- 8 cups shredded cabbage
- 1 lb. smoked kielbasa, cut into ½-in. slices
- 1 can (14½ oz.) stewed tomatoes
- ½ cup water
- 4 tsp. caraway seeds
- 1 tsp. paprika

In a Dutch oven, saute onion in butter. Add remaining ingredients; bring to a boil. Reduce the heat; cover and simmer for 30 minutes or until cabbage is tender. Serve with a slotted spoon.

1 cup: 115 cal., 6g fat (0 sat. fat), 30mg chol., 454mg sod., 8g carb. (0 sugars, 0 fiber), 8g pro. **Diabetic exchanges:** 1½ vegetable, 1 meat.

BLUE CHEESE-MUSHROOM STUFFED TENDERLOIN

Here's my go-to entree for most special events. Filled with a savory stuffing, the sliced tenderloin looks and tastes like it comes from an upscale restaurant.
—Joyce Conway, Westerville, OH

- -

Prep: 25 min. • **Bake:** 40 min. + standing
Makes: 8 servings

- 2 **Tbsp. butter**
- ½ **lb. sliced baby portobello mushrooms**
- 1 **Tbsp. Worcestershire sauce**
- 3 **Tbsp. horseradish mustard or spicy brown mustard**
- 1 **Tbsp. coarsely ground pepper**
- 1 **Tbsp. olive oil**
- 1 **tsp. salt**
- 1 **beef tenderloin roast (4 lbs.)**
- ¾ **cup crumbled blue cheese, divided**
- 1½ **cups french-fried onions Additional French-fried onions, optional**

1. Preheat oven to 425°. In a small skillet, heat butter over medium-high heat. Add mushrooms and Worcestershire sauce; cook and stir until mushrooms are tender, 6-8 minutes. In a small bowl, mix mustard, pepper, oil and salt.

2. Cut lengthwise through the center of roast to within ½ in. of bottom. Open roast and cut lengthwise through the center of each half to within ½ in. of bottom. Open roast flat; cover with plastic wrap. Pound with a meat mallet to ¾-in. thickness.

3. Remove plastic. Spread mushrooms down center of roast to within ½ in. of ends; top with ½ cup cheese and onions. Starting at a long side, roll up jelly-roll style; tie at 1½-in. intervals with kitchen string. Secure ends with toothpicks.

4. Place on a rack in a shallow roasting pan; spread with mustard mixture. Roast until the meat reaches desired doneness (for medium-rare, a thermometer should read 135°; medium, 140°; medium-well, 145°), 40-50 minutes.

5. Remove roast from oven; tent with foil. Let stand 15 minutes before slicing. Remove string and toothpicks. Top servings with the remaining cheese. If desired, warm the additional onions in microwave and sprinkle over tops.

1 serving: 499 cal., 28g fat (11g sat. fat), 116mg chol., 636mg sod., 7g carb. (1g sugars, 1g fiber), 52g pro.

PEPPERCORN BEEF TOP LOIN ROAST

A red wine sauce complements the caramelized brown sugar coating on the crust of this special-occasion roast. The down-home flavor makes it the ultimate entree when hosting a dinner party.
—*Taste of Home* Test Kitchen

- -

Prep: 30 min. • **Bake:** 1 hour + standing
Makes: 10 servings (1½ cups sauce)

```
 1   beef top round roast (4 lbs.)
⅓   cup packed brown sugar
 3   Tbsp. whole peppercorns, crushed
 4   garlic cloves, minced
¾   tsp. salt
 1   large onion, finely chopped
 1   Tbsp. olive oil
 2   Tbsp. tomato paste
 2   tsp. Worcestershire sauce
1½  cups port wine
1½  cups dry red wine
```

1. Preheat oven to 325° Trim fat from the roast. If desired, tie roast with kitchen twine every 1½-2 in. to help beef maintain shape while cooking. In a small bowl, combine the brown sugar, peppercorns, garlic and salt. Rub over meat. Place roast in a shallow roasting pan.

2. Bake until a thermometer meat reaches desired doneness (for medium-rare, should read 135°; medium, 140°; medium-well, 145°), 1-1½ hours. Remove the roast from oven, tent with foil and let stand 15 minutes before slicing.

3. Meanwhile, in a large saucepan, saute onion in oil until tender. Stir in tomato paste and Worcestershire sauce until blended. Add wines. Bring to a boil; cook until liquid is reduced to about 1½ cups. Serve with the roast.

5 oz.: 444 cal., 26g fat (10g sat. fat), 99mg chol., 275mg sod., 12g carb. (9g sugars, 0 fiber), 32g pro.

GRAM'S FRIED CHICKEN

As a boy, I wolfed down my grandmother's fried chicken. I never knew how she made it, but my recipe using crispy potato flakes is pretty close.
—David Nelson, Lincolnton, NC

- -

Prep: 20 min. + chilling • **Cook:** 10 min.
Makes: 4 servings

```
 1   large egg
 1   cup 2% milk
 2   cups mashed potato flakes
 1   Tbsp. garlic powder
 1   Tbsp. each dried oregano, parsley
     flakes and minced onion
½   tsp. salt
¼   tsp. coarsely ground pepper
 4   boneless skinless chicken
     breast halves (6 oz. each)
     Oil for frying
```

1. In a shallow bowl, whisk egg and milk. In another shallow bowl, toss potato flakes with seasonings. Remove half of the potato mixture and reserve (for a second coat of breading).

2. Pound chicken with a meat mallet to ½-in. thickness. Dip chicken in egg mixture, then in potato mixture, patting to help coating adhere. Arrange chicken in an even layer on a large plate. Cover and refrigerate chicken and remaining egg mixture 1 hour. Discard remaining used potato mixture.

3. In a 12-in. cast-iron or other deep skillet, heat ½ in. of oil over medium heat to 350°. For the second coat of breading, dip chicken in remaining egg mixture, then in unused potato mixture; pat to coat. Fry chicken 4-5 minutes on each side or until golden brown and chicken is no longer pink. Drain on paper towels.

1 chicken breast half: 469 cal., 28g fat (3g sat. fat), 121mg chol., 269mg sod., 16g carb. (3g sugars, 2g fiber), 38g pro.

GREEK-STYLE LEMON-GARLIC CHICKEN

I love celebrating my Greek heritage with this super simple and scrumptious Sunday dinner. Prep time is a breeze, and the ingredient list is relatively short for such a flavorful one-dish meal. Each time I make this, it reminds me of my yaya (grandma), who used to let me squeeze the lemons when she made it.
—Lisa Renshaw, Kansas City, MO

- -

Prep: 15 min. • **Bake:** 1 hour
Makes: 8 servings

- 8 medium Yukon Gold potatoes (about 3 lbs.)
- 1 cup pitted Greek olives
- 8 bone-in chicken thighs (about 3 lbs.)
- ½ cup olive oil
- 3 Tbsp. lemon juice
- 6 garlic cloves, minced
- 2 tsp. salt
- 2 tsp. dried oregano
- ½ tsp. pepper
- 1½ cups reduced-sodium chicken broth

1. Preheat oven to 375°. Scrub potatoes; cut each into 8 wedges and place in a shallow roasting pan. Top with olives and chicken. In a small bowl, whisk oil, lemon juice, garlic, salt, oregano and pepper until blended. Drizzle over chicken and potatoes. Pour chicken broth around chicken into roasting pan.
2. Bake, uncovered, 60-70 minutes or until a thermometer inserted in chicken reads 170°-175° and potatoes are tender. Serve with pan juices.
1 chicken thigh with 8 potato wedges and about ⅓ cup pan juices: 602 cal., 33g fat (6g sat. fat), 81mg chol., 1071mg sod., 48g carb. (4g sugars, 4g fiber), 29g pro.

PARMESAN FISH STICKS

I wanted a healthier approach to fish sticks and developed a baked tilapia with a slightly peppery bite. The entire family loves the crispy coating.
—Candy Summerhill, Alexander, AR

- -

Takes: 25 min. • **Makes:** 4 servings

- ⅓ cup all-purpose flour
- ½ tsp. salt
- ⅛ to ¼ tsp. pepper
- 2 large eggs
- 1 cup panko (Japanese) bread crumbs
- ⅓ cup grated Parmesan cheese
- 2 Tbsp. garlic-herb seasoning blend
- 1 lb. tilapia fillets
  Cooking spray

1. Preheat oven to 450°. In a shallow bowl, mix flour, salt and pepper. In another bowl, whisk eggs. In a third bowl, toss the bread crumbs with cheese and seasoning blend.
2. Cut fillets into 1-in.-wide strips. Dip fish in flour mixture to coat both sides; shake off excess. Dip in eggs, then in crumb mixture, patting to help coating adhere.
3. Place on a foil-lined baking sheet coated with cooking spray. Spritz tops with cooking spray until crumbs appear moistened. Bake 10-12 minutes or until golden brown and fish just begins to flake easily with a fork.
1 serving: 281 cal., 11g fat (3g sat. fat), 154mg chol., 641mg sod., 16g carb. (1g sugars, 1g fiber), 28g pro. **Diabetic exchanges:** 3 lean meat, 1 starch, 1 fat.

NEW ENGLAND LAMB BAKE

This dish is hearty and perfect for warming up on a chilly winter evening. The aroma is almost as delightful as the dish itself.
—Frank Grady, Fort Kent, ME

- -

Prep: 25 min. • **Bake:** 1½ hours
Makes: 8 servings

- 1 Tbsp. canola oil
- 2 lbs. boneless leg of lamb, cut into 1-in. cubes
- 1 large onion, chopped
- ¼ cup all-purpose flour
- 3 cups chicken broth
- 2 large leeks (white portion only), cut into ½-in. slices
- 2 large carrots, sliced
- 2 Tbsp. minced fresh parsley, divided
- ½ tsp. dried rosemary, crushed
- ½ tsp. salt
- ¼ tsp. pepper
- ¼ tsp. dried thyme
- 3 large potatoes, peeled and sliced
- 3 Tbsp. butter, melted and divided

1. Preheat oven to 375°. In a Dutch oven, heat oil over medium heat. Add lamb and onion; cook and stir until meat is no longer pink. Stir in flour until blended. Gradually add the broth. Bring to a boil; cook until thickened, 1-2 minutes, stirring to loosen browned bits from pan. Add leeks, carrots, 1 Tbsp. parsley, rosemary, salt, pepper and thyme.
2. Spoon into a greased 13x9-in. or 3-qt. baking dish. Cover with potato slices; brush with 2 Tbsp. melted butter. Bake 1 hour; brush potatoes with remaining butter. Return to oven; bake until meat is tender and potatoes are golden, 30 minutes to 1 hour longer. Cool briefly; sprinkle with remaining parsley.

Freeze option: Remove baking dish from oven; cool completely. Before adding remaining parsley, cover dish and freeze. Freeze parsley separately. To use, partially thaw lamb in refrigerator overnight. Remove from refrigerator 30 minutes before baking; thaw remaining parsley. Preheat oven to 350°. Reheat, covered, until a thermometer reads 165°, about 1 hour. Sprinkle with remaining parsley.

1 serving: 356 cal., 13g fat (5g sat. fat), 82mg chol., 631mg sod., 34g carb. (4g sugars, 4g fiber), 25g pro. **Diabetic exchanges:** 3 starch, 3 lean meat, 1½ fat.

"Thanks for reminding me about this dish. I made this years ago, and I forgot how good it was. Now I saved this for fall meals."
—WALKERJO, TASTEOFHOME.COM

ROASTED SAGE TURKEY WITH VEGETABLE GRAVY

There's no place like home when roasting the big bird. Try stuffing the turkey with fresh sage and thyme sprigs.
—Beth Jacobson, Milwaukee, WI

Prep: 30 min. + chilling
Bake: 2 hours 10 min. + standing
Makes: 16 servings (3½ cups gravy)

- 1 **turkey (14 to 16 lbs.)**
- 1 **Tbsp. kosher salt**
- 1 **tsp. ground sage**
- ½ **tsp. garlic powder**
- 1 **large onion, chopped**
- 3 **celery ribs, chopped**
- 3 **medium carrots, chopped**
- 1¼ **cups water, divided**
- 3 **Tbsp. canola oil**
- ½ **tsp. freshly ground pepper**
- ¾ **cup white wine**
- 3 **fresh sage sprigs**
- 4 **fresh thyme sprigs**

GRAVY
- 1 **to 1½ cups reduced-sodium chicken broth or homemade chicken stock**
- ¼ **cup all-purpose flour**
- ¼ **tsp. minced fresh sage**
- ¼ **tsp. freshly ground pepper**

1. Remove giblets and neck from turkey. Reserve turkey neck; refrigerate, covered, overnight. Place turkey in a 15x10-in. baking pan, breast side up. Secure skin to the underside of neck cavity with toothpicks. Mix salt, sage and garlic powder. Tuck wings under turkey; tie drumsticks together. Pat turkey dry. Rub outside of turkey with the salt mixture. Refrigerate turkey, loosely covered, overnight.

2. Preheat oven to 475°. Place onion, celery, carrots and reserved neck in bottom of a broiler pan; add ½ cup water. Place broiler pan rack over top; transfer turkey to rack. Rub outside of turkey with oil; sprinkle with pepper. Pour wine and remaining water into turkey cavity; add sage and thyme sprigs.

3. Place turkey in oven, legs facing toward back of the oven. Roast, uncovered, for 40 minutes.

4. Reduce oven setting to 350°. Cover breast tightly with a double thickness of foil. Roast until a thermometer inserted in thickest part of thigh reads 170°-175° (thermometer should not touch bone or fat), 1½-2 hours longer.

5. Remove turkey from oven. Let stand, uncovered, 20 minutes before carving. Using a turkey baster, remove liquid from turkey cavity to a large measuring cup. Line a strainer or colander with cheesecloth; place over measuring cup. With a slotted spoon, remove vegetables from bottom of broiler pan, reserving 1¼ cups. Discard turkey neck. Strain the cooking liquid into measuring cup. Skim fat, reserving ¼ cup fat. Add enough broth to the cooking liquid to measure 2 cups.

6. In a large saucepan, mix the flour and reserved fat until smooth; gradually whisk in the broth mixture. Bring to a boil over medium-high heat, stirring constantly; cook and stir until thickened, 1-2 minutes. Add half of the reserved vegetables. Puree gravy using an immersion blender; or, cool gravy slightly and puree in a blender. Stir in sage, pepper and remaining vegetables; heat through. Serve with turkey.

9 oz. cooked turkey with about ¼ cup gravy: 514 cal., 24g fat (6g sat. fat), 215mg chol., 562mg sod., 4g carb. (1g sugars, 1g fiber), 64g pro.

DOUBLE-DUTY CITRUS HAM

You'll want to remember this recipe for both Easter and Christmas. It's special to me because it's based on the ham my grandma and mom used to make. Leftovers can be frozen up to 3 months.
—Penny Hawkins, Mebane, NC

Prep: 15 min. • **Bake:** 1¾ hours + standing
Makes: 9 servings plus leftovers

  1 **fully cooked bone-in ham (6 to 8 lbs.)**
     Whole cloves
1¼ **cups orange soda**
1¼ **cups orange marmalade**
 ½ **cup packed brown sugar**
 ¼ **cup Dijon mustard**

1. Place ham on a rack in a shallow roasting pan. Score the surface of the ham, making diamond shapes ½ in. deep; insert a clove in the center of each diamond. Loosely cover ham with foil. Bake at 325° for 1½ hours.
2. In a small saucepan, combine the soda, marmalade and brown sugar. Bring to a boil; cook until liquid is reduced by half, about 15 minutes. Stir in mustard.
3. Brush the ham with some of the glaze; bake 15-30 minutes longer or until a thermometer reads 140°, basting occasionally with remaining glaze. Let stand 10 minutes before slicing.
4 oz. cooked ham: 345 cal., 6g fat (2g sat. fat), 106mg chol., 1422mg sod., 38g carb. (35g sugars, 0 fiber), 36g pro.

GRAN'S SWEDISH MEATBALLS

My mother made these hearty meatballs when we were growing up, and now my kids love them, too. My daughter likes to help toss the meatballs in the flour.
—Karin Ness, Big Lake, MN

- -

Takes: 30 min. • **Makes:** 4 servings

- 1   **large egg, lightly beaten**
- ½   **cup crushed saltines (about 10 crackers)**
- ¼   **tsp. seasoned salt**
- ¼   **tsp. pepper**
- ½   **lb. ground beef**
- ½   **lb. bulk pork sausage**
- ¼   **cup plus 2 Tbsp. all-purpose flour, divided**
- 2½   **cups reduced-sodium beef broth, divided**
      Hot mashed potatoes
      Minced fresh parsley, optional

1. Mix the first 4 ingredients. Add beef and sausage; mix lightly but thoroughly. Shape into 1-in. balls; gently toss with ¼ cup flour, coating lightly.
2. In a large skillet, brown meatballs over medium-high heat. Add 2 cups broth; bring to a boil. Reduce heat; simmer, covered, 5-6 minutes or until the meatballs are cooked through.
3. Remove meatballs with a slotted spoon. Mix the remaining flour and broth until smooth; add to pan. Bring to a boil; cook and stir until thickened, 1-2 minutes. Return meatballs to pan; heat through. Serve with mashed potatoes. If desired, sprinkle with minced parsley.

1 serving: 348 cal., 21g fat (7g sat. fat), 115mg chol., 846mg sod., 17g carb. (1g sugars, 1g fiber), 21g pro.

PARMESAN CHICKEN

The savory coating on this chicken has the satisfying flavor of Parmesan cheese. It's easy enough to be a family weekday meal yet impressive enough to serve to guests. When I make this chicken for dinner, we never have any leftovers.
—Schelby Thompson, Camden Wyoming, DE

- -

Prep: 10 min. • **Bake:** 25 min.
Makes: 6 servings

- ½   **cup butter, melted**
- 2   **tsp. Dijon mustard**
- 1   **tsp. Worcestershire sauce**
- ½   **tsp. salt**
- 1   **cup dry bread crumbs**
- ½   **cup grated Parmesan cheese**
- 6   **boneless skinless chicken breast halves (7 oz. each)**

1. Preheat oven to 350°. In a shallow bowl, combine butter, mustard, Worcestershire sauce and salt. Place bread crumbs and cheese in another shallow bowl. Dip chicken in butter mixture, then in bread crumb mixture, patting to help coating adhere.
2. Place in an ungreased 15x10x1-in. baking pan. Drizzle with any remaining butter mixture. Bake chicken, uncovered, until a thermometer inserted in chicken reads 165°, 25-30 minutes.

1 chicken breast half: 270 cal., 16g fat (9g sat. fat), 82mg chol., 552mg sod., 10g carb. (1g sugars, 0 fiber), 21g pro.

GRANDMA'S PIZZA MEAT LOAF

Good food and memories are made in the kitchen, particularly when that kitchen is Grandma's. This recipe came from my grandma, and we all love it to this day.
—Nicholas King, Duluth, MN

- -

Prep: 20 min. • **Bake:** 55 min. + standing
Makes: 8 servings

- 1 **large egg, lightly beaten**
- 1½ **cups seasoned bread crumbs**
- 1 **can (4¼ oz.) chopped ripe olives, drained**
- 1 **can (4 oz.) mushroom stems and pieces, drained**
- 1 **cup shredded part-skim mozzarella cheese**
- 1 **small green pepper, chopped**
- 1 **small onion, chopped**
- 2 **Tbsp. onion soup mix**
- 1 **cup pizza sauce, divided**
- 2 **lbs. ground beef**
- ¼ **cup grated Parmesan cheese**

1. In a large bowl, combine the egg, bread crumbs, olives, mushrooms, mozzarella cheese, pepper, onion, soup mix and ½ cup pizza sauce. Crumble beef over mixture and mix well. Shape into a 10x6-in. rectangle and place in a greased 15x10x1-in. baking pan; Spoon remaining pizza sauce over top.
2. Bake, uncovered, at 350° for 45 minutes. Sprinkle with Parmesan cheese. Bake until no pink remains and a thermometer reads 160°, 10-15 minutes longer. Let stand for 10 minutes before slicing.
1 slice: 417 cal., 22g fat (8g sat. fat), 114mg chol., 1037mg sod., 23g carb. (4g sugars, 3g fiber), 32g pro.

COMPANY STUFFED PORK CHOPS

These comforting pork chops bake to a perfect golden brown, and the stuffing is incredibly moist. It's one of my favorite dishes to serve guests because I know they'll simply love it.
—Lorraine Darocha, Mountain City, TN

- -

Prep: 40 min. • **Bake:** 30 min.
Makes: 6 servings

2 **celery ribs, diced**
1 **small onion, chopped**
1 **tsp. olive oil**
9 **slices white bread, cubed**
¼ **cup minced fresh parsley**
¼ **tsp. salt**
¼ **tsp. rubbed sage**
⅛ **tsp. white pepper**
⅛ **tsp. dried marjoram**
⅛ **tsp. dried thyme**
¾ **cup reduced-sodium chicken broth**
PORK CHOPS
6 **pork rib chops (7 oz. each)**
2 **tsp. olive oil**
¼ **tsp. salt**
¼ **tsp. pepper**

1. In a large skillet coated with cooking spray, saute celery and onion in 1 tsp. oil until tender; remove from the heat. In a large bowl, combine bread and seasonings. Add celery mixture and broth; toss to coat. Set aside.

2. Cut a pocket in each pork chop by making a horizontal slice almost to the bone. Coat the same skillet with cooking spray. Cook chops in oil in batches over medium-high heat until browned, 1-2 minutes on each side. Carefully fill chops with bread mixture; secure with toothpicks if necessary.

3. Transfer stuffed chops to a 13x9-in. baking dish coated with cooking spray. Sprinkle with salt and pepper. Cover and bake at 350° for 15 minutes. Uncover; bake until a thermometer inserted in pork chops reads at least 145°, 15-20 minutes longer. Discard the toothpicks and let stand for 5 minutes before serving.

1 pork chop: 314 cal., 12g fat (4g sat. fat), 64mg chol., 526mg sod., 20g carb. (3g sugars, 1g fiber), 29g pro. **Diabetic exchanges:** 4 lean meat, 1 starch.

SWIFT WAY TO STUFF

When creating the pockets in pork chops, use a paring knife to make a slit in the chop's fatty side. Cut almost to the bone. (If using boneless chops, cut toward the other side but not through the chop.) Spoon the stuffing mixture into the pocket and secure the opening with some toothpicks.

BEEF TENDERLOIN IN MUSHROOM SAUCE

This is a recipe my mother-in-law has been using for more than 30 years. I prepare it for my husband as part of special menus when our kids are away.
—Denise McNab, Warminster, PA

- -

Takes: 25 min. • **Makes:** 2 servings

- 4 Tbsp. butter, divided
- 1 tsp. canola oil
- 2 beef tenderloin steaks (1 in. thick and 4 oz. each)
- 1 cup sliced fresh mushrooms
- 1 Tbsp. chopped green onion
- 1 Tbsp. all-purpose flour
- ⅛ tsp. salt
  Dash pepper
- ⅔ cup chicken or beef broth
- ⅛ tsp. browning sauce, optional

1. In a large skillet, heat 2 Tbsp. butter and oil over medium-high heat; cook steaks to desired doneness (for medium-rare, a thermometer should read 135°; medium, 140°), 5-6 minutes per side. Remove from pan, reserving drippings; keep warm.
2. In same pan, heat the drippings and remaining butter over medium-high heat; saute mushrooms and green onion until tender. Stir in flour, salt and pepper until blended; gradually stir in broth and, if desired, browning sauce. Bring to a boil, stirring constantly; cook and stir until thickened, 1-2 minutes. Serve with steaks.
1 serving: 417 cal., 32g fat (17g sat. fat), 112mg chol., 659mg sod., 5g carb. (1g sugars, 1g fiber), 26g pro.

CROWN ROAST OF PORK WITH MUSHROOM DRESSING

My entire family loves this succulent pork and savory bread stuffing. It looks so elegant that everyone thinks I really fussed but it's actually so easy! The biggest challenge is to remember to order the crown roast from the meat department ahead of time.
—Betty Claycomb, Alverton, PA

- -

Prep: 15 min. • **Bake:** 2 hours
Makes: 10 servings

- 1 pork loin crown roast (10 to 12 ribs, about 6 to 8 lbs.)
- ½ tsp. seasoned salt
  MUSHROOM DRESSING
- ¼ cup butter, cubed
- 1 cup sliced fresh mushrooms
- ½ cup diced celery
- 3 cups cubed day-old bread
- ¼ tsp. salt
- ¼ tsp. pepper
- ⅓ cup apricot preserves

1. Preheat oven to 350°. Place roast, rib ends up, in a shallow roasting pan; sprinkle with seasoned salt. Cover rib ends with foil. Bake, uncovered, for 1¼ hours.
2. Meanwhile, melt butter over medium-high heat. Add mushrooms and celery; saute until tender. Stir in bread cubes, salt and pepper. Spoon around roast. Brush sides of roast with preserves. Bake until a thermometer inserted into meat between ribs reads 145°, 45-60 minutes. Remove foil; let meat stand 10 minutes before slicing.
1 pork rib plus stuffing: 404 cal., 17g fat (7g sat. fat), 106mg chol., 314mg sod., 16g carb. (7g sugars, 1g fiber), 45g pro.

INDIVIDUAL TURKEY POTPIES

These savory, creamy potpies may seem like a lot of work, but frozen puff pastry sheets make them simple to assemble.
—Victoria Bond, Tempe, AZ

Prep: 50 min. • **Bake:** 20 min.
Makes: 6 servings

- 2½ cups cubed peeled potatoes
- 1 cup chopped onion
- ¾ cup sliced fresh carrots
- ½ cup chopped celery
- 1 Tbsp. olive oil
- 2 garlic cloves, minced
- 2 cups cubed cooked turkey
- ½ cup fresh peas
- ½ tsp. minced fresh thyme or ⅛ tsp. dried thyme
- ½ tsp. minced fresh rosemary or ⅛ tsp. dried rosemary, crushed
- ¼ tsp. salt
- ⅛ tsp. pepper

SAUCE
- ¼ cup butter, cubed
- 6 Tbsp. all-purpose flour
- 2 cups 2% milk
- 1 cup chicken broth
- ½ cup heavy whipping cream
- 3 Tbsp. Dijon mustard
- 1 Tbsp. capers, drained
- 1 tsp. minced fresh tarragon or ¼ tsp. dried tarragon
- 1 tsp. minced fresh thyme or ¼ tsp. dried thyme
- 1 tsp. minced fresh rosemary or ¼ tsp. dried rosemary, crushed
- ½ tsp. rubbed sage
- ½ tsp. dried marjoram
- ¼ tsp. ground nutmeg
- ⅛ tsp. salt
- ⅛ tsp. pepper

CRUST
- 1 sheet frozen puff pastry, thawed

1. In a large skillet, saute the potatoes, chopped onion, carrots and celery in oil for 8 minutes. Add garlic; cook 1 minute longer. Stir in the turkey, peas, thyme, rosemary, salt and pepper; heat through.

2. In a large saucepan, melt butter. Stir in flour until smooth; gradually add milk, broth and cream. Bring to a boil; cook and stir for 1-2 minutes or until thickened. Stir in the Dijon mustard, capers, herbs, nutmeg, salt, pepper and potato mixture. Divide among 6 greased 10-oz. ramekins.

3. On a lightly floured surface, roll out puff pastry into a 13x9-in. rectangle. Cut into 6 squares. Place 1 pastry over each ramekin; pressing to seal edges. Beat egg and water; brush over pastry. Sprinkle with cheese.

4. Place ramekins on a baking sheet. Bake, uncovered, at 400° for 20-25 minutes or until golden brown.

1 potpie: 620 cal., 34g fat (15g sat. fat), 126mg chol., 864mg sod., 55g carb. (8g sugars, 6g fiber), 25g pro.

MAPLE-GLAZED CORNED BEEF

Passed down by my great-grandmother, this corned beef recipe offers a touch of sweetness with a maple syrup glaze. Even people who say they don't care for corned beef will ask for seconds!
—Gayle Macklin, Vail, AZ

Prep: 25 minutes • **Cook:** 2½ hours
Makes: 12 servings

- 2 **corned beef briskets with spice packets (3 lbs. each)**
- 1 **large sweet onion, sliced**
- 12 **garlic cloves, peeled and halved**
- ¼ **cup kosher salt**
- ¼ **cup whole peppercorns**
- 8 **bay leaves**
- 2 **Tbsp. dried basil**
- 2 **Tbsp. dried oregano**
- 4 **qt. water**
- 3 **cups beef broth**
- ¼ **cup maple syrup**
- ⅓ **cup packed brown sugar**

1. Place briskets and contents of the spice packets in a stockpot. Add onion, garlic, salt, peppercorns, bay leaves, basil and oregano. Pour in water and beef broth. Bring to a boil. Reduce heat; cover and simmer for 2½-3 hours or until the meat is tender.

2. Transfer meat to a broiler pan. Brush with maple syrup; sprinkle with brown sugar. Broil 4-6 in. from the heat for 2-3 minutes or until beef is glazed. Thinly slice meat across the grain.

4 oz. cooked beef: 439 cal., 30g fat (10g sat. fat), 156mg chol., 2014mg sod., 11g carb. (10g sugars, 0 fiber), 29g pro.

HONEY WALLEYE

This recipe has always been a quick way to prepare the fresh walleye hooked by the anglers in our family.
—Kitty McCue, St. Louis Park, MN

Takes: 20 min. • **Makes:** 6 servings

- 1 **large egg**
- 2 **tsp. honey**
- 2 **cups crushed Ritz crackers (about 45 to 50)**
- ½ **tsp. salt**
- 1½ **lbs. walleye fillets**
- ⅓ **to ½ cup canola oil**
  Optional: Lemon wedge and minced fresh parsley

1. In a shallow bowl, beat egg; add honey. In a shallow dish, combine crackers and salt. Dip fish in the egg mixture, then in cracker mixture; turn until coated.

2. In a cast-iron or other heavy skillet, cook fillets in oil over medium heat until golden and fish flakes easily with a fork, 3-5 minutes on each side. If desired, top with parsley and serve with lemon wedges.

3 oz. cooked fish: 389 cal., 22g fat (3g sat. fat), 133mg chol., 514mg sod., 23g carb. (5g sugars, 1g fiber), 25g pro.

BARLEY RISOTTO & BEEF STROGANOFF

I miss my Russian grandma's barley porridge and stroganoff, so I combined the two dishes. Cook the barley using the risotto method to keep the grains whole and irresistibly chewy.
—Tatiana Kireeva, New York, NY

- -

Prep: 25 min. + marinating • **Cook:** 45 min.
Makes: 4 servings

- 1 beef top sirloin steak
  (1 lb.), cut into 1-in. cubes
- 3 Tbsp. Cognac or brandy
- 3 Tbsp. butter, divided
- 1 Tbsp. all-purpose flour
- 2 cups chicken stock
- 1 tsp. Dijon mustard
- 1 medium beefsteak tomato
- 1 tsp. coarsely ground pepper
- ¼ tsp. salt
- 2 Tbsp. sour cream
- 1 medium onion, sliced

BARLEY RISOTTO

- 5 cups water
- 1 medium onion, finely chopped
- ½ tsp. salt
- 1 Tbsp. white wine, optional
- 1 cup medium pearl barley
- 2 Tbsp. minced fresh parsley

1. In a shallow dish, toss beef with Cognac. Refrigerate, covered, 2 hours. In a small saucepan, melt 1 Tbsp. butter over medium heat. Stir in flour until smooth; gradually whisk in chicken stock and mustard. Bring to a boil, stirring constantly; cook and stir until thickened, 3-5 minutes. Reduce heat; simmer, uncovered, 5 minutes.

2. Meanwhile, cut tomato into thick strips. In a large skillet over medium-low heat, cook tomato until softened, 3-5 minutes. Stir into mustard sauce; add coarsely ground pepper and salt. Stir in sour cream.

3. In same skillet, melt 1 Tbsp. butter over medium-high heat. Drain beef and pat dry. Add sliced onion and beef to pan; cook and stir until onions are softened and meat is no longer pink, 6-8 minutes. Add mustard sauce; reduce heat to low and simmer, uncovered, until the mixture is thickened, about 15 minutes. Keep warm until serving.

4. For risotto, bring water to a boil in a large saucepan. Reduce heat to maintain simmer. In another large saucepan, melt remaining butter over medium heat. Add chopped onion, salt and, if desired, white wine. Cook and stir until liquid evaporates. Add barley; toast in pan.

5. Stir hot water into barley 1 cup at a time, waiting until liquid has almost absorbed before adding more. Cook 15-20 minutes or until barley is softened but still slightly chewy; stir in parsley. Serve immediately with beef.

4 oz. cooked steak with 1 cup barley: 463 cal., 15g fat (8g sat. fat), 74mg chol., 859mg sod., 48g carb. (4g sugars, 9g fiber), 33g pro.

SPECIAL SLOW-COOKED BEEF

This hearty entree is easy to prepare for Sunday dinner. While the beef cooks, the chef has time to attend to other details. With mashed potatoes on the side, it's the sort of comforting meal everyone craves.
—Juli George, Grandville, MI

- -

Prep: 35 min. • **Cook:** 6 hours
Makes: 8 servings

- 1 **boneless beef chuck roast (3 lbs.), cubed**
- 1 **Tbsp. canola oil**
- 1 **Tbsp. Italian seasoning**
- 1 **tsp. salt**
- 1 **garlic clove, minced**
- ½ **cup sliced ripe olives, drained**
- ⅓ **cup oil-packed sun-dried tomatoes, drained and chopped**
- 1 **cup beef broth**
- ½ **cup fresh pearl onions, peeled**
- 1 **Tbsp. cornstarch**
- 2 **Tbsp. cold water**

1. In a large skillet, brown meat in oil in batches; drain. Transfer to a 5-qt. slow cooker. Sprinkle with Italian seasoning, salt and garlic; top with olives and tomatoes. Add broth and onions. Cook, covered, on low until meat is tender, 6-8 hours.
2. With a slotted spoon, remove beef and onions to a serving platter and keep warm. Pour cooking juices into a small saucepan; skim fat.
3. Combine cornstarch and water until smooth; gradually stir into cooking juices. Bring to a boil; cook and stir until thickened, about 2 minutes. Spoon over beef mixture.
1 serving: 332 cal., 20g fat (7g sat. fat), 111mg chol., 551mg sod., 3g carb. (0 sugars, 1g fiber), 34g pro.

CHICKEN DIVAN

This great recipe was given to me by a friend years ago, and it's been a family favorite ever since. My daughters enjoy making this dish in their own homes now, and they always get the same enthusiastic compliments I received!
—Mary Pat Lucia, North East, PA

- -

Prep: 20 min. • **Bake:** 35 min.
Makes: 10 servings

- ¼ **cup plus 1 Tbsp. butter, divided**
- ¼ **cup all-purpose flour**
- 1½ **cups half-and-half cream**
- ½ **cup cooking sherry or water**
- 2 **cans (10¾ oz. each) condensed cream of chicken soup, undiluted**
- 2 **pkg. (10 oz. each) frozen cut or chopped broccoli, thawed**
- 1 **cup cooked rice**
- 3 **to 4 cups cubed cooked chicken**
- 2 **cups shredded cheddar cheese**
- 1 **cup soft bread crumbs**

1. In a small saucepan, melt ¼ cup butter. Add flour, stirring until blended. Stir in the cream and cooking sherry or water; cook and stir until thickened and bubbly. Cook and stir 2 more minutes. Blend in the soup until smooth; remove from the heat and set aside.
2. Place broccoli in an ungreased 13x9-in. baking dish. Cover with rice and then half of the sauce. Top with chicken. Stir shredded cheese into remaining sauce; pour over the chicken.
3. Melt the remaining butter and toss with bread crumbs. Sprinkle over the casserole. Bake, uncovered, at 350° for 35-45 minutes or until heated through.
1 cup: 412 cal., 24g fat (12g sat. fat), 98mg chol., 798mg sod., 20g carb. (3g sugars, 3g fiber), 22g pro.

HONEY HOISIN CHICKEN & POTATOES

When I was young, Tutu (my grandma) cooked up this blend of Asian and American flavors. The potatoes are delicious drizzled with pan juices.
—Janet Yee, Phoenix, AZ

- -

Prep: 10 min. • **Bake:** 50 min.
Makes: 4 servings

- 4 medium Yukon Gold potatoes (about 1¾ lbs.), cut into 1-in. pieces
- 1 large onion, cut into 1-in. pieces
- ½ cup hoisin sauce
- 3 Tbsp. honey
- ½ tsp. salt, divided
- ½ tsp. pepper, divided
- 4 bone-in chicken thighs (about 1½ lbs.)

1. Preheat oven to 400°. Place potatoes and onion in a greased 13x9-in. baking pan. In a small bowl, mix hoisin, honey, ¼ tsp. salt and ¼ tsp. pepper; add to potato mixture and toss to coat.

2. Place chicken over vegetables; sprinkle with remaining salt and pepper. Roast for 50-60 minutes or until potatoes are tender and a thermometer inserted in chicken reads 170°-175°, basting occasionally with pan juices.

1 chicken thigh with 1 cup potato mixture and 3 Tbsp. sauce: 561 cal., 16g fat (4g sat. fat), 82mg chol., 910mg sod., 75g carb. (27g sugars, 6g fiber), 29g pro.

TRADITIONAL LASAGNA

My family tasted this rich lasagna at a friend's home on Christmas Eve, and it became our holiday tradition, too. My sister's Italian in-laws request it often.
—Lorri Foockle, Granville, IL

- -

Prep: 30 min. + simmering
Bake: 70 min. + standing
Makes: 12 servings

- 1 **lb. ground beef**
- ¾ **lb. bulk pork sausage**
- 3 **cans (8 oz. each) tomato sauce**
- 2 **cans (6 oz. each) tomato paste**
- 2 **garlic cloves, minced**
- 2 **tsp. sugar**
- 1 **tsp. Italian seasoning**
- ½ **to 1 tsp. salt**
- ¼ **to ½ tsp. pepper**
- 3 **large eggs**
- 3 **Tbsp. minced fresh parsley**
- 3 **cups 4% small-curd cottage cheese**
- 1 **carton (8 oz.) ricotta cheese**
- ½ **cup grated Parmesan cheese**
- 9 **lasagna noodles, cooked and drained**
- 6 **slices provolone cheese (about 6 oz.)**
- 3 **cups shredded part-skim mozzarella cheese, divided**

1. In a large skillet over medium heat, cook and crumble beef and sausage until no longer pink; drain. Add next 7 ingredients. Bring to a boil. Reduce the heat; simmer, uncovered, 1 hour, stirring occasionally. Adjust seasoning with additional salt and pepper, if desired.

2. Meanwhile, in a large bowl, lightly beat eggs. Add parsley; stir in cottage cheese, ricotta and Parmesan cheese.

3. Preheat oven to 375°. Spread 1 cup meat sauce in an ungreased 13x9-in. baking dish. Layer with 3 noodles, provolone cheese, 2 cups cottage cheese mixture, 1 cup mozzarella, 3 noodles, 2 cups meat sauce, remaining cottage cheese mixture and 1 cup mozzarella. Top with remaining noodles, meat sauce and mozzarella (dish will be full).

4. Cover; bake 50 minutes. Uncover; bake until heated through, 20 minutes. Let stand 15 minutes before cutting.

1 piece: 503 cal., 27g fat (13g sat. fat), 136mg chol., 1208mg sod., 30g carb. (9g sugars, 2g fiber), 36g pro.

TEST KITCHEN TIP

Want to add mushrooms or onions? Before adding any vegetable to your lasagna, it's best to cook it first. Be sure to strain out any excess liquid from the cooking process. Not doing so might make your lasagna a bit watery.

BEST EVER MAC & CHEESE

To make this amazing mac, I make a sauce loaded with three different cheeses to toss with the noodles. When baked, it's ooey, gooey and cheesy good. And don't get me started on the crunchy topping!
—Beth Jacobson, Milwaukee, WI

- -

Prep: 40 min. • **Bake:** 10 min.
Makes: 12 servings

1 pkg. (16 oz.) uncooked elbow macaroni
4 slices hearty white bread (4 oz.), torn into large pieces
6 Tbsp. butter, cubed and divided
½ cup grated Parmesan cheese
1 tsp. salt, divided
1 tsp. pepper, divided
¼ cup finely chopped onion
1 tsp. ground mustard
¼ tsp. cayenne pepper
¼ cup all-purpose flour
3 cups whole milk
2 cups half-and-half cream
1 cup (4 oz.) cubed process cheese (Velveeta)
1 block (8 oz.) sharp cheddar cheese, shredded
1 block (8 oz.) Monterey Jack cheese, shredded
1 tsp. Worcestershire sauce

1. Preheat oven to 400°. In a stockpot or Dutch oven, cook pasta according to package directions for al dente; drain and return to pan. Pulse bread, 2 Tbsp. butter, Parmesan, ½ tsp. salt and ½ tsp. pepper in a food processor until coarsely ground.

2. Meanwhile, in a large skillet over medium heat, melt remaining butter. Add onions and cook until tender, about 3 minutes. Add ground mustard and cayenne; stir until blended. Stir in flour until smooth, about 3 minutes. Slowly whisk in milk and cream; bring to a boil. Reduce heat to medium-low; simmer, stirring constantly, until thickened, about 5 minutes. Remove from heat; stir in Velveeta. Slowly add remaining cheeses a handful at a time, stirring until cheese is melted. Add Worcestershire and remaining salt and pepper. Pour over the pasta; toss to coat.

3. Transfer to a greased 13x9-in baking dish. Sprinkle bread crumbs over top of the casserole. Bake until topping is golden brown and sauce is bubbly, 10-12 minutes.

1 cup: 762 cal., 43g fat (25g sat. fat), 134mg chol., 1138mg sod., 61g carb. (10g sugars, 3g fiber), 32g pro.

TWIST UP THE TOPPING

Substitute any (or all) of the following for the bread crumb topping:
- 2 cups coarsely crushed pork rinds
- 2 cups coarsely crushed potato chips
- 2 cups coarsely crushed Ritz crackers

GERMAN BEEF

I like to serve this slow-cooked entree with potato pancakes and vegetables. Crushed gingersnaps, lemon and vinegar give the marinated slow-cooked beef and gravy their appetizing sweet-sour flavor.
—Susan Garoutte, Georgetown, TX

- -

Prep: 10 min. + marinating
Cook: 6 hours 10 min. • **Makes:** 12 servings

1½ cups water, divided
1¼ cups cider vinegar, divided
2 large onions, sliced, divided
1 medium lemon, sliced
15 whole cloves, divided
6 bay leaves, divided
6 whole peppercorns
2 Tbsp. sugar
2 tsp. salt
1 beef sirloin tip roast
   (3 lbs.), cut in half
¼ tsp. pepper
12 gingersnap cookies, crumbled

1. In a large shallow dish, combine 1 cup water, 1 cup vinegar, half of the onions, sliced lemon, 10 whole cloves, 4 bay leaves, peppercorns, sugar and salt; mix well. Add roast. Turn to coat; cover and refrigerate overnight, turning occasionally.

2. Drain and discard marinade. Place roast in a 5-qt. slow cooker; add pepper and remaining water, vinegar, onions, cloves and bay leaves. Cover and cook on low until meat is tender, 6-8 hours.

3. Remove roast and keep warm. Discard bay leaves. Stir in gingersnaps. Cover and cook on high for 10-15 minutes or until gravy is thickened. Slice roast; serve with the gravy.

3 oz. cooked beef: 214 cal., 7g fat (2g sat. fat), 71mg chol., 495mg sod., 12g carb. (0 sugars, 1g fiber), 26g pro. **Diabetic exchanges:** 3 lean meat, ½ starch.

GREAT-GRANDMA'S ITALIAN MEATBALLS

A classic Italian dish isn't complete without homemade meatballs, but this versatile recipe can also be used in any dish that stars meatballs.
—Audrey Colantino, Winchester, MA

- -

Prep: 30 min. • **Bake:** 20 min.
Makes: 8 servings

- 2 tsp. olive oil
- 1 medium onion, chopped
- 3 garlic cloves, minced
- ¾ cup seasoned bread crumbs
- ½ cup grated Parmesan cheese
- 2 large eggs, lightly beaten
- 1 tsp. each dried basil, oregano and parsley flakes
- ¾ tsp. salt
- 1 lb. lean ground turkey
- 1 lb. lean ground beef (90% lean)
  Optional: Hot cooked pasta and pasta sauce

1. Preheat oven to 375°. In a small skillet, heat oil over medium-high heat. Add onion; cook and stir until tender, 3-4 minutes. Add garlic; cook 1 minute longer. Cool slightly.
2. In a large bowl, combine bread crumbs, cheese, eggs, seasonings and onion mixture. Add turkey and beef; mix lightly but thoroughly. Shape into 1½-in. balls.
3. Place meatballs on a rack coated with cooking spray in a 15x10x1-in. baking pan. Bake until lightly browned and cooked through, 18-22 minutes. If desired, serve with pasta and pasta sauce.
1 serving: 271 cal., 13g fat (5g sat. fat), 125mg chol., 569mg sod., 10g carb. (1g sugars, 1g fiber), 27g pro. **Diabetic exchanges:** 4 lean meat, 1 fat, ½ starch.

FLOUNDER WITH SHRIMP STUFFING

The delicious shrimp-herb stuffing makes this flounder recipe special enough for company. But it really isn't hard to make. Our family enjoys it, so we eat it often.
—Marie Forte, Raritan, NJ

- -

Prep: 30 min. • **Bake:** 20 min.
Makes: 6 servings

STUFFING
- 6 Tbsp. butter, cubed
- 1 small onion, finely chopped
- ¼ cup finely chopped celery
- ¼ cup finely chopped green pepper
- 1 lb. uncooked shrimp, peeled, deveined and chopped
- ¼ cup beef broth
- 1 tsp. diced pimientos, drained
- 1 tsp. Worcestershire sauce
- ½ tsp. dill weed
- ½ tsp. minced chives
- ⅛ tsp. salt
- ⅛ tsp. cayenne pepper
- 1½ cups soft bread crumbs

FISH
- 6 flounder fillets (3 oz. each)
- 5 Tbsp. butter, melted
- 2 Tbsp. lemon juice
- 1 tsp. minced fresh parsley
- ½ tsp. paprika
  Salt and pepper to taste

1. Preheat oven to 375°. In a large skillet, melt butter. Add onion, celery and green pepper; saute until tender. Add shrimp; cook and stir until shrimp turn pink. Add broth, pimientos, Worcestershire sauce, dill, chives, salt and cayenne; heat through. Remove from heat; stir in bread crumbs.
2. Spoon about ½ cup stuffing onto each fillet; roll up. Place seam side down in a greased 13x9-in. baking dish. Drizzle with butter and lemon juice. Sprinkle with seasonings. Bake, uncovered, until fish flakes easily with a fork, 20-25 minutes.
1 stuffed fillet: 357 cal., 23g fat (14g sat. fat), 187mg chol., 476mg sod., 9g carb. (1g sugars, 1g fiber), 28g pro.

SWEET & SOUR PORK

My grandmother made this for me on Valentine's Day when I was a child. Now I make it for my children on Valentine's. I usually make brown rice or rice noodles and add thinly sliced bok choy to up the vegetable intake. I've never had leftovers.
—Barbara Hinterberger, Buffalo, NY

Prep: 20 min. • **Cook:** 15 min.
Makes: 4 servings

- 1 can (20 oz.) unsweetened pineapple chunks
- ⅓ cup water
- ⅓ cup cider vinegar
- 3 Tbsp. brown sugar
- 2 Tbsp. cornstarch
- 1 Tbsp. reduced-sodium soy sauce
- 1 tsp. Worcestershire sauce
- ½ tsp. salt
- 1 lb. pork tenderloin, cut into ½-in. pieces
- 1 tsp. paprika
- 1 Tbsp. canola oil
- 1 medium green pepper, thinly sliced
- 1 small onion, thinly sliced
- 2 cups hot cooked brown rice

1. Drain pineapple, reserving ⅔ cup juice; set pineapple aside. In a small bowl, mix water, vinegar, brown sugar, cornstarch, soy sauce, Worcestershire sauce, salt and reserved pineapple juice until smooth; set aside.

2. Sprinkle pork with paprika. In a large skillet coated with cooking spray, brown pork in oil.

3. Stir cornstarch mixture and add to pan. Bring to a boil; cook and stir 1 minute or until thickened. Add green pepper, onion and pineapple. Reduce heat; simmer, covered, 6-8 minutes or until pork is tender. Serve with rice.

1¼ cups pork mixture with ½ cup cooked rice: 428 cal., 9g fat (2g sat. fat), 63mg chol., 519mg sod., 61g carb. (30g sugars, 4g fiber), 26g pro.

COMPANY POTPIE

Here's our smart spin on potpie, filled with turkey, autumn vegetables and a creamy herb sauce. Best of all, there's no crust to make—just top with conveniently prepared phyllo dough.
—*Taste of Home* Test Kitchen

- -

Prep: 1 hour • **Bake:** 10 min.
Makes: 6 servings

- ½ lb. sliced baby portobello mushrooms
- 2 shallots, chopped
- 2 tsp. olive oil
- 2 cups cubed peeled butternut squash
- 1 cup chopped sweet red pepper
- ½ cup sliced fennel bulb
- 2 cups reduced-sodium chicken broth, divided
- ⅓ cup all-purpose flour
- ½ cup 2% milk
- 3 cups cubed cooked turkey breast
- 2 Tbsp. sherry or additional reduced-sodium chicken broth
- 1 tsp. rubbed sage
- ½ tsp. salt
- ½ tsp. dried thyme
- ¼ tsp. pepper
- 10 sheets phyllo dough (14x9-in. size) Refrigerated butter-flavored spray

1. In a large skillet, saute mushrooms and shallots in oil until tender. Add the squash, red pepper and fennel; saute 5 minutes longer. Add ¼ cup broth. Cover and cook over medium-low heat until vegetables are tender, about 15 minutes.

2. Sprinkle flour over vegetables; cook and stir for 1 minute. Gradually add milk and remaining broth. Bring to a boil; cook and stir until thickened, 1-2 minutes. Stir in the turkey, sherry and seasonings; heat through. Transfer to a 2-qt. baking dish coated with cooking spray.

3. Stack all 10 phyllo sheets. Roll up, starting with a long side; cut into ½-in. strips. Place strips in a large bowl and toss to separate; spritz with butter-flavored spray. Arrange over turkey mixture; spritz again. Bake, uncovered, at 425° until golden brown, 10-15 minutes.

1 cup: 275 cal., 4g fat (1g sat. fat), 62mg chol., 544mg sod., 33g carb. (6g sugars, 5g fiber), 28g pro. **Diabetic exchanges:** 3 lean meat, 2 starch.

TEST KITCHEN TIP
Fennel is an aromatic herb with a large pale green bulb, celery-like stems and feathery leaves. Sliced thinly, the fennel bulb can be used in all sorts of baked dishes as well as salads.

PRIME RIB WITH FRESH HERB SAUCE

Nothing says special occasion like a perfectly seasoned prime rib. Savory, succulent, tender, it's the ideal choice when you want to share something truly divine.
—Tonya Burkhard, Palm Coast, FL

- -

Prep: 40 min. • **Bake:** 3¼ hours + standing
Makes: 10 servings (1½ cups sauce)

- 1 **bone-in beef rib roast (6 to 8 lbs.)**
- 1 **tsp. kosher salt**
- 1 **tsp. freshly ground pepper**
- 3 **cups water**
- 2 **small onions, halved**
- 7 **garlic cloves, crushed**
- 5 **fresh sage sprigs**
- 5 **fresh thyme sprigs**
- 2 **bay leaves**

SAUCE

- 2 **Tbsp. butter**
- 2 **shallots, thinly sliced**
- 4 **garlic cloves, thinly sliced**
- 5 **fresh sage sprigs**
- 5 **fresh thyme sprigs**
- 2 **bay leaves**
- 1 **Tbsp. all-purpose flour**
- 2 **Tbsp. cracked black pepper**
- ¼ **tsp. kosher salt**
- 1½ **to 2½ cups beef stock, divided**
- ½ **cup dry red wine or beef stock**
- ½ **tsp. red wine vinegar**
  Fresh thyme sprigs, optional

1. Preheat oven to 450°. Place roast in a shallow roasting pan, fat side up; rub with salt and pepper. Add 1 cup water, onions, garlic and herbs to roasting pan. Roast 15 minutes.

2. Reduce oven setting to 325°. Roast 3-3½ hours longer or until meat reaches desired doneness (for medium-rare, a thermometer should read 135°; medium, 140°; medium-well, 145°), adding 1 cup water every hour.

3. For sauce, in a large saucepan, heat butter over medium-high heat. Add shallots; cook and stir 5-6 minutes or until tender. Add garlic and herbs; cook 1 minute longer. Stir in flour, pepper and salt until blended. Gradually stir in 1½ cups stock. Remove from heat.

4. Remove roast to a serving platter; tent with foil. Let stand 15 minutes before carving. Meanwhile, strain any pan juices through a sieve into a measuring cup; discard onions and herbs. Skim fat from pan juices. If necessary, add additional stock to pan juices to measure 1 cup. Add to the shallot mixture.

5. Place roasting pan over 2 burners; add wine. Bring to a boil; cook 2-3 minutes, stirring to loosen browned bits from pan. Add to the sauce. Bring to a boil, stirring occasionally; cook until mixture is reduced to about 1½ cups, 10-15 minutes.

6. Stir in vinegar; strain, discarding shallots and herbs. Serve with roast and, if desired, garnish with thyme.

5 oz. cooked beef with 2 Tbsp. sauce: 353 cal., 20g fat (9g sat. fat), 6mg chol., 430mg sod., 2g carb. (1g sugars, 0g fiber), 37g pro.

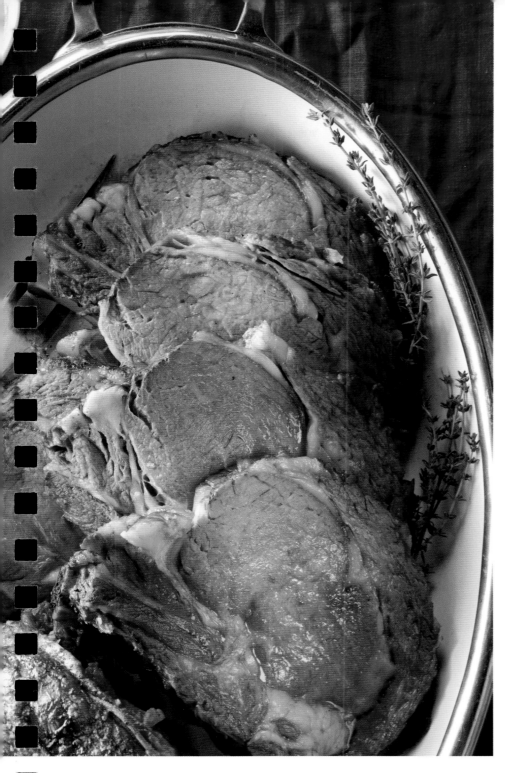

OLD-WORLD STUFFED PORK CHOPS

Years ago, a relative ran a restaurant in downtown Milwaukee, where several well-known German restaurants still operate. This is one of the recipes she developed. The savory stuffing and juicy pork chops are always a hit.
—Jeanne Schuyler, Wauwatosa, WI

- -

Prep: 15 min. • **Bake:** 1 hour
Makes: 4 servings

    4   pork chops (½ in. thick)
    1   to 2 Tbsp. canola oil
        Salt and pepper to taste
    3   cups dry unseasoned bread cubes
    1   can (16 oz.) cream-style corn
    1   large egg, lightly beaten
    1   tsp. grated onion
    ½   tsp. rubbed sage
    ½   tsp. dried basil
    ½   tsp. salt
    ¼   tsp. pepper

In a skillet, brown pork chops in oil on both sides; sprinkle with salt and pepper. Meanwhile, in a bowl, combine remaining ingredients and mix well. Alternate the pork chops and stuffing lengthwise in a greased 3-qt. or 11x7-in. baking dish. Bake, uncovered, at 350° for 1 hour.

1 serving: 591 cal., 25g fat (8g sat. fat), 158mg chol., 995mg sod., 50g carb. (6g sugars, 3g fiber), 45g pro.

HAM WITH PINEAPPLE SAUCE

We serve this dish during the holidays because everyone is crazy about it. But we also enjoy it all year long because it's super simple to prepare.
—Terry Roberts, Yorktown, VA

Prep: 10 min. • **Cook:** 6 hours
Makes: 12 servings

- 1 fully cooked boneless ham (4 to 5 lbs.)
- 1 Tbsp. cornstarch
- 2 Tbsp. lemon juice
- 1 cup packed brown sugar
- 1 Tbsp. yellow mustard
- ¼ tsp. salt
- 1 can (20 oz.) unsweetened crushed pineapple, undrained

1. Place ham in a 5-qt. slow cooker. In a small saucepan, mix cornstarch and lemon juice until smooth. Stir in the remaining ingredients; bring to a boil, stirring occasionally. Pour over ham, covering completely.
2. Cook, covered, on low 6-8 hours (a thermometer inserted in ham should read at least 140°).
Note: This recipe is not recommended for a spiral-sliced ham.
4 oz. ham with ¼ cup sauce: 262 cal., 6g fat (2g sat. fat), 77mg chol., 1638mg sod., 27g carb. (25g sugars, 0 fiber), 28g pro.

TURKEY A LA KING

This is a smart way to use up leftover turkey. It's so quick and easy, you might want to make a double batch!
—Mary Gaylord, Balsam Lake, WI

Takes: 25 min. • **Makes:** 6 servings

- 1 medium onion, chopped
- ¾ cup sliced celery
- ¼ cup diced green pepper
- ¼ cup butter, cubed
- ¼ cup all-purpose flour
- 1 tsp. sugar
- 1½ cups chicken broth
- ¼ cup half-and-half cream
- 3 cups cubed cooked turkey or chicken
- 1 can (4 oz.) sliced mushrooms, drained
- 6 slices bread, toasted

1. In a large skillet, saute the onion, celery and green pepper in butter until tender. Stir in flour and sugar until a paste forms.
2. Gradually stir in the broth. Bring to a boil; boil until thickened, about 1 minute. Reduce heat. Add cream, turkey and mushrooms; heat through. Serve with toast.
1 serving: 297 cal., 13g fat (7g sat. fat), 98mg chol., 591mg sod., 21g carb. (4g sugars, 2g fiber), 24g pro.

SHORT RIB COBBLER

This supper is as down-home as it gets. It was my family's love of beef stew and biscuits that inspired me to create this savory meal. After years of making the two separately, I put the biscuits on top of the stew like a cobbler and this was the result!
—Janine Talley, Orlando, FL

- -

Prep: 45 min. • **Bake:** 3 hours
Makes: 8 servings

- ½ cup plus 3 Tbsp.
     all-purpose flour, divided
- 1¼ tsp. salt, divided
- ½ tsp. pepper
- 2 lbs. well-trimmed boneless beef
     short ribs, cut into 1½-in. pieces
- 5 Tbsp. olive oil, divided
- 1 large onion, chopped
- 1 medium carrot, chopped
- 1 celery rib, chopped
- 1 garlic clove, minced
- 2 Tbsp. tomato paste
- 5 cups beef stock
- 1 cup dry red wine or
     additional beef stock
- 1 tsp. poultry seasoning
- 1 bay leaf
- 1 pkg. (14 oz.) frozen pearl
     onions, thawed
- 4 medium carrots, cut
     into 2-in. pieces

COBBLER TOPPING
- 2 cups biscuit/baking mix
- ⅔ cup 2% milk
     Fresh thyme leaves

1. Preheat oven to 350°. In a shallow bowl, mix ½ cup flour, ¾ tsp. salt and pepper. Dip short ribs in flour mixture to coat all sides; shake off excess.
2. In a Dutch oven, heat 3 Tbsp. oil over medium heat. Brown the beef in batches. Remove from pan.
3. In same pan, heat remaining oil over medium heat. Add onion, chopped carrot and celery; cook and stir until tender, 2-3 minutes. Add garlic; cook 1 minute longer. Stir in tomato paste and remaining flour until blended. Gradually stir in stock and wine until smooth. Return beef to pan; stir in poultry seasoning, bay leaf and remaining salt. Bring to a boil.
4. Bake, covered, 1¾ hours. Stir in pearl onions and carrot pieces. Bake, covered, 30-45 minutes longer or until the beef and onions are tender. Skim the fat and remove the bay leaf.
5. In a small bowl, mix biscuit mix and milk just until a soft dough forms. Drop by scant ¼ cupfuls over beef mixture. Bake, uncovered, until topping is golden brown, 40-45 minutes longer. Sprinkle with thyme.
1 serving: 452 cal., 22g fat (6g sat. fat), 48mg chol., 929mg sod., 40g carb. (9g sugars, 3g fiber), 23g pro.

HAM & CHEESE PASTA

Whenever we had leftover ham, we could look forward to my mother preparing her yummy, comforting pasta. Horseradish gives it a nice tangy taste. I quickened the preparation by using process cheese instead of making a cheese sauce from scratch. Now my kids love it, too.
—Karen Kopp, Indianapolis, IN

Prep: 15 min. • **Bake:** 30 min.
Makes: 4 servings

8	oz. uncooked medium pasta shells
1	lb. process cheese (Velveeta), cubed
½	cup whole milk
2	Tbsp. ketchup
1	Tbsp. prepared horseradish
2	cups cubed fully cooked ham
1	pkg. (8 oz.) frozen peas, thawed

1. Cook pasta according to the package directions. Meanwhile, in a microwave-safe bowl, combine cheese and milk. Cover and microwave on high for 2 minutes; stir. Heat 1-2 minutes longer or until smooth, stirring twice. Stir in ketchup and horseradish until well blended.

2. Drain pasta and place in a large bowl. Stir in the ham, peas and cheese sauce.

3. Transfer to a greased 2-qt. baking dish. Cover and bake at 350° for 30-35 minutes or until bubbly.

1 cup: 761 cal., 36g fat (20g sat. fat), 114mg chol., 2425mg sod., 63g carb. (16g sugars, 5g fiber), 47g pro.

MEAT SAUCE FOR SPAGHETTI

Here's a hearty meat sauce that turns ordinary spaghetti and garlic bread into a feast. If you don't have spaghetti noodles, no problem! I've successfully swirled up this sauce with nearly every pasta shape in my pantry.
—Mary Tallman, Arbor Vitae, WI

Prep: 30 min. • **Cook:** 8 hours
Makes: 9 servings

- 1 lb. ground beef
- 1 lb. bulk Italian sausage
- 1 can (28 oz.) crushed tomatoes, undrained
- 1 medium green pepper, chopped
- 1 medium onion, chopped
- 2 medium carrots, finely chopped
- 1 cup water
- 1 can (8 oz.) tomato sauce
- 1 can (6 oz.) tomato paste
- 1 Tbsp. brown sugar
- 1 Tbsp. Italian seasoning
- 2 garlic cloves, minced
- ½ tsp. salt
- ¼ tsp. pepper
  Hot cooked spaghetti

1. In a large skillet, cook beef and sausage over medium heat until meat is no longer pink; drain.

2. Transfer to a 5-qt. slow cooker. Stir in the tomatoes, green pepper, onion, carrots, water, tomato sauce, tomato paste, brown sugar, Italian seasoning, garlic, salt and pepper. Cover and cook on low until bubbly, 8-10 hours. Serve with spaghetti.

1 cup sauce: 286 cal., 17g fat (6g sat. fat), 58mg chol., 767mg sod., 17g carb. (9g sugars, 4g fiber), 18g pro.

SPECIAL-OCCASION BEEF BOURGUIGNON

I've found many rich and satisfying variations for beef bourguignon, including an intriguing peasant version that used beef cheeks for the meat and a rustic table wine. To make this stew gluten-free, use white rice flour instead of all-purpose.
—Leo Cotnoir, Johnson City, NY

Prep: 50 min. • **Bake:** 2 hours
Makes: 8 servings

- 4   bacon strips, chopped
- 1   beef sirloin tip roast (2 lbs.), cut into 1½-in. cubes and patted dry
- ¼   cup all-purpose flour
- ½   tsp. salt
- ½   tsp. pepper
- 1   Tbsp. canola oil
- 2   medium onions, chopped
- 2   medium carrots, coarsely chopped
- ½   lb. medium fresh mushrooms, quartered
- 4   garlic cloves, minced
- 1   Tbsp. tomato paste
- 2   cups dry red wine
- 1   cup beef stock
- 2   bay leaves
- ½   tsp. dried thyme
- 8   oz. uncooked egg noodles
     Minced fresh parsley

1. Preheat oven to 325°. In a Dutch oven, cook bacon over medium-low heat until crisp, stirring occasionally. Remove with a slotted spoon, reserving drippings; drain on paper towels.

2. In batches, brown beef in drippings over medium-high heat; remove from pan. Toss with flour, salt and pepper.

3. In same pan, heat 1 Tbsp. oil over medium heat; saute onions, carrots and mushrooms 4-5 minutes or until onions are tender. Add garlic and tomato paste; cook and stir 1 minute. Add wine and stock, stirring to loosen browned bits from pan. Add herbs, bacon and beef; bring to a boil.

4. Transfer to oven; bake, covered, until meat is tender, 2-2¼ hours. Remove the bay leaves.

5. To serve, cook noodles according to package directions; drain. Serve stew with noodles; sprinkle with parsley.

Freeze option: Freeze cooled stew in freezer containers. To use, partially thaw in refrigerator overnight. Heat through in a saucepan, stirring occasionally and adding a little stock or broth if necessary.

⅔ cup stew with ⅔ cup noodles: 422 cal., 14g fat (4g sat. fat), 105mg chol., 357mg sod., 31g carb. (4g sugars, 2g fiber), 31g pro.
Diabetic exchanges: 4 lean meat, 2 fat, 1½ starch, 1 vegetable.

GRANDMA'S FAVORITE

SUNDAY DINNERS

Gather around the table and settle in for the kind of meal made famous at Grandma's house. Here, you'll find complete lineups for casual yet cheery suppers as well as impressive menus sure to make memories for years to come.

MENU

CHICKEN DINNER

Roast Chicken with
Creole Stuffing, p. 267

Oven-Roasted
Asparagus, p. 267

Special Radicchio-
Spinach Salad, p. 268

Perfect Dinner
Rolls, p. 268

Honey Pear
Cheesecake, p. 269

ROAST CHICKEN WITH CREOLE STUFFING

I've used this recipe ever since I roasted my first chicken. Our whole family looks forward to it. The combination of shrimp, sausage, ham, vegetables and seasonings makes the stuffing unique and delicious.
—Ruth Bates, Temecula, CA

- -

Prep: 50 min. • **Bake:** 3 hours
Makes: 8 servings (8 cups stuffing)

- 1½ cups uncooked brown rice
- 2 Italian sausage links
- 2 Tbsp. vegetable oil
- 1 cup chopped onion
- 5 garlic cloves, minced
- ½ cup diced green pepper
- ½ cup diced sweet red pepper
- 1 can (14½ oz.) diced tomatoes, undrained
- 1 Tbsp. lemon juice
- 1 tsp. dried basil
- ½ tsp. sugar
- ½ tsp. hot pepper sauce
- ½ tsp. chicken bouillon granules
- ¼ tsp. chili powder
- ¼ tsp. pepper
- ⅛ tsp. dried thyme
- 1¼ tsp. salt, divided
- 1 cup diced fully cooked ham
- 1 cup cooked small shrimp, peeled and deveined, optional
- 3 Tbsp. minced fresh parsley
- 1 roasting chicken (5 to 6 lbs.)
- ½ tsp. paprika
  Dash pepper

1. In a large saucepan, cook rice according to the package directions. Meanwhile, in a skillet, cook the sausage links in oil until a thermometer reads 160°. Remove the sausages, reserving drippings. When cool enough to handle, cut the sausages in half lengthwise, then into ¼-in. pieces; set aside.

2. Saute the onion, garlic and peppers in drippings until tender, about 4 minutes. Add the diced tomatoes, lemon juice, basil, sugar, hot pepper sauce, chicken bouillon, chili powder, pepper, thyme and 1 tsp. salt; cook and stir for 5 minutes. Add to the cooked rice. Stir in ham, shrimp, if desired, parsley and sausage; mix lightly.

3. Just before baking, stuff the chicken with about 3½ cups stuffing. Place remaining stuffing in a greased 1½-qt. baking dish; cover and refrigerate. Place chicken on a rack in a roasting pan; tie the drumsticks together. Combine paprika, pepper and remaining salt; rub over chicken.

4. Bake, uncovered, at 350° for 1½ hours, basting every 30 minutes. Cover and bake 1½ hours longer or until juices run clear. Bake the additional stuffing for the last 40 minutes of baking time, uncovering during the last 10 minutes.

1 serving: 472 cal., 24g fat (6g sat. fat), 106mg chol., 766mg sod., 27g carb. (3g sugars, 2g fiber), 36g pro.

OVEN-ROASTED ASPARAGUS

Asparagus never tasted so good! Simply seasoned with butter and green onions, they taste fresh and keep their bright green color, too. They're so good, you might want to make extra.
—Jody Fisher, Stewartstown, PA

- -

Takes: 20 min. • **Makes:** 6 servings

- 2 lbs. fresh asparagus, trimmed
- ¼ cup butter, melted
- 2 to 4 green onions, chopped
- ½ tsp. salt

1. Preheat oven to 425°. Place asparagus in a 15x10x1-in. pan. Toss with melted butter and green onions; spread evenly. Sprinkle with salt.

2. Roast until crisp-tender, 10-15 minutes.

1 serving: 87 cal., 8g fat (5g sat. fat), 20mg chol., 266mg sod., 4g carb. (1g sugars, 1g fiber), 2g pro.

SPECIAL RADICCHIO-SPINACH SALAD

When you hear of mint, chipotle pepper and honey blended together, you may wonder how it will taste. Well, prepare to be amazed. My spicy-sweet salad is simply delicious and a lovely change of pace.
—Roxanne Chan, Albany, CA

- -

Takes: 20 min. • **Makes:** 12 servings

- 6 cups fresh baby spinach
- 1 head radicchio, torn
- 2 cups fresh raspberries
- ½ cup raisins
- ¼ cup pine nuts, toasted
- ¼ cup thinly sliced red onion
- ¼ cup minced fresh mint
- 3 Tbsp. lime juice
- 2 Tbsp. olive oil
- 2 tsp. honey
- 1½ to 3 tsp. chopped chipotle pepper in adobo sauce
- ¼ tsp. salt
- ½ cup crumbled feta cheese

In a large salad bowl, combine the first 7 ingredients. In a small saucepan, combine the lime juice, oil, honey, chipotle pepper and salt. Cook and stir until blended and heated through. Immediately pour over salad; toss to coat. Sprinkle with cheese.
¾ cup: 92 cal., 5g fat (1g sat. fat), 3mg chol., 117mg sod., 11g carb. (6g sugars, 3g fiber), 3g pro. **Diabetic exchanges:** 1 vegetable, 1 fat, ½ fruit.

PERFECT DINNER ROLLS

These rolls melt in your mouth. I loved them as a child, and I'm happy to bake them for my kids because I know I am creating those same wonderful memories my mom made for me!
—Gayleen Grote, Battleview, ND

- -

Prep: 30 min. + rising • **Bake:** 15 min.
Makes: 2 dozen

- 1 Tbsp. active dry yeast
- 2¼ cups warm water (110° to 115°)
- ⅓ cup sugar
- ⅓ cup shortening
- ¼ cup powdered nondairy creamer
- 2¼ tsp. salt
- 6 to 7 cups bread flour

1. In a large bowl, dissolve yeast in warm water. Add the sugar, shortening, creamer, salt and 5 cups flour. Beat until smooth. Stir in enough remaining flour to form a soft dough (dough will be sticky).
2. Turn onto a floured surface; knead until smooth and elastic, 6-8 minutes. Place in a bowl coated with cooking spray, turning once to coat the top. Cover and let rise in a warm place until doubled, about 1 hour.
3. Punch dough down. Turn onto a lightly floured surface; divide into 24 pieces. Shape each into a roll. Place 2 in. apart on baking sheets coated with cooking spray. Cover and let rise until doubled, about 30 minutes.
4. Meanwhile, preheat oven to 350°. Bake until lightly browned, 12-15 minutes. Remove from pans to wire racks.
1 roll: 142 cal., 3g fat (1g sat. fat), 0 chol., 222mg sod., 25g carb. (3g sugars, 1g fiber), 4g pro.

HONEY PEAR CHEESECAKE

We grow pear trees, so I'm always dabbling in pear desserts. I like to stir a little bit of crystallized ginger into the filling.
—Nancy Zimmerman,
Cape May Court House, NJ

- -

Prep: 25 min. • **Bake:** 1½ hours + chilling
Makes: 12 servings

- 1½ cups crushed gingersnap cookies (about 30)
- ¼ cup sugar
- 4 to 6 Tbsp. butter, melted

FILLING
- 3 pkg. (8 oz. each) cream cheese, softened
- 1 cup honey, divided
- 1 Tbsp. lemon juice
- 2 tsp. minced fresh gingerroot
- 4 large eggs, lightly beaten
- 3 peeled and chopped medium pears (about 1½ cups), divided
- ⅓ cup golden raisins
- 1 Tbsp. butter
- 1 cup chopped pecans, toasted

1. Preheat oven to 325°. Securely wrap a double thickness of heavy-duty foil (about 18 in. square) around and under a greased 9-in. springform pan. In a bowl, combine the crushed gingersnaps and sugar; stir in 4 Tbsp. butter, adding more as necessary. Press onto bottom and 1½ in. up sides of prepared pan.

2. Beat cream cheese until fluffy, gradually adding ⅔ cup honey, lemon juice and minced ginger. Add eggs; beat on low speed just until blended. Fold in 1 cup chopped pears and raisins. Pour into crust. Place springform pan in a larger baking pan; add 1 in. of hot water to larger pan. Bake until the center is just set and top appears dull, 1½-1¾ hours. Remove from oven; remove springform from water bath.

3. Cool the cheesecake on a wire rack for 10 minutes. Loosen sides from pan with a knife; remove foil. Cool 1 hour longer. Refrigerate overnight, covering when completely cooled. Remove rim from pan.

4. In a large skillet, melt butter over medium heat. Add remaining honey and pears; cook and stir until pears are tender. Stir in the pecans. Top cake with pear-pecan mixture.

Note: To toast nuts, bake in a shallow pan in a 350° oven for 5-10 minutes or cook in a skillet over low heat until lightly browned, stirring occasionally.

1 slice: 552 cal., 36g fat (17g sat. fat), 142mg chol., 374mg sod., 54g carb. (40g sugars, 3g fiber), 8g pro.

TEST KITCHEN TIP

For this cheesecake, try using honey with a mild flavor, such as orange blossom, clover or alfalfa honey. This will help the flavor of the pears shine through a bit more. Speaking of which, try Bartlett pears in this recipe. Their flavor is stronger than most other pears and can stand up to the other tastes in this homey dessert.

CLASSIC COMFORTS

Traditional
Meat Loaf, p. 271

Roasted Vegetables
with Sage, p. 271

Five-Cheese
Rigatoni, p.272

Olive & Onion
Quick Bread, p. 273

Lemon Ginger
Icebox Cake, p.273

TRADITIONAL MEAT LOAF

Homemade meat loaf is a must-have comfort food. It freezes well, too, so we increase the recipe and stash a loaf aside for busy nights.
—Gail Graham, Maple Ridge, BC

Prep: 15 min. • **Bake:** 1 hour + standing
Makes: 6 servings

3	slices bread
1	large egg, lightly beaten
⅔	cup 2% milk
1	cup shredded cheddar cheese
1	medium onion, finely chopped
½	cup finely shredded carrot
1	tsp. salt
¼	tsp. pepper
1½	lbs. ground beef

GLAZE
¼	cup packed brown sugar
¼	cup ketchup
1	Tbsp. prepared mustard

1. Preheat oven to 350°. Tear bread into 2-in. pieces; place in a blender. Cover and pulse to form coarse crumbs; transfer to a large bowl. Stir in egg, milk, cheese, onion, carrot, salt and pepper. Add the beef; mix lightly but thoroughly. Transfer to a greased 9x5-in. loaf pan.
2. In a small bowl, mix glaze ingredients; spread over loaf. Bake 60-75 minutes or until a thermometer reads 160°. Let stand 10 minutes before slicing.
Freeze option: Bake meat loaf without glaze. Securely wrap cooled meat loaf in plastic wrap and foil, then freeze. To use, partially thaw meat loaf in refrigerator overnight. Prepare and spread glaze over top; reheat on a greased shallow baking pan in a preheated 350° oven until heated through and a thermometer inserted in center reads 165°.
1 slice: 394 cal., 21g fat (10g sat. fat), 128mg chol., 843mg sod., 23g carb. (15g sugars, 1g fiber), 28g pro.

ROASTED VEGETABLES WITH SAGE

When I can't decide what vegetable to serve, I just roast a bunch. That's how we boost our love of veggies at our house.
—Betty Fulks, Onia, AR

Prep: 20 min. • **Bake:** 35 min.
Makes: 8 servings

5	cups cubed peeled butternut squash
½	lb. fingerling potatoes (about 2 cups)
1	cup fresh Brussels sprouts, halved
1	cup fresh baby carrots
3	Tbsp. butter
1	Tbsp. minced fresh sage or 1 tsp. dried sage leaves
1	garlic clove, minced
½	tsp. salt

1. Preheat oven to 425°. Place vegetables in a large bowl. In a microwave, melt butter; stir in the remaining ingredients. Add to the vegetables and toss to coat.
2. Transfer to a greased 15x10x1-in. baking pan. Roast 35-45 minutes or until tender, stirring occasionally.
¾ cup: 122 cal., 5g fat (3g sat. fat), 11mg chol., 206mg sod., 20g carb. (4g sugars, 3g fiber), 2g pro. **Diabetic exchanges:** 1 starch, 1 fat.

FIVE-CHEESE RIGATONI

Who can resist cheesy pasta hot from the oven? This ooey-gooey rigatoni boasts a homemade creamy Swiss sauce that comes together in just a few minutes.
—Shirley Foltz, Dexter, KS

- -

Prep: 25 min. • **Bake:** 25 min.
Makes: 9 servings

- 1   **pkg. (16 oz.) rigatoni or large tube pasta**
- 2   **Tbsp. butter**
- 3   **Tbsp. all-purpose flour**
- 1   **tsp. salt**
- ½   **tsp. pepper**
- 2½ **cups whole milk**
- ½   **cup shredded Swiss cheese**
- ½   **cup shredded fontina cheese**
- ½   **cup shredded part-skim mozzarella cheese**
- ½   **cup grated Parmesan cheese, divided**
- ½   **cup grated Romano cheese, divided**

TEST KITCHEN TIP
To keep pasta from sticking together when cooking, use a large pot with plenty of water. Add a little cooking oil if desired (this also prevents boiling over).

1. Cook the rigatoni according to the package directions.
2. Preheat oven to 375°. In a large saucepan, melt butter. Stir in the flour, salt and pepper until smooth. Gradually stir in milk; bring to a boil. Cook and stir 1-2 minutes or until thickened. Stir in Swiss, fontina, mozzarella, ¼ cup Parmesan and ¼ cup Romano cheese until melted.

3. Drain rigatoni; stir in cheese sauce. Transfer to a greased 13x9-in. baking dish. Sprinkle with remaining Parmesan and Romano cheeses. Cover and bake for 20 minutes. Uncover; bake 5-10 minutes longer or until bubbly.
¾ cup: 362 cal., 14g fat (8g sat. fat), 40mg chol., 586mg sod., 42g carb. (5g sugars, 2g fiber), 18g pro.

OLIVE & ONION QUICK BREAD

I've been baking for over 50 years and I never get tired of trying new recipes for my family and friends. Baking actually relaxes me. I feel like an artist creating a masterpiece of love. This savory loaf also makes a great gift.
—Paula Marchesi, Lenhartsville, PA

- -

Prep: 15 min. • **Bake:** 45 min. + cooling
Makes: 1 loaf (12 slices)

- 1 Tbsp. canola oil
- 1 medium onion, finely chopped
- 2 cups all-purpose flour
- 1 Tbsp. minced fresh rosemary
- 1 tsp. baking soda
- ½ tsp. salt
- 2 large eggs, room temperature
- 1 cup buttermilk
- 2 Tbsp. butter, melted
- ¼ cup plus 2 Tbsp. sharp cheddar cheese, divided
- ¼ cup each chopped pitted green and ripe olives

1. Preheat oven to 350°. In a skillet, heat oil over medium-high heat. Add onion; cook and stir until tender, 2-3 minutes. Remove from heat.
2. In a large bowl, whisk the flour, rosemary, baking soda and salt. In another bowl, whisk the eggs, buttermilk and melted butter until blended. Add to flour mixture; stir just until moistened. Fold in ¼ cup cheese, olives and onion.
3. Transfer to a greased 8x4-in. loaf pan. Bake 40 minutes. Sprinkle remaining cheese over top. Bake until a toothpick inserted in the center comes out clean, 5-10 minutes longer. Cool in the pan 10 minutes before removing to a wire rack to cool.
1 slice: 150 cal., 6g fat (2g sat. fat), 41mg chol., 373mg sod., 18g carb. (1g sugars, 1g fiber), 5g pro.

LEMON GINGER ICEBOX CAKE

Everyone searches for grand desserts that have easy ingredients and minimal effort. My lemony ginger icebox cake is the answer. It's a real lifesaver.
—Suzanne Banfield, Basking Ridge, NJ

- -

Prep: 20 min. + chilling • **Makes:** 12 servings

- 1 pkg. (8 oz.) cream cheese, softened
- 2 tsp. grated lemon zest
- 1 jar (10 oz.) lemon curd
- 2 cups heavy whipping cream
- 2 pkg. (5¼ oz. each) thin ginger cookies
- 2 Tbsp. chopped crystallized ginger

1. In a large bowl, beat cream cheese and lemon zest until creamy. Beat in lemon curd until smooth. Gradually add the cream, beating on medium-high speed until soft peaks form.
2. Line bottom of an 8-in. square dish with 9 cookies; spread with about ⅔ cup cream cheese mixture. Repeat the layers 6 times. Sprinkle with crystallized ginger. Refrigerate, covered, 2 hours or overnight.
Note: This recipe was tested with Anna's Ginger Thins Swedish cookies.
1 piece: 521 cal., 31g fat (19g sat. fat), 93mg chol., 340mg sod., 54g carb. (34g sugars, 0 fiber), 4g pro.

PERFECT FOUR-CHEESE LASAGNA

Lasagna is one of my favorite meals, and this is the recipe I've been making since I was a teenager. It's a tantalizing combo of pasta, meat sauce, cheese (and more cheese) that really lives up to its name!
—Lauren Delaney-Wallace, Glen Carbon, IL

Prep: 25 min. • **Bake:** 50 min. + standing
Makes: 12 servings

- 1 lb. ground beef
- 1 medium onion, chopped
- 2 garlic cloves, minced
- 1 tsp. dried oregano
- 1 tsp. dried basil
- 2 cans (15 oz. each) tomato sauce
- 2 large eggs, lightly beaten
- 2 cups 4% cottage cheese
- ⅔ cup grated Parmesan cheese
- ¼ cup shredded cheddar cheese
- 1½ cups shredded part-skim mozzarella cheese, divided
- 12 no-cook lasagna noodles (about 7 oz.)
- 1 tsp. Italian seasoning

1. Preheat oven to 350°. In a large skillet, cook and crumble the beef with the onion and garlic over medium-high heat until browned, 5-7 minutes; drain. Stir in herbs and tomato sauce. In a bowl, mix the eggs, cottage cheese, Parmesan cheese, cheddar cheese and ½ cup mozzarella cheese.
2. Spread 1 cup meat sauce into a greased 13x9-in. baking dish; layer with 4 noodles, cottage cheese mixture, an additional 4 noodles and half of the remaining meat sauce. Repeat the last 2 layers. Sprinkle with Italian seasoning and the remaining mozzarella cheese.
3. Cover with greased foil; bake until the cheese is melted, 50-55 minutes. Let stand 10 minutes before serving.
1 piece: 279 cal., 13g fat (6g sat. fat), 72mg chol., 662mg sod., 22g carb. (4g sugars, 2g fiber), 20g pro.

EASY ORANGE & RED ONION SALAD

Here's a unique salad that's so easy to prepare when you're short on time. The combination of red onions and oranges may seem unusual, but it's surprisingly delightful. Give it a try!
—Edie DeSpain, Logan, UT

Takes: 20 min. • **Makes:** 10 servings

- 6 Tbsp. canola oil
- 2 Tbsp. white wine vinegar
- ½ tsp. grated orange zest
- 2 Tbsp. orange juice
- 1 Tbsp. sugar
- ⅛ tsp. ground cloves
  Dash salt
  Dash pepper
- 6 medium navel oranges, peeled and sliced
- 1 medium red onion, thinly sliced and separated into rings

For dressing, whisk together the first 8 ingredients. Place oranges and onion in a large bowl; toss gently with dressing. Refrigerate, covered, until serving.
¾ cup: 127 cal., 9g fat (1g sat. fat), 0 chol., 148mg sod., 13g carb. (9g sugars, 2g fiber), 1g pro. **Diabetic exchanges:** ½ fruit, 1½ fat.

SAVORY BISCUIT-BREADSTICKS

I love to experiment in the kitchen with simple ingredients such as refrigerated biscuits. The results usually are a big hit, like these super quick breadsticks.
—Billy Hensley, Mount Carmel, TN

- -

Takes: 20 min. • **Makes:** 10 breadsticks

- ½ cup grated Parmesan cheese
- 2 tsp. dried minced garlic
- ¼ tsp. crushed red pepper flakes
- 1 tube (12 oz.) refrigerated buttermilk biscuits
- 2 Tbsp. olive oil

Preheat oven to 400°. In a shallow bowl, mix cheese, garlic and pepper flakes. Roll each biscuit into a 6-in. rope. Brush lightly with oil; roll in the cheese mixture. Place on a greased baking sheet. Bake until golden brown, 8-10 minutes.

1 breadstick: 142 cal., 8g fat (2g sat. fat), 3mg chol., 353mg sod., 16g carb. (2g sugars, 0 fiber), 3g pro.

HAM & SWISS LAYERED SALAD

Layered salads rank among the classics in the potluck hall of fame. In this one, the combination of ham, cheese, egg and bacon is like a deconstructed sandwich, making it hearty enough for a main course.
—Stacy Huggins, Valley Center, CA

- -

Takes: 30 min. • **Makes:** 12 servings

- 2 cups mayonnaise
- 1 cup sour cream
- ½ tsp. sugar
- ⅛ tsp. salt
- ⅛ tsp. pepper
- 8 cups fresh baby spinach (about 6 oz.)
- 6 hard-boiled large eggs, chopped
- ½ lb. sliced fully cooked ham, cut into strips
- 4 cups torn iceberg lettuce (about ½ head)
- 2½ cups frozen petite peas (about 10 oz.), thawed, optional
- 1 small red onion, halved and thinly sliced
- 8 oz. sliced Swiss cheese, cut into strips
- ½ lb. bacon strips, cooked and crumbled

For dressing, mix first 5 ingredients. In a 3-qt. or larger glass bowl, layer spinach, eggs, ham, lettuce, peas, if desired, and onion. Spread with dressing. Sprinkle with cheese and bacon. Refrigerate, covered, until serving.

1 cup: 501 cal., 43g fat (12g sat. fat), 137mg chol., 665mg sod., 11g carb. (5g sugars, 3g fiber), 19g pro.

MOM'S CITRUS BUTTERMILK CAKE

Everyone raves over this lovely lemon cake. It's divine with fresh raspberries and a scoop of vanilla ice cream on the side.
—Joan Hallford, North Richland Hills, TX

Prep: 25 min. • **Bake:** 45 min. + cooling
Makes: 12 servings

- 1 cup shortening
- 2 cups sugar
- 4 large eggs, room temperature
- 2 tsp. lemon extract
- 3 cups all-purpose flour
- 1 tsp. baking powder
- ½ tsp. baking soda
- ½ tsp. salt
- 1 cup buttermilk

GLAZE

- 1½ cups confectioners' sugar
- 1 Tbsp. grated orange zest
- 5 Tbsp. orange juice
- 1 Tbsp. grated lemon zest
- 5 Tbsp. lemon juice
- ¼ tsp. salt

1. Preheat oven to 350°. Grease and flour a 10-in. fluted tube pan.
2. Cream shortening and sugar until light and fluffy. Add 1 egg at a time, beating well after each addition. Beat in the extract. In another bowl, whisk together flour, baking powder, salt and baking soda; add to the creamed mixture alternately with the buttermilk, beating after each addition.
3. Transfer to prepared pan. Bake until a toothpick inserted in center comes out clean, 45-50 minutes.
4. Poke holes in warm cake using a fork or wooden skewer. Mix glaze ingredients; spoon slowly over cake. Cool 15 minutes before removing from pan to a wire rack; cool completely.

1 slice: 488 cal., 18g fat (5g sat. fat), 63mg chol., 304mg sod., 75g carb. (50g sugars, 1g fiber), 6g pro.

TEST KITCHEN TIP
To remove cakes easily, start by greasing plain and fluted tube pans with solid shortening.

MENU
OLD WORLD

GRAMP'S GERMAN-STYLE POT ROAST

Grandpa was of German heritage and loved the Old Country recipes given to him by his mother. I made a few changes to make this dish in the slow cooker and to give it a slightly updated flavor.
—Nancy Heishman, Las Vegas, NV

Prep: 20 min. • **Cook:** 6 hours
Makes: 8 servings

- 4   **thick-sliced bacon strips**
- 1   **lb. baby Yukon Gold potatoes**
- 4   **medium carrots, sliced**
- 1   **can (14 oz.) sauerkraut, rinsed and well drained**
- ¾   **cup chopped dill pickles**
- 1   **tsp. smoked paprika**
- 1   **tsp. ground allspice**
- ½   **tsp. kosher salt**
- ½   **tsp. pepper**
- 1   **boneless beef chuck roast (3 lbs.)**
- 2   **pkg. (14.40 oz. each) frozen pearl onions, thawed**
- 4   **garlic cloves, minced**
- ½   **cup stout beer or beef broth**
- ⅓   **cup Dusseldorf mustard**
- ½   **cup sour cream**
- ½   **cup minced fresh parsley**

1. In a large skillet, cook bacon over medium heat until crisp. Carefully remove to paper towels to drain.

2. Meanwhile, place potatoes, carrots, sauerkraut and pickles in a 7-qt. slow cooker. Mix paprika, allspice, salt and pepper; rub over roast. Brown roast in drippings over medium heat. Transfer to slow cooker. Add onions and garlic to drippings; cook and stir 1 minute. Stir in beer and mustard; pour over meat. Crumble bacon; add to slow cooker.

3. Cook, covered, on low until meat and vegetables are tender, 6-8 hours. Remove roast; let stand 10 minutes before slicing. Strain cooking juices. Reserve vegetables and juices; skim fat. Return the reserved vegetables and cooking juices to the slow cooker. Stir in sour cream; heat through. Serve with roast; sprinkle with parsley.

1 serving: 552 cal., 31g fat (12g sat. fat), 127mg chol., 926mg sod., 28g carb. (9g sugars, 6g fiber), 39g pro.

FLAKY BUTTERHORN ROLLS

My grandchildren have renamed these Grandma's Croissants. The dinner rolls are slightly sweet and so very flaky. Originally my mother's recipe, it's simple to prepare because you don't have to knead it.
—Bernice Smith, Sturgeon Lake, MN

Prep: 30 min. + rising • **Bake:** 10 min./batch
Makes: 4 dozen

- 4   **cups all-purpose flour**
- ½   **cup sugar**
- 1   **tsp. salt**
- 1   **cup cold butter, cubed, or shortening**
- 1   **pkg. (¼ oz.) active dry yeast**
- ¼   **cup warm water (110° to 115°)**
- ¾   **cup warm whole milk (110° to 115°)**
- 1   **large egg, room temperature, lightly beaten**
- 4   **Tbsp. butter, melted, divided**

1. In a large bowl, combine the flour, sugar and salt. Cut in the butter until the mixture resembles coarse crumbs. In another bowl, dissolve yeast in warm water; add to crumb mixture. Add milk and egg; mix well. Cover and refrigerate overnight.

2. Divide dough into 4 equal portions. On a lightly floured surface, roll 1 portion into a 12-in. circle. Brush with 1 Tbsp. melted butter; cut into 12 wedges.

3. Roll up dough, beginning with the wide end; place on greased baking sheets. Repeat with remaining dough. Cover and let rise in a warm place until nearly doubled, about 1 hour.

4. Bake at 375° for 10-12 minutes or until golden brown. Remove to wire racks.

1 roll: 92 cal., 5g fat (3g sat. fat), 18mg chol., 101mg sod., 10g carb. (2g sugars, 0 fiber), 1g pro.

MASHED CAULIFLOWER AU GRATIN

My grandchildren love the cheesy, creamy side dish. Unless someone tells you, you might not know that it's cauliflower. It tastes like buttery mashed potatoes.
—Sandie Parker, Elk Rapids, MI

Prep: 40 min. • **Cook:** 40 min.
Makes: 12 servings

- 2 **large heads cauliflower, broken into florets**
- 1½ **cups shredded Parmesan cheese**
- 1 **cup shredded Colby-Monterey Jack cheese**
- 6 **Tbsp. butter, cubed**
- ¾ **tsp. garlic salt**
- ½ **tsp. Montreal steak seasoning**
- TOPPING
- 1 **cup (4 oz.) Italian-style panko (Japanese) bread crumbs**
- ¼ **cup butter, melted**

NOTHING BUT THE BEST

When purchasing fresh heads of cauliflower, look for compact florets that are free from yellow or brown spots. The leaves should be crisp and green, not withered or discolored.

1. Preheat oven to 350°. Place cauliflower in a stockpot; add water to cover. Bring to a boil. Reduce heat; simmer, uncovered, until very tender, 10-12 minutes. Drain; transfer to a large bowl. Mash the cauliflower; stir in the cheeses, cubed butter and seasonings. Transfer to a greased 3-qt. or 13x9-in. baking dish.

2. In a small bowl, mix bread crumbs and melted butter until evenly coated; sprinkle over cauliflower mixture. Bake, uncovered, until heated through and topping is golden brown, 40-50 minutes.

Freeze option: Cool unbaked casserole; cover and freeze. To use, partially thaw in the refrigerator overnight. Remove from refrigerator 30 minutes before baking. Preheat oven to 350°. Bake casserole as directed, increasing time as necessary to heat through and for a thermometer inserted in center to read 165°.

¾ cup: 238 cal., 17g fat (10g sat. fat), 41mg chol., 612mg sod., 14g carb. (3g sugars, 4g fiber), 9g pro.

Swiss Mashed Cauliflower: Cook and mash cauliflower as directed. Add 1 cup shredded Swiss cheese, 2 Tbsp. butter, 1 tsp. salt, ½ tsp. pepper, ¼ tsp. garlic powder and ¼-⅓ cup 2% milk.

DATE-NUT PINWHEELS

To me, pinwheel cookies with dates and walnuts are a family treasure. There are a few steps when prepping, so I sometimes freeze the dough and bake later.
—Frieda Whiteley, Lisbon, CT

Prep: 30 min. + chilling • **Bake:** 10 min./batch
Makes: about 9 dozen

  1 **cup butter, softened**
  1 **cup sugar**
  1 **cup packed brown sugar**
  2 **large eggs, room temperature**
  4 **cups all-purpose flour**
  ½ **tsp. baking soda**

FILLING

  2 **pkg. (8 oz. each) pitted dates**
  1 **cup water**
  ½ **cup sugar**
  ½ **cup chopped walnuts**

1. In a large bowl, cream butter and sugars until light and fluffy. Beat in eggs. In another bowl, whisk flour and baking soda; gradually beat into creamed mixture. Divide dough into 3 portions. Shape each into a disk; wrap in plastic. Refrigerate 1 hour or until firm enough to roll.
2. For filling, place dates, water and sugar in a large saucepan. Bring to a boil. Reduce heat; simmer, uncovered, until dates are tender and liquid is almost evaporated. Stir in walnuts; cool completely.
3. Roll each portion of dough between 2 sheets of waxed paper into a 12x10-in. rectangle. Refrigerate 30 minutes. Remove the waxed paper. Spread a third of the filling over each rectangle. Roll up tightly jelly-roll style, starting with a long side. Wrap in plastic. Refrigerate until firm.
4. Preheat oven to 350°. Unwrap and cut dough crosswise into ⅓-in. slices. Place 2 in. apart on greased baking sheets. Bake until set, 10-12 minutes. Remove from pans to wire racks to cool.
1 cookie: 67 cal., 2g fat (1g sat. fat), 8mg chol., 21mg sod., 12g carb. (7g sugars, 1g fiber), 1g pro.

HONEY COFFEE

For a simple yet soothing dinner finale, sip this pleasantly sweet coffee. Flavored with rich earthy seasonings, it's a heartwarming end to a long day.
—*Taste of Home* Test Kitchen

Takes: 10 min. • **Makes:** 4 servings

  2 **cups hot strong brewed coffee**
     (French or other dark roast)
  ½ **cup whole milk**
  ¼ **cup honey**
  ⅛ **tsp. ground cinnamon**
     Dash ground nutmeg
  ¼ **tsp. vanilla extract**

In a small saucepan, combine the coffee, milk, honey, cinnamon and nutmeg. Cook and stir until heated through. (Do not boil.) Remove from the heat; stir in vanilla. Pour into cups or mugs; serve immediately.
½ cup: 86 cal., 1g fat (1g sat. fat), 4mg chol., 18mg sod., 19g carb. (18g sugars, 0 fiber), 1g pro.

MENU
PORK DINNER

Italian Herb-Crusted
Pork Loin, p. 283

Quick & Easy au Gratin
Potatoes, p. 284

Roasted Italian Green
Beans & Tomatoes, p. 284

Spinach Salad
with Raspberries &
Candied Walnuts, p. 285

Pina Colada
Bundt Cake, p. 283

ITALIAN HERB-CRUSTED PORK LOIN

I like to change things up by roasting pork loin with my favorite herbs and veggies. This dish is a showpiece that really dazzles my entire family.
—Kim Palmer, Kingston, GA

- -

Prep: 15 min. + chilling
Bake: 50 min. + standing • **Makes:** 8 servings

- 3 Tbsp. olive oil
- 5 garlic cloves, minced
- 1 tsp. salt
- 1 tsp. each dried basil, thyme and rosemary, crushed
- ½ tsp. Italian seasoning
- ½ tsp. pepper
- 1 boneless pork loin roast (3 to 4 lbs.)
- 8 medium carrots, halved lengthwise
- 2 medium onions, quartered

1. In a small bowl, mix olive oil, garlic and seasonings; rub over roast. Arrange carrots and onions on bottom of a 13x9-in. baking pan. Place roast over vegetables, fat side up. Refrigerate, covered, 1 hour.

2. Preheat oven to 475°. Roast the pork for 20 minutes.

3. Decrease heat to 425°. Roast pork until a thermometer reads 145° and vegetables are tender, 30-40 minutes longer. Remove roast from oven; tent with foil. Let stand for 20 minutes before slicing.

1 serving: 295 cal., 13g fat (4g sat. fat), 85mg chol., 388mg sod., 9g carb. (4g sugars, 2g fiber), 34g pro. **Diabetic exchanges:** 5 lean meat, 1 vegetable, 1 fat.

PINA COLADA BUNDT CAKE

We named this cake a pina colada because it has coconut, pineapple and rum. It's a soothing finish at the end of a big spread.
—Debra Keil, Owasso, OK

- -

Prep: 15 min. • **Bake:** 45 min. + cooling
Makes: 12 servings

- 1 pkg. white cake mix (regular size)
- 1 pkg. (3.4 oz.) instant coconut cream pudding mix
- 1 cup canola oil
- ¾ cup water
- 2 large eggs, room temperature
- ¼ cup rum
- 1 cup drained crushed pineapple

GLAZE

- 2 cups confectioners' sugar, divided
- 2 Tbsp. unsweetened pineapple juice
- ¼ cup cream of coconut
- 1 Tbsp. rum
- ¼ cup sweetened shredded coconut

1. Preheat oven to 350°. Grease and flour a 10-in. fluted tube pan.

2. In a large bowl, combine the cake mix, pudding mix, oil, water, eggs and rum; beat on low speed 30 seconds. Beat on medium 2 minutes. Stir in pineapple. Transfer batter to prepared pan. Bake 45-50 minutes or until a toothpick inserted in center comes out clean. Cool in pan 15 minutes before removing to a wire rack.

3. In a small bowl, mix 1 cup confectioners' sugar and pineapple juice; brush over warm cake. Cool cake completely.

4. In another bowl, mix cream of coconut, rum and remaining confectioners' sugar; drizzle over cake. Sprinkle with coconut.

1 slice: 495 cal., 25g fat (5g sat. fat), 31mg chol., 357mg sod., 64g carb. (47g sugars, 1g fiber), 3g pro.

QUICK & EASY AU GRATIN POTATOES

A friend serves these creamy, cheesy potatoes whenever we all get together to celebrate with our lifelong friends and our grown children.
—Carol Blue, Barnesville, PA

- -

Prep: 10 min. • **Bake:** 50 min.
Makes: 12 servings

2   cups sour cream
1   can (10¾ oz.) condensed cream
    of chicken soup, undiluted
½   tsp. salt
¼   tsp. pepper
1   pkg. (30 oz.) frozen shredded
    hash brown potatoes, thawed
2   cups shredded cheddar cheese
1   small onion, chopped
2   cups crushed cornflakes
¼   cup butter, melted

1. Preheat oven to 350°. In a large bowl, mix sour cream, condensed soup, salt and pepper; stir in potatoes, cheese and onion. Transfer to a greased 13x9-in. baking dish.
2. In a small bowl, mix crushed cornflakes and melted butter; sprinkle over potato mixture. Bake, uncovered, 50-60 minutes or until golden brown.
¾ cup: 394 cal., 22g fat (14g sat. fat), 70mg chol., 680mg sod., 36g carb. (5g sugars, 2g fiber), 11g pro.

ROASTED ITALIAN GREEN BEANS & TOMATOES

When you roast green beans and tomatoes, the flavors really shine through. I think the vibrant colors light up any table.
—Brittany Allyn, Mesa, AZ

- -

Takes: 25 min. • **Makes:** 8 servings

1½ lbs. fresh green beans,
    trimmed and halved
1   Tbsp. olive oil
1   tsp. Italian seasoning
½   tsp. salt
2   cups grape tomatoes, halved
½   cup grated Parmesan cheese

1. Preheat oven to 425°. Place the green beans in a 15x10x1-in. baking pan coated with cooking spray. Mix oil, Italian seasoning and salt; drizzle over beans. Toss to coat. Roast 10 minutes, stirring once.
2. Add tomatoes to pan. Roast until the beans are crisp-tender and tomatoes are softened, 4-6 minutes longer. Sprinkle with Parmesan cheese.
¾ cup: 70 cal., 3g fat (1g sat. fat), 4mg chol., 231mg sod., 8g carb. (3g sugars, 3g fiber), 4g pro. **Diabetic exchanges:** 1 vegetable, ½ fat.

SPINACH SALAD WITH RASPBERRIES & CANDIED WALNUTS

I created this bright spinach salad with raspberries for a big family dinner, and it fit right in with the overall meal. Even those who don't like spinach change their mind at the very first bite.
—Robert Aucelluzzo, Simi Valley, CA

Prep: 15 min. • **Bake:** 25 min. + cooling
Makes: 8 servings

- 1 large egg white
- ¾ tsp. vanilla extract
- 2 cups walnut halves
- ½ cup sugar

DRESSING
- ¼ cup canola oil
- 2 Tbsp. cider vinegar
- 1 Tbsp. sugar
- 1½ tsp. light corn syrup
- 1 tsp. poppy seeds
- ¼ tsp. salt
- ¼ tsp. ground mustard

SALAD
- 8 oz. fresh baby spinach (about 10 cups)
- 1½ cups fresh raspberries

1. Preheat oven to 300°. In a small bowl, whisk egg white and vanilla until frothy. Stir in walnuts. Sprinkle with sugar; toss to coat evenly. Spread in a single layer in a greased 15x10x1-in. baking pan.

2. Bake for 25-30 minutes or until lightly browned, stirring every 10 minutes. Spread on waxed paper to cool completely.

3. In a small bowl, whisk the dressing ingredients until blended. Place spinach in a large bowl. Drizzle with dressing; toss to coat. Sprinkle with raspberries and 1 cup candied walnuts. (Save remaining walnuts for another use.)

1½ cups: 171 cal., 13g fat (1g sat. fat), 0 chol., 100mg sod., 12g carb. (9g sugars, 3g fiber), 3g pro. **Diabetic exchanges:** 1½ fat, 1 starch, 1 vegetable.

SEASONED RIBEYE ROAST

This is an especially savory way to prepare a boneless beef roast. Gravy made from the drippings is exceptional.
—Evelyn Gebhardt, Kasilof, AK

- -

Prep: 10 min. • **Bake:** 1¾ hours + standing
Makes: 8 servings

- 1½ tsp. lemon-pepper seasoning
- 1½ tsp. paprika
- ¾ tsp. garlic salt
- ½ tsp. dried rosemary, crushed
- ¼ tsp. cayenne pepper
- 1 beef ribeye roast (3 to 4 lbs.)

1. Preheat oven to 350°. Mix seasonings. Place roast on a rack in a roasting pan, fat side up; rub with seasonings.
2. Roast, uncovered, until meat reaches desired doneness (for medium-rare, a thermometer should read 135°; medium, 140°), 1½-2 hours. Remove from oven; tent with foil. Let stand for 10 minutes before slicing.

4 oz. cooked beef: 372 cal., 27g fat (11g sat. fat), 100mg chol., 321mg sod., 0 carb. (0 sugars, 0 fiber), 30g pro.

> "This is so, so good. I have made it many times and continue to be asked to prepare it for family and friends. I would recommend it to anyone."
>
> —A13, TASTEOFHOME.COM

ROSEMARY GARLIC SHRIMP

Delicate shrimp take on fabulous flavor when simmered in chicken broth mixed with garlic and ripe olives.
—*Taste of Home* Test Kitchen

- -

Takes: 20 min. • **Makes:** 8 servings

- 1¼ cups chicken or vegetable broth
- 3 Tbsp. chopped ripe olives
- 1 small cayenne or other fresh red chili pepper, finely chopped
- 2 Tbsp. lemon juice
- 1 Tbsp. minced fresh rosemary or 1 tsp. dried rosemary, crushed
- 4 garlic cloves, minced
- 2 tsp. Worcestershire sauce
- 1 tsp. paprika
- ½ tsp. salt
- ¼ to ½ tsp. pepper
- 2 lbs. uncooked shrimp (31-40 per lb.), peeled and deveined

1. In a large skillet, combine all ingredients except the shrimp; bring to a boil. Cook, uncovered, until liquid is reduced by half.
2. Stir in shrimp; return just to a boil. Reduce heat; simmer, uncovered, until shrimp turn pink, 3-4 minutes, stirring occasionally.

Note: Wear disposable gloves when cutting hot peppers; the oils can burn skin. Avoid touching your face.

½ cup: 110 cal., 2g fat (0 sat. fat), 139mg chol., 473mg sod., 3g carb. (1g sugars, 0 fiber), 19g pro. **Diabetic exchanges:** 3 lean meat.

GRUYERE MASHED POTATOES

Here, Gruyere cheese and chives take mashed potatoes to a whole new level. Don't have chives? Just use extra green onion instead.
—Preci D'Silva, Dubai, AA

Takes: 25 min. • **Makes:** 8 servings

- 2 lbs. potatoes, peeled and cubed
- ¼ cup butter, cubed
- ½ cup sour cream
- ⅓ cup 2% milk, warmed
- 1 garlic clove, minced
- ¼ cup shredded Gruyere or Swiss cheese
- ¼ cup minced fresh chives
- 2 green onions, chopped
- ½ tsp. garlic salt
- ¼ tsp. pepper

1. Place potatoes in a 6-qt. stockpot; add water to cover. Bring to a boil. Reduce heat; cover, uncovered, until potatoes are tender, 10-15 minutes.

2. Drain; return to pot. Mash potatoes, gradually adding sour cream, milk and garlic. Stir in remaining ingredients.

¾ cup: 169 cal., 10g fat (6g sat. fat), 23mg chol., 206mg sod., 17g carb. (2g sugars, 1g fiber), 3g pro.

PARSNIP & CELERY ROOT BISQUE

With its smooth texture and earthy vegetable flavors, this simple yet elegant soup makes a tempting first course. Try chives and pomegranate seeds on top.
—Merry Graham, Newhall, CA

- -

Prep: 25 min. • **Cook:** 45 min.
Makes: 8 servings (2 qt.)

- 2 Tbsp. olive oil
- 2 medium leeks (white portion only), chopped (about 2 cups)
- 1½ lbs. parsnips, peeled and chopped (about 4 cups)
- 1 medium celery root, peeled and cubed (about 1½ cups)
- 4 garlic cloves, minced
- 6 cups chicken stock
- 1½ tsp. salt
- ¾ tsp. coarsely ground pepper
- 1 cup heavy whipping cream
- 2 Tbsp. minced fresh parsley
- 2 tsp. lemon juice
- 2 Tbsp. minced fresh chives
  Pomegranate seeds, optional

1. In a large saucepan, heat olive oil over medium-high heat; saute leeks 3 minutes. Add parsnips and celery root; cook and stir 4 minutes. Add garlic; cook and stir for 1 minute. Stir in stock, salt and pepper; bring to a boil. Reduce heat; simmer, covered, until vegetables are tender, 25-30 minutes.
2. Puree soup using an immersion blender. Or, cool slightly and puree soup in batches in a blender; return to pan. Stir in cream, parsley and lemon juice; heat through. Garnish with minced chives and, if desired, pomegranate seeds.
1 cup: 248 cal., 15g fat (7g sat. fat), 34mg chol., 904mg sod., 25g carb. (8g sugars, 5g fiber), 6g pro.

OLD-FASHIONED CHOCOLATE PUDDING

One of the nice things about this from-scratch pudding is how easy it is. I even make it into a pie with a graham cracker crust that our grandchildren just love.
—Amber Sampson, Somonauk, IL

- -

Prep: 10 min. • **Cook:** 30 min. + chilling
Makes: 4 servings

- 2 cups whole milk
- 2 Tbsp. butter
- 2 oz. unsweetened chocolate, chopped
- ⅔ cup sugar
- ⅓ cup all-purpose flour
- ¼ tsp. salt
- 2 large egg yolks, beaten
- ½ tsp. vanilla extract
  Whipped cream, optional

1. In a double boiler or metal bowl over simmering water, heat the milk, butter and chocolate until chocolate is melted (chocolate may appear curdled).
2. Combine sugar, flour and salt. Sprinkle over chocolate mixture (do not stir). Cover and continue to cook in a double boiler over medium-low heat for 20 minutes. With a wooden spoon, stir until smooth. Remove from the heat.
3. Stir a small amount of hot mixture into egg yolks; return all to the pan, stirring constantly. Cook and stir until mixture is thickened and a thermometer reads 160°. Remove from heat; stir in vanilla. Cool for 15 minutes, stirring occasionally. Transfer to dessert dishes.
4. Cover and refrigerate for 1 hour. If desired, top with whipped cream.
⅔ cup: 413 cal., 20g fat (11g sat. fat), 120mg chol., 254mg sod., 52g carb. (40g sugars, 3g fiber), 8g pro.

MENU

TAMALE NIGHT

Chicken Tamales, p. 291

Topsy-Turvy Sangria, p. 291

Homemade
Guacamole, p. 292

Southwestern Rice, p. 292

Tres Leches Cake, p. 293

CHICKEN TAMALES

Homemade tamales take time to assemble, but they are so worth the effort. My family requests them somewhat regularly, so I like to make a big batch and stash them away in the freezer.
—Cindy Pruitt, Grove, OK

Prep: 2½ hours + soaking • **Cook:** 50 min.
Makes: 20 tamales

- 24 dried corn husks
- 1 broiler/fryer chicken (3 to 4 lbs.), cut up
- 1 medium onion, quartered
- 2 tsp. salt
- 1 garlic clove, crushed
- 3 qt. water

DOUGH
- 1 cup shortening
- 3 cups masa harina

FILLING
- 6 Tbsp. canola oil
- 6 Tbsp. all-purpose flour
- ¾ cup chili powder
- ½ tsp. salt
- ¼ tsp. garlic powder
- ¼ tsp. pepper
- 2 cans (2¼ oz. each) sliced ripe olives, drained
  Hot water

1. Cover corn husks with cold water; soak until softened, at least 2 hours.
2. Place chicken, onion, salt and garlic in a 6-qt. stockpot. Pour in 3 qt. water; bring to a boil. Reduce heat; simmer, covered, until chicken is tender, 45-60 minutes. Remove chicken from broth. When cool enough to handle, remove bones and skin; discard. Shred chicken. Strain cooking juices; skim fat. Reserve 6 cups stock.
3. For dough, beat shortening until light and fluffy, about 1 minute. Beat in small amounts of masa harina alternately with small amounts of reserved stock, using no more than 2 cups stock. Drop a small amount of dough into a cup of cold water; dough should float. If not, continue beating, rechecking every 1-2 minutes.
4. For filling, heat oil in a Dutch oven; stir in flour until blended. Cook and stir over medium heat 7-9 minutes or until lightly browned. Stir in seasonings, chicken and remaining stock; bring to a boil. Reduce the heat; simmer, uncovered, stirring occasionally, until thickened, about 45 minutes.
5. Drain the corn husks and pat dry; tear 4 husks to make 20 strips for tying tamales. (To prevent husks from drying out, cover with a damp towel until ready to use.) On wide end of each remaining husk, spread 3 Tbsp. dough to within ½ in. of side edges; top each with 2 Tbsp. chicken filling and 2 tsp. olives. Fold long sides of husk over filling, overlapping slightly. Fold over the narrow end of husk; tie with a strip of husk to secure.
6. Place a large steamer basket in the stockpot over water; place tamales upright in steamer. Bring to a boil; steam, covered, adding hot water as needed, until dough peels away from husk, about 45 minutes.
2 tamales: 564 cal., 35g fat (7g sat. fat), 44mg chol., 835mg sod., 43g carb. (2g sugars, 7g fiber), 20g pro.

TOPSY-TURVY SANGRIA

I got this recipe from a friend a few years ago. It's perfect for relaxed get-togethers.
—Tracy Field, Bremerton, WA

Takes: 10 min.
Makes: 10 servings (about 2 qt.)

- 1 bottle (750 ml) merlot
- 1 cup sugar
- 1 cup orange liqueur
- ½ to 1 cup brandy
- 3 cups cold lemon-lime soda
- 1 cup sliced fresh strawberries
- 1 medium orange, sliced
- 1 medium lemon, sliced
- 1 medium peach, sliced
  Ice cubes

In a pitcher, stir first 4 ingredients until sugar is dissolved. Stir in soda and fruit. Serve over ice.
¾ cup: 292 cal., 0 fat (0 sat. fat), 0 chol., 11mg sod., 42g carb. (39g sugars, 0 fiber), 0 pro.

HOMEMADE GUACAMOLE

Ever wonder how to make guacamole? I get the most delicious guacamole with this easy recipe.
—Joan Hallford, North Richland Hills, TX

Takes: 10 min. • **Makes:** 2 cups

- 3 medium ripe avocados, peeled and cubed
- 1 garlic clove, minced
- ¼ to ½ tsp. salt
- 2 medium tomatoes, seeded and chopped, optional
- 1 small onion, finely chopped
- ¼ cup mayonnaise, optional
- 1 to 2 Tbsp. lime juice
- 1 Tbsp. minced fresh cilantro

Mash avocados with garlic and salt. Stir in remaining ingredients.

¼ cup: 90 cal., 8g fat (1g sat. fat), 0 chol., 78mg sod., 6g carb. (1g sugars, 4g fiber), 1g pro. **Diabetic exchanges:** 1½ fat.

> ### TEST KITCHEN TIP
> You can use lemon and lime juice interchangeably in this recipe to achieve a different flavor. To add in orange juice, however, you'll need to keep a little lemon or lime to spark up the flavor.

SOUTHWESTERN RICE

I created this colorful side dish after eating something similar at a restaurant. I think it complements any southwestern meal wonderfully. Sometimes I add cubes of grilled chicken breast to the rice to make it an entree.
—Michelle Dennis, Clarks Hill, IN

Takes: 30 min. • **Makes:** 8 servings

- 1 Tbsp. olive oil
- 1 medium green pepper, diced
- 1 medium onion, chopped
- 2 garlic cloves, minced
- 1 cup uncooked long grain rice
- ½ tsp. ground cumin
- ⅛ tsp. ground turmeric
- 1 can (14½ oz.) reduced-sodium chicken broth
- 2 cups frozen corn (about 10 oz.), thawed
- 1 can (15 oz.) black beans, rinsed and drained
- 1 can (10 oz.) diced tomatoes and green chiles, undrained

1. In a large nonstick skillet, heat oil over medium-high heat; saute the pepper and onion 3 minutes. Add garlic; cook and stir for 1 minute.

2. Stir in rice, spices and broth; bring to a boil. Reduce heat; simmer, covered, until rice is tender, about 15 minutes. Stir in remaining ingredients; cook, covered, until heated through.

¾ cup: 198 cal., 3g fat (1g sat. fat), 1mg chol., 339mg sod., 37g carb. (0 sugars, 5g fiber), 7g pro.

TRES LECHES CAKE

A classic in Mexican kitchens for many generations, this cake gets its name from the three types of milk—evaporated, sweetened condensed and heavy whipping cream—used to create a wonderfully moist and tender texture.
—*Taste of Home* Test Kitchen

- -

Prep: 45 min. • **Bake:** 20 min. + chilling
Makes: 10 servings

  4 **large eggs, separated, room temperature**

⅔ **cup sugar, divided**
⅔ **cup cake flour**
   Dash salt
¾ **cup heavy whipping cream**
¾ **cup evaporated milk**
¾ **cup sweetened condensed milk**
 2 **tsp. vanilla extract**
¼ **tsp. rum extract**

TOPPING

1¼ **cups heavy whipping cream**
 3 **Tbsp. sugar**
   Optional: Sliced fresh strawberries and dulce de leche

1. Place egg whites in a large bowl. Meanwhile, line the bottom of a 9-in. springform pan with parchment; grease the paper.

2. Meanwhile, preheat oven to 350°. In another large bowl, beat egg yolks until slightly thickened. Gradually add ⅓ cup sugar, beating on high speed until thick and lemon-colored. Fold in flour, a third at a time.

3. Add the salt to egg whites; with clean beaters, beat on medium until soft peaks form. Gradually add the remaining sugar, 1 Tbsp. at a time, beating on high after each addition until sugar is dissolved. Continue beating until soft glossy peaks form. Fold a third of the whites into batter, then fold in the remaining whites. Gently spread into prepared pan.

4. Bake until top springs back when lightly touched, 20-25 minutes. Cool 10 minutes before removing from pan to a wire rack to cool completely.

5. Place cake on a rimmed serving plate. Poke holes in top with a skewer. In a small bowl, mix the cream, evaporated milk, sweetened condensed milk and extracts; brush slowly over the cake. Refrigerate, covered, 2 hours.

6. For topping, beat cream until it begins to thicken. Add sugar; beat until peaks form. Spread over top of cake. If desired, top with sliced strawberries and dulce de leche just before serving.

1 slice: 392 cal., 23g fat (14g sat. fat), 142mg chol., 104mg sod., 40g carb. (33g sugars, 0 fiber), 8g pro.

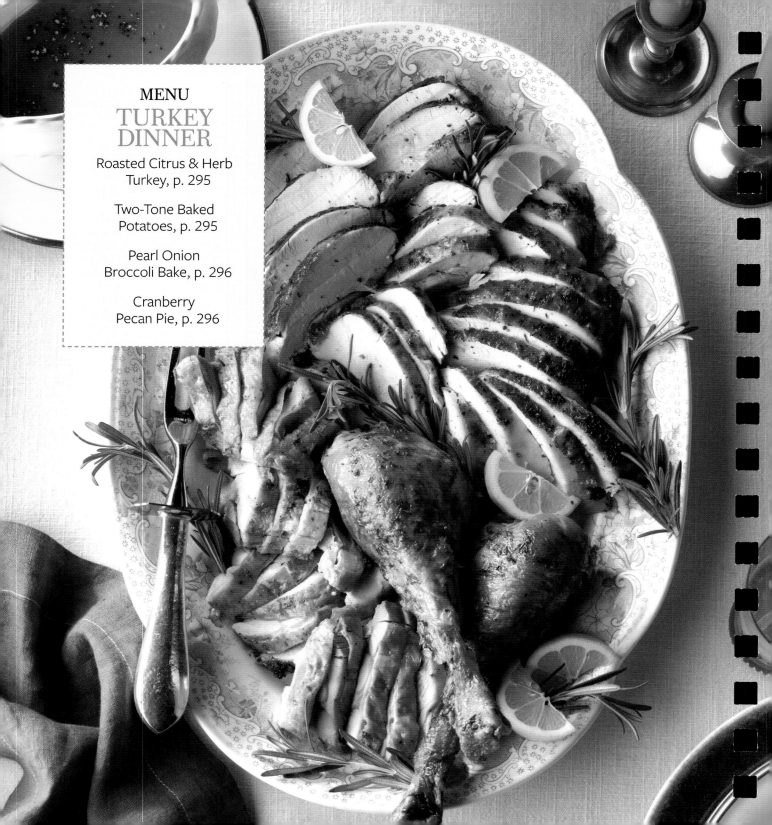

MENU
TURKEY DINNER

Roasted Citrus & Herb
Turkey, p. 295

Two-Tone Baked
Potatoes, p. 295

Pearl Onion
Broccoli Bake, p. 296

Cranberry
Pecan Pie, p. 296

ROASTED CITRUS & HERB TURKEY

This is a true showstopper that never fails to impress in both presentation and flavor.
—Nancy Niemerg, Dieterich, IL

Prep: 30 min. • **Bake:** 3½ hours + standing
Makes: 16 servings (2 cups gravy)

- ¼ cup butter, softened
- 2 Tbsp. Italian seasoning
- 1 turkey (14 to 16 lbs.)
- 2 tsp. salt
- 2 tsp. pepper
- 1 large onion, quartered
- 1 medium orange, quartered
- 1 medium lemon, quartered
- 3 fresh rosemary sprigs
- 3 fresh sage sprigs
- 3 cups chicken broth, divided
- 3 to 4 Tbsp. all-purpose flour
- ⅛ tsp. browning sauce, optional

1. Preheat oven to 325°. Mix butter and Italian seasoning.
2. Place the turkey on a rack in a roasting pan, breast side up; pat dry. With fingers, carefully loosen skin from turkey breast; rub half of the butter mixture under the skin. Secure skin to underside of breast with toothpicks. Rub cavity with salt and pepper; fill with onion, orange, lemon and herbs. Tuck the wings under turkey; tie the drumsticks together.
3. Melt remaining butter mixture; brush over outside of turkey. Add 2 cups broth to roasting pan.
4. Roast, uncovered, until a thermometer inserted in the thickest part of thigh reads 170°-175°, 3½-4 hours, basting occasionally with pan drippings. (Cover loosely with foil if turkey browns too quickly.)
5. Remove turkey from oven; tent with foil. Let stand 20 minutes before carving.
6. Pour pan drippings into a small saucepan; skim fat. Mix the flour, remaining broth and, if desired, browning sauce until smooth; whisk into pan. Bring to a boil; cook and stir until thickened, 1-2 minutes. Serve with turkey.

7 oz. cooked turkey with 2 Tbsp. gravy: 500 cal., 24g fat (8g sat. fat), 223mg chol., 653mg sod., 2g carb. (0 sugars, 0 fiber), 64g pro.

TWO-TONE BAKED POTATOES

I think this recipe is doubly wonderful as far as spud lovers are concerned. I have a reputation at home and at work for trying out new recipes. Everyone is glad I took a chance on this one.
—Sherree Stahn, Central City, NE

Prep: 30 min. • **Bake:** 1¼ hours
Makes: 12 servings

- 6 medium russet potatoes (about 8 oz. each)
- 6 medium sweet potatoes (about 8 oz. each)
- ⅔ cup sour cream, divided
- ⅓ cup 2% milk
- ¾ cup shredded cheddar cheese
- 4 Tbsp. minced fresh chives, divided
- 1½ tsp. salt, divided

1. Preheat oven to 400°. Scrub russet and sweet potatoes; pierce several times with a fork. Place in foil-lined 15x10x1-in. pans;

bake until tender, 60-70 minutes. Reduce oven setting to 350°.
2. When cool enough to handle, cut a third off the top of each russet potato (discard top or save for another use). Scoop out the pulp, leaving ½-in.-thick shells. In a bowl, mash pulp, adding ⅓ cup sour cream, milk, cheese, 2 Tbsp. chives and ¾ tsp. salt.
3. Cut a thin slice off the top of each sweet potato; discard slice. Scoop out the pulp, leaving ½-in. thick shells. Mash pulp with remaining sour cream, chives and salt.
4. Spoon russet potato mixture into half of each russet and sweet potato skin. Spoon the sweet potato mixture into other half. Return to pans. Bake until heated through, 15-20 minutes.

1 stuffed potato: 237 cal., 5g fat (3g sat. fat), 11mg chol., 365mg sod., 42g carb. (11g sugars, 5g fiber), 6g pro.

CRANBERRY PECAN PIE

I first prepared this pie at Thanksgiving to share with my co-workers. It was such a success! Now I freeze cranberries while they are in season, so that I can make it year-round.
—Dawn Liet Hartman, Miffinburg, PA

- -

Prep: 25 min. + chilling
Bake: 45 min. + chilling • **Makes:** 8 servings

- 6 Tbsp. shortening
- 1½ tsp. buttermilk
- 2 Tbsp. hot water
- 1 cup all-purpose flour
- ½ tsp. salt
FILLING
- 3 large eggs
- 1 cup light or dark corn syrup
- ⅔ cup sugar
- ¼ cup butter, melted
- 1 tsp. vanilla extract
- 2 cups fresh or frozen cranberries, thawed
- 1 cup chopped pecans
   Sweetened whipped cream, optional

1. Beat the shortening and buttermilk until blended. Gradually add water, beating until light and fluffy. Beat in flour and salt. Shape into a disk. Wrap in plastic; refrigerate for 4 hours or overnight.
2. Preheat oven to 425°. On a lightly floured surface, roll dough to a ⅛-in.-thick circle; transfer to a 9-in. pie plate. Trim crust to ½ in. beyond edge of plate; flute edge.
3. In a large bowl, whisk the first 5 filling ingredients until blended. Stir in cranberries and pecans. Pour into crust.
4. Bake on a lower oven rack 10 minutes. Reduce oven setting to 350°; bake until filling is almost set, 35-40 minutes. Cool completely on a wire rack. Refrigerate, covered, overnight before serving. If desired, serve with whipped cream.
1 slice: 514 cal., 27g fat (7g sat. fat), 85mg chol., 250mg sod., 68g carb. (52g sugars, 3g fiber), 5g pro.

PEARL ONION BROCCOLI BAKE

With its creamy white cheese sauce and buttery crumb topping, this dish is pure comfort food. If you're looking for a mild way to dress up broccoli, this is the recipe.
—Charles Keating, Manchester, MD

- -

Prep: 20 min. • **Bake:** 25 min.
Makes: 12 servings

- 2 pkg. (16 oz. each) frozen broccoli florets
- 1 pkg. (14.4 oz.) pearl onions
- ½ cup butter, divided
- ¼ cup all-purpose flour
- ¾ tsp. salt
- ⅛ tsp. pepper
- 2 cups 2% milk
- 6 oz. cream cheese, cubed
- 1 cup shredded cheddar cheese
- 2 cups soft bread crumbs

1. Preheat oven to 350°. Cook broccoli in 1 in. of water until almost tender; drain. Cook pearl onions in 1 in. of water until almost tender; drain. Transfer both to a greased 13x9-in. baking dish.
2. In a large saucepan, melt ¼ cup butter; whisk in flour, salt and pepper until smooth. Gradually whisk in milk. Bring to a boil; cook and stir until thickened, 1-2 minutes. Reduce heat; stir in the cream cheese until blended. Add to the vegetables; stir gently to coat. Sprinkle with cheddar cheese.
3. Melt remaining butter; toss with bread crumbs. Sprinkle over casserole. Bake, uncovered, until topping is golden brown, 25-30 minutes.
Note: To make soft bread crumbs, tear bread into pieces and place in a food processor or blender. Cover and pulse until crumbs form. One slice of bread yields ½-¾ cup crumbs.
¾ cup: 241 cal., 17g fat (10g sat. fat), 47mg chol., 389mg sod., 15g carb. (5g sugars, 3g fiber), 7g pro.

MENU

SPRING SUPPER

Bourbon-Spiced
Glazed Ham, p. 299

Easy Biscuit Muffins, p. 299

Warm Fava Bean &
Pea Salad, p. 300

Buttery Carrots, p. 300

Strawberry Shortcake
Puffs, p. 300

BOURBON-SPICED GLAZED HAM

This bourbon-spiked ham makes a wonderful main course for a holiday feast. Leftovers (if there are any, that is) make great sandwiches.
—Karen Sublett- Young, Princeton, IN

- -

Prep: 20 min. + marinating • **Bake:** 3 hours
Makes: 16 servings

7 to 9 lbs. fully cooked bone-in ham
1 cup packed brown sugar
1 cup orange juice
1 cup bourbon
1½ tsp. ground cloves

1. Place the ham in a large resealable plastic bag. Whisk together remaining ingredients until blended; pour into bag. Seal the bag and turn ham to coat. Refrigerate 8 hours or overnight.
2. Preheat oven to 325°. Remove ham from marinade and place on a rack in a roasting pan; reserve remaining marinade, placing it in the refrigerator until ready to baste.
3. Using a sharp knife, score surface of ham with ¼-in.-deep cuts in a diamond pattern. Bake, covered, 2 hours. Baste ham with about half of the reserved marinade. Bake, uncovered, 1-1½ hours, basting the ham 2 more times during the first half hour, until a thermometer reads 140°.
4 oz. cooked ham: 182 cal., 5g fat (2g sat. fat), 87mg chol., 1,042mg sod., 4g carb. (3g sugars, 0 fiber), 29g pro.

EASY BISCUIT MUFFINS

Simple homemade biscuits, made with readily available ingredients — you'd never know there's mayonnaise in them! It's easy to adapt this recipe for jumbo-sized muffin tins—just give them more baking time.
—Taryn Ellis, Wyoming, MI

- -

Prep: 10 min. • **Bake:** 25 min.
Makes: 1 dozen

3 cups all-purpose flour
4 tsp. baking powder
1½ tsp. sugar
1 tsp. salt
1½ cups whole milk
½ cup mayonnaise

1. Preheat oven to 350°. Whisk together first 4 ingredients. In another bowl, whisk milk and mayonnaise until blended; add to dry ingredients, stirring just until moistened (batter will be thick).
2. Spoon ¼ cup mixture into each of 12 greased or paper-lined muffin cups. Bake until golden brown, 25-30 minutes. Cool 5 minutes before removing from pan to a wire rack. Serve warm.
1 muffin: 194 cal., 8g fat (2g sat. fat), 4mg chol., 417mg sod., 26g carb. (2g sugars, 1g fiber), 4g pro.

WARM FAVA BEAN & PEA SALAD

This is a springtime staple in my house; my mom has been making it forever. I know that when favas are at the market I can always find this refreshing and tasty salad in her fridge! If fresh favas or peas are not available, frozen is fine—but if you use frozen favas, be sure to take off the tough outer skin.
—Francesca Ferenczi, New York, NY

Prep: 55 min. • **Cook:** 25 min.
Makes: 12 servings

- 3 cups shelled fresh fava beans (about 4 lbs. unshelled) or 1 pkg. (28 oz.) frozen fava beans, thawed
- 8 cups shelled fresh peas (about 8 lbs. unshelled) or 8 cups frozen peas (about 32 oz.)
- 3 Tbsp. olive oil, divided
- 4 oz. diced pancetta
- 8 shallots, thinly sliced
- ½ tsp. salt
- ¼ tsp. pepper

1. For fresh fava beans, add beans to a large pot of boiling water; return to a boil. Cook, uncovered, until tender, 4-5 minutes. Using a strainer, remove beans to a bowl of ice water to cool. Drain cooled beans; squeeze gently to remove skins. (If using frozen fava beans, prepare according to package directions.)

2. For fresh peas, add peas to boiling water; return to a boil. Cook, uncovered, just until tender, 2-4 minutes. Drain well; place in a large bowl. (If using frozen peas, cook according to package directions.)

3. In a large skillet, heat 1 Tbsp. oil over medium heat. Add pancetta; cook and stir until crisp, about 5 minutes. Drain on paper towels, reserving drippings.

4. In same pan, heat the remaining oil and reserved drippings over medium heat. Add the shallots; cook and stir until tender and lightly browned, 5-6 minutes. Stir in fava beans and heat through. Add to peas; stir in salt, pepper and pancetta. Serve warm.
Note: Three cups frozen shelled edamame may be substituted for fava beans; prepare according to package directions.
¾ cup: 293 cal., 7g fat (2g sat. fat), 8mg chol., 282mg sod., 49g carb. (35g sugars, 8g fiber), 10g pro.

BUTTERY CARROTS

My mother made this recipe often when I was growing up. She got it from a friend who was a chef at a local restaurant my parents frequented. The onions really bring out the sweetness of the carrots. When I have carrots fresh from the garden, I don't even peel them—I just scrub them well before cutting.
—Mary Ellen Chambers, Lakewood, OH

Takes: 20 min.
Makes: 12 servings

- 3 lbs. medium carrots, halved crosswise and cut into strips
- 2 medium onions, halved and thinly sliced
- ½ cup butter, melted
- ½ cup chopped fresh parsley
- ½ tsp. salt
  Coarsely ground pepper, optional

1. Place 2 in. of water in a 6-qt. stockpot. Add carrots and onions; bring to a boil. Reduce heat; simmer, covered, until carrots are crisp-tender, 10-12 minutes.

2. Drain vegetables. Toss with remaining ingredients.
¾ cup: 123 cal., 8g fat (5g sat. fat), 20mg chol., 240mg sod., 13g carb. (6g sugars, 4g fiber), 1g pro.

STRAWBERRY SHORTCAKE PUFFS

When a friend brought me a pint of strawberries, I decided to make strawberry shortcake with my own spin. The light and airy puff pastry stacks let the fruit shine.
—Jenny Dubinsky, Inwood, WV

Prep: 25 min. • **Bake:** 15 min. + cooling
Makes: 12 servings

- 1 sheet frozen puff pastry, thawed
- 4 cups fresh strawberries, sliced
- ¼ cup plus 3 Tbsp. sugar, divided
- 1½ cups heavy whipping cream
- ½ tsp. vanilla extract

1. Preheat oven to 400°. On a lightly floured surface, roll puff pastry to a 10-in. square; cut into 12 rectangles (approx. 3x2½ in.). Place on ungreased baking sheets. Bake until golden brown, 12-15 minutes. Remove to wire racks; cool completely.

2. In a large bowl, toss strawberries with ¼ cup sugar. Let stand 30 minutes, stirring occasionally. In another bowl, beat cream until it begins to thicken. Add vanilla and the remaining sugar; beat until stiff peaks form.

3. To serve, split pastries horizontally in half. Top each bottom half with 2 Tbsp. whipped cream and 1 Tbsp. strawberries; replace top half. Top with remaining whipped cream and strawberries.
1 serving: 246 cal., 16g fat (8g sat. fat), 34mg chol., 76mg sod., 23g carb. (11g sugars, 2g fiber), 3g pro.

GRANDMA'S FAVORITE

COOKIES, BROWNIE'S & BARS

Grandma's cookie jar is as full of memories as it is with yummy home-baked treats. Turn here whenever you need a sweet escape, a bite to share or a delicious remembrance of simply happy times.

GRANDMA'S STAR COOKIES

My husband's grandma would only make these butter cutouts with a star cookie cutter. I love them, but I do use various other shapes for celebrations we host throughout the year.
—Jenny Brown, West Lafayette, IN

- -

Prep: 1 hour + chilling
Bake: 10 min./batch + cooling
Makes: about 7 dozen

1½ cups butter, softened
½   cup shortening
1   cup sugar
1   cup packed brown sugar
2   large eggs, room temperature
¼   cup thawed orange
    juice concentrate
1   tsp. vanilla extract
5   cups all-purpose flour
1   tsp. baking soda
1   tsp. salt
FROSTING
3   cups confectioners' sugar
¼   cup butter, melted
1½ tsp. thawed orange
    juice concentrate
1   tsp. vanilla extract
3   to 4 Tbsp. whole milk
    Optional: Food coloring and
    sprinkles or colored sugar

1. In a large bowl, cream softened butter, shortening and sugars until light and fluffy. Add 1 egg at a time, beating well after each addition. Beat in orange juice concentrate and vanilla. Combine the flour, baking soda and salt; gradually add to creamed mixture and mix well. Cover and refrigerate until easy to handle, about 2 hours.

2. On a lightly floured surface, roll out dough to ¼-in. thickness. Cut with a 3-in. star-shaped cookie cutter dipped in flour. Place 1 in. apart on ungreased baking sheets. Bake at 350° until edges are firm, 7-8 minutes. Remove to wire racks to cool.

3. For frosting, combine the confectioners' sugar, butter, orange juice concentrate, vanilla and enough milk to reach spreading consistency. Tint with food coloring if desired. Frost cookies; decorate as desired.

1 cookie: 111 cal., 5g fat (3g sat. fat), 15mg chol., 77mg sod., 15g carb. (9g sugars, 0 fiber), 1g pro.

GUMDROP COOKIES

These cookies were my mother's special treat. They are great for keeping children busy—they can cut up the gumdrops and eat all the black ones so they don't turn the dough gray.
—Letah Chilston, Riverton, WY

- -

Prep: 15 min. + chilling • **Bake:** 10 min./batch
Makes: about 7 dozen

1½ cups spice gumdrops
¾ cup coarsely chopped walnuts
½ cup golden raisins
1¾ cups all-purpose flour, divided
½ cup shortening
1 cup packed brown sugar
1 large egg, room temperature
¼ cup buttermilk
½ tsp. baking soda
½ tsp. salt

1. Cut gumdrops into small pieces; place in a bowl. Add walnuts, raisins and ¼ cup flour and toss to coat.
2. In a large bowl, beat the shortening and brown sugar until blended. Beat in the egg, then buttermilk. In another bowl, whisk the remaining flour, baking soda and salt; gradually beat into shortening mixture. Stir in gumdrop mixture. Refrigerate, covered, 1 hour.
3. Preheat oven to 400°. Drop dough by rounded teaspoonfuls 2 in. apart onto ungreased baking sheets. Bake until golden brown, 8-10 minutes. Cool on pans for 2 minutes. Remove to wire racks to cool.
1 cookie: 53 cal., 2g fat (0 sat. fat), 2mg chol., 26mg sod., 9g carb. (5g sugars, 0 fiber), 1g pro.

CHEWY PECAN PIE BARS

This is one of my husband's favorite recipes. I've been making it for many years, and we still can't get enough of it.
—Judy Taylor, Shreveport, LA

Prep: 10 min. • **Bake:** 30 min. + cooling
Makes: 2 dozen

- ¼   cup butter, melted
- 2   cups packed brown sugar
- ⅔   cup all-purpose flour
- 4   large eggs, room temperature
- 2   tsp. vanilla extract
- ¼   tsp. baking soda
- ¼   tsp. salt
- 2   cups chopped pecans
     Confectioners' sugar, optional

1. Preheat oven to 350°. Pour the butter into a 13x9-in. baking pan. In a large bowl, combine next 6 ingredients; mix well. Stir in pecans. Spread over the butter.
2. Bake 30-35 minutes. Remove from oven. If desired, immediately dust with confectioners' sugar. Cool before cutting.
1 bar: 180 cal., 10g fat (2g sat. fat), 41mg chol., 75mg sod., 22g carb. (18g sugars, 1g fiber), 2g pro.

"I've made this several times, and each time it is a big hit with family and friends. I made it for a party and it was the most eaten dessert. It is simple and fast to make."
—SHABAYEB, TASTEOFHOME.COM

CHOCOLATE SNOWBALLS

This is one of my favorite cookie recipes. They remind me of the snowballs I'd pack as a child during winters here in Wisconsin.
—Dee Derezinski, Waukesha, WI

Prep: 30 min. • **Bake:** 15 min./batch + cooling **Makes:** about 4 dozen

- ¾   cup butter, softened
- ½   cup sugar
- ½   tsp. salt
- 1   large egg, room temperature
- 2   tsp. vanilla extract
- 2   cups all-purpose flour
- 1   cup chopped pecans or walnuts
- 1   cup (6 oz.) chocolate chips
     Confectioners' sugar

1. Preheat oven to 350°. In a large bowl, cream butter, sugar and salt until light and fluffy. Beat in egg and vanilla. Gradually beat in flour. Stir in pecans and chocolate chips.
2. Shape dough into 1-in. balls; place 2 in. apart on ungreased baking sheets. Bake until set and bottoms are lightly browned, 15-20 minutes. Cool on pans 2 minutes. Roll warm cookies in confectioners' sugar. Cool completely on wire racks. If desired, reroll cookies in confectioners' sugar.
1 cookie: 92 cal., 6g fat (3g sat. fat), 12mg chol., 49mg sod., 10g carb. (5g sugars, 1g fiber), 1g pro.

CRANBERRY PECAN TASSIES

A traditional pecan tassie is a small tart with nuts, and this festive version adds cranberries.
—Peggy West, Georgetown, DE

- -

Prep: 25 min. + chilling
Bake: 20 min. + cooling • **Makes:** 2 dozen

- ½ cup butter, softened
- 3 oz. cream cheese, softened
- 1 cup all-purpose flour
- 1 large egg, room temperature
- ⅔ cup packed brown sugar
- 1 Tbsp. butter, melted
- 1 tsp. grated orange zest
- ½ cup chopped pecans
- ½ cup fresh or frozen cranberries, thawed

1. In a small bowl, beat butter and cream cheese until smooth; gradually beat in flour. Refrigerate, covered, 30 minutes or until firm enough to shape.
2. Preheat oven to 325°. Shape dough into 1-in. balls; place in greased mini-muffin cups. Press evenly onto bottoms and up sides of cups.
3. In a small bowl, beat the egg, brown sugar, melted butter and orange zest until blended. Stir in pecans. Spoon 1½ tsp. filling into each cup; top with cranberries.
4. Bake 20-25 minutes or until the crust is golden and filling is set. Cool in pans for 2 minutes. Remove to wire racks to cool.
Freeze option: Freeze cookies, layered between waxed paper, in freezer containers. To use, thaw before serving.
1 tassie: 113 cal., 7g fat (4g sat. fat), 23mg chol., 50mg sod., 11g carb. (6g sugars, 0 fiber), 1g pro.

LEMON COCONUT SQUARES

The tangy lemon flavor of this no-fuss bar is especially delicious on a warm day. It reminds me of selling lemonade on the sidewalk as a little girl.
—Donna Biddle, Elmira, NY

- -

Prep: 25 min. • **Bake:** 20 min. + cooling
Makes: 4 dozen

- 1½ cups all-purpose flour
- ½ cup confectioners' sugar
- ¾ cup cold butter, cubed
- 4 large eggs, room temperature
- 1½ cups sugar
- ½ cup lemon juice
- 1 tsp. baking powder
- ¾ cup sweetened shredded coconut

1. In a small bowl, combine the flour and confectioners' sugar; cut in the butter until crumbly. Press into a lightly greased 13x9-in. baking pan. Bake at 350° for 15 minutes.
2. Meanwhile, in another small bowl, beat the eggs, sugar, lemon juice and baking powder until combined. Pour over crust; sprinkle with coconut.
3. Bake at 350° for 20-25 minutes or until golden brown. Cool on a wire rack. Cut into bars.
1 serving: 82 cal., 4g fat (2g sat. fat), 25mg chol., 46mg sod., 11g carb. (8g sugars, 0 fiber), 1g pro.

HAZELNUT CHOCOLATE CHIP COOKIE

These nutty cookies are popular with the ladies at my craft club. I grew up during the Depression, and my mother taught me to use what was available, and these cookies use the nuts that are plentiful here.
—Selmer Looney, Eugene, OR

Takes: 25 min. • **Makes:** 3 dozen

- 1 cup butter, softened
- ½ cup sugar
- 1 cup packed brown sugar
- 2 large eggs, room temperature
- 1 tsp. vanilla extract
- 2⅓ cups all-purpose flour
- 1 tsp. baking soda
- ½ tsp. salt
- 1 cup (6 oz.) semisweet chocolate chips
- ¾ cup chopped hazelnuts

1. In a large bowl, cream butter and sugars on medium speed for 3 minutes. Add 1 egg at a time, beating well after each addition. Add vanilla. Combine the flour, baking soda and salt; gradually add to batter. Fold in the chocolate chips and nuts.

2. Drop by heaping tablespoonfuls 3 in. apart onto lightly greased baking sheets. Flatten lightly with a fork. Bake at 350° for 10-12 minutes or until light brown. Remove to a wire rack to cool.

1 cookie: 299 cal., 17g fat (8g sat. fat), 51mg chol., 251mg sod., 37g carb. (23g sugars, 1g fiber), 4g pro.

GINGER-CREAM BARS

I rediscovered this nearly forgotten old-time recipe recently and found that it's still everyone's favorite. Even 4-year-olds have asked for these frosted bars as their nursery treats.
—Carol Nagelkirk, Holland, MI

Prep: 20 min. • **Bake:** 20 min.
Makes: 5 dozen

- 1 cup butter, softened
- 1 cup sugar
- 2 cups all-purpose flour
- 1 tsp. salt
- 2 tsp. baking soda
- 1 Tbsp. ground cinnamon
- 1 Tbsp. ground cloves
- 1 Tbsp. ground ginger
- 2 large eggs, room temperature
- ½ cup molasses
- 1 cup hot brewed coffee

FROSTING

- ½ cup butter, softened
- 3 oz. cream cheese, softened
- 2 cups confectioners' sugar
- 2 tsp. vanilla extract
  Chopped nuts, optional

1. Preheat oven to 350°. Cream butter and granulated sugar. Sift together flour, salt, baking soda and spices; add to creamed mixture. Add 1 egg at a time, beating well after each addition, and molasses. Blend in coffee. Spread in a 15x10x1-in. baking pan.

2. Bake 20-25 minutes. Cool. For frosting, cream butter and cream cheese; add the confectioners' sugar and vanilla. Spread over bars. If desired, top with nuts.

1 bar: 101 cal., 5g fat (3g sat. fat), 20mg chol., 126mg sod., 13g carb. (9g sugars, 0 fiber), 1g pro.

CHERRY COCONUT TREATS

My great-grandmother created this recipe more than 100 years ago, so it's made many appearances at family parties. Add a bit of flair by using both red and green maraschino cherries.
—Anne Mullen, Windsor, ON

- -

Prep: 15 min. • **Bake:** 35 min. + chilling
Makes: 2 dozen

- 1½ cups all-purpose flour
- 1 cup graham cracker crumbs
- ⅔ cup packed brown sugar
- 1 tsp. baking powder
- ½ tsp. salt
- 1 cup butter, melted

FILLING
- 4 cups unsweetened finely shredded coconut
- 2 cans (14 oz. each) sweetened condensed milk
- 2 jars (10 oz. each) maraschino cherries, drained and chopped
- 2 tsp. vanilla extract
- 1 tsp. almond extract

1. Preheat oven to 325°. In a small bowl, mix the first 5 ingredients; stir in melted butter. Press onto bottom of a greased 13x9-in. baking pan.

2. In another bowl, mix filling ingredients; pour over crust. Bake until edges are lightly browned, 35-40 minutes. Cool on a wire rack 1 hour. Refrigerate, covered, 4 hours before cutting. Store in an airtight container in the refrigerator.

Note: Look for unsweetened coconut in the baking or health food section.

1 bar: 362 cal., 20g fat (14g sat. fat), 32mg chol., 202mg sod., 45g carb. (35g sugars, 3g fiber), 5g pro.

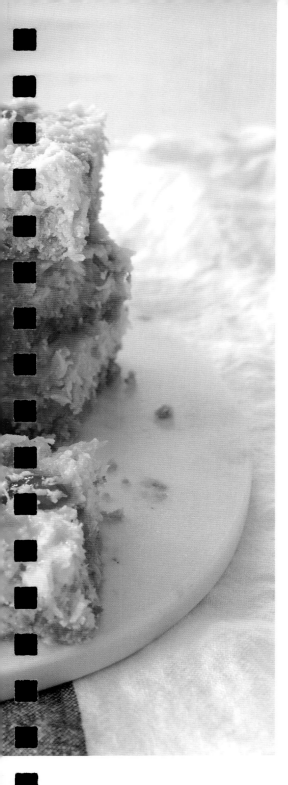

GRANDMA'S RASPBERRY RUGELACH

I remember sitting on the couch in my great-grandmother's house with a pad and pen as she told me each ingredient and measurement for her special rugelach. Some of the ingredients are different from the typical version. My whole family cherishes this heirloom recipe.
—Dalya Rubin, Boca Raton, FL

- -

Prep: 45 min. + chilling
Bake: 25 min./batch + cooling
Makes: about 5 dozen

1½   **cups margarine, softened**
⅓   **cup sugar**
3   **tsp. vanilla extract**
    Pinch salt
1   **cup heavy whipping cream**
4   **to 4½ cups all-purpose flour**
1   **cup seedless raspberry jam**
OPTIONAL GLAZE
1   **cup confectioners' sugar**
4   **tsp. 2% milk**

1. In a large bowl, beat the margarine, sugar, vanilla and salt on medium-low until combined. Slowly beat in whipping cream. Gradually beat in enough flour until dough is no longer sticky. Divide the dough into 4 portions, then flatten into disks. Wrap in plastic; refrigerate dough at least 2 hours or overnight.

2. Preheat oven to 350°. On a lightly floured surface, roll each portion of the dough into a 12-in. circle; spread each with ¼ cup raspberry jam. Cut each circle of dough into 16 wedges.

3. Gently roll up the wedges from the wide ends. Place 2 in. apart on parchment-lined baking sheets, point side down. Bake until light golden, 25-30 minutes. Remove to wire racks to cool.

4. If desired, combine confectioners' sugar and milk until smooth. Drizzle glaze over cooled rugelach.

1 cookie: 96 cal., 6g fat (2g sat. fat), 4mg chol., 53mg sod., 10g carb. (4g sugars, 0 fiber), 1g pro.

Grandma's Apricot Rugelach: Substitute apricot filling for the raspberry jam. In a small bowl, combine ½ cup sugar and 1 Tbsp. ground cinnamon. Spread ¼ cup apricot jam over dough; sprinkle with 2 Tbsp. cinnamon sugar. Proceed as directed.

GRANDMA BRUBAKER'S ORANGE COOKIES

My family has enjoyed these light, delicate, orange-flavored cookies for at least two generations, if not more.
—Sheri DeBolt, Huntington, IN

Prep: 20 min.
Bake: 10 min./batch + cooling
Makes: about 6 dozen

- 1 cup shortening
- 2 cups sugar
- 2 large eggs, room temperature, separated
- 1 cup buttermilk
- 5 cups all-purpose flour
- 2 tsp. baking powder
- 2 tsp. baking soda
  Pinch salt
  Juice and grated zest of 2 medium navel oranges

ICING
- 2 cups confectioners' sugar
- ¼ cup orange juice
- 1 Tbsp. butter
- 1 Tbsp. grated orange zest

1. Preheat oven to 325°. In a bowl, cream shortening and sugar. Beat in the egg yolks and buttermilk. Sift together flour, baking powder, soda and salt; add to creamed mixture alternately with orange juice and zest. Add egg whites and beat until smooth.
2. Drop by rounded teaspoonfuls onto greased cookie sheets. Bake until set, about 10 minutes. Remove cookies to wire racks to cool completely.
3. For icing, combine all ingredients and beat until smooth. Frost cooled cookies.
1 cookie: 97 cal., 3g fat (1g sat. fat), 6mg chol., 58mg sod., 16g carb. (9g sugars, 0 fiber), 1g pro.

CHOCOLATE MAPLE BARS

My family runs a maple syrup operation, and I'm always looking for new ways to incorporate our syrup into my cooking and baking. These bars are a delicious success!
—Cathy Schumacher, Alto, MI

Prep: 20 min.
Bake: 25 min. + cooling
Makes: 3 dozen

- ½ cup shortening
- ¾ cup maple syrup
- ½ cup sugar
- 3 large eggs, room temperature
- 3 Tbsp. whole milk
- 1 tsp. vanilla extract
- 1¼ cups all-purpose flour
- ¼ tsp. baking powder
- ¼ tsp. salt
- 1½ oz. unsweetened chocolate, melted
- ½ cup chopped pecans
- ½ cup sweetened shredded coconut

FROSTING
- ¼ cup butter, softened
- 1 cup confectioners' sugar
- ½ cup baking cocoa
- ½ cup maple syrup
- 1 cup miniature marshmallows

1. In a large bowl, cream the shortening, syrup and sugar until light and fluffy. Beat in the eggs, milk and vanilla. Combine the flour, baking powder and salt; add to the creamed mixture and mix well. Remove half of the batter to another bowl.
2. Combine melted chocolate and pecans; stir into 1 bowl of batter. Spread into a greased 13x9-in. baking pan. Add coconut to remaining batter. Spread carefully over chocolate batter.
3. Bake at 350° until a toothpick inserted in center comes out clean, about 25 minutes. Cool completely on a wire rack.
4. For the frosting, in a small bowl, beat butter until smooth. Gradually add the confectioners' sugar and cocoa. Gradually add syrup, beating until smooth. Fold in the marshmallows. Frost bars.
1 bar: 143 cal., 7g fat (3g sat. fat), 21mg chol., 43mg sod., 20g carb. (14g sugars, 1g fiber), 2g pro.

CHOCOLATE BUTTERMILK SQUARES

Every time I take a pan of these squares to a potluck, it comes back clean! At home, they vanish as fast as I make them.
—Clarice Baker, Stromsburg, NE

- -

Prep: 20 min. • **Bake:** 20 min.
Makes: 15 servings

- 1 cup butter, cubed
- ¼ cup baking cocoa
- 1 cup water
- 2 cups all-purpose flour
- 2 cups sugar
- 1 tsp. baking soda
- ½ tsp. salt
- ½ cup buttermilk
- 2 large eggs, room temperature, beaten
- 1 tsp. vanilla extract
- 3 to 4 drops red food coloring, optional

FROSTING
- ½ cup butter, cubed
- ¼ cup baking cocoa
- ¼ cup buttermilk
- 3¾ cups confectioners' sugar
- 1 tsp. vanilla extract
  Dash salt
- ¾ cup chopped almonds, optional

1. In a large saucepan, bring butter, cocoa and water just to a boil. Cool.

2. Meanwhile, in a large bowl, combine the flour, sugar, baking soda and salt. Add cocoa mixture and buttermilk; mix well. Beat in the eggs, vanilla and, if desired, food coloring. Pour into a greased and floured 15x10x1-in. baking pan.

3. Bake at 350° for 20 minutes. For frosting, melt butter with cocoa and buttermilk. Stir in the confectioners' sugar, vanilla and salt. Spread over the warm cake. Garnish with chopped almonds if desired.

1 piece: 466 cal., 19g fat (12g sat. fat), 78mg chol., 380mg sod., 72g carb. (55g sugars, 1g fiber), 4g pro.

TEST KITCHEN TIP

For different flavor thrills, try substituting almond, rum or mint extract for the vanilla in the batter and frosting. (Mint extract packs quite a punch, however, so be sure to reduce it from 1 tsp. to ¼ tsp.) As long as you're trying new flavors, consider topping the bars with toffee bits or crushed candy bars instead of the chopped almonds. Yum!

BAKI'S OLD-WORLD COOKIES

My maternal grandmother mixed up many batches of these pretty treats. My uncles called them "cupcake cookies" because of the unique way they're baked.
—Marilyn Louise Riggenbach, Ravenna, OH

- -

Prep: 25 min. + chilling
Bake: 20 min./batch
Makes: 3 dozen

1	cup butter, softened
1	cup sugar
2	large eggs, room temperature
1	cup ground walnuts
1½	cups all-purpose flour
1½	tsp. ground cinnamon
1	tsp. ground cloves
2	tsp. vanilla extract
	Confectioners' sugar

1. Preheat oven to 350°. Cream butter and sugar until light and fluffy. Add 1 egg at a time, beating well after each addition. Add nuts. In another bowl, sift together flour, cinnamon and cloves; add with vanilla to creamed mixture. Refrigerate, covered, for 1 hour.

2. Fill 36 generously greased cups of a muffin tin or individual 3-in. tins one-third to half full. Press the dough around sides, leaving a depression in center. (If dough is too soft, add flour.)

3. Bake until light brown, about 18 minutes. Cool 2 minutes; tap tins to remove cookies. Dust with confectioners' sugar.

1 cookie: 105 cal., 7g fat (3g sat. fat), 24mg chol., 45mg sod., 10g carb. (6g sugars, 0 fiber), 1g pro.

JAM-FILLED WREATHS

My mother found this recipe some 30 years ago, and I continue to make it today. The beautiful wreath-shaped cookies with jewel-red centers are perfect at Christmas. The dusting of powdered sugar gives them a snowy look.
—Monica Wilson, Pomona, NY

- -

Prep: 25 min. + chilling
Bake: 10 min./batch + cooling
Makes: about 3 dozen wreaths

¾	cup butter, softened
1	cup sugar
2	large eggs, room temperature
1½	cups all-purpose flour
1	tsp. baking powder
1	tsp. ground cinnamon
½	tsp. ground allspice
1	cup quick-cooking oats
¾	cup finely chopped nuts
1	jar (18 oz.) seedless raspberry jam
	Confectioners' sugar

1. In a bowl, cream the butter and sugar. Add 1 egg at a time, beating well after each addition. Combine the flour, baking powder, cinnamon and allspice; add to the creamed mixture. Stir in the oats and nuts; mix well. Refrigerate for 3 hours or until the dough is easy to handle.

2. On a floured surface, roll out dough to ⅛-in. thickness. Cut with a 2½-in. round cookie cutter. Using a 1-in. round cookie cutter, cut out the center of half of the cookies. Place solid and window cookies on lightly greased baking sheets.

3. Bake at 400° for 6-8 minutes or until lightly browned. Cool on wire racks.

4. Spread 1 tsp. jam over bottoms of solid cookies; top with window cookies. Dust with confectioners' sugar. Fill centers with additional jam if desired.

1 cookie: 166 cal., 7g fat (3g sat. fat), 25mg chol., 58mg sod., 25g carb. (17g sugars, 1g fiber), 2g pro.

LEMON SNOWDROPS

I save my snowdrop cookies for special occasions. The crunchy, buttery sandwich cookie has a tart yet lovely lemon filling.
—Bernice Martinoni, Petaluma, CA

- -

Prep: 40 min. + chilling
Bake: 10 min./batch + cooling
Makes: 2 dozen

- 1   cup butter, softened
- ½   cup confectioners' sugar
- ¼   tsp. salt
- 1   tsp. lemon extract
- 2   cups all-purpose flour
-     Sugar

FILLING

- 1   large egg, room temperature, lightly beaten
- ⅔   cup sugar
- 2   tsp. grated lemon zest
- 3   Tbsp. lemon juice
- 4   tsp. butter
-     Additional confectioners' sugar, optional

1. Preheat oven to 350°. Cream the butter, confectioners' sugar and salt until light and fluffy. Beat in extract. Gradually beat in the flour. Shape teaspoonfuls of dough into balls (if necessary, refrigerate the dough, covered, until firm enough to shape). Place balls 1 in. apart on ungreased baking sheets; flatten slightly with bottom of a glass dipped in granulated sugar. Bake until light brown, 10-12 minutes. Remove cookies from pans to wire racks to cool completely.

2. For filling, whisk together the egg, sugar, lemon zest and lemon juice in a small heavy saucepan over medium-low heat until blended. Add butter; cook over medium heat, whisking constantly, until thickened and a thermometer reads at least 170°, about 20 minutes. Remove from heat immediately (do not allow to boil). Transfer to a small bowl; cool. Press plastic wrap onto surface of filling. Refrigerate until cold, about 1 hour.

3. To serve, spread lemon filling on half of cookies; cover with remaining cookies. If desired, dust with confectioners' sugar. Store leftovers in refrigerator.

Freeze option: Freeze the cookies, (unfilled and undecorated) in freezer containers. To use, thaw cookies in covered containers. Fill and decorate as directed.

1 sandwich cookie: 147 cal., 9g fat (5g sat. fat), 30mg chol., 94mg sod., 16g carb. (8g sugars, 0 fiber), 1g pro.

ALMOND TASSIES

I make so many of these fancy tassies, I go through a 7-pound container of almond paste every year. They're one of my family's all-time favorites.
—Donna Westhouse, Dorr, MI

- -

Prep: 30 min.
Bake: 15 min./batch + cooling
Makes: 4 dozen

- 1   cup butter, softened
- 6   oz. cream cheese, softened
- 2   cups all-purpose flour

FILLING

- 2   cans (8 oz. each) almond paste
- 1½ cups sugar
- 3   large eggs, room temperature, lightly beaten
- 3   Tbsp. orange juice
- 3   Tbsp. heavy whipping cream
- 1   Tbsp. all-purpose flour
- ¼   cup sliced almonds

1. In a large bowl, cream butter and cream cheese until light and fluffy. Gradually add flour and mix well. Shape into 48 balls. With floured fingers, press onto the bottom and up sides of greased miniature muffin cups.
2. For filling, in a large bowl, combine the almond paste, sugar, eggs, orange juice, cream and flour. Fill the prepared cups three-fourths full. Sprinkle with almonds.
3. Bake at 400° for 12-13 minutes or until lightly browned. Cool for 10 minutes before carefully removing from pans to wire racks to cool completely.
1 tassie: 144 cal., 9g fat (4g sat. fat), 26mg chol., 47mg sod., 15g carb. (10g sugars, 1g fiber), 2g pro.

CHOCOLATE-COCONUT LAYER BARS

For fun, I reinvented no-bake Nanaimo bars by amping up the coconut.
—Shannon Dobos, Calgary, AB

- -

Prep: 20 min. + chilling • **Makes:** 3 dozen

- ¾   cup butter, cubed
- 3   cups Oreo cookie crumbs
- 2   cups sweetened shredded coconut
- ½   cup cream of coconut

FILLING

- ⅓   cup butter, softened
- 3   Tbsp. cream of coconut
- ¼   tsp. coconut extract
- 3   cups confectioners' sugar
- 1   to 2 Tbsp. 2% milk

TOPPING

- 1½ cups semisweet chocolate chips
- 4   tsp. canola oil
- 3   Mounds candy bars (1¾ oz. each), coarsely chopped, optional

1. Microwave butter on high until melted; stir until smooth. Stir in cookie crumbs, shredded coconut and cream of coconut until blended (mixture will be wet). Spread onto bottom of an ungreased 13x9-in. baking pan. Refrigerate until set, about 30 minutes.
2. For filling, beat butter, cream of coconut and extract until smooth. Gradually beat in the confectioners' sugar and enough milk to reach a spreading consistency. Spread over the crust.
3. For topping, microwave the semisweet chocolate chips and oil until melted; stir until smooth. Cool slightly; spread over filling. If desired, sprinkle with chopped Mounds candy bars. Refrigerate.
1 bar: 229 cal., 13g fat (8g sat. fat), 15mg chol., 124mg sod., 28g carb. (23g sugars, 1g fiber), 1g pro.

WINNING APRICOT BARS

This recipe is down-home baking at its best. It's even won blue ribbons at county fairs and contests in several states. The treat is easy to make, and it's perfect for potluck suppers, bake sales, lunch boxes, or just plain snacking.
—Jill Moritz, Irvine, CA

- -

Prep: 15 min. • **Bake:** 30 min. + cooling
Makes: 2 dozen

- ¾ cup butter, softened
- 1 cup sugar
- 1 large egg, room temperature
- ½ tsp. vanilla extract
- 2 cups all-purpose flour
- ¼ tsp. baking powder
- 1⅓ cups sweetened shredded coconut
- ½ cup chopped walnuts
- 1 jar (10 to 12 oz.) apricot preserves

1. Preheat oven to 350°. In a large bowl, cream butter and sugar until light and fluffy. Beat in the egg and vanilla. In a small bowl, whisk flour and baking powder; gradually add to creamed mixture, mixing well. Fold in coconut and walnuts.

2. Press two-thirds of the dough onto the bottom of a greased 13x9-in. baking pan. Spread with preserves; crumble remaining dough over preserves. Bake 30-35 minutes or until golden brown. Cool completely in pan on a wire rack. Cut into bars.

1 bar: 195 cal., 10g fat (6g sat. fat), 23mg chol., 72mg sod., 27g carb. (16g sugars, 1g fiber), 2g pro.

FIG & ALMOND COOKIES

In our family, cookies—such as these nutty fig types—are a big deal. I'm so proud to pass on this Italian tradition to my boys.
—Angela Lemoine, Howell, NJ

Prep: 50 min. + chilling
Bake: 10 min./batch + cooling
Makes: about 6½ dozen

- 2 **large eggs, room temperature**
- 1 **Tbsp. cold water**
- 2 **tsp. vanilla extract**
- 2¾ **cups all-purpose flour**
- 1½ **cups confectioners' sugar**
- 3 **tsp. baking powder**
- ¼ **tsp. salt**
- 6 **Tbsp. cold butter, cubed**

FILLING
- 8 **oz. dried figs (about 1⅓ cups)**
- 3 **Tbsp. unblanched almonds**
- 2 **Tbsp. apricot preserves**
- 4 **tsp. orange juice**

GLAZE
- 1 **cup confectioners' sugar**
- 2 **Tbsp. 2% milk**
- ½ **tsp. vanilla extract**

1. In a small bowl, whisk eggs, cold water and vanilla until blended. Place the flour, confectioners' sugar, baking powder and salt in a food processor; pulse until blended. Add the cold butter; pulse until crumbly. While pulsing, add the egg mixture just until combined.

2. Divide dough in half. Shape each into a disk; cover. Refrigerate 1 hour or until firm enough to roll.

3. Wipe food processor clean. Add the figs and almonds; pulse until chopped. Add the preserves and juice; pulse until combined.

4. Preheat oven to 350°. On a lightly floured surface, roll each portion of dough into a 10x8-in. rectangle; cut each lengthwise into four 2-in.-wide strips.

5. Spread about 2 Tbsp. filling down center of each strip. Fold dough over filling; pinch edges to seal. Roll each gently to shape into a log; cut crosswise into 1-in. pieces.

6. Place 1 in. apart on parchment-lined baking sheets. Bake until cookies are light brown, 10-12 minutes. Remove from pans to wire racks to cool completely.

7. In a small bowl, mix glaze ingredients until smooth. Drizzle over the cookies. Let stand until set.

1 cookie: 51 cal., 1g fat (1g sat. fat), 7mg chol., 33mg sod., 9g carb. (5g sugars, 0 fiber), 1g pro.

CHOCOLATE-COVERED CHERRY THUMBPRINTS

These thumbprints elicit sweet memories. When I dig out my best cookie recipes, I'm always reminded of baking when my children were little.
—Deborah Puette, Lilburn, GA

- -

Prep: 30 min. + chilling
Bake: 15 min. + cooling • **Makes:** 2 dozen

- ¼ cup butter, softened
- ¼ cup shortening
- ¼ cup packed brown sugar
- ¼ tsp. salt
- 1 large egg, room temperature, separated
- ½ tsp. vanilla extract
- 1 cup all-purpose flour
- 1 cup finely chopped salted roasted almonds

FILLING
- ⅓ cup confectioners' sugar
- 1 Tbsp. maraschino cherry juice
- 2 tsp. butter, softened
- 1 tsp. 2% milk

TOPPINGS
- 24 maraschino cherries
- 4 oz. milk chocolate candy coating, melted

1. Preheat oven to 350°. In a large bowl, cream butter, shortening, brown sugar and salt until light and fluffy. Beat in egg yolk and vanilla. Gradually beat flour into creamed mixture. Refrigerate, covered, until easy to handle, 30 minutes.

2. Preheat oven to 350°. Shape dough into 1¼-in. balls. In a shallow bowl, whisk egg white until foamy. Place the almonds in a separate shallow bowl. Dip the balls in egg white; roll in almonds.

3. Place 2 in. apart on ungreased baking sheets. Press a deep indentation in center of each with your thumb. Bake until edges are light brown, 10-12 minutes. Remove from pans to wire racks.

4. In a small bowl, beat confectioners' sugar, cherry juice, butter and milk until smooth. Fill each cookie with ¼ tsp. filling; top with 1 cherry. Drizzle with candy coating. Let stand until set.

1 cookie: 145 cal., 9g fat (3g sat. fat), 14mg chol., 75mg sod., 15g carb. (10g sugars, 1g fiber), 2g pro.

CARAMEL PEANUT BARS

Here, rich chocolate, crunchy peanuts and gooey caramel peek out from between golden oat and crumb layers. Delicious!
—Ardyce Piehl, Wisconsin Dells, WI

Prep: 25 min. • **Bake:** 15 min. + cooling
Makes: 3 dozen

- 1½ cups quick-cooking oats
- 1½ cups all-purpose flour
- 1¼ cups packed brown sugar
- ¾ tsp. baking soda
- ¼ tsp. salt
- ¾ cup butter, melted
- 1 pkg. (14 oz.) caramels
- ½ cup heavy whipping cream
- 1½ cups (9 oz.) semisweet chocolate chips
- ¾ cup chopped peanuts

1. In a bowl, combine the first 5 ingredients; stir in butter. Set aside 1 cup for topping. Press remaining mixture into a greased 13x9-in. baking pan. Bake at 350° until lightly browned, about 10 minutes.
2. In a heavy saucepan or microwave, melt the caramels with cream, stirring often. Sprinkle chocolate chips and peanuts over the crust; top with the caramel mixture. Sprinkle with reserved oat mixture. Bake for 15-20 minutes or until topping is golden brown. Cool completely on a wire rack. Cut into bars.
Note: This recipe was tested with Hershey's caramels.
1 bar: 197 cal., 10g fat (5g sat. fat), 16mg chol., 113mg sod., 27g carb. (19g sugars, 1g fiber), 3g pro.

BLACKBERRY PEEKABOO COOKIES

I'm so happy my grandmother bakes these cookies regularly. She uses homemade blackberry jam that she makes fresh every summer. These cookies are so delicious!
—Jacquie Franklin, Hot Springs, MT

Prep: 15 min. + chilling
Bake: 10 min./batch + cooling
Makes: about 3 dozen

- ½ cup butter, softened
- ½ cup shortening
- 2 cups packed brown sugar
- 2 large eggs, room temperature
- 1 tsp. vanilla extract
- 4 cups all-purpose flour
- 1½ tsp. baking soda
- 1½ tsp. salt
- ¾ cup seedless blackberry spreadable fruit

1. Cream butter, shortening and brown sugar until light and fluffy. Add 1 egg at a time, beating well after each addition. Beat in vanilla. In another bowl, whisk the flour, baking soda and salt; gradually beat into creamed mixture. Divide dough in half. Shape each into a disk; cover. Refrigerate until firm enough to roll, about 30 minutes.
2. Preheat oven to 350°. On a lightly floured surface, roll each portion of dough to ⅛-in. thickness. Cut with a floured 2-in. round cookie cutter. Place half of the circles onto parchment-lined baking sheets. Spread 1 tsp. spreadable fruit in the center of each circle; top with remaining circles, pressing edges lightly to seal.
3. Bake until light brown, 10-12 minutes. Remove from pans to wire racks to cool.
1 cookie: 162 cal., 6g fat (2g sat. fat), 17mg chol., 179mg sod., 26g carb. (15g sugars, 0 fiber), 2g pro.

GROSSMUTTER'S PEPPERNUTS

Before Christmas, my grandmother would bake peppernuts and store them until the big day. When we'd come home from school, the whole house would smell like anise and we knew the holiday season was about to begin.
—Marilyn Kutzli, Clinton, IA

Prep: 40 min. + chilling
Bake: 10 min./batch + cooling
Makes: about 30 dozen

- 3 large eggs, room temperature
- 2 cups sugar
- 2¾ cups all-purpose flour
- 1 tsp. anise extract or crushed aniseed

1. Beat eggs and sugar at medium speed for 15 minutes. Reduce speed; gradually add flour and anise. Beat until well combined. On a lightly floured surface, shape dough into ½-in.-thick ropes. Refrigerate, covered, for 1 hour.
2. Preheat oven to 350°. Cut ropes into ½-in. pieces; place on greased baking sheets. Bake until set, 6-8 minutes. Cool completely on baking sheets on wire racks. Cookies will harden upon standing. Store in airtight containers.
6 pieces: 51 cal., 0 fat (0 sat. fat), 9mg chol., 4mg sod., 11g carb. (7g sugars, 0 fiber), 1g pro. **Diabetic exchanges:** 1 starch.

NO-BAKE CORNFLAKE COOKIES

I grew up on a farm where we hand-milked cows and had plenty of milk and cream to use for baking. Sometimes we'd substitute light cream for the evaporated milk in this recipe. We'd rarely let these cookies cool before sampling them, and a batch never lasted a day!
—Denise Marnell, Hereford, TX

Takes: 25 min. • **Makes:** about 4 dozen

- 4 cups cornflakes
- 1½ cups sweetened shredded coconut
- ¾ cup chopped pecans
- 1½ cups sugar
- ½ cup light corn syrup
- ½ cup evaporated milk
- ¼ cup butter
  Dash salt

Combine cornflakes, shredded coconut and pecans; set aside. In a small heavy saucepan, combine the remaining ingredients. Cook, stirring constantly, over medium heat until a candy thermometer reads 240° (soft-ball stage). Add the syrup mixture to the dry ingredients; stir well. Drop the mixture by tablespoonfuls onto waxed paper. Let stand until set.

1 cookie: 81 cal., 3g fat (2g sat. fat), 3mg chol., 68mg sod., 13g carb. (11g sugars, 0 fiber), 1g pro.

PEPPERMINT BROWNIES

My grandmother encouraged me to enter these mint brownies in the county fair, and they earned top honors!
—Marcy Greenblatt, Redding, CA

Prep: 15 min. • **Bake:** 35 min. + cooling
Makes: 2 dozen

- 1⅓ cups all-purpose flour
- 1 cup baking cocoa
- 1 tsp. salt
- 1 tsp. baking powder
- ¾ cup canola oil
- 2 cups sugar
- 2 tsp. vanilla extract
- 4 large eggs, room temperature
- ⅔ cup crushed peppermint candies

GLAZE
- 1 cup (6 oz.) semisweet chocolate chips
- 1 Tbsp. shortening
- 2 Tbsp. crushed peppermint candies

1. Preheat oven to 350°. Line a 13x9-in. baking pan with foil; grease foil.
2. In a bowl, whisk together the first 4 ingredients. In a large bowl, beat oil and sugar until blended. Beat in the vanilla and 1 egg at a time, beating well after each addition. Gradually add flour mixture; stir in crushed peppermint candies. Spread into prepared pan.
3. Bake until a toothpick inserted in center comes out clean, 35-40 minutes. Cool in pan on a wire rack.
4. In a microwave, melt chocolate chips and shortening; stir until smooth. Spread over brownies; sprinkle with candies.

1 brownie: 222 cal., 11g fat (3g sat. fat), 35mg chol., 128mg sod., 31g carb. (22g sugars, 1g fiber), 3g pro.

SWEDISH ALMOND RUSKS

Not too sweet, these nutty, crunchy cookies go well with a cup of hot coffee. They travel well in care packages, too!
—Judy Videen, Moorehead, MN

Prep: 20 min. • **Bake:** 40 min.
Makes: 6 dozen

1	cup butter, softened
1¾	cups sugar
2	large eggs, room temperature
2	tsp. almond extract
5	cups all-purpose flour
1	tsp. ground cardamom
1	tsp. baking soda
1	cup sour cream
1	cup finely chopped almonds

1. In a bowl, cream the butter and sugar. Add 1 egg at a time, beating well after each addition. Stir in extract. Sift together flour, cardamom and baking soda; add alternately with sour cream to creamed mixture. Fold in almonds.

2. Divide the dough into 6 parts; shape into logs (like refrigerated cookie dough). Place 3 each on 2 greased baking sheets. Bake at 350° for about 30 minutes or until light brown. Remove logs to cutting board. Using a sharp knife, slice logs diagonally ½ in. thick. Place cookies on sheets; return to oven and bake until light brown. Cool; store in tightly covered containers.

2 rusks: 184 cal., 8g fat (4g sat. fat), 30mg chol., 93mg sod., 24g carb. (10g sugars, 1g fiber), 3g pro.

STRAWBERRY CREAM COOKIES

These delicate cream cheese cookies look lovely on a tea tray or dessert platter. Feel free to experiment with other jam flavors such as raspberry, blueberry or apricot.
—Glenna Aberle, Sabetha, KS

Prep: 25 min. + chilling • **Bake:** 10 min./batch
Makes: 5 dozen

1	cup butter, softened
3	oz. cream cheese, softened
1	cup sugar
1	large egg yolk, room temperature
3	tsp. vanilla extract
2½	cups all-purpose flour
	Seedless strawberry jam

1. In a large bowl, cream the butter, cream cheese and sugar until light and fluffy. Beat in egg yolk and vanilla. Add flour and mix well. Cover and refrigerate for 1 hour or until easy to handle.

2. Shape dough into 1-in. balls. Place 2 in. apart on ungreased baking sheets. Using the end of a wooden spoon handle, make a ½-in.-deep indentation in the center of each ball; fill with about ¼ tsp. jam. Bake at 350° for 10-12 minutes or until set. Remove to wire racks to cool.

2 cookies: 139 cal., 7g fat (4g sat. fat), 27mg chol., 71mg sod., 17g carb. (9g sugars, 0 fiber), 1g pro.

GREAT-GRANDMA'S OATMEAL COOKIES

This recipe originated with my great-grandmother. Sometimes we'd add colored sugar for a festive touch. They are always a favorite with my husband.
—Mary Ann Konechne, Kimball, SD

- -

Prep: 35 min. • **Bake:** 15 min./batch + cooling
Makes: about 12 dozen

- 1½ cups shortening
- 2 cups sugar
- 4 large eggs, room temperature
- 4 tsp. water
- 4 cups all-purpose flour
- 2 tsp. baking soda
- 2 tsp. ground cinnamon
- ½ tsp. salt
- 4 cups quick-cooking oats
- 2 cups chopped raisins
- 1 cup chopped walnuts
  Additional sugar or colored sugar

1. Preheat oven to 350°. Cream shortening and sugar until light and fluffy. Add 1 egg at a time, beating well after each addition. Beat in water. In another bowl, whisk together flour, baking soda, cinnamon and salt; add to creamed mixture, and mix well. Stir in oats, raisins and walnuts.

2. On a surface sprinkled with additional sugar, roll dough to ¼-in. thickness. Cut dough with a floured 2½-in. cookie cutter in desired shapes. Place 2 in. apart on greased baking sheets. Bake until set, 12-15 minutes. Remove to wire racks to cool.

1 cookie: 63 cal., 3g fat (1g sat. fat), 5mg chol., 28mg sod., 9g carb. (4g sugars, 0 fiber), 1g pro.

TEST KITCHEN TIP
If you want to add a finishing touch to these cookies, mix 1 cup confectioners' sugar with ¼ tsp. cinnamon and 5-6 tsp. water to make a quick glaze.

SPRITZ COOKIES

It was a tradition to make these cookies with my grandmother every year. Now my daughters help me make them for extra special occasions.
—Sharon Claussen, Wheat Ridge, CO

- -

Prep: 25 min. • **Bake:** 15 min.
Makes: 11 dozen

2	cups butter, softened
1	cup sugar
2	large eggs, room temperature
2	tsp. vanilla extract
4	cups all-purpose flour
1	tsp. baking powder
½	cup light corn syrup
	Colored sugar

1. In a large bowl, cream butter and sugar until light and fluffy. Add 1 egg at a time, beating well after each addition. Beat in the vanilla. Combine the flour and baking powder; add to the creamed mixture and mix well.

2. Using a cookie press fitted with the disk of your choice, press dough 2 in. apart onto ungreased baking sheets. Bake at 325° for 11-12 minutes or until set (do not brown). Remove to wire racks to cool.

3. Microwave corn syrup for 6-8 seconds or until thinned. Working with a few cookies at a time, brush corn syrup over the surface and dip into sugar. Reheat the corn syrup as necessary. Let stand until set.

2 cookies: 91 cal., 6g fat (4g sat. fat), 21mg chol., 65mg sod., 9g carb. (3g sugars, 0 fiber), 1g pro.

PECAN PUFFS

I just had to share my mom's recipe for these drop cookies. The light-as-a-cloud puffs are just heavenly.
—Leslie Link-Terry, Greendale, WI

Prep: 15 min. • **Bake:** 50 min.
Makes: 3 dozen

- 3 large egg whites, room temperature
  Pinch salt
- 1 cup packed brown sugar
- ½ tsp. vanilla extract
- 1 cup chopped pecans

In a bowl, beat egg whites and salt until soft peaks form. Gradually add the brown sugar, beating until stiff peaks form, 5-8 minutes. Fold in vanilla and chopped pecans. Drop by well-rounded teaspoonfuls onto greased baking sheets. Bake at 225° until firm to the touch, 50-55 minutes. Store cookies in an airtight container.

2 puffs: 95 cal., 5g fat (0 sat. fat), 0 chol., 22mg sod., 13g carb. (12g sugars, 1g fiber), 1g pro.

BANANA-SPLIT BROWNIES

How's this for a treat? All of the joy of a banana split without the mess! Everything in my recipe fits into one pan of delectable brownie bars.
—Constance Sheckler, Chestertown, MD

- -

Prep: 45 min. • **Bake:** 40 min. + cooling
Makes: 2 dozen

- 8 oz. unsweetened chocolate, chopped
- ¾ cup butter, cubed
- 3 large eggs, room temperature
- 2 cups sugar
- 1 tsp. vanilla extract
- 1 cup plus 2 Tbsp. all-purpose flour
- 1 cup maraschino cherries, chopped

TOPPING

- 1 pkg. (8 oz.) cream cheese, softened
- ½ cup mashed ripe banana (about 1 medium)
- ⅓ cup strawberry preserves
- 1 large egg, room temperature, lightly beaten
- ¼ cup chopped salted peanuts
  Optional: Sliced bananas and additional chopped maraschino cherries

1. Preheat oven to 350°. In a microwave, melt unsweetened chocolate and butter; stir until smooth.

2. In a large bowl, beat eggs and sugar on high speed 10 minutes. Stir in vanilla and chocolate mixture. Gradually stir in flour. Fold in cherries. Spread into a greased 13x9-in. baking pan.

3. For topping, in a small bowl, beat cream cheese until smooth. Beat in the mashed banana and preserves. Add egg; beat on low speed just until blended. Spread over brownie batter; sprinkle with peanuts.

4. Bake until topping is set and a toothpick inserted in the brownie portion comes out mostly clean, 40-45 minutes. Cool completely on a wire rack.

5. Cut into bars. If desired, serve bars topped with banana slices and additional cherries. Store in an airtight container in the refrigerator.

1 brownie: 262 cal., 16g fat (9g sat. fat), 57mg chol., 101mg sod., 31g carb. (23g sugars, 2g fiber), 4g pro.

LEMON BUTTER COOKIES

These tender cutout cookies have a slight lemon flavor that makes them stand out from the rest. They're very easy to roll out compared to other sugar cookies I've worked with. I know you'll enjoy them as much as we do.
—Judy McCreight, Springfield, IL

- -

Prep: 20 min. + chilling • **Bake:** 10 min./batch
Makes: about 13 dozen

    1   cup butter, softened
    2   cups sugar
    2   large eggs, room temperature,
        lightly beaten
    ¼   cup whole milk
    2   tsp. lemon extract
 4½   cups all-purpose flour
    2   tsp. baking powder
    ½   tsp. salt
    ¼   tsp. baking soda
        Colored sugar, optional

1. In a large bowl, cream butter and sugar until light and fluffy. Beat in the eggs, milk and extract. Combine the dry ingredients; gradually add to creamed mixture and mix well. Cover and chill for 2 hours.
2. Roll out on a lightly floured surface to ⅛-in. thickness. Cut with a 2-in. cookie cutter dipped in flour. Place 2 in. apart on ungreased baking sheets. Sprinkle with colored sugar if desired.
3. Bake at 350° for 8-9 minutes or until the edges just begin to brown. Remove to wire racks to cool.
2 cookies: 70 cal., 3g fat (2g sat. fat), 12mg chol., 55mg sod., 11g carb. (5g sugars, 0 fiber), 1g pro.

SILVER BELLS

My mom and grandma are known for their Christmas cookies, so here's my take on an favorite. Edible shimmer dust gives them a shine. Look for it in the cake decorating section of craft or grocery stores.
—Crystal Schlueter, Northglenn, CO

- -

Prep: 20 min. + chilling
Bake: 15 min./batch + cooling
Makes: about 4 dozen

 1½   cups butter, softened
    3   cups sugar
    4   large eggs, room temperature
    1   tsp. peppermint extract
    1   tsp. vanilla extract
    5   cups all-purpose flour
    2   tsp. baking powder
    1   tsp. salt
    1   pkg. (10 to 12 oz.) white
        baking chips
    1   Tbsp. shortening
        Black paste food coloring, optional
        Silver edible shimmer dust or sugar

1. Cream butter and sugar until light and fluffy. Beat in eggs and extracts. In another bowl, whisk flour, baking powder and salt; gradually beat into creamed mixture. Divide dough into quarters. Shape each into a disk; cover. Refrigerate until firm enough to roll, about 2 hours.
2. Preheat oven to 350°. On a lightly floured surface, roll each portion of dough to ⅛-in. thickness. Cut dough with a floured 2½-in. bell-shaped cookie cutter. Place 1 in. apart on greased baking sheets. Bake until edges begin to brown, 12-15 minutes. Remove from pans to wire racks to cool completely.
3. In a microwave, melt the chips and shortening; stir until smooth. If desired, tint with food coloring. Spread over the cookies. Let stand until set; brush with shimmer dust.
1 cookie: 188 cal., 8g fat (5g sat. fat), 32mg chol., 126mg sod., 26g carb. (16g sugars, 0 fiber), 2g pro.

MINTY CHOCOLATE CREAM CHEESE BARS

I always looked forward to my grandma's gooey rich cream cheese bars when I was growing up. This version includes mint, which is one of my favorite flavor add-ins.
—Jill Lutz, Woodbury, MN

- -

Prep: 15 min. • **Bake:** 30 min. + cooling
Makes: 2 dozen

1 pkg. chocolate cake mix (regular size)
½ cup butter, softened
1 tsp. almond extract
1 tsp. vanilla extract
4 large eggs, room temperature, divided use
1 pkg. (10 oz.) Andes creme de menthe baking chips, divided
8 oz. cream cheese, softened
1⅔ cups confectioners' sugar

1. Preheat oven to 350°. In a large bowl, beat cake mix, butter, extracts and 2 eggs until blended. Spread into a greased 13x9-in. baking pan. Sprinkle with ¾ cup baking chips.
2. In a small bowl, beat cream cheese and confectioners' sugar until smooth. Add remaining eggs; beat on low speed just until blended. Pour over chocolate layer, spreading evenly; sprinkle with remaining baking chips.
3. Bake 30-35 minutes or until edges begin to brown. Cool in pan on a wire rack. Cut into bars. Refrigerate leftovers.

1 bar: 260 cal., 14g fat (9g sat. fat), 56mg chol., 219mg sod., 33g carb. (25g sugars, 1g fiber), 3g pro.

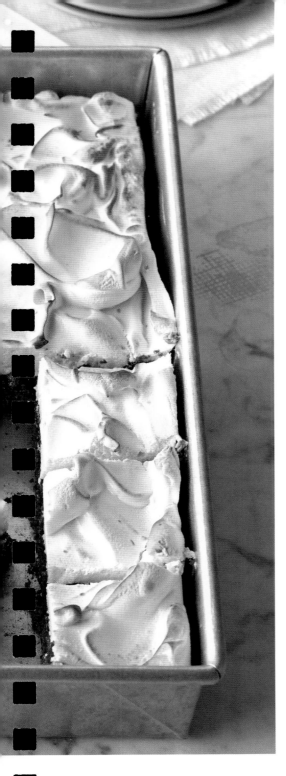

GINGERBREAD MERINGUE BARS

For the best of both worlds, I combined my grandmother's gingerbread recipe with my aunt's special brown sugar meringue. The result? These lovable bars.

—Eden Dranger, Los Angeles, CA

- -

Prep: 20 min. • **Bake:** 30 min. + cooling
Makes: 2 dozen

- ¼ cup butter, softened
- 1 cup molasses
- 2 large egg yolks, room temperature
- 1 large egg, room temperature
- ¼ cup canned pumpkin
- 1 tsp. vanilla extract
- 1½ cups whole wheat flour
- 2½ tsp. ground cinnamon
- 2 tsp. ground ginger
- 1 tsp. baking powder
- 1 tsp. baking soda
- ¾ tsp. ground allspice
- ¼ tsp. salt
- 1 cup miniature marshmallows
- ½ cup chopped pecans
- ½ cup semisweet chocolate chips

MERINGUE
- 4 large egg whites, room temperature
- ½ cup packed brown sugar

1. In a large bowl, beat butter and molasses until blended. Add egg yolks and egg, 1 at a time, beating well after each addition. Beat in pumpkin and vanilla.

2. In a small bowl, combine the flour, cinnamon, ginger, baking powder, baking soda, allspice and salt. Gradually add to the molasses mixture. Pour into a greased 13x9-in. baking pan. Sprinkle with miniature marshmallows, pecans and chocolate chips. Bake at 350° for 20 minutes.

3. Meanwhile, in a small bowl, beat egg whites on medium speed until soft peaks form. Gradually beat in the brown sugar, 1 Tbsp. at a time, on high until stiff glossy peaks form and sugar is dissolved.

4. Remove gingerbread from oven; spread with meringue. Bake until the meringue is lightly browned, 9-11 minutes longer. Cool completely. Cut into bars.

1 bar: 135 cal., 4g fat (2g sat. fat), 31mg chol., 129mg sod., 24g carb. (15g sugars, 1g fiber), 2g pro. **Diabetic exchanges:** 1½ starch, 1 fat.

CHOCOLATY DOUBLE CRUNCHERS

I first tried these crispy sandwich cookies at a family picnic when I was a child. Packed with oats, cornflakes and coconut, they quickly became a regular at our house. Years later, I still make them for my very own family.

—Cheryl Johnson, Upper Marlboro, MD

Prep: 20 min.
Bake: 10 min./batch + cooling
Makes: 2 dozen

- ½ cup butter, softened
- ½ cup sugar
- ½ cup packed brown sugar
- 1 large egg, room temperature
- ½ tsp. vanilla extract
- 1 cup all-purpose flour
- ½ tsp. baking soda
- ¼ tsp. salt
- 1 cup quick-cooking oats
- 1 cup crushed cornflakes
- ½ cup sweetened shredded coconut

FILLING

- 6 oz. cream cheese, softened
- 1½ cups confectioners' sugar
- 2 cups (12 oz.) semisweet
    chocolate chips, melted

1. In a large bowl, cream butter and sugars until light and fluffy. Beat in egg and vanilla. Combine the flour, baking soda and salt; gradually add to creamed mixture and mix well. Stir in oats, cornflakes and coconut.
2. Shape into 1-in. balls and place 2 in. apart on greased baking sheets. Flatten with a glass dipped lightly in flour. Bake at 350° for 8-10 minutes or until lightly browned. Remove to wire racks to cool.
3. For filling, beat cream cheese and sugar until smooth. Beat in chocolate. Spread about 1 Tbsp. on half of the cookies and top each with another cookie. Store in the refrigerator.

1 sandwich cookie: 234 cal., 10g fat (6g sat. fat), 23mg chol., 138mg sod., 35g carb. (25g sugars, 1g fiber), 3g pro.

"These are very easy to make and super tasty!"
—MOMOF4KIDS, TASTEOFHOME.COM

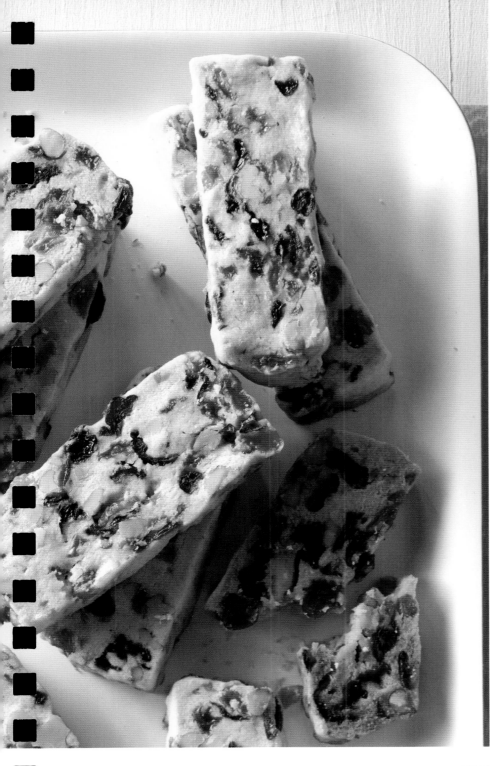

NANNY'S FRUITCAKE COOKIES

My grandmother always made a holiday fruitcake. I took her recipe and turned it into a cookie that's perfect any time of year with a cup of tea.
—Amanda Digges, South Windsor, CT

Prep: 35 min. + chilling • **Bake:** 15 min./batch
Makes: about 4 dozen

1⅔	cups chopped pecans or walnuts
1⅓	cups golden raisins
1	cup pitted dried plums, chopped
⅔	cup dried apricots, finely chopped
½	cup dried cranberries
¼	cup Triple Sec
1	cup butter, softened
½	cup sugar
⅓	cup packed light brown sugar
½	tsp. ground nutmeg
1	large egg, room temperature
2⅔	cups all-purpose flour

1. Place the first 5 ingredients in a large bowl. Drizzle with Triple Sec and toss to combine. Let stand, covered, overnight.
2. In a large bowl, cream butter, sugars and nutmeg until light and fluffy. Beat in egg. Gradually beat in flour. Stir in fruit mixture.
3. Divide the dough in half; shape each into a 12x3x1-in. rectangular log. Cover; refrigerate overnight or until firm.
4. Preheat oven to 350°. Uncover and cut dough crosswise into ½-in. slices. Place 2 in. apart on ungreased baking sheets. Bake until edges are light brown, 13-16 minutes. Remove from pans to wire racks to cool.
1 cookie: 131 cal., 7g fat (3g sat. fat), 14mg chol., 37mg sod., 17g carb. (9g sugars, 1g fiber), 2g pro.

CHEWY CHOCOLATE COOKIES

This cookie recipe—a favorite of our children—has been in my collection for years. Sometimes I will substitute mint-flavored chips for the semisweet chocolate ones. Either way, the cookies always seem to disappear quickly.
—Sheri Ziesemer, Olympia, WA

Prep: 20 min. • **Bake:** 10 min./batch
Makes: about 4½ dozen

1¼ cups butter, softened
2 cups sugar
2 large eggs, room temperature
2 tsp. vanilla extract
2 cups all-purpose flour
¾ cup baking cocoa
1 tsp. baking soda
½ tsp. salt
2 cups (12 oz.) semisweet chocolate chips

1. Preheat oven to 350°. In a large bowl, cream butter and sugar until light and fluffy. Beat in eggs and vanilla. In another bowl, whisk flour, cocoa, baking soda and salt; gradually add to creamed mixture. Stir in chocolate chips.
2. Drop by teaspoonfuls onto lightly greased baking sheets. Bake 8-10 minutes (do not overbake). Cool on pans 1 minute. Remove to wire racks to cool.
2 cookies: 238 cal., 13 g fat (8 g sat. fat), 38 mg chol., 182 mg sod., 31 g carb., 1 g fiber, 2 g pro.

MINCEMEAT COOKIE BARS

My daughter won the grand champion title at the Alaska State Fair with these bars when she was 10. The topping is delicious but can be a bit crumbly—for neatly edged cookies, freeze before cutting.
—Mary Bohanan, Sparks, NV

Prep: 15 min. • **Bake:** 30 min. + cooling
Makes: 3 dozen

1 tsp. butter
2 cups all-purpose flour
1 cup sugar
½ tsp. baking soda
½ tsp. salt
½ cup canola oil
¼ cup 2% milk
1 jar (28 oz.) prepared mincemeat
1 cup chopped pecans

1. Preheat oven to 400°. Line an 8-in. square baking pan with foil; grease foil with butter. In a large bowl, whisk flour, sugar, baking soda and salt. Stir in the oil and milk. Reserve 1 cup for topping. Press remaining crumb mixture onto bottom of prepared pan. Spread with mincemeat. Stir pecans into reserved crumb mixture; sprinkle over top. Bake 30-35 minutes or until topping is golden brown.
2. Cool completely in pan on a wire rack. Cut into bars.
1 bar: 134 cal., 6g fat (1g sat. fat), 0 chol., 59mg sod., 20g carb. (13g sugars, 1g fiber), 1g pro.

OLD-FASHIONED GINGERSNAPS

I discovered this recipe many years ago, and it's been a favorite among our family and friends since. Who doesn't like cookies during the holidays?
—Francis Stoops, Stoneboro, PA

Prep: 15 min. + chilling
Bake: 10 min./batch + cooling
Makes: about 4 dozen

- ¾ **cup butter, softened**
- 1 **cup sugar**
- 1 **large egg, room temperature**
- ¼ **cup molasses**
- 2 **cups all-purpose flour**
- 2 **tsp. baking soda**
- 1 **tsp. ground cinnamon**
- 1 **tsp. ground cloves**
- 1 **tsp. ground ginger**
- ¼ **tsp. salt**
  Additional sugar

1. In a bowl, cream the butter and sugar. Beat in the egg and molasses. Combine the flour, baking soda, cinnamon, cloves, ginger and salt; gradually add to creamed mixture. Chill.

2. Roll into 1¼-in. balls and dip into sugar. Place 2 in. apart on ungreased baking sheets. Bake at 375° for about 10 minutes or until set and surface cracks. Cool on wire racks.

2 cookies: 150 cal., 8g fat (5g sat. fat), 29mg chol., 211mg sod., 19g carb. (10g sugars, 0 fiber), 1g pro.

GRANDMA'S PECAN RUM BARS

My grandmother handed down the recipe for these gooey bars, which we all love. The candied cherries are a must.
—Deborah Pennington, Cullman, AL

- -

Prep: 20 min. • **Bake:** 1 hour + cooling
Makes: 2 dozen

    4   large eggs
    4   cups chopped pecans, divided
    1   cup butter, softened
 2¼   cups packed brown sugar
    2   Tbsp. vanilla extract
    1   cup all-purpose flour
 2¼   cups red candied cherries
 1½   cups chopped candied pineapple
    ½   cup chopped candied citron
    ⅓   cup rum

1. Let eggs stand at room temperature for 30 minutes. Sprinkle 3 cups pecans over a greased 15x10x1-in. baking pan.
2. Preheat oven to 350°. Cream butter and brown sugar until light and fluffy. Add 1 egg at a time, beating well after each addition. Beat in the vanilla. Gradually add flour to the creamed mixture, beating well.
3. Spread the batter into prepared pan. Combine candied fruit and the remaining pecans. Spread the fruit and pecans evenly over creamed mixture; press gently to help mixtures adhere. Bake until a toothpick inserted in center comes out clean, about 1 hour. Sprinkle rum over the top; cool completely in pan on a wire rack. Cut into bars. Store in an airtight container.
1 bar: 401 cal., 22g fat (6g sat. fat), 51mg chol., 123mg sod., 49g carb. (40g sugars, 2g fiber), 4g pro.

TEST KITCHEN TIP
This holiday treat tastes like a cross between rum cake, fruitcake and pecan pie. For a decadent twist, serve these bars over a swirl of creme anglaise or vanilla sauce.

GRANDMA KRAUSE'S COCONUT COOKIES

When my daughters were young, their great-grandma made them cookies with oats and coconut. Thankfully, she shared the recipe.
—Debra Dorn, Homosassa, FL

- -

Prep: 40 min. + freezing
Bake: 10 min./batch
Makes: about 4 dozen

- 1 cup shortening
- 1 cup sugar
- 1 cup packed brown sugar
- 2 large eggs, room temperature
- 1 tsp. vanilla extract
- 2 cups all-purpose flour
- 1 tsp. baking powder
- 1 tsp. baking soda
- ¼ tsp. salt
- 1 cup old-fashioned oats
- 1 cup sweetened shredded coconut

1. In a large bowl, beat shortening and sugars until blended. Beat in eggs and vanilla. In another bowl, whisk flour, baking powder, baking soda and salt; gradually beat into sugar mixture. Stir in oats and coconut.
2. Divide dough into 4 portions. On a lightly floured surface, shape each portion into a 6-in.-long log. Wrap logs in plastic; freeze 2 hours or until firm.
3. Preheat oven to 350°. Unwrap and cut dough crosswise into ½-in. slices, reshaping as needed. Place 2 in. apart on ungreased baking sheets. Bake 10-12 minutes or until golden brown. Cool on pans for 5 minutes. Remove to wire racks to cool.
Freeze option: Place wrapped logs in freezer container; return to freezer. To use, unwrap frozen logs and cut into slices. If necessary, let dough stand a few minutes at room temperature before cutting. Prepare and bake as directed.
1 cookie: 109 cal., 5g fat (2g sat. fat), 8mg chol., 56mg sod., 15g carb. (10g sugars, 0 fiber), 1g pro.

SWEET POTATO CHEESECAKE BARS

Your whole house will be filled with the aroma of pumpkin spice when you bake these wonderful bars. They might seem a bit complicated, but are so easy that you can whip up a batch anytime.
—Nancy Whitford, Edwards, NY

- -

Prep: 20 min. • **Bake:** 25 min. + chilling
Makes: 2 dozen

- 1 pkg. yellow cake mix (regular size)
- ½ cup butter, softened
- 1 large egg, room temperature

FILLING
- 1 can (15 oz.) sweet potatoes, drained
- 1 pkg. (8 oz.) cream cheese, cubed
- ½ cup plus ¼ cup sugar, divided
- 1 large egg, room temperature
- 1½ tsp. pumpkin pie spice
- 1 cup sour cream
- ¼ tsp. vanilla extract

TOPPING
- 1¼ cups granola without raisins
- ½ cup white baking chips
- ¼ tsp. pumpkin pie spice

1. In a large bowl, beat cake mix, butter and egg until crumbly. Press onto the bottom of a greased 13x9-in. baking dish.
2. Place the sweet potatoes, cream cheese, ½ cup sugar, egg and pie spice in a food processor; cover and process until blended. Spread over crust.
3. Bake at 350° until center is almost set, 20-25 minutes. Meanwhile, in a small bowl, combine the sour cream, vanilla and the remaining sugar. Spread over the filling. Combine topping ingredients; sprinkle over top. Bake just until set, 5-8 minutes longer. Cool on a wire rack.
4. Refrigerate for at least 2 hours. Cut into bars.
1 bar: 259 cal., 13g fat (7g sat. fat), 45mg chol., 217mg sod., 34g carb. (22g sugars, 2g fiber), 4g pro.

DATE OATMEAL BARS

In no time at all, you can treat your family to these bars. They'll be surprised at how light and tasty the snacks are.
—Helen Cluts, Eden Prairie, MN

Prep: 20 min. • **Bake:** 20 min. + cooling
Makes: 16 servings

1	cup chopped dates
½	cup water
¼	cup sugar
1½	cups quick-cooking oats
1	cup all-purpose flour
1	cup packed brown sugar
½	tsp. baking soda
¼	tsp. salt
⅓	cup butter, melted
1	large egg white, room temperature

1. Preheat oven to 350°. Place dates, water and sugar in a small saucepan; bring to a boil, stirring constantly. Reduce the heat; simmer, uncovered, until thickened, about 5 minutes, stirring constantly.

2. In a large bowl, mix oats, flour, brown sugar, baking soda and salt; stir in melted butter and egg white. Press half of the mixture into an 8-in. square baking pan coated with cooking spray. Spread carefully with date mixture; top with the remaining oat mixture.

3. Bake for 20-25 minutes or until lightly browned. Cool in pan on a wire rack. Cut into bars.

1 bar: 182 cal., 4g fat (3g sat. fat), 10mg chol., 114mg sod., 35g carb. (23g sugars, 2g fiber), 2g pro. **Diabetic exchanges:** 1½ starch, ½ fruit, 1 fat.

CHRISTMAS CUTOUTS

Making and decorating these tender sugar cookies left a lasting impression on our children. Now that they're grown, they've all asked for my recipe, and are baking new memories with my grandchildren.
—Shirley Kidd, New London, MN

- -

Prep: 25 min. + chilling
Bake: 10 min./batch + cooling
Makes: about 3½ dozen

- 1 cup butter, softened
- 1½ cups confectioners' sugar
- 1 large egg, room temperature
- 1 tsp. vanilla extract
- ½ tsp. almond extract
- 2½ cups all-purpose flour
- 1 tsp. baking soda
- 1 tsp. cream of tartar

FROSTING
- 3¾ cups confectioners' sugar
- 3 Tbsp. butter, softened
- 1 tsp. vanilla extract
- 2 to 4 Tbsp. 2% milk
  Optional: Liquid or paste food coloring and assorted sprinkles

1. Cream butter and confectioners' sugar until light and fluffy. Beat in the egg and extracts. In another bowl, whisk together the flour, baking soda and cream of tartar; gradually beat into creamed mixture. Shape into a disk; wrap in plastic. Refrigerate until firm enough to roll, 2-3 hours.

2. Preheat oven to 375°. On a lightly floured surface, roll dough to ⅛-in. thickness. Cut with floured 2-in. cookie cutters. Place on ungreased baking sheets.

3. Bake until the edges begin to brown, 7-8 minutes. Remove from pan to wire racks; cool completely.

4. For frosting, beat confectioners' sugar, butter, vanilla and enough milk to reach desired consistency; tint with food coloring if desired. Spread over cookies. Decorate cookies as desired.

1 cookie: 134 cal., 5g fat (3g sat. fat), 18mg chol., 74mg sod., 21g carb. (15g sugars, 0 fiber), 1g pro.

HARDWORKING LAZY SUSANS

Use a lazy Susan for your next cookie-decorating extravaganza. It's a handy way to keep icings, sugars and sprinkles all at the ready without lots of mess and reaching.

SWEDISH GINGERBREAD COOKIES

Making Swedish pepparkakor—or gingerbread cookies—is a holiday tradition for our family. I entered these at the Iowa State Fair and took home a blue ribbon.
—Kathleen Olesen, Des Moines, IA

Prep: 15 min. + chilling
Bake: 10 min./batch + cooling
Makes: about 3 dozen

- 1 cup butter, softened
- 1 cup sugar
- ½ cup molasses
- 1 large egg, room temperature
- 3¼ cups all-purpose flour
- 1 Tbsp. ground ginger
- 1 Tbsp. ground cinnamon
- 2 tsp. ground cloves
- 1 tsp. baking soda

FROSTING
- 3 cups confectioners' sugar
- ¾ cup shortening
- 1 Tbsp. vanilla extract
- 3 to 5 Tbsp. water
    Red Hots, optional

1. In a large bowl, cream butter and sugar until light and fluffy. Beat in the molasses and egg. In another bowl, whisk the flour, ginger, cinnamon, cloves and baking soda; gradually beat into creamed mixture. Divide dough in half. Shape each portion into a disk; wrap in plastic. Refrigerate 1 hour or until firm enough to roll.

2. Preheat oven to 350°. On a lightly floured surface, roll each portion of dough to ¼-in. thickness. Cut dough with a floured 3½-in. gingerbread man cookie cutter. Place 1 in. apart on greased baking sheets. Bake until edges are firm, 8-10 minutes. Cool on pans for 2 minutes. Remove cookies to wire racks to cool completely.

3. For the frosting, in a bowl, beat the confectioners' sugar, shortening, vanilla and enough water to reach spreading consistency. Decorate cookies with frosting and, if desired, Red Hots.

Freeze option: Transfer wrapped disks to a resealable plastic freezer bag; freeze. To use, thaw dough in refrigerator overnight or until it is soft enough to roll. Prepare, bake and decorate cookies as directed.

1 cookie: 201 cal., 9g fat (4g sat. fat), 19mg chol., 80mg sod., 28g carb. (19g sugars, 0 fiber), 1g pro.

BLACK WALNUT COOKIES

Black walnuts have a more distinctive flavor than the traditional English walnuts. Black walnuts have a short shelf life and it's best to store them in the freezer.
—Doug Black, Conover, NC

- -

Prep: 20 min. + chilling • **Bake:** 15 min./batch
Makes: 10 dozen

- 1   cup butter, softened
- 2   cups packed brown sugar
- 2   large eggs, room temperature
- 1   tsp. vanilla extract
- 3½ cups all-purpose flour
- 1   tsp. baking soda
- ¼   tsp. salt
- 2   cups chopped black walnuts
     or walnuts, divided

1. In a large bowl, cream butter and brown sugar until light and fluffy. Beat in eggs and vanilla. Combine the flour, baking soda and salt; gradually add to creamed mixture. Stir in 1¼ cups black walnuts. Finely chop the remaining nuts.

2. Shape dough into two 15-in. rolls. Roll in chopped nuts, pressing gently. Wrap each in plastic wrap. Refrigerate for 2 hours or until firm.

3. Unwrap dough; cut into ¼-in. slices. Place 2 in. apart on greased baking sheets. Bake at 300° until cookies are lightly browned, about 12 minutes. Remove to wire racks.

1 cookie: 55 cal., 3g fat (1g sat. fat), 7mg chol., 30mg sod., 7g carb. (4g sugars, 0 fiber), 1g pro.

GRANDMA'S FAVORITE

CAKES & PIES

- -

A slice of Grandma's from-scratch dessert is like a big warm hug just when you need it most. Relish every last bite of these heavenly treats that always make the day just a tiny bit brighter.

GRANDPA'S MAPLE WALNUT CAKE

My beloved grandpa made delicious maple syrup when I was a child. This cake honors his memory, and it has proven to be a real favorite with family and friends.
—Lori Fee, Middlesex, NY

Prep: 45 min. • **Bake:** 15 min. + cooling
Makes: 16 servings

- ½ cup unsalted butter, softened
- 1½ cups packed light brown sugar
- 3 large eggs, room temperature
- 1 tsp. maple flavoring or maple syrup
- 2 cups all-purpose flour
- 1 tsp. baking powder
- 1 tsp. baking soda
- ¼ tsp. salt
- 1 cup buttermilk

CANDIED WALNUTS

- 1 Tbsp. unsalted butter
- 1½ cups coarsely chopped walnuts
- 1 Tbsp. maple syrup
- ¼ tsp. salt

FROSTING

- 2 cups unsalted butter, softened
- 1 tsp. maple flavoring or maple syrup
- ¼ tsp. salt
- 5 cups confectioners' sugar
- ¼ to ½ cup half-and-half cream
- 3 Tbsp. maple syrup, divided

1. Preheat oven to 350°. Line the bottoms of 3 greased 9-in. round baking pans with parchment; grease parchment.

2. Cream butter and brown sugar until light and fluffy. Add 1 egg at a time, beating well after each addition. Beat in maple flavoring. In another bowl, whisk together the flour, baking powder, baking soda and salt; add to the creamed mixture alternately with buttermilk, beating after each addition.

3. Transfer to prepared pans. Bake until a toothpick inserted in the center comes out clean, 11-13 minutes. Cool in pans for 10 minutes before removing to wire racks; remove paper. Cool completely.

4. For candied walnuts, in a large skillet, melt butter over medium heat; saute walnuts until toasted, about 5 minutes. Stir in maple syrup and salt; cook and stir 1 minute. Spread onto foil; cool completely.

5. For frosting, beat butter until creamy. Beat in maple flavoring and salt. Gradually beat in confectioners' sugar and enough cream to reach desired consistency.

6. Place 1 cake layer on a serving plate; spread with 1 cup frosting. Sprinkle with ½ cup candied walnuts and drizzle with 1 Tbsp. maple syrup. Repeat layers.

7. Top with remaining layer. Frost top and sides of cake. Top with remaining walnuts and syrup.

1 slice: 653 cal., 38g fat (20g sat. fat), 116mg chol., 275mg sod., 75g carb. (61g sugars, 1g fiber), 5g pro.

FAVORITE DUTCH APPLE PIE

Everything about this dessert makes it a top request at gatherings. The delightful crust cuts beautifully to reveal a filling of diced apple. You just cannot beat this delectable pie.
—Brenda DuFresne, Midland, MI

Prep: 20 min. • **Bake:** 40 min. + cooling
Makes: 8 servings

- 2 cups all-purpose flour
- 1 cup packed brown sugar
- ½ cup quick-cooking oats
- ¾ cup butter, melted

FILLING
- ⅔ cup sugar
- 3 Tbsp. cornstarch
- 1¼ cups cold water
- 4 cups chopped peeled tart apples (about 2 large)
- 1 tsp. vanilla extract

1. Preheat oven to 350°. Mix flour, brown sugar, oats and butter; reserve 1½ cups mixture for topping. Press remaining mixture onto bottom and up sides of an ungreased 9-in. pie plate.

2. In a large saucepan, mix sugar, cornstarch and water until smooth; bring to a boil. Cook and stir 2 minutes or until thickened. Remove from heat; stir in apples and vanilla. Pour into the crust. Crumble the topping over filling.

3. Bake until crust is golden brown and filling is bubbly, 40-45 minutes. Cool on a wire rack.

1 piece: 494 cal., 18g fat (11g sat. fat), 46mg chol., 146mg sod., 81g carb. (49g sugars, 2g fiber), 4g pro.

TILLIE'S GINGER CRUMB CAKE

Made in a cast-iron skillet, this cake goes back as far as my grandmother, who was born in the early 1900s. Our sons and I enjoy eating it in a bowl with milk poured over it—much to the dismay of my husband, who prefers it plain.
—Kathy Nienow Clark, Byron, MI

- -

Prep: 20 min. • **Bake:** 35 min.
Makes: 16 servings

4	cups all-purpose flour
2	cups sugar
1	cup cold butter
½	tsp. ground ginger
¼	tsp. ground cloves
½	tsp. ground cinnamon
½	tsp. ground nutmeg
1	cup plus 2 Tbsp. buttermilk
1¼	tsp. baking soda
2	large eggs, room temperature

1. In a large bowl, combine flour and sugar; cut in butter until crumbly. Set aside 2 cups. Combine remaining crumb mixture with the remaining ingredients.

2. Sprinkle 1 cup of the reserved crumbs into a greased 12-in. cast-iron skillet or 13x9-in. baking dish. Pour batter over crumbs and sprinkle with the remaining crumbs. Bake at 350° until a toothpick inserted in the center comes out clean, about 35 minutes.

1 piece: 330 cal., 13g fat (8g sat. fat), 54mg chol., 232mg sod., 50g carb. (26g sugars, 1g fiber), 5g pro.

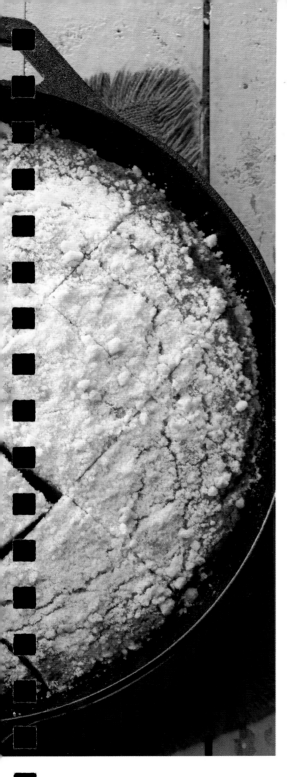

MARBLE CHIFFON CAKE

This towering treat won a blue ribbon for best chiffon cake at our country fair. The delicate-flavored orange cake has ribbons of chocolate swirled throughout.
—Sharon Evans, Clear Lake, IA

- -

Prep: 20 min. • **Bake:** 70 min. + cooling
Makes: 16 servings

- 7 large eggs, separated
- ⅓ cup baking cocoa
- ¼ cup boiling water
- 1½ cups plus 3 Tbsp. sugar, divided
- ½ cup plus 2 Tbsp. canola oil, divided
- 2¼ cups all-purpose flour
- 1 Tbsp. baking powder
- 1 tsp. salt
- ¾ cup water
- ½ tsp. cream of tartar
- 2 tsp. grated orange zest

ORANGE GLAZE

- 2 cups confectioners' sugar
- ⅓ cup butter, melted
- 3 to 4 Tbsp. orange juice
- ½ tsp. grated orange zest

1. Let eggs stand at room temperature for 30 minutes. In a large bowl, whisk the cocoa, boiling water, 3 Tbsp. sugar and 2 Tbsp. oil; cool. and set aside.
2. In a large bowl, combine the flour, baking powder, salt and remaining sugar. In another bowl, whisk the egg yolks, water and remaining oil. Add to dry ingredients; beat until well blended. In another bowl, beat egg whites and cream of tartar until stiff peaks form; fold into batter.
3. Remove 2 cups of batter; stir into cocoa mixture. To the remaining batter, add the orange zest. Alternately spoon the batters into an ungreased 10-in. tube pan. Swirl with a knife.
4. Gently spoon into an ungreased 10-in. tube pan. Cut through batter with a knife to remove air pockets. Bake on the lowest oven rack at 325° for 70-75 minutes or until cake springs back when lightly touched. Immediately invert pan; cool completely, about 1 hour.
5. Run a knife around side and center tube of pan. Remove cake to a serving plate.
6. For glaze, in a small bowl, combine the sugar, butter and enough orange juice to reach desired drizzling consistency. Add orange zest; Drizzle over cake.

1 piece: 354 cal., 15g fat (4g sat. fat), 92mg chol., 300mg sod., 51g carb. (36g sugars, 1g fiber), 5g pro.

GRAN'S APPLE CAKE

My grandmother occasionally brought over this wonderful cake warm from the oven. The spicy apple flavor combined with the sweet cream cheese frosting made this dessert a treasured recipe. Even though I've lightened it up, it's still a family favorite.
—Lauris Conrad, Turlock, CA

Prep: 20 min. • **Bake:** 35 min. + cooling
Makes: 18 servings

- 1⅔ cups sugar
- 2 large eggs, room temperature
- ½ cup unsweetened applesauce
- 2 Tbsp. canola oil
- 2 tsp. vanilla extract
- 2 cups all-purpose flour
- 2 tsp. baking soda
- 2 tsp. ground cinnamon
- ¾ tsp. salt
- 6 cups chopped peeled tart apples
- ½ cup chopped pecans

FROSTING
- 4 oz. reduced-fat cream cheese
- 2 Tbsp. butter, softened
- 1 tsp. vanilla extract
- 1 cup confectioners' sugar

1. Preheat oven to 350°. Coat a 13x9-in. baking pan with cooking spray.
2. In a large bowl, beat the sugar, eggs, applesauce, oil and vanilla until well blended. In another bowl, whisk flour, baking soda, cinnamon and salt; gradually beat into sugar mixture. Fold in apples and pecans.
3. Transfer to prepared pan. Bake until top is golden brown and a toothpick inserted in center comes out clean, 35-40 minutes. Cool the cake completely in the pan on a wire rack.
4. In a small bowl, beat cream cheese, butter and vanilla until smooth. Gradually beat in the confectioners' sugar (mixture will be soft). Spread over cake. Refrigerate leftover cake.

1 piece: 241 cal., 7g fat (2g sat. fat), 29mg chol., 284mg sod., 42g carb. (30g sugars, 1g fiber), 3g pro.

BANANA CREAM PIE

Made from our farm-fresh dairy products, this pie was a creamy treat anytime Mom served it. Her recipe is a real treasure, and I've never found one that tastes better.
—Bernice Morris, Marshfield, MO

Prep: 20 min. + cooling • **Makes:** 8 servings

- ¾ cup sugar
- ⅓ cup all-purpose flour
- ¼ tsp. salt
- 2 cups whole milk
- 3 large egg yolks, room temperature, lightly beaten
- 2 Tbsp. butter
- 1 tsp. vanilla extract
- 3 medium, firm bananas
- 1 pastry shell (9 in.), baked
  Optional: Whipped cream and additional sliced bananas

1. In a saucepan, combine sugar, flour and salt; stir in milk and mix well. Cook over medium-high heat until mixture is thickened and bubbly. Cook and stir for 2 minutes longer. Remove from the heat. Stir a small amount into egg yolks; return all to the saucepan. Bring to a gentle boil. Cook and stir 2 minutes; remove from the heat. Add butter and vanilla; cool slightly.
2. Slice the bananas into pastry shell; pour filling over top. Cool on wire rack for 1 hour. Store in the refrigerator. If desired, before serving, garnish with whipped cream and sliced bananas.

1 slice: 338 cal., 14g fat (7g sat. fat), 101mg chol., 236mg sod., 49g carb. (30g sugars, 1g fiber), 5g pro.

TEST KITCHEN TIP

To ensure a smooth, lump-free filling, stir sugar mixture constantly during cooking, and scrape the sides and bottom of the saucepan with a heatproof rubber spatula.

GRANDMA'S LEMON POPPY SEED CAKE

This is from a collection of family recipes. My granddaughter, Riley, likes that it tastes like lemons and is refreshingly sweet. It's always wonderful.
—Phyllis Harmon, Nelson, WI

- -

Prep: 20 min. • **Bake:** 30 min. + cooling
Makes: 15 servings

- 1 **pkg. lemon cake mix (regular size)**
- 1 **pkg. (3.4 oz.) instant vanilla pudding mix**
- 4 **large eggs, room temperature**
- 1 **cup water**
- ½ **cup canola oil**
- ¼ **cup poppy seeds**

DRIZZLE
- 2 **cups confectioners' sugar**
- 2 **Tbsp. water**
- 2 **Tbsp. lemon juice**

1. In a large bowl, combine the cake mix, pudding mix, eggs, water and oil; beat on low speed for 30 seconds. Beat on medium for 2 minutes. Fold in poppy seeds. Transfer to a greased and floured 13x9-in. baking pan. Bake at 350° for 30-35 minutes or until a toothpick inserted in the center comes out clean. Cool on a wire rack.

2. For drizzle, in a small bowl, combine the confectioners' sugar, water and lemon juice; drizzle over cake.

1 piece: 320 cal., 12g fat (2g sat. fat), 56mg chol., 335mg sod., 51g carb. (36g sugars, 0 fiber), 3g pro.

GLAZED CHOCOLATE ANGEL FOOD CAKE

Light as air and loaded with big chocolate flavor, this low-fat dessert will become a standby at all your gatherings. Add fresh strawberries or raspberries and a dollop of sweetened whipped cream if you'd like!
—Mary Relyea, Canastota, NY

- -

Prep: 20 min. • **Bake:** 40 min. + cooling
Makes: 12 servings

1½ **cups egg whites (about 10 large)**
1   **cup cake flour**
2   **cups sugar, divided**
½   **cup baking cocoa**
1   **tsp. cream of tartar**
1   **tsp. vanilla extract**
¼   **tsp. salt**
GLAZE
½   **cup semisweet chocolate chips**
3   **Tbsp. half-and-half cream**

1. Place egg whites in a large bowl; let stand at room temperature 30 minutes.
2. Preheat oven to 350°. Sift flour, 1 cup sugar and cocoa together twice.
3. Add cream of tartar, vanilla and salt to egg whites; beat on medium speed until soft peaks form. Gradually add remaining sugar, 2 Tbsp. at a time, beating on high after each addition until sugar is dissolved. Continue beating the mixture until stiff glossy peaks form. Gradually fold in flour mixture, about ½ cup at a time.
4. Gently transfer to an ungreased 10-in. tube pan. Cut through batter with a knife to remove air pockets. Bake on lowest oven rack until top springs back when lightly touched and cracks feel dry, 40-50 minutes. Immediately invert pan; cool completely in pan, about 1 hour.
5. Run a knife around sides and center tube of pan. Remove cake to a serving plate. For glaze, in a microwave, melt chocolate chips with cream; stir until smooth. Drizzle over the cake.

1 slice: 235 cal., 3g fat (2g sat. fat), 2mg chol., 102mg sod., 49g carb. (37g sugars, 1g fiber), 5g pro.

LEMON LAYER CAKE

This citrusy cake with a luscious cream cheese frosting will garner plenty of raves. The flavor, a duet of sweet and tangy notes, really sings.
—Summer Goddard, Springfield, VA

Prep: 35 min. • **Bake:** 25 min. + cooling
Makes: 12 servings

- 1 cup butter, softened
- 1½ cups sugar
- 2 large eggs, room temperature
- 3 large egg yolks, room temperature
- 1 Tbsp. grated lemon zest
- 2 Tbsp. lemon juice
- ¾ cup sour cream
- ¼ cup 2% milk
- 2½ cups all-purpose flour
- 1 tsp. salt
- 1 tsp. baking powder
- ½ tsp. baking soda

SYRUP

- ½ cup sugar
- ½ cup lemon juice

FROSTING

- 2 pkg. (8 oz. each) cream cheese, softened
- 1 cup butter, softened
- 4 cups confectioners' sugar
- 1½ tsp. lemon juice
- ⅛ tsp. salt
  Optional: Lemon slices or edible flowers

1. Preheat oven to 350°. Line bottoms of 2 greased 9-in. round baking pans with parchment; grease parchment.

2. Cream butter and sugar until light and fluffy. Add eggs and egg yolks, 1 at a time, beating well after each addition. Beat in lemon zest and juice. In a small bowl, mix sour cream and milk. In another bowl, whisk together the flour, salt, baking powder and baking soda; add to the creamed mixture alternately with sour cream mixture.

3. Transfer to prepared pans. Bake until a toothpick inserted in center comes out clean, 24-28 minutes. Cool in pans for 10 minutes before removing to wire racks; remove paper. Cool slightly.

4. For the syrup, in a small saucepan, combine sugar and lemon juice. Bring to a boil; cook until the liquid is reduced by half. Cool completely.

5. For frosting, beat the cream cheese and butter until smooth; beat in confectioners' sugar, lemon juice and salt until blended.

6. Using a long serrated knife, cut each cake horizontally in half. Brush layers with warm syrup; cool completely.

7. Place 1 cake layer on a serving plate; spread with 1 cup frosting. Repeat layers twice. Top with remaining cake layer. Frost top and sides with remaining frosting. If desired, top with lemon slices or edible flowers. Refrigerate leftovers.

1 slice: 841 cal., 48g fat (30g sat. fat), 219mg chol., 656mg sod., 96g carb. (72g sugars, 1g fiber), 8g pro.

SAUERKRAUT CHOCOLATE CAKE

For an old-fashioned yet adventurous cake, try this recipe home bakers have relied on for generations. People might need a little coaxing, but once they try it, they'll love it.
—*Taste of Home* Test Kitchen

- -

Prep: 20 min. • **Bake:** 35 min. + cooling
Makes: 16 servings

½ cup butter, softened
1½ cups sugar
3 large eggs, room temperature
1 tsp. vanilla extract
2 cups all-purpose flour
½ cup baking cocoa
1 tsp. baking powder
1 tsp. baking soda
½ tsp. salt
1 cup water
¾ cup sauerkraut, drained, squeezed dry and chopped

SILK CHOCOLATE FROSTING

1⅓ cups butter, softened
4 oz. unsweetened chocolate, melted
1½ tsp. vanilla extract
4 cups confectioners' sugar
¼ cup whole milk

1. In a bowl, cream the butter and sugar. Add 1 egg at a time, beating well after each. Add vanilla. Combine flour, cocoa, baking powder, baking soda and salt; add to the creamed mixture alternately with water. Stir in sauerkraut. Pour into 2 greased and floured 8-in. round baking pans.
2. Bake at 350° for 35-40 minutes or until a toothpick inserted in the center comes out clean. Cool in pans for 10 minutes before removing to wire racks to cool completely.
3. For frosting, beat butter, chocolate and vanilla in a bowl; add sugar and beat well. Add milk; beat until smooth and fluffy. Spread between layers and over top and sides of cake.
1 slice: 505 cal., 26g fat (16g sat. fat), 91mg chol., 412mg sod., 65g carb. (49g sugars, 2g fiber), 5g pro.

SKILLET PINEAPPLE UPSIDE-DOWN CAKE

For a change of pace, you can substitute fresh or frozen peach slices for the pineapple in this old-fashioned recipe.
—Bernardine Melton, Paola, KS

Prep: 20 min. • **Bake:** 30 min. + cooling
Makes: 8 servings

- ½   cup butter
- 1   cup packed brown sugar
- 1   can (20 oz.) sliced pineapple
- ½   cup chopped pecans
- 3   large eggs, room temperature, separated
- 1   cup sugar
- 1   tsp. vanilla extract
- 1   cup all-purpose flour
- 1   tsp. baking powder
- ¼   tsp. salt
     Maraschino cherries

1. Preheat oven to 375°. Melt butter in a 9- or 10-in. ovenproof skillet. Add brown sugar; mix well until sugar is melted. Drain pineapple, reserving ⅓ cup juice. Arrange about 8 pineapple slices in a single layer over sugar (refrigerate remaining slices for another use). Sprinkle pecans over pineapple; set aside.
2. In a large bowl, beat egg yolks until thick and lemon-colored. Gradually add sugar, beating well. Blend in vanilla and reserved pineapple juice. Combine the flour, baking powder and salt; gradually add to batter and mix well.
3. In a small bowl, beat egg whites on high speed until stiff peaks form; fold into batter. Spoon into skillet.
4. Bake until a toothpick inserted in the center comes out clean, 30-35 minutes (cover loosely with foil if cake browns too quickly). Let stand 10 minutes before inverting onto serving plate. Place cherries in center of pineapple slices.
1 slice: 380 cal., 15g fat (7g sat. fat), 88mg chol., 224mg sod., 59g carb. (48g sugars, 1g fiber), 4g pro.

SHOOFLY PIE

Shoofly pie is to the Amish as pecan pie is to a Southerner. My grandmother made the absolute best shoofly pie in the tradition of the Pennsylvania Dutch.
—Mark Morgan, Waterford, WI

Prep: 20 min. + chilling
Bake: 65 min. + cooling
Makes: 8 servings

- Pastry for single-crust pie (9 in.)
- ½   cup packed brown sugar
- ½   cup molasses
- 1   large egg, room temperature
- 1½ tsp. all-purpose flour
- ½   tsp. baking soda
- 1   cup boiling water
- 1   large egg yolk, room temperature, lightly beaten

TOPPING
- 1½ cups all-purpose flour
- ¾   cup packed brown sugar
- ¾   tsp. baking soda
     Dash salt
- 6   Tbsp. cold butter, cubed

1. On a floured surface, roll dough to fit a 9-in. deep-dish pie plate. Trim and flute edge. Refrigerate at least 30 minutes.
2. Meanwhile, preheat oven to 425°. For the filling, mix brown sugar, molasses, egg, flour and baking soda. Gradually stir in boiling water; cool completely.
3. Line the unpricked crust with a double thickness of foil. Fill with pie weights, dried beans or uncooked rice. Bake on a lower oven rack 15 minutes. Remove foil and pie weights; brush crust with egg yolk. Bake 5 minutes. Cool on a wire rack. Reduce oven setting to 350°.
4. In another bowl, whisk together the first 4 topping ingredients. Cut in butter until crumbly. Add filling to crust; sprinkle with topping. Cover edge of pie with foil.
5. Bake until filling is set and golden brown, 45-50 minutes. Cool on a wire rack. Store in the refrigerator.
Note: Let pie weights cool before storing. Beans and rice may be reused for pie weights, but not for cooking.
1 piece: 540 cal., 22g fat (13g sat. fat), 99mg chol., 630mg sod., 82g carb. (49g sugars, 1g fiber), 6g pro.

MOCHA HAZELNUT TORTE

I make this pretty cake on birthdays and other special occasions because it looks and tastes so amazing. The combination of mild hazelnut and coffee flavors is simply impossible to resist.

—Christina Pope, Speedway, IN

- -

Prep: 35 min. • **Bake:** 25 min. + cooling
Makes: 16 servings

- ¾ cup butter, softened
- 1¼ cups packed brown sugar
- 1 cup sugar
- 3 large eggs, room temperature
- 3 oz. unsweetened chocolate, melted and cooled slightly
- 2 tsp. vanilla extract
- 2¼ cups all-purpose flour
- 1 Tbsp. instant espresso powder
- 1 tsp. baking soda
- ½ tsp. baking powder
- ¼ tsp. salt
- 1½ cups 2% milk

FROSTING

- 1 cup butter, softened
- 1 cup Nutella
- 4 cups confectioners' sugar
- 1 tsp. vanilla extract
- 3 to 4 Tbsp. 2% milk
- ½ cup chopped hazelnuts, toasted

1. Preheat oven to 350°. Line bottoms of 2 greased 9-in. round baking pans with parchment; grease parchment.

2. In a large bowl, cream butter and sugars until light and fluffy. Add 1 egg at a time, beating well after each addition. Beat in melted chocolate and vanilla. In another bowl, whisk flour, espresso powder, baking soda, baking powder and salt; add to the creamed mixture alternately with milk, beating well after each addition.

3. Transfer batter to prepared pans. Bake 25-30 minutes or until a toothpick inserted in center comes out clean. Cool in pans for 10 minutes before removing to wire racks; remove paper. Cool completely.

4. For frosting, in a large bowl, beat butter and Nutella until blended. Gradually beat in confectioners' sugar, vanilla and enough milk to reach desired consistency.

5. Place 1 cake layer on a serving plate; spread with 1 cup frosting. Sprinkle with ¼ cup hazelnuts. Top with remaining cake layer. Frost top and sides with remaining frosting. Sprinkle with remaining hazelnuts.

Note: To toast nuts, bake in a shallow pan in a 350° oven for 5-10 minutes or cook in a skillet over low heat until lightly browned, stirring occasionally.

1 slice: 639 cal., 32g fat (16g sat. fat), 94mg chol., 311mg sod., 88g carb. (69g sugars, 2g fiber), 6g pro.

"My family absolutely loved the hazelnut buttercream frosting. It's really a keeper for any cake."

—LAURELISINTHEKITCHEN, TASTEOFHOME.COM

WHITE TEXAS SHEET CAKE

My mother-in-law introduced this rich sheet cake to me. With its creamy frosting and light almond flavor, no one can stop at just one piece!
—Joanie Ward, Brownsburg, IN

- -

Prep: 20 min. • **Bake:** 20 min. + cooling
Makes: 20 servings

2	cups all-purpose flour
2	cups sugar
1	tsp. baking powder
1	tsp. salt
¼	tsp. baking soda
1	cup butter, cubed
1	cup water
2	large eggs, room temperature
½	cup sour cream
1	tsp. almond extract

FROSTING

½	cup butter, cubed
¼	cup 2% milk
4½	cups confectioners' sugar
½	tsp. almond extract
1	cup chopped walnuts

1. Grease a 15x10x1-in. baking pan. Preheat oven to 375°.

2. In a large bowl, whisk first 5 ingredients. In a small saucepan, combine butter and water; bring just to a boil. Stir into the flour mixture. In a small bowl, whisk eggs, sour cream and extract until blended; add to flour mixture, whisking constantly.

3. Transfer to prepared pan. Bake until golden brown and a toothpick inserted in center comes out clean, 18-22 minutes. Cool on a wire rack 20 minutes.

4. For frosting, combine butter and milk in a large saucepan; bring just to a boil. Remove from heat; gradually stir in confectioners' sugar and extract. Stir in walnuts. Spread over warm cake.

1 piece: 409 cal., 19g fat (10g sat. fat), 62mg chol., 304mg sod., 58g carb. (45g sugars, 1g fiber), 4g pro.

BLUEBERRY PIE WITH LEMON CRUST

I just had to share this recipe. Mom and I have fun making it together, and I hope one day to be as great a baker as she is.
—Sara West, Broken Arrow, OK

Prep: 30 min. + chilling
Bake: 40 min. + cooling
Makes: 8 servings

- 2 cups all-purpose flour
- 1 tsp. salt
- ½ tsp. grated lemon zest
- ⅔ cup shortening
- 1 Tbsp. lemon juice
- 4 to 6 Tbsp. cold water

FILLING

- 4 cups fresh blueberries
- ¾ cup sugar
- 3 Tbsp. all-purpose flour
- ½ tsp. grated lemon zest
  Dash salt
- 1 to 2 tsp. lemon juice
- 1 Tbsp. butter

1. In a large bowl, combine the flour, salt and lemon zest. Cut in shortening until crumbly. Add lemon juice. Gradually add water, tossing with a fork until a ball forms. Cover and refrigerate for 1 hour.
2. Divide dough in half. On a lightly floured surface, roll out 1 portion to fit a 9-in. pie plate. Transfer crust to pie plate; trim to 1 in. beyond edge of plate.
3. In a large bowl, combine the blueberries, sugar, flour, lemon zest and salt; spoon into crust. Drizzle with lemon juice; dot with the butter. Roll out remaining dough; place over the filling. Seal and flute edges. Cut slits in top crust.
4. Bake at 400° for 40-45 minutes or until crust is golden brown and filling is bubbly. Cool on a wire rack. Store in refrigerator.

1 piece: 398 cal., 18g fat (5g sat. fat), 4mg chol., 329mg sod., 56g carb. (26g sugars, 3g fiber), 4g pro.

HOLIDAY HONEY CAKE

Thirty-five years ago, I gave a friend of mine a platter of my assorted home-baked Christmas cookies. The next day, she brought over slices of this delicious cake, which she made for Hanukkah. Naturally, we exchanged recipes, and my family and I have been enjoying this moist and flavorful honey cake ever since. I top my cake with a creamy caramel glaze.
—Kristine Chayes, Smithtown, NY

- -

Prep: 20 min. + standing
Bake: 50 min. + cooling
Makes: 12 servings

- 3   large eggs, separated
- 3½ cups all-purpose flour
- 1   cup sugar
- 2½ tsp. baking powder
- 1   tsp. baking soda
- 1   tsp. ground cinnamon
- ½   tsp. salt
- ½   tsp. ground cloves
- ¼   tsp. ground ginger
- 1⅓ cups brewed coffee
- 1⅓ cups honey
- ¼   cup canola oil
- ¼   tsp. cream of tartar

CARAMEL GLAZE
- 3   Tbsp. butter
- ⅓   cup packed brown sugar
- 2   Tbsp. 2% milk
- ¾   cup confectioners' sugar
- 1   tsp. vanilla extract

1. Place egg whites in a large bowl; let stand at room temperature 30 minutes.
2. Meanwhile, preheat oven to 350°. Sift flour, sugar, baking powder, baking soda, cinnamon, salt, cloves and ginger together twice; place in another large bowl.
3. In a small bowl, whisk egg yolks, coffee, honey and oil until smooth. Add to flour mixture; beat until well blended.
4. Add cream of tartar to egg whites; with clean beaters, beat on high speed just until stiff but not dry. Fold a fourth of the whites into batter, then fold in remaining whites.
5. Gently transfer to an ungreased 10-in. tube pan. Bake on lowest oven rack until top springs back when lightly touched, 50-60 minutes. Immediately invert pan; cool completely, about 1½ hours.
6. In a small heavy saucepan, melt butter. Stir in brown sugar and milk. Bring to a boil; cook over medium heat until sugar is dissolved. Stir in confectioners' sugar and vanilla; cook until thickened, about 5 minutes.
7. Run a knife around sides and center tube of pan. Remove cake to a serving plate and add glaze.

1 glazed slice: 452 cal., 9g fat (3g sat. fat), 54mg chol., 350mg sod., 89g carb. (61g sugars, 1g fiber), 6g pro.

LEMON SUPREME PIE

A friend and I often visit a local restaurant for pie and coffee. When they stopped carrying our favorite, I got busy in the kitchen and created this version, which we think tastes even better! The combination of the refreshing cream cheese and tart lemon is just wonderful.
—Jana Beckman, Wamego, KS

- -

Prep: 25 min. + cooling
Bake: 25 min. + chilling
Makes: 8 servings

Pastry for deep-dish pie (9 in.)
LEMON FILLING
- 1¼ cups sugar, divided
- 6 Tbsp. cornstarch
- ½ tsp. salt
- 1¼ cups water
- 2 Tbsp. butter
- 2 tsp. grated lemon zest
- 4 to 5 drops yellow food coloring, optional
- ½ cup lemon juice

CREAM CHEESE FILLING
- 11 oz. cream cheese, softened
- ¾ cup confectioners' sugar
- 1½ cups whipped topping, thawed
- 1 Tbsp. lemon juice
  Additional frozen whipped topping, optional

1. On a lightly floured surface, roll pie dough to a ⅛-in.-thick circle; transfer to a 9-in. deep dish pie plate. Trim crust to ½ in. beyond rim of plate; flute edge. Refrigerate 30 minutes.
2. Preheat oven to 425°. Line crust with a double thickness of foil. Fill with pie weights, dried beans or uncooked rice. Bake on a lower oven rack 20-25 minutes or until edges are golden brown. Remove the foil and weights; bake 3-6 minutes longer or until bottom is golden brown. Cool on a wire rack.
3. For lemon filling, combine ¾ cup sugar, cornstarch and salt in a small saucepan. Stir in water until smooth. Bring to a boil over medium-high heat. Reduce heat; add the remaining sugar. Cook and stir until mixture is thickened and bubbly, about 2 minutes. Remove from heat; stir in butter, lemon zest and, if desired, food coloring. Gently stir in lemon juice. Cool to room temperature, about 1 hour.
4. For cream cheese filling, beat cream cheese and confectioners' sugar until smooth. Fold in whipped topping and lemon juice. Spread over pie shell.
5. Cover cream cheese filling with lemon filling. Refrigerate pie overnight.
6. If desired, dollop additional whipped topping over lemon filling. Refrigerate until serving.

1 slice: 735 cal., 42g fat (26g sat. fat), 107mg chol., 604mg sod., 84g carb. (48g sugars, 1g fiber), 7g pro.

Pastry for deep-dish pie (9 in.): Combine 2½ cups all-purpose flour and ½ tsp. salt; cut in 1 cup cold butter until crumbly. Gradually add ⅓ to ⅔ cup ice water, tossing with a fork until dough holds together when pressed. Shape into a disk; wrap in plastic wrap. Refrigerate 1 hour or overnight.

COCOA COLA CAKE

I love this old-time cola cake because I usually have the ingredients on hand and it mixes up in a jiffy. The rich fudge frosting is easy to prepare, and the chopped pecans add a nice little crunch.

—Ellen Champagne, New Orleans, LA

Prep: 15 min. + standing
Bake: 35 min. + cooling
Makes: 15 servings

1	pkg. white cake mix (regular size)
1	cup cola
2	large eggs, room temperature
½	cup buttermilk
½	cup butter, melted
¼	cup baking cocoa
1	tsp. vanilla extract
1½	cups miniature marshmallows

FUDGE FROSTING

¼	cup baking cocoa
½	cup butter, cubed
⅓	cup cola
4	cups confectioners' sugar
1	cup chopped pecans, toasted

1. In a large bowl, combine the first 7 ingredients; beat mixture on low speed for 30 seconds. Beat on medium for 2 minutes. Fold in marshmallows.

2. Pour into a greased 13x9-in. baking pan. Bake at 350° for 35-40 minutes or until a toothpick inserted in the center comes out clean. Cool on a wire rack for 15 minutes.

3. Meanwhile, for frosting, combine cocoa and butter in a small saucepan. Cook over low heat until butter is melted. Stir in cola until blended. Bring to a boil, stirring constantly. Remove from the heat; stir in confectioners' sugar until smooth. Fold in pecans. Spread over cake. Let stand for 20 minutes before cutting.

1 piece: 479 cal., 22g fat (9g sat. fat), 61mg chol., 363mg sod., 69g carb. (50g sugars, 2g fiber), 4g pro.

RHUBARB UPSIDE-DOWN CAKE

I've baked this cake every spring for many years, and my family loves it! At potlucks it gets eaten up quickly, even by folks who don't normally go for rhubarb. Use your own fresh rhubarb, hit up a farmers market or find a neighbor who is willing to trade a few stalks for the recipe!
—Helen Breman, Mattydale, NY

- -

Prep: 20 min. • **Bake:** 35 min.
Makes: 10 servings

- 3 cups sliced fresh or frozen rhubarb
- 1 cup sugar
- 2 Tbsp. all-purpose flour
- ¼ tsp. ground nutmeg
- ¼ cup butter, melted

BATTER

- ¼ cup butter, melted
- ¾ cup sugar
- 1 large egg, room temperature
- 1½ cups all-purpose flour
- 2 tsp. baking powder
- ½ tsp. ground nutmeg
- ¼ tsp. salt
- ⅔ cup whole milk
  Sweetened whipped cream, optional

1. Place rhubarb in a greased 10-in. heavy ovenproof skillet. Combine sugar, flour and nutmeg; sprinkle over rhubarb. Drizzle with butter; set aside. For batter, in a large bowl, beat the butter and sugar until blended. Beat in the egg. Combine the flour, baking powder, nutmeg and salt. Gradually add to egg mixture alternately with milk, beating well after each addition.
2. Spread over rhubarb mixture. Bake at 350° for 35 minutes or until a toothpick inserted in the center comes out clean. Loosen edges immediately and invert onto a serving dish. Serve warm. Serve with whipped cream if desired.
1 piece: 316 cal., 10g fat (6g sat. fat), 48mg chol., 248mg sod., 53g carb. (36g sugars, 1g fiber), 4g pro.

GRANDMA PRUIT'S VINEGAR PIE

This historic pie has been in our family for many generations and is always at all of the family get-togethers.
—Suzette Pruit, Houston, TX

- -

Prep: 40 min. • **Bake:** 1 hour + cooling
Makes: 8 servings

- 2 cups sugar
- 3 Tbsp. all-purpose flour
- ¼ to ½ tsp. ground nutmeg
  Pastry for double-crust pie (9 in.)
- ½ cup butter, cubed
- ⅔ cup white vinegar
- 1 qt. hot water

1. Preheat oven to 450°. Whisk together sugar, flour and nutmeg; set aside. On a lightly floured surface, roll one-third of pie dough to a ⅛-in.-thick circle; cut into 2x1-in. strips. Layer a deep 12-in. enamel-coated cast-iron skillet or ovenproof casserole with half the strips; sprinkle with half the sugar mixture. Dot with half the butter. Repeat sugar and butter layers.
2. Roll remaining two-thirds of pie dough to a ⅛-in.-thick circle. Place over filling, pressing against sides of skillet or casserole. Cut a slit in top. Add vinegar to hot water; slowly pour vinegar mixture through slit. Liquid may bubble up through crust; this is normal. To catch spills, line an oven rack with foil.
3. Bake until crust is golden brown, about 1 hour. Cover edge loosely with foil during the last 15-20 minutes if needed to prevent overbrowning. Remove foil. Cool pie on a wire rack.
1 slice: 545 cal., 25g fat (13g sat. fat), 41mg chol., 316mg sod., 78g carb. (50g sugars, 0 fiber), 2g pro.
Pastry for double-crust pie (9 in.): Combine 2½ cups all-purpose flour and ½ tsp. salt; cut in 1 cup cold butter until crumbly. Gradually add ⅓ to ⅔ cup ice water, tossing with a fork until the dough holds together when pressed. Divide dough in thirds. Shape each into a disk; wrap in plastic. Refrigerate at least 1 hour.

RAISIN PECAN PIE

I remember my Grandmother Voltie and Great-Aunt Ophelia making this southern-style pie. It was always one of the many cakes and pies lined up for dessert.
—Angie Price, Bradford, TN

Prep: 20 min. + chilling
Bake: 35 min. + cooling
Makes: 8 servings

Pastry for single-crust pie (9 in.)
- ½ cup boiling water
- ½ cup golden raisins
- 3 large eggs, room temperature
- 1½ cups sugar
- ½ cup butter, melted
- 2 tsp. cider vinegar
- 1 tsp. vanilla extract
- ½ tsp. ground cinnamon
- ½ tsp. ground cloves
- ¼ tsp. ground nutmeg
- ½ cup chopped pecans

1. On a lightly floured surface, roll dough to a ⅛-in.-thick circle; transfer to a 9-in. pie plate. Trim crust to ½ in. beyond rim of plate; flute edge. Refrigerate 30 minutes. Preheat oven to 350°.

2. Pour boiling water over raisins in a small bowl; let stand 5 minutes. Drain. In a large bowl, beat the eggs, sugar, melted butter, vinegar, vanilla and spices until blended. Stir in pecans and drained raisins. Pour into crust.

3. Bake on a lower oven rack until filling is set, 35-40 minutes. Cool on a wire rack. Refrigerate leftovers.

1 piece: 524 cal., 30g fat (16g sat. fat), 130mg chol., 275mg sod., 61g carb. (44g sugars, 2g fiber), 6g pro.

Pastry for single-crust pie (9 in.): Combine 1¼ cups all-purpose flour and ¼ tsp. salt; cut in ½ cup cold butter until crumbly. Gradually add 3-5 Tbsp. ice water, tossing with a fork until the dough holds together when pressed. Cover dough and refrigerate 1 hour.

CONTEST-WINNING RHUBARB MERINGUE PIE

My husband's grandmother was a great cook and didn't always share her secrets, so we are fortunate to have her recipe for rhubarb cream pie. I added one of my favorite crusts and a never-fail meringue.
—Elaine Sampson, Colesburg, IA

- -

Prep: 50 min. + chilling
Bake: 65 min. + cooling
Makes: 8 servings

- ¾ cup all-purpose flour
- ¼ tsp. salt
- ¼ tsp. sugar
- ¼ cup shortening
- 1 Tbsp. beaten egg, room temperature
- ¼ tsp. white vinegar
- 3 to 4½ tsp. cold water

FILLING

- 3 cups chopped fresh or frozen rhubarb
- 1 cup sugar
- 3 Tbsp. all-purpose flour
  Dash salt
- 3 large egg yolks, room temperature
- 1 cup heavy whipping cream

MERINGUE

- 4 tsp. plus ⅓ cup sugar, divided
- 2 tsp. cornstarch
- ⅓ cup water
- 3 large egg whites, room temperature
- ⅛ tsp. cream of tartar

1. In a small bowl, combine the flour, salt and sugar; cut in shortening until crumbly. Combine egg and vinegar; sprinkle over crumb mixture. Gradually add water, tossing with a fork until a ball forms. Cover and chill for 1 hour or until easy to handle.

2. On a lightly floured surface, roll out dough to fit a 9-in. pie plate. Trim to ½ in. beyond edge of plate; flute edges.

3. Place rhubarb in crust. Whisk the sugar, flour, salt, egg yolks and cream; pour over rhubarb. Bake at 350° until the filling is set and the pie jiggles when gently shaken, 50-60 minutes.

4. Meanwhile, in a small saucepan, combine 4 tsp. sugar and cornstarch. Gradually stir in water. Bring to a boil, stirring constantly; cook until thickened, 1-2 minutes. Cool to room temperature.

5. In a small bowl, beat the egg whites and cream of tartar until frothy. Add cornstarch mixture; beat on high until soft peaks form. Gradually beat in remaining sugar, 1 Tbsp. at a time, on high until stiff glossy peaks form and sugar is dissolved.

6. Spread evenly over hot filling, sealing edges to crust. Bake until meringue is golden brown, about 15 minutes. Cool on a wire rack for 1 hour. Store in the refrigerator.

Note: If using frozen rhubarb, measure the rhubarb while still frozen, then thaw completely. Drain in a colander, but do not press liquid out.

1 piece: 388 cal., 19g fat (9g sat. fat), 129mg chol., 131mg sod., 50g carb. (37g sugars, 1g fiber), 5g pro.

BLACK FOREST CHOCOLATE TORTE

If you're thinking about pulling out all the stops for a dessert that says "wow," look no further. This cherry-crowned beauty stacked with layers of chocolate cake and cream filling keeps everyone talking.
—Doris Grotz, York, NE

Prep: 1 hour • **Bake:** 15 min. + cooling
Makes: 16 servings

- ⅔ cup butter, softened
- 1¾ cups sugar
- 4 large eggs, room temperature
- 1¼ cups water
- 4 oz. unsweetened chocolate, chopped
- 1 tsp. vanilla extract
- 1¾ cups all-purpose flour
- 1 tsp. baking powder
- ¼ tsp. baking soda

CHOCOLATE FILLING
- 6 oz. German sweet chocolate, chopped
- ¾ cup butter, cubed
- ½ cup sliced almonds, toasted

WHIPPED CREAM
- 2 cups heavy whipping cream
- 1 Tbsp. sugar
- 1½ tsp. vanilla extract

TOPPING
- 1½ cups sliced almonds, toasted
- 1 cup cherry pie filling

1. Preheat oven to 350°. Line bottoms of 4 greased 9-in. round baking pans with parchment; grease parchment.
2. Cream the butter and sugar until light and fluffy. Add 1 egg at a time, beating well after each addition. Beat in the water just until blended.
3. In a microwave, melt unsweetened chocolate; stir until smooth. Stir in vanilla. In a small bowl, whisk together flour, baking powder and baking soda; add to creamed mixture alternately with chocolate mixture, beating after each addition. Divide batter among prepared pans.

4. Bake until a toothpick inserted in center comes out clean, 15-20 minutes. Cool for 10 minutes before removing from pans to wire racks; remove paper. Cool completely.
5. For chocolate filling, melt chocolate in a microwave; stir until smooth. Stir in butter until blended. Stir in almonds.
6. For whipped cream, in a small bowl, beat cream until it begins to thicken. Add sugar and vanilla; beat until soft peaks form.
7. To assemble, place 1 cake layer on a serving plate; spread with ⅓ cup chocolate filling and 1 cup whipped cream. Repeat layers twice. Top with the remaining cake and chocolate filling.
8. Spread remaining whipped cream over sides of cake. Press almonds onto sides. Spoon cherry pie filling over top of cake. Refrigerate until serving.

Note: To toast nuts, bake in a shallow pan in a 350° oven for 5-10 minutes or cook in a skillet over low heat until lightly browned, stirring occasionally.

1 slice: 596 cal., 41g fat (22g sat. fat), 124mg chol., 210mg sod., 46g carb. (26g sugars, 3g fiber), 8g pro.

GRANDMA'S TANDY KAKE

My grandmother made this for all our family gatherings. Everyone loves it, and now I make it for every party we attend or host.

—John Morgan, Lebanon, PA

Prep: 20 min. • **Bake:** 20 min + chilling
Makes: 24 servings

- 4 large eggs, room temperature
- 2 cups sugar
- 1 cup 2% milk
- 1 tsp. vanilla extract
- 2 cups all-purpose flour
- 1 tsp. baking powder
- ¼ tsp. salt
- 1¾ cups creamy peanut butter
- 5 milk chocolate candy bars (1.55 oz. each), chopped
- 2 Tbsp. butter

1. Preheat oven to 350°. In a large bowl, beat the eggs and sugar until thick and lemon-colored. Beat in milk and vanilla. In another bowl, combine flour, baking powder and salt; gradually add to egg mixture and mix well.

2. Spread into a greased 15x10x1-in. baking pan. Bake 20-25 minutes or until lightly browned. Cool 15 minutes on a wire rack. Spread peanut butter over top; cool the cake completely.

3. In a double boiler or metal bowl over simmering water, melt chocolate and butter; stir until smooth. Gently spread over peanut butter. Refrigerate 30 minutes or until firm.

1 piece: 290 cal., 14g fat (5g sat. fat), 36mg chol., 156mg sod., 35g carb. (24g sugars, 2g fiber), 7g pro.

MOLASSES-BOURBON PECAN PIE

Guests' mouths water when they get a glimpse of this southern charmer. Its flaky crust perfectly complements the rich, nutty filling.

—Charlene Chambers, Ormond Beach, FL

Prep: 35 min. + chilling
Bake: 55 min. + cooling
Makes: 8 servings

- 1½ cups all-purpose flour
- ¾ tsp. salt
- 6 Tbsp. shortening
- 5 to 6 Tbsp. ice water
  FILLING
- ¾ cup packed brown sugar
- ¾ cup corn syrup
- ½ cup molasses
- 3 Tbsp. butter
- ½ tsp. salt
- 3 large eggs, room temperature, beaten
- 2 Tbsp. bourbon
- 2 tsp. vanilla extract
- 2 cups pecan halves
  Whipped cream

1. In a large bowl, combine flour and salt; cut in shortening until crumbly. Gradually add water, tossing with a fork until dough forms a ball. Wrap in plastic. Refrigerate for 1-1½ hours or until easy to handle.

2. Roll out dough to fit a 9-in. pie plate. Transfer crust to pie plate. Trim crust to ½ in. beyond edge of plate; flute the edge. Refrigerate.

3. Meanwhile, in a large saucepan, combine the brown sugar, corn syrup, molasses, butter and salt; bring to a simmer over medium heat. Cook and stir for 2-3 minutes or until sugar is dissolved. Remove from the heat and cool to room temperature. (The mixture will be thick when cooled.)

4. Preheat oven to 350°. Stir eggs, bourbon and vanilla into molasses mixture. Stir in pecans. Pour into crust. Bake 55-60 minutes or until a knife inserted in the center comes out clean. Cover edges with foil during the last 30 minutes to prevent overbrowning if necessary.

5. Cool on a wire rack. Serve with whipped cream. Refrigerate leftovers.

1 slice: 653 cal., 35g fat (7g sat. fat), 91mg chol., 489mg sod., 81g carb. (41g sugars, 3g fiber), 7g pro.

OMA'S APFELKUCHEN

For more than 150 years, members of my husband's German family have shared this scrumptious apple cake recipe. Try it with any apples you have on hand, but I like to use Granny Smith.
—Amy Kirchen, Loveland, OH

- -

Prep: 20 min. • **Bake:** 45 min. + cooling
Makes: 10 servings

- 5 large egg yolks
- 2 medium tart apples, peeled, cored and halved
- 1 cup plus 2 Tbsp. unsalted butter, softened
- 1¼ cups sugar
- 2 cups all-purpose flour
- 2 Tbsp. cornstarch
- 2 tsp. cream of tartar
- 1 tsp. baking powder
- ½ tsp. salt
- ¼ cup 2% milk
  Confectioners' sugar

1. Preheat oven to 350°. Let the egg yolks stand at room temperature for 30 minutes. Starting ½ in. from 1 end, cut apple halves lengthwise into ¼-in. slices, leaving them attached at the top so they fan out slightly. Set aside.

2. Cream butter and sugar until light and fluffy. Add 1 egg yolk at a time, beating well after each addition. In another bowl, sift flour, cornstarch, cream of tartar, baking powder and salt twice. Gradually beat into creamed mixture. Add milk; mix well (batter will be thick).

3. Spread the batter into a greased 9-in. springform pan wrapped in a sheet of heavy-duty foil. Gently press apples, round side up, into batter. Bake until a toothpick inserted in the center comes out with moist crumbs, 45-55 minutes. Cool on a wire rack 10 minutes. Loosen sides from pan with knife; remove foil. Cool 1 hour longer. Carefully remove rim from pan. Dust with confectioners' sugar.

1 slice: 422 cal., 23g fat (14g sat. fat), 148mg chol., 177mg sod., 50g carb. (28g sugars, 1g fiber), 4g pro.

PEEL, CORE, SLICE…

Using a sharp knife, peel a washed apple and cut in half. Use a spoon or small scoop to remove the center seeds and membranes. Slice each apple half into wedges or as desired. You can also core a whole apple simply using an apple corer.

SMOOTH CHOCOLATE PIE

My mom and I made this pie, and the whole family enjoyed it. We think you will, too.
—Steve Riemersma, Allegan, MI

Prep: 25 min. + freezing • **Makes:** 8 servings

1½ cups finely crushed chocolate
    wafers (about 24 wafers)
⅓ cup butter, melted
3 oz. cream cheese, softened
2 Tbsp. sugar
4 oz. German sweet
    chocolate, melted
⅓ cup 2% milk
1 carton (8 oz.) frozen
    whipped topping, thawed
    Additional melted German sweet
    chocolate, optional

1. In a small bowl, mix wafer crumbs and melted butter. Press onto bottom and up sides of an ungreased 9-in. pie plate.
2. In a bowl, beat cream cheese and sugar until blended. Gradually beat in the melted chocolate and milk. Refrigerate 10 minutes.
3. Fold whipped topping into chocolate mixture; spoon into crust. Freeze 4 hours or until firm. If desired, drizzle with melted chocolate before serving.
1 piece: 383 cal., 24g fat (15g sat. fat), 33mg chol., 293mg sod., 39g carb. (23g sugars, 2g fiber), 4g pro.

GRANDMA'S APPLE PIE

You'll elicit plenty of smiles every time you serve slices of this classic apple pie. The crisp crust is a nice complement to the tender apples.
—Carole Davis, Keene, NH

Prep: 20 min. • **Bake:** 50 min.
Makes: 8 servings

	Pastry for a double-crust pie (9 in.)
6	to 7 cups thinly sliced peeled tart apples (about 2½ lbs.)
1	Tbsp. lemon juice
1	cup sugar
2	Tbsp. all-purpose flour
½	tsp. ground cinnamon
	Dash ground nutmeg
2	Tbsp. butter
2%	milk
	Additional sugar

1. Line a 9-in. pie plate with bottom crust; trim the crust even with edge of pie plate. Set aside.

2. In a large bowl, toss apples with lemon juice. Combine the sugar, flour, cinnamon and nutmeg. Arrange half of the apples in pastry shell; sprinkle with half of the sugar mixture. Repeat layers. Dot with butter.

3. Roll out remaining pastry to fit top of pie; place over filling. Trim, seal and flute edges. Cut slits in pastry. Brush with milk and sprinkle with additional sugar.

4. Cover the edges loosely with foil. Bake at 425° for 20 minutes. Remove foil; bake for 30-35 minutes longer or until crust is golden brown and filling is bubbly. Serve warm if desired or cool on a wire rack.

1 piece: 417 cal., 17g fat (8g sat. fat), 18mg chol., 229mg sod., 65g carb. (36g sugars, 2g fiber), 2g pro.

Apple Crumb Pie: Use pastry for a single-crust pie; line pie plate and fill as directed. Combine ½ cup all-purpose flour and ½ cup sugar; cut in ¼ cup cold butter until crumbly. Sprinkle over apples. Bake at 375° for 45-50 minutes or until filling is bubbly and apples are tender.

MARVELOUS MARBLE CAKE

Pound cake and chocolate go together to make the best marble cake ever.
—Ellen Riley, Murfreesboro, TN

Prep: 45 min. • **Bake:** 20 min. + cooling
Makes: 16 servings

- 4 oz. bittersweet chocolate, chopped
- 3 Tbsp. plus 1¼ cups butter, softened, divided
- 2 cups sugar
- 5 large eggs, room temperature
- 3 tsp. vanilla extract
- 2¼ cups all-purpose flour
- 2 tsp. baking powder
- ½ tsp. salt
- ½ cup sour cream
- ½ cup miniature semisweet chocolate chips, optional

FROSTING
- ¾ cup butter, softened
- 6¾ cups confectioners' sugar
- 2 tsp. vanilla extract
- ½ to ⅔ cup 2% milk
- 2 Tbsp. miniature semisweet chocolate chips

1. In top of a double boiler or a metal bowl over barely simmering water, melt the chocolate and 3 Tbsp. butter; stir until smooth. Cool to room temperature.
2. Preheat oven to 375°. Line bottoms of 3 greased 8-in. round baking pans with parchment; grease parchment.
3. In a large bowl, cream remaining butter and sugar until light and fluffy. Add 1 egg at a time, beating well after each addition. Beat in the vanilla. Whisk the flour, baking powder and salt; add to creamed mixture alternately with the sour cream, beating well after each addition.
4. Remove 2 cups batter to a small bowl; stir in cooled chocolate mixture and, if desired, chocolate chips, until blended. Drop plain and chocolate batters by tablespoonfuls into prepared pans, dividing batters evenly among pans. To make batter level in pans, bang cake pans several times on counter.
5. Bake until a toothpick inserted in center comes out clean, 20-25 minutes. Cool in pans 10 minutes before removing to wire racks; remove parchment. Cool completely.
6. For frosting, in a large bowl, beat the butter until smooth. Gradually beat in the confectioners' sugar, vanilla and enough milk to reach desired consistency.
7. If cake layers have rounded tops, trim with a serrated knife to make level. In a microwave, melt chocolate chips; stir until smooth. Cool slightly.
8. Place 1 cake layer on a serving plate; spread with ½ cup frosting. Repeat layers. Top with remaining cake layer. Frost top and sides of cake.
9. Drop the cooled melted chocolate by ½ teaspoonfuls over frosting. Using a large offset spatula, smear chocolate to create a marble design in frosting.

1 slice: 683 cal., 33g fat (20g sat. fat), 138mg chol., 330mg sod., 97g carb. (79g sugars, 1g fiber), 5g pro.

ORANGE CHOCOLATE RICOTTA PIE

I love this traditional Italian dessert that's often served for special occasions. The orange and chocolate flavors make a classic pairing in this pie.
—Trisha Kruse, Eagle, ID

Prep: 20 min. • **Bake:** 40 min. + cooling
Makes: 8 servings

- 2 cartons (15 oz. each) whole-milk ricotta cheese
- 2 large eggs, room temperature, lightly beaten
- ½ cup dark chocolate chips
- ⅓ cup sugar
- 1 Tbsp. grated orange zest
- 2 Tbsp. orange liqueur, optional
  Pastry for double-crust pie (9 in.)

1. In a large bowl, combine the ricotta cheese, eggs, chocolate chips, sugar, orange zest and, if desired, orange liqueur.
2. Roll out half of the dough to fit a 9-in. pie plate; transfer crust to pie plate. Fill with ricotta mixture.
3. Roll out remaining dough into an 11-in. circle; cut into 1-in.-wide strips. Lay half of the strips across the pie, about 1 in. apart. Fold back every other strip halfway. Lay another strip across center of pie at a right angle. Unfold strips over center strip. Fold back the alternate strips; place a second strip across the pie. Continue to add strips until pie is covered with lattice. Trim, seal and flute edges.
4. Bake at 425° until crust is golden brown, 40-45 minutes. Refrigerate leftovers.

1 slice: 525 cal., 31g fat (16g sat. fat), 106mg chol., 346mg sod., 49g carb. (23g sugars, 0 fiber), 17g pro.

.

LEMON CREAM CUPCAKES

Delicate cupcakes like these are sure to disappear at your next potluck or bake sale.
—Ruth Ann Stelfox, Raymond, AB

Prep: 20 min. • **Bake:** 25 min. + cooling
Makes: about 2½ dozen

- 1 cup butter, softened
- 2 cups sugar
- 3 large eggs, room temperature
- 2 tsp. grated lemon zest
- 1 tsp. vanilla extract
- 3½ cups all-purpose flour
- 1 tsp. baking soda
- ½ tsp. baking powder
- ½ tsp. salt
- 2 cups sour cream

FROSTING

- 3 Tbsp. butter, softened
- 2¼ cups confectioners' sugar
- 2 Tbsp. lemon juice
- ¾ tsp. vanilla extract
- ¼ tsp. grated lemon zest
- 1 to 2 Tbsp. whole milk
  Additional lemon zest, optional

1. In a large bowl, cream butter and sugar until light and fluffy. Add 1 egg at a time, beating well after each addition. Beat in lemon zest and vanilla. Combine the flour, baking soda, baking powder and salt; add to creamed mixture alternately with sour cream, beating well after each addition (batter will be thick).
2. Fill greased or paper-lined muffin cups with ¼ cup of batter. Bake at 350° until a toothpick inserted in the center comes out clean, 25-30 minutes. Cool for 10 minutes before removing from pans to wire racks to cool completely.
3. For the frosting, cream the butter and confectioners' sugar in a small bowl until light and fluffy. Add the lemon juice, vanilla, lemon zest and milk; beat until smooth. Frost cupcakes. If desired, sprinkle with additional lemon zest.

1 cupcake: 244 cal., 11g fat (6g sat. fat), 48mg chol., 178mg sod., 34g carb. (22g sugars, 0 fiber), 3g pro.

RICH RUM CAKE

We like a touch of rum for the holidays, and this orangey rum cake is decadent alone or with big dollops of whipped cream.
—Nancy Heishman, Las Vegas, NV

- -

Prep: 35 min. • **Bake:** 25 min. + cooling
Makes: 12 servings

- 4 **large eggs, room temperature, separated**
- 2½ **cups confectioners' sugar**
- ¾ **cup orange juice**
- ¼ **cup butter, cubed**
- ¾ **cup rum**
- 1 **cup all-purpose flour**
- 1 **tsp. baking powder**
- ½ **tsp. ground cinnamon**
- ¼ **tsp. salt**
- ¼ **tsp. ground nutmeg**
- ½ **cup packed brown sugar, divided**
- 1 **tsp. vanilla extract**
- ¾ **cup butter, melted**
  Optional: Whipped cream and finely chopped glazed pecans

1. Place the egg whites in a large bowl; let stand at room temperature 30 minutes. For the sauce, in a saucepan, combine the confectioners' sugar, juice and ¼ cup cubed butter; cook and stir over medium-low heat until sugar is dissolved. Remove from heat; stir in rum. Reserve ¾ cup for serving.
2. Preheat oven to 375°. Grease and flour a 10-in. tube pan. Sift flour, baking powder, cinnamon, salt and nutmeg together twice; set aside.
3. In a bowl, beat egg whites on medium until soft peaks form. Gradually add ¼ cup brown sugar, 1 Tbsp. at a time, beating on high after each addition until the sugar is dissolved. Continue beating until stiff peaks form.
4. In another bowl, beat egg yolks until slightly thickened. Gradually add ¼ cup remaining brown sugar and the vanilla, beating on high speed until thick. Fold a fourth of the egg whites into batter. Alternately fold in the flour mixture and remaining whites. Fold in melted butter.
5. Transfer to prepared pan. Bake on lowest oven rack 25-30 minutes or until top springs back when lightly touched. Immediately poke holes in cake with a fork; slowly pour remaining sauce over cake, allowing sauce to absorb into cake. Cool completely in pan on a wire rack. Invert onto a serving plate. Serve with reserved sauce and, if desired, whipped cream and glazed pecans.

Note: To remove cakes easily, use solid shortening to grease plain and fluted tube pans.

1 slice: 371 cal., 17g fat (10g sat. fat), 103mg chol., 233mg sod., 44g carb. (35g sugars, 0 fiber), 3g pro.

IRISH COFFEE PIE

Even though we aren't Irish, my mom made this pie for my dad every St. Patrick's Day.
—Holly Nauroth, Fruita, CO

- -

Prep: 25 min. + chilling • **Makes:** 4 servings

⅔ cup graham cracker crumbs
2 Tbsp. sugar
2 Tbsp. butter, melted
4 oz. cream cheese, softened
¼ cup sugar
¼ cup water
1 Tbsp. whiskey, optional
2 tsp. instant coffee granules
1 carton (8 oz.) frozen whipped topping, thawed

1. Combine the cracker crumbs, sugar and butter; press onto the bottom and up the sides of a greased 7-in. pie plate. Bake at 375° for 8-10 minutes or until lightly browned. Cool on a wire rack.

2. In a small bowl, beat the cream cheese and sugar until smooth. Combine the water, whiskey if desired and coffee granules; beat into cream cheese mixture until smooth. Fold in whipped topping.

3. Spoon into crust. Cover and refrigerate the pie for at least 2 hours before serving. Refrigerate leftovers.

1 slice: 448 cal., 26g fat (19g sat. fat), 46mg chol., 209mg sod., 43g carb. (29g sugars, 0 fiber), 3g pro.

CRANBERRY-FILLED ORANGE POUND CAKE

I made this for a special dinner with my family. Everyone loved the cran-orange flavor and the sweet glaze drizzled on top. For a fun variation, add ⅔ cup flaked sweetened coconut when including the orange juice to the batter. Sprinkle the finished cake with toasted coconut.
—Patricia Harmon, Baden, PA

Prep: 25 min. • **Bake:** 50 min. + cooling
Makes: 12 servings

- 1 cup butter, softened
- 1 pkg. (8 oz.) reduced-fat cream cheese
- 2 cups sugar
- 6 large eggs, room temperature
- 3 Tbsp. orange juice, divided
- 4 tsp. grated orange zest
- 3 cups all-purpose flour
- 1 tsp. baking powder
- ½ tsp. baking soda
- ½ tsp. salt
- 1 can (14 oz.) whole-berry cranberry sauce
- ½ cup dried cherries

GLAZE
- 1 cup confectioners' sugar
- ¼ tsp. grated orange zest
- 4 to 5 tsp. orange juice

"This cake is delicious. It came out just perfect! Nice flavor. I used a few maraschino cherries instead of dried cherries and the filling was delicious."
—CARL, TASTEOFHOME.COM

1. Preheat oven to 350°. Grease and flour a 10-in. fluted tube pan.
2. In a large bowl, cream the butter, cream cheese and sugar until light and fluffy. Add 1 egg at a time, beating well after each addition. Beat in 2 Tbsp. orange juice and the orange zest. In another bowl, whisk the flour, baking powder, baking soda and salt; gradually add to creamed mixture, beating just until combined.
3. In a small bowl, mix the cranberry sauce, cherries and remaining orange juice. Spoon two-thirds of the batter into prepared pan. Spread with cranberry mixture. Top with remaining batter.
4. Bake 50-60 minutes or until a toothpick inserted in center comes out clean. Loosen sides from pan with a knife. Cool in pan for 10 minutes before removing to a wire rack to cool completely.
5. In a small bowl, mix confectioners' sugar, orange zest and enough orange juice to reach desired consistency. Pour the glaze over top of cake, allowing it to flow over the sides.

1 slice: 573 cal., 22g fat (13g sat. fat), 147mg chol., 447mg sod., 87g carb. (57g sugars, 2g fiber), 9g pro.

SPICED DEVIL'S FOOD CAKE

One of my mom's friends gave her this recipe when I was a child and it has been a family favorite ever since. When your sweet tooth acts up, this chocolaty treat hits the spot!

—Linda Yeamans, Ashland, OR

Prep: 25 min. • **Bake:** 30 min. + cooling
Makes: 12 servings

- 1 cup butter, softened
- 1½ cups sugar
- 3 large eggs, room temperature
- 1 tsp. vanilla extract
- 2 cups all-purpose flour
- ¼ cup baking cocoa
- 1 tsp. baking powder
- 1 tsp. baking soda
- 1 tsp. ground cinnamon
- ½ to 1 tsp. ground nutmeg
- ¼ to ½ tsp. ground cloves
- 1 cup buttermilk

MOCHA ICING
- 3¾ cups confectioners' sugar
- ¼ cup baking cocoa
- 6 Tbsp. strong brewed coffee
- 6 Tbsp. butter, melted
- 1 tsp. vanilla extract
  Toasted whole or chopped almonds, optional

1. Preheat oven to 350°. Cream butter and sugar until light and fluffy. Add 1 egg at a time, beating well after each addition. Add the vanilla.

2. Sift together all of the dry ingredients; add to creamed mixture alternately with buttermilk. Pour into 2 greased and floured 9-in. round baking pans.

3. Bake until a toothpick inserted in center comes out clean, 30-35 minutes. Cool on wire racks for 10 minutes before removing from pans.

4. In a small bowl, combine all of the icing ingredients except nuts. Spread frosting between layers and over the top and sides of cake. If desired, top with almonds.

1 slice: 543 cal., 23g fat (14g sat. fat), 110mg chol., 389mg sod., 82g carb. (61g sugars, 1g fiber), 5g pro.

HOLIDAY EGGNOG PIE

When I created this pie, I was just trying to use up a few things I had on hand. Everyone loved it the result. With pumpkin pie spice and eggnog, the creamy, dreamy pie has fantastic holiday flavor.

—Shirley Darger, Colorado City, AZ

Prep: 15 min. + freezing • **Makes:** 8 servings

- 4 oz. cream cheese, softened
- 1 Tbsp. butter, softened
- ½ cup confectioners' sugar
- ¼ cup eggnog
- 2 Tbsp. sour cream
- 1 tsp. pumpkin pie spice
- 1½ cups whipped topping
- 1 graham cracker crust (9 in.)
- ⅛ tsp. ground nutmeg

1. In a small bowl, beat the cream cheese, butter and confectioners' sugar until smooth. Beat in the eggnog, sour cream and pie spice. Fold in whipped topping; spread into crust. Sprinkle with nutmeg.

2. Cover and freeze for 4 hours or until firm. Remove the pie from the freezer 15 minutes before slicing.

Note: This recipe was tested with commercially prepared eggnog.

1 slice: 253 cal., 15g fat (8g sat. fat), 27mg chol., 179mg sod., 26g carb. (19g sugars, 0 fiber), 2g pro.

GRANDMA'S CARROT CAKE

My grandma was very special to me. She had a big country kitchen that was full of wonderful aromas anytime we visited. This was one of her prized cake recipes, which continues to be a favorite from generation to generation.
—Denise Strasz, Detroit, MI

- -

Prep: 30 min. • **Bake:** 50 min. + cooling
Makes: 16 servings

2	cups sugar
1½	cups canola oil
4	large eggs, room temperature
2	tsp. vanilla extract
2½	cups all-purpose flour
1½	tsp. baking soda
½	tsp. salt
1	tsp. ground cinnamon
3	cups shredded carrots (about 6 medium)
1	cup chopped walnuts

FROSTING

1	pkg. (8 oz.) cream cheese, softened
¼	cup butter, softened
3	cups confectioners' sugar

1. Preheat oven to 350°. Grease and flour a 10-in. fluted tube pan.
2. Beat first 4 ingredients until well blended. Whisk together flour, baking soda, salt and cinnamon; gradually beat into the sugar mixture. Stir in carrots and walnuts.
3. Transfer to prepared pan. Bake until a toothpick inserted in center comes out clean, 50-60 minutes. Cool in the pan for 10 minutes before removing to a wire rack; cool completely.
4. For frosting, beat cream cheese and butter until smooth. Gradually beat in confectioners' sugar. Spread over cake.
Note: To remove cakes easily, use solid shortening to grease plain and fluted tube pans.
1 slice: 593 cal., 35g fat (7g sat. fat), 68mg chol., 292mg sod., 67g carb. (49g sugars, 2g fiber), 6g pro.

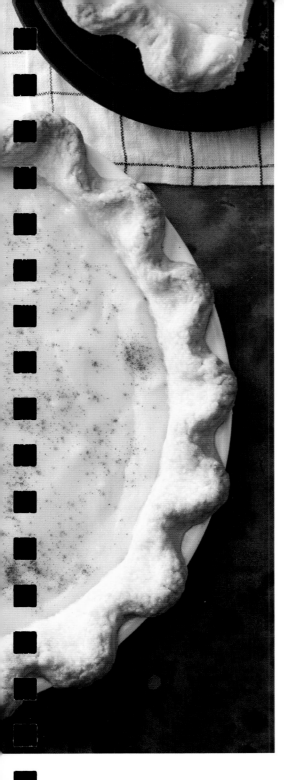

SUGAR CREAM PIE

I love creamy sugar pie, especially the one that my grandma made for me. Here in Indiana, we serve it warm or chilled.
—Laura Kipper, Westfield, IN

- -

Prep: 20 min. • **Bake:** 15 min. + chilling
Makes: 8 servings

	Pastry for single-crust pie (9 in.)
1	**cup sugar**
¼	**cup cornstarch**
2	**cups 2% milk**
½	**cup butter, cubed**
1	**tsp. vanilla extract**
¼	**tsp. ground cinnamon**

1. Preheat oven to 450°. Roll out dough to fit a 9-in. pie plate. Transfer crust to pie plate. Trim crust to ½ in. beyond rim of plate; flute edge. Line unpricked crust with a double thickness of heavy-duty foil. Fill with pie weights, dried beans or uncooked rice.
2. Bake 8 minutes. Remove foil and weights; bake 5-7 minutes longer or until light brown. Cool on a wire rack. Reduce the oven setting to 375°.
3. Meanwhile, in a large saucepan, combine sugar and cornstarch; stir in the milk until smooth. Bring to a boil. Reduce heat; cook and stir 2 minutes or until thickened and bubbly. Remove from heat; stir in butter and vanilla. Transfer to crust; sprinkle with cinnamon. Bake for 15-20 minutes or until golden brown. Cool the pie on a wire rack; refrigerate until chilled.

1 slice: 418 cal., 24g fat (15g sat. fat), 66mg chol., 275mg sod., 47g carb. (28g sugars, 1g fiber), 4g pro.

TEST KITCHEN TIP

For a change of pace, try baking this pie in a crumb crust. Graham crackers, gingersnaps and vanilla wafer cookies all taste delicious.

DECADENT FUDGE CAKE

Whenever I serve this, people seem to love the rich flavor. Four types of chocolate make it particularly decadent.
—Anna Hogge, Yorktown, VA

Prep: 20 min. • **Bake:** 1¼ hours
Makes: 16 servings

- 1 cup butter, softened
- 1½ cups sugar
- 4 large eggs, room temperature
- 1 cup buttermilk
- ½ tsp. baking soda
- 2½ cups all-purpose flour
- 8 oz. German sweet chocolate, melted
- 1 cup chocolate syrup
- 2 tsp. vanilla extract
- 1¼ cups miniature semisweet chocolate chips, divided
- 4 oz. white baking chocolate, chopped
- 2 Tbsp. plus 1 tsp. shortening, divided

1. Cream butter in a large bowl. Gradually mix in sugar. Add 1 egg at a time, beating well after each addition. Combine the buttermilk and baking soda; add to creamed mixture alternately with flour, beginning and ending with flour. Add melted chocolate, chocolate syrup and vanilla. Stir in 1 cup miniature chocolate chips. Pour into a greased and floured 10-in. fluted tube pan. Bake at 325° for 1 hour and 15 minutes or until a toothpick comes out clean. Immediately invert cake onto a serving plate; cool completely.
2. Meanwhile, in a microwave, melt the white chocolate and 2 Tbsp. shortening; stir until smooth. Cool slightly; drizzle over cake. Melt remaining chips and shortening in a small saucepan over low heat, stirring until smooth. Remove from the heat; cool slightly. Drizzle over white chocolate.
1 piece: 519 cal., 25g fat (15g sat. fat), 78mg chol., 192mg sod., 63g carb. (44g sugars, 2g fiber), 7g pro.

CRANBERRY WALNUT PIE

With its ruby-red color and a golden lattice crust, this pie looks as good as it tastes.
—Diane Everett, Dunkirk, NY

Prep: 20 min. • **Bake:** 50 min. + cooling
Makes: 8 servings

- 1 pkg. (12 oz.) fresh or frozen cranberries, thawed
- 1½ cups packed brown sugar
- 1 cup chopped walnuts
- ¼ cup butter, melted
- 4½ tsp. all-purpose flour
- 2 tsp. grated orange zest
  Dash salt
  Pastry for double-crust pie (9 in.)

1. Preheat oven to 375°. Place cranberries in a food processor; cover and process until finely chopped. Transfer to a large bowl; stir in brown sugar, walnuts, melted butter, flour, orange zest and salt.
2. On a lightly floured surface, roll 1 half of pastry dough to a ⅛-in.-thick circle; transfer to a 9-in. pie plate. Trim the crust to ½ in. beyond rim of plate. Add filling.
3. Roll remaining dough to a ⅛-in.-thick circle; cut into ½-in.-wide strips. Arrange over filling in a lattice pattern. Trim and seal strips to edge of bottom crust; flute edge. Cover edges loosely with foil.
4. Bake 30 minutes. Remove foil; bake until crust is golden brown and filling is bubbly, 20-25 minutes. Cool on a wire rack.
Note: To add a little sparkle to pie crusts, brush with an egg wash and sprinkle with coarse sugar before baking.
1 slice: 672 cal., 38g fat (19g sat. fat), 75mg chol., 391mg sod., 79g carb. (43g sugars, 4g fiber), 7g pro.
Pastry for double-crust pie (9 in.): Combine 2½ cups all-purpose flour and ½ tsp. salt; cut in 1 cup cold butter until crumbly. Gradually add ⅓ to ⅔ cup ice water, tossing with a fork until dough holds together when pressed. Divide dough in half and shape into disks; wrap in plastic wrap and refrigerate 1 hour.

GRANDMA'S BLACKBERRY CAKE

This dessert is a lovely change-of-pace treat. A lightly seasoned spice cake lets the wonderful flavor of fresh blackberries shine through.
—Diana Martin, Moundsville, WV

- -

Prep: 15 min. • **Bake:** 45 min. + cooling
Makes: 9 servings

- 1 cup fresh blackberries
- 2 cups all-purpose flour, divided
- ½ cup butter, softened
- 1 cup sugar
- 2 large eggs, room temperature
- 1 tsp. baking soda
- 1 tsp. ground cinnamon
- 1 tsp. ground nutmeg
- ½ tsp. salt
- ¼ tsp. ground cloves
- ¼ tsp. ground allspice
- ¾ cup buttermilk
  Whipped cream, optional

1. Toss blackberries with 2 Tbsp. of flour; set aside. In a large bowl, cream the butter and sugar until light and fluffy. Beat in the eggs. Combine the baking soda, cinnamon, nutmeg, salt, cloves, allspice and remaining flour; add to creamed mixture alternately with buttermilk, beating well after each addition. Fold in blackberries.
2. Pour into a greased and floured 9-in. square baking pan. Bake at 350° until a toothpick inserted in the center comes out clean, 45-50 minutes. Cool on a wire rack. Serve with whipped cream if desired.

1 piece: 312 cal., 12g fat (7g sat. fat), 75mg chol., 410mg sod., 47g carb. (24g sugars, 2g fiber), 5g pro.

COCONUT CREAM PIE

My husband and I grow 500 acres of wheat on the actual farm his family homesteaded in 1889. I grind my own flour and love to use it in this recipe. The easy, pat-in crust has a rich grain flavor. It's simply irresistible topped with old-fashioned coconut cream and a fluffy meringue.
—Roberta Foster, Kingfisher, OK

- -

Prep: 40 min. • **Bake:** 15 min. + chilling
Makes: 8 servings

- 1½ cups whole wheat flour
- 2 tsp. sugar
- ½ tsp. salt
- ½ cup canola oil
- 2 Tbsp. whole milk

FILLING

- ½ cup sugar
- 3 Tbsp. cornstarch
- 1 Tbsp. all-purpose flour
- ½ tsp. salt
- 2¼ cups whole milk
- 3 large egg yolks, room temperature
- 1 Tbsp. butter
- ½ cup sweetened shredded coconut
- 1 tsp. vanilla extract

MERINGUE

- 3 large egg whites, room temperature
- 1 cup marshmallow creme
- ¼ cup sweetened shredded coconut

1. Preheat oven to 350°. In a bowl, mix flour, sugar and salt. In another bowl, whisk the oil and milk. Gradually add to flour mixture, tossing with a fork until moistened (mixture will be crumbly). Press onto bottom and up sides of an ungreased 9-in. pie plate. Bake 20 minutes. Cool on a wire rack.

2. For filling, in a heavy saucepan, mix sugar, cornstarch, flour and salt. Gradually whisk in milk. Bring to a boil; cook and stir roughly 2 minutes or until thickened. Remove from the heat.

3. In a small bowl, whisk a small amount of hot mixture into egg yolks; return all to pan, whisking constantly. Bring to a gentle boil; cook and stir 2 minutes. Remove from heat; stir in butter, coconut and vanilla.

4. For meringue, in a bowl, beat egg whites until soft peaks form. Gradually add the marshmallow creme, beating on high speed. Continue beating mixture until stiff glossy peaks form.

5. Transfer hot filling to crust. Spread meringue evenly over filling, sealing to edge of crust. Sprinkle with coconut. Bake until meringue is golden brown, 12-15 minutes. Cool 1 hour on a wire rack. Refrigerate at least 3 hours before serving.

1 slice: 437 cal., 23g fat (7g sat. fat), 80mg chol., 395mg sod., 51g carb. (29g sugars, 3g fiber), 8g pro.

TEST KITCHEN TIP
Jazz up homemade pie crusts by mixing a bit of orange or lemon zest into the flour.

GERMAN CHOCOLATE CAKE

This from-scratch cake is my husband's favorite! Every bite has a light crunch from the pecans, a sweet taste of coconut and a lovely drizzle of chocolate.
—Joyce Platfoot, Wapakoneta, OH

Prep: 30 min. • **Bake:** 30 min. + cooling
Makes: 12 servings

- 4 oz. German sweet chocolate, chopped
- ½ cup water
- 1 cup butter, softened
- 2 cups sugar
- 4 large eggs, room temperature, separated
- 1 tsp. vanilla extract
- 2½ cups cake flour
- 1 tsp. baking soda
- ½ tsp. salt
- 1 cup buttermilk

FROSTING
- 1½ cups sugar
- 1½ cups evaporated milk
- ¾ cup butter
- 5 large egg yolks, room temperature, beaten
- 2 cups sweetened shredded coconut
- 1½ cups chopped pecans
- 1½ tsp. vanilla extract

ICING
- 1 tsp. shortening
- 2 oz. semisweet chocolate

1. Line 3 greased 9-in. round baking pans with waxed paper. Grease waxed paper and set aside. In small saucepan, melt chocolate with water over low heat; cool.

2. Preheat oven to 350°. In a large bowl, cream butter and sugar until light and fluffy. Beat in 4 egg yolks, 1 at a time, beating well after each addition. Blend in the melted chocolate and vanilla. Combine flour, baking soda and salt; add to the creamed mixture alternately with buttermilk, beating well after each addition.

3. In a small bowl and with clean beaters, beat the 4 egg whites until stiff peaks form. Fold a fourth of the egg whites into the creamed mixture; fold in remaining whites.

4. Pour batter into prepared pans. Bake 24-28 minutes or until a toothpick inserted in center comes out clean. Cool 10 minutes before removing from pans to wire racks to cool completely.

5. For frosting, in a small saucepan, heat the sugar, milk, butter and egg yolks over medium-low heat until mixture is thickened and golden brown, stirring constantly. Remove from heat. Stir in coconut, pecans and vanilla extract. Cool until thick enough to spread. Spread a third of the frosting over each cake layer and stack the layers.

6. In a microwave, melt the chocolate and shortening; stir until smooth. Drizzle over the cake.

1 slice: 910 cal., 53g fat (28g sat. fat), 237mg chol., 511mg sod., 103g carb. (76g sugars, 4g fiber), 11g pro.

CHERRY PUDDING CAKE

A cross between a cake and a cobbler, this cherry dessert is awesome. Add it to your list of trusty potluck recipes, because this one is sure to go fast.
—Brenda Parker, Kalamazoo, MI

- -

Prep: 10 min. • **Bake:** 40 min.
Makes: 12 servings

  2   **cups all-purpose flour**
2½ **cups sugar, divided**
  4   **tsp. baking powder**
  1   **cup whole milk**
  2   **Tbsp. canola oil**
  2   **cans (14½ oz. each) water-packed pitted tart red cherries, well drained**
  2   **to 3 drops red food coloring, optional**
 ⅛ **tsp. almond extract**
      Optional: Whipped cream or ice cream

1. In a bowl, combine flour, 1 cup of sugar, baking powder, milk and oil; pour into a greased shallow 3-qt. baking dish. In a bowl, combine cherries, food coloring, if desired, extract and remaining sugar; spoon over the batter.
2. Bake at 375° for 40-45 minutes or until a toothpick inserted in the cake portion comes out clean. Serve warm, with whipped cream or ice cream if desired.
1 serving: 296 cal., 3g fat (1g sat. fat), 3mg chol., 147mg sod., 65g carb. (48g sugars, 1g fiber), 3g pro.

GOLDEN PEACH PIE

Years ago, I entered this pie in a county fair, and it won a first-place blue ribbon—plus a purple ribbon for Best All Around. Family and friends agree with the judges—it's a perfectly peachy pie.
—Shirley Olson, Polson, MT

Prep: 20 min. • **Bake:** 50 min. + cooling
Makes: 8 servings

- 2 **sheets refrigerated pie crust**
- 5 **cups sliced peeled fresh peaches (about 5 medium)**
- 2 **tsp. lemon juice**
- ½ **tsp. grated orange zest**
- ⅛ **tsp. almond extract**
- 1 **cup sugar**
- ¼ **cup cornstarch**
- ¼ **tsp. ground nutmeg**
- ⅛ **tsp. salt**
- 2 **Tbsp. butter**

1. Line a 9-in. pie plate with 1 crust; trim, leaving a 1-in. overhang around edge. Set aside. In a large bowl, combine the peaches, lemon juice, grated orange zest and extract. Combine the sugar, cornstarch, nutmeg and salt. Add to peach mixture; toss gently to coat. Pour into crust; dot with butter.
2. Roll out remaining crust to a ⅛-in.-thick circle; cut into strips of various widths. Arrange the over filling in a lattice pattern. Trim and seal strips to bottom crust; fold overhang over. Lightly press or flute edge. Cover the edges loosely with foil.
3. Bake at 400° for 40 minutes. Remove foil; bake until crust is golden brown and filling is bubbly, 10-15 minutes longer. Cool on a wire rack. Store in the refrigerator.
1 slice: 425 cal., 17g fat (8g sat. fat), 18mg chol., 267mg sod., 67g carb. (36g sugars, 2g fiber), 3g pro.

CHOCOLATE CAKE WITH CHOCOLATE FROSTING

I once sent this rich chocolate cake to my kids' teachers, and it vanished, so I had to make another one!
—Megan Moelbert, Springville, NY

Prep: 40 min. • **Bake:** 30 min. + cooling
Makes: 16 servings

- 2 **cups sugar**
- 2 **cups water**
- ⅔ **cup canola oil**
- 2 **Tbsp. white vinegar**
- 2 **tsp. vanilla extract**
- 3 **cups all-purpose flour**
- ⅓ **cup plus 1 Tbsp. baking cocoa, sifted**
- 2 **tsp. baking soda**
- 1 **tsp. salt**

FROSTING
- 3¾ **cups confectioners' sugar**
- ⅓ **cup baking cocoa**
- 1 **cup butter, softened**
- 1 **tsp. vanilla extract**
- 3 **to 5 Tbsp. 2% milk**

1. Preheat oven to 350°. Line bottoms of 2 greased 9-in. round baking pans with parchment; grease parchment.
2. In a large bowl, beat sugar, water, oil, vinegar and vanilla until well blended. In another large bowl, whisk the flour, sifted cocoa, baking soda and salt; gradually add to sugar mixture, beating until smooth.
3. Transfer batter to prepared pans. Bake until a toothpick inserted in center comes out clean, 30-35 minutes. Cool in pans for 10 minutes before removing to wire racks; remove parchment. Cool completely.
4. For frosting, sift confectioners' sugar and cocoa together. In a large bowl, beat butter and vanilla extract until blended. Beat in the confectioners' sugar mixture alternately with enough milk to reach desired spreading consistency. Spread frosting between layers and over top and sides of cake.
1 slice: 491 cal., 22g fat (8g sat. fat), 31mg chol., 399mg sod., 74g carb. (53g sugars, 1g fiber), 3g pro.
For chocolate sheet cake: Make batter as directed and transfer to a greased 13x9-in. baking pan. Bake in a preheated 350° oven for 30-35 minutes or until a toothpick inserted in center comes out clean. Frosting recipe may be halved.

GINGERY PUMPKIN PIE

My birthday is in late November so my mom often morphed the Thanksgiving pumpkin pie into my birthday cake and had all the family sing for me. This is an update on her recipe, adding a lot more of our mutual favorite ingredient, ginger. The pie is best after it's nice and chilled. Birthday candles optional.

—Emily Tyra, Traverse City, MI

- -

Prep: 30 min. + chilling • **Bake:** 50 min.
Makes: 8 servings (1½ cups whipped cream)

- 1¼ **cups all-purpose flour**
- 1 **Tbsp. minced fresh gingerroot**
- ¼ **tsp. ground allspice**
- ¼ **tsp. salt**
- ½ **cup butter, cubed**
- 3 **to 5 Tbsp. ice water**

FILLING
- 2 **large eggs, room temperature**
- 1 **large egg yolk, room temperature**
- 1 **can (15 oz.) solid-pack pumpkin**
- 1¼ **cups heavy whipping cream**
- ⅔ **cup packed brown sugar**
- 1 **tsp. ground cinnamon**
- 1 **tsp. minced fresh gingerroot**
- 1 **tsp. molasses**
- ¼ **tsp. ground ginger**
- ¼ **tsp. ground allspice**
- ⅛ **tsp. ground cardamom**
- ⅛ **tsp. ground cloves**

WHIPPED CREAM
- ¾ **cup heavy whipping cream**
- 1 **Tbsp. maple syrup**
- ¼ **tsp. ground cinnamon**

1. In a small bowl, mix the flour, ginger, allspice and salt; cut in butter until crumbly. Gradually add ice water, tossing with a fork until dough holds together when pressed. Shape into a disk; cover and refrigerate at least 1 hour or overnight.

2. Preheat oven to 375°. On a lightly floured surface, roll dough to a ⅛-in.-thick circle; transfer to a 9-in. pie plate. Trim crust to ½ in. beyond rim of plate; flute edge. In a large bowl, whisk filling ingredients until blended; pour into crust.

3. Bake on a lower oven rack 50-60 minutes or until a knife inserted in the center comes out clean. Cool pie on a wire rack; serve or refrigerate within 2 hours.

4. For whipped cream, in a small bowl, beat cream until it begins to thicken. Add maple syrup and cinnamon; beat until soft peaks form. Serve with pie.

1 slice with 3 Tbsp. whipped cream:
504 cal., 36g fat (22g sat. fat), 182mg chol., 226mg sod., 42g carb. (22g sugars, 2g fiber), 6g pro.

GRANDMA'S CHOCOLATE MERINGUE PIE

My grandmother served chocolate meringue pie after Sunday dinner each week, usually apologizing that it was too runny or something else was wrong with it. Of course, it was never less than perfect!
—Donna Vest Tilley, Chesterfield, VA

- -

Prep: 30 min. • **Bake:** 15 min.
Makes: 8 servings

- ¾ cup sugar
- 5 Tbsp. baking cocoa
- 3 Tbsp. cornstarch
- ¼ tsp. salt
- 2 cups whole milk
- 3 large egg yolks, room temperature, beaten
- 1 tsp. vanilla extract
- 1 pastry shell (9 in.), baked

MERINGUE

- 3 large egg whites, room temperature
- ¼ tsp. cream of tartar
- 6 Tbsp. sugar

1. In a saucepan, mix sugar, cocoa, cornstarch and salt; gradually add milk. Cook and stir over medium-high heat until thickened and bubbly. Reduce heat; cook and stir 2 minutes more. Remove from heat. Stir about 1 cup of the hot filling into the egg yolks. Return to saucepan and bring to a gentle boil. Cook and stir 2 minutes. Remove from the heat and stir in vanilla. Pour hot filling into pie crust.
2. For meringue, immediately beat egg whites with cream of tartar until soft peaks form. Gradually add sugar and continue to beat until stiff and glossy. Spread evenly over hot filling, sealing meringue to pie crust. Bake at 350° for 12-15 minutes or until golden.

1 piece: 317 cal., 11g fat (5g sat. fat), 93mg chol., 227mg sod., 49g carb. (31g sugars, 1g fiber), 6g pro.

ZUCCHINI CUPCAKES

I asked my grandmother for this recipe after trying these irresistible spice cupcakes at her home. I just love the creamy caramel frosting. They're such a scrumptious dessert you actually forget you're eating your vegetables, too!
—Virginia Lapierre, Greensboro Bend, VT

- -

Prep: 20 min. • **Bake:** 20 min. + cooling
Makes: about 1½ dozen

- 3 large eggs, room temperature
- 1⅓ cups sugar
- ½ cup canola oil
- ½ cup orange juice
- 1 tsp. almond extract
- 2½ cups all-purpose flour
- 2 tsp. ground cinnamon
- 2 tsp. baking powder
- 1 tsp. baking soda
- 1 tsp. salt
- ½ tsp. ground cloves
- 1½ cups shredded zucchini

FROSTING

- 1 cup packed brown sugar
- ½ cup butter, cubed
- ¼ cup 2% milk
- 1 tsp. vanilla extract
- 1½ to 2 cups confectioners' sugar

1. Preheat oven to 350°. Beat the first 5 ingredients. Combine dry ingredients; gradually add to egg mixture and blend well. Stir in zucchini.
2. Fill paper-lined muffin cups two-thirds full. Bake until a toothpick inserted in center comes out clean, 20-25 minutes. Cool for 10 minutes before removing to a wire rack.
3. For frosting, combine the brown sugar, butter and milk in a large saucepan. Bring to a boil over medium heat; cook and stir until thickened, 1-2 minutes. Remove from heat; stir in vanilla. Cool to lukewarm.
4. Gradually beat in confectioners' sugar until frosting reaches desired spreading consistency. Frost cupcakes.

1 cupcake: 327 cal., 12g fat (4g sat. fat), 45mg chol., 305mg sod., 52g carb. (38g sugars, 1g fiber), 3g pro.

DESSERTS

From cobblers and crisps to tortes and trifles,
old-fashioned desserts always get thumbs-up approval.
Turn here for cheesecakes, frozen treats, pastries,
puddings and more, and end your meals on
a sweet note just as Grandma always did.

SPUMONI BAKED ALASKA

For a refreshing end to a rich meal, try this impressive frosty finale.
—*Taste of Home* Test Kitchen

Prep: 50 min. + freezing
Bake: 5 min.
Makes: 12 servings

- ½ cup butter, cubed
- 2 oz. unsweetened chocolate, chopped
- 1 cup sugar
- 1 tsp. vanilla extract
- 2 large eggs, room temperature
- ¾ cup all-purpose flour
- ½ tsp. baking powder
- ½ tsp. salt
- 1 cup chopped hazelnuts
- 2 qt. vanilla ice cream, softened, divided
- ½ cup chopped pistachios
- ½ tsp. almond extract
- 6 drops green food coloring, optional
- ⅓ cup chopped maraschino cherries
- 1 Tbsp. maraschino cherry juice
- 1 Tbsp. rum

MERINGUE
- 8 large egg whites, room temperature
- 1 cup sugar
- 1 tsp. cream of tartar

1. Preheat oven to 350°. In a microwave-safe bowl, melt butter and chocolate; stir until smooth. Stir in the sugar and vanilla. Add 1 egg at a time, beating well after each addition. Combine the flour, baking powder and salt; gradually stir into the chocolate mixture. Stir in hazelnuts.

2. Spread into a greased 8-in. round baking pan. Bake 35-40 minutes or until a toothpick inserted in the center comes out with moist crumbs (do not overbake). Cool 10 minutes before removing from pan to a wire rack to cool completely.

3. Meanwhile, line an 8-in. round bowl (1½ qt.) with foil. In a smaller bowl, place 1 qt. ice cream; add the pistachios, almond extract and, if desired, green food coloring. Quickly spread ice cream over bottom and up sides of foil-lined bowl, leaving the center hollow; cover and freeze for 30 minutes.

4. In a small bowl, combine cherries, cherry juice, rum and remaining ice cream. Pack the ice cream into hollow center of 8-in. bowl; cover and freeze.

5. In a large heavy saucepan, combine egg whites, sugar and cream of tartar. With a hand mixer, beat on low speed 1 minute. Continue beating over low heat until egg mixture reaches 160°, about 8 minutes. Transfer to a bowl; beat until stiff glossy peaks form and sugar is dissolved.

6. Place brownie on an ungreased foil-lined baking sheet; top with inverted ice cream mold. Remove foil. Immediately spread meringue over ice cream, sealing to edges of brownie. Freeze until ready to serve, up to 24 hours.

7. Preheat oven to 400°. Bake 2-5 minutes or until meringue is lightly browned. Quickly and carefully transfer to a serving plate; serve immediately.

1 piece: 554 cal., 29g fat (13g sat. fat), 94mg chol., 314mg sod., 68g carb. (52g sugars, 3g fiber), 11g pro.

STICKY TOFFEE RICE PUDDING WITH CARAMEL CREAM

The once-simple rice pudding gets a makeover with this upscale recipe. It has just the right amount of thickness for soaking up a hot caramel topping.
—Janice Elder, Charlotte, NC

- -

Prep: 45 min. • **Bake:** 35 min. + cooling
Makes: 16 servings

- 3 cups water
- 1 cup uncooked medium grain rice
- ¼ tsp. salt
- 3 cups pitted dates, chopped
- 3 cups 2% milk
- 2 tsp. vanilla extract
- 1 cup packed brown sugar
- 1½ cups heavy whipping cream, divided
- ¼ cup butter, cubed
- ½ cup sour cream
- ¼ cup hot caramel ice cream topping

1. In a large saucepan, bring the water, rice and salt to a boil. Reduce heat; cover and simmer for 12-15 minutes or until rice is tender. Add dates and milk; cook and stir for 10 minutes. Remove from the heat; stir in vanilla. Set aside.

2. In a small saucepan, combine the brown sugar, 1 cup cream and butter. Bring to a boil. Reduce heat; simmer, uncovered, for 2 minutes, stirring constantly. Stir into rice mixture. Transfer to a greased 13x9-in. baking dish. Bake, uncovered, at 350° for 35-40 minutes or until bubbly. Cool for 15 minutes.

3. Meanwhile, in a small bowl, beat the sour cream, caramel topping and remaining cream until slightly thickened. Serve with warm rice pudding. Refrigerate leftovers.

½ cup rice pudding with 1 Tbsp. topping:
329 cal., 14g fat (8g sat. fat), 38mg chol., 112mg sod., 50g carb. (37g sugars, 2g fiber), 4g pro.

STRAWBERRY BAVARIAN TORTE

This beautiful make-ahead dessert is deliciously light...the perfect ending to any meal.
—Christine Azzarello, Elmhurst, IL

Prep: 15 min. + chilling
Makes: 12 servings

- 1   pkg. (6 oz.) strawberry gelatin
- 1   cup boiling water
- 2   qt. fresh strawberries, sliced
- ½ pint heavy whipping cream, whipped
- 1   sponge cake, cut into cubes
  Additional whipped cream
  Whole strawberries for garnish

In a bowl, dissolve gelatin in water. Add berries; allow to thicken partially. Fold in whipped cream. Fold in cake cubes; stir until well coated. Spread into a greased springform pan; cover and chill overnight. Remove from pan and place on a torte plate. Frost with whipped cream and garnish with berries.

1 slice: 258 cal., 9g fat (5g sat. fat), 66mg chol., 133mg sod., 43g carb. (34g sugars, 2g fiber), 4g pro.

MOM'S BEST PUMPKIN CHEESECAKE

Pumpkin swirls not only turn this fall cheesecake into a showstopper, but they also make it more delicious!
—Jami Geittmann, Greendale, WI

- -

Prep: 35 min. • **Bake:** 55 min. + chilling
Makes: 12 servings

1½   cups graham cracker crumbs
¼   cup sugar
⅓   cup butter, melted
FILLING
4   pkg. (8 oz. each) cream
    cheese, softened
1½   cups sugar
2   Tbsp. cornstarch
2   tsp. vanilla extract
4   large eggs, room temperature,
    lightly beaten
1   cup canned pumpkin
2   tsp. ground cinnamon
1½   tsp. ground nutmeg
TOPPINGS
    Optional: Whipped cream,
    additional ground cinnamon
    and caramel syrup

1. Preheat oven to 325°. Place a greased 9-in. springform pan on a double thickness of heavy-duty foil (about 18 in. square). Securely wrap foil around pan.
2. Combine crumbs and ¼ cup sugar; stir in butter. Press onto bottom and 1½ in. up the sides of prepared pan. Place on a baking sheet. Bake until set, 10-15 minutes. Cool on a wire rack.
3. For filling, beat 1 pkg. of cream cheese, ½ cup sugar and cornstarch until smooth, about 2 minutes. Beat in remaining cream cheese, 1 package at a time, until smooth. Beat in the remaining sugar and the vanilla. Add the eggs; beat on low speed just until combined. Place 2 cups filling in a small bowl; stir in the canned pumpkin, cinnamon and nutmeg.
4. Pour half of plain filling over the crust; dollop with half of the pumpkin filling. Cut through with a knife to swirl. Repeat the layers and swirling.
5. Place springform pan in a large baking pan; add 1 in. hot water to larger pan. Bake until center is just set and top appears dull, 55-65 minutes. Remove springform pan from water bath. Cool on a wire rack for 10 minutes. Carefully run a knife around edge of pan to loosen; cool 1 hour longer. Refrigerate overnight, covering when completely cooled. Remove rim from pan. If desired, top with whipped cream and cinnamon or caramel sauce.

1 slice: 518 cal., 34g fat (19g sat. fat), 152mg chol., 361mg sod., 47g carb. (36g sugars, 1g fiber), 8g pro.

PEACH & BERRY COBBLER

This is one of my favorite summer recipes because it features in-season peaches and berries, but is just as delicious with frozen fruit. The quick biscuit topping brings it all together quite nicely.
—Lauren Knoelke, Des Moines, IA

Prep: 20 min. • **Bake:** 40 min.
Makes: 8 servings

- ½ cup sugar
- 3 Tbsp. cornstarch
- ½ tsp. ground cinnamon
- ¼ tsp. ground cardamom
- 10 medium peaches, peeled and sliced (about 6 cups)
- 2 cups mixed blackberries, raspberries and blueberries
- 1 Tbsp. lemon juice

TOPPING

- 1 cup all-purpose flour
- ¼ cup sugar
- 2 tsp. grated orange zest
- ¾ tsp. baking powder
- ¼ tsp. salt
- ¼ tsp. baking soda
- 3 Tbsp. cold butter
- ¾ cup buttermilk
  Vanilla ice cream, optional

1. Preheat oven to 375°. In a large bowl, mix the sugar, cornstarch, cinnamon and cardamom. Add the peaches, berries and lemon juice; toss to combine. Transfer to a 10-in. cast-iron or other ovenproof skillet.
2. In a small bowl, whisk the first 6 topping ingredients; cut in butter until the mixture resembles coarse crumbs. Add buttermilk; stir just until moistened. Drop mixture by tablespoonfuls over peach mixture.
3. Bake, uncovered, until topping is golden brown, 40-45 minutes. Serve warm. If desired, top with vanilla ice cream.

1 serving: 279 cal., 5g fat (3g sat. fat), 12mg chol., 238mg sod., 57g carb. (38g sugars, 5g fiber), 4g pro.

GRANDMA'S ENGLISH TRIFLE

This trifle recipe was my grandmother's. I remember Mother telling me stories of how her mother made this dessert for Saturday night dinners, when they had guests. If there were leftovers, they'd have the trifle for dessert every night that week until it was gone! Today this recipe goes over big with my husband and our children.
—Ruth Verratti, Gasport, NY

Prep: 30 min. + chilling • **Makes:** 10 servings

- 1 prepared loaf pound cake or 1 pkg. (10¾ oz.) frozen pound cake, thawed
- ¼ to ½ cup raspberry jam
- 1 pkg. (3 to 3½ oz.) regular or instant vanilla pudding mix
- 2½ cups 2% milk
- 1 cup chilled heavy whipping cream
- 3 Tbsp. confectioners' sugar
  Slivered almonds
  Maraschino cherries, halved

Slice pound cake in half horizontally. Spread with jam and replace top of cake. Slice cake into 9 pieces. Line the sides and fill center of a 2-qt. glass serving bowl with cake pieces. Prepare pudding with milk. Pour over cake. Chill. Beat cream and sugar until soft peaks form; spread over cake and pudding. Chill at least 4 hours. Garnish with slivered almonds and cherries.

1 serving: 292 cal., 16g fat (10g sat. fat), 76mg chol., 176mg sod., 31g carb. (24g sugars, 0 fiber), 4g pro.

FRESH PLUM KUCHEN

In the summer when plums are in season, this tender fruit-topped dessert is always welcomed. For variety, you can use fresh pears or apples instead.
—Anna Daley, Montague, PE

- -

Prep: 20 min. • **Bake:** 40 min. + cooling
Makes: 12 servings

- ¼ **cup butter, softened**
- ¾ **cup sugar**
- 2 **large eggs, room temperature**
- 1 **cup all-purpose flour**
- 1 **tsp. baking powder**
- ¼ **cup whole milk**
- 1 **tsp. grated lemon zest**
- 2 **cups sliced fresh plums (about 4 medium)**
- ½ **cup packed brown sugar**
- 1 **tsp. ground cinnamon**

1. In a small bowl, cream butter and sugar until light and fluffy. Beat in eggs. Combine the flour and baking powder; add to the creamed mixture alternately with the milk, beating well after each addition. Add lemon zest. Pour into a greased 10-in. springform pan. Arrange plums on top; gently press into batter. Sprinkle with the brown sugar and cinnamon.

2. Place pan on a baking sheet. Bake at 350° for 40-50 minutes or until top is golden and a toothpick inserted in the center comes out clean. Cool for 10 minutes. Run a knife around edge of pan; remove sides. Cool on a wire rack.

1 piece: 185 cal., 5g fat (3g sat. fat), 46mg chol., 89mg sod., 33g carb. (24g sugars, 1g fiber), 3g pro.

FROZEN CHRISTMAS SALAD

My mom's use of red and green cherries to decorate dishes at Christmastime inspired me to create a holiday gelatin. It's cool, creamy and fun to serve guests.
—Pat Habiger, Spearville, KS

- -

Prep: 25 min. + freezing
Makes: 10 servings

- 1 **can (20 oz.) crushed pineapple, drained**
- 2 **cups miniature marshmallows**
- 1 **pkg. (8 oz.) cream cheese, softened**
- ½ **cup mayonnaise**
- 12 **red maraschino cherries, chopped and patted dry**
- 12 **green maraschino cherries, chopped and patted dry**
- ½ **cup chopped walnuts**
- 1 **cup heavy whipping cream**

1. In a small bowl, combine the crushed pineapple and marshmallows. Set aside until marshmallows are softened, about 15 minutes.

2. Meanwhile, in another small bowl, beat the cream cheese and mayonnaise until smooth. Stir into marshmallow mixture. Fold in cherries and walnuts.

3. In a bowl, beat whipping cream until soft peaks form. Fold into pineapple mixture. Spoon into a 6-cup mold; freeze overnight. Let salad stand at room temperature for 15-20 minutes; unmold onto a serving plate.

1 serving: 371 cal., 28g fat (12g sat. fat), 51mg chol., 142mg sod., 29g carb. (24g sugars, 1g fiber), 3g pro.

THELMA'S CHOCOLATE ECLAIR DESSERT

I love eclairs but making the actual pastry is difficult, so I came up with this recipe as a substitute. It still satisfies my cravings with the same wonderful flavors.
—Thelma Beam, Esbon, KS

- -

Prep: 20 min. + chilling • **Makes:** 15 servings

- 14 to 15 whole graham crackers
- 3½ cups 2% milk
- 2 pkg. (3.4 oz. each) instant vanilla pudding mix
- 1 carton (8 oz.) frozen whipped topping, thawed

TOPPING
- 2 oz. semisweet chocolate
- 2 Tbsp. butter
- 1½ cups confectioners' sugar
- 3 Tbsp. 2% milk
- 1 tsp. light corn syrup
- 1 tsp. vanilla extract

1. Line a 13x9-in. dish with half of the graham crackers, breaking crackers to fit as needed.
2. Whisk milk and pudding mixes 2 minutes; let stand until soft-set, about 2 minutes. Fold in whipped topping; spread evenly over crackers. Top with remaining crackers.
3. In a microwave-safe bowl, microwave chocolate and butter until melted; stir until blended. Stir in the remaining ingredients. Spread over top. Refrigerate, covered, at least 8 hours or overnight.
1 piece: 238 cal., 8g fat (5g sat. fat), 12mg chol., 229mg sod., 38g carb. (26g sugars, 1g fiber), 3g pro.

> **TEST KITCHEN TIP**
> Fold ½ cup canned pumpkin and 1 tsp. pumpkin pie spice into the filling for a no-fuss fall take on this classic treat.

CHERRY RHUBARB CRUNCH

This recipe was given to me by my husband's grandmother, along with a bunch of rhubarb, when we were first married. I never cared for rhubarb, but after trying this dessert, I changed my mind. Now my children dig in, too!
—Sharon Wasikowski, Middleville, MI

- -

Prep: 20 min. • **Bake:** 45 min.
Makes: 15 servings

- 1 cup rolled oats
- 1 cup packed brown sugar
- 1 cup all-purpose flour
- ¼ tsp. salt
- ½ cup cold butter, cubed
- 4 cups diced rhubarb
- 1 cup sugar
- 2 Tbsp. cornstarch
- 1 cup water
- 1 tsp. almond extract
- 1 can (21 oz.) cherry pie filling
- ½ cup finely chopped walnuts
  Vanilla ice cream

1. Preheat oven to 350°. In a large bowl, combine oats, brown sugar, flour and salt; stir well. Cut in butter until crumbly. Pat 2 cups of mixture into a greased 13x9-in. baking dish; cover with rhubarb.
2. In a saucepan, combine the sugar and cornstarch. Stir in water; cook until mixture is thickened and clear. Stir in the extract and cherry filling; spoon over rhubarb. Combine nuts with reserved crumb mixture; sprinkle over cherries. Bake until filling is bubbly and topping is lightly browned, 40-45 minutes. If desired, serve with ice cream.
1 serving: 294 cal., 9g fat (4g sat. fat), 16mg chol., 116mg sod., 52g carb. (38g sugars, 2g fiber), 3g pro.

LAYERED CHRISTMAS GELATIN

My jewel-toned ribbon salad always makes an appearance during our Christmas feast. Filled with cranberries and pineapple, the sweet-tart gelatin could even serve as a sweet side dish.
—Diane Schefelker, Ireton, IA

- -

Prep: 30 min. + chilling • **Makes:** 10 servings

- 1 **pkg. (3 oz.) lime gelatin**
- 1 **cup boiling water**
- ⅓ **cup unsweetened pineapple juice**
- 1 **cup crushed pineapple, drained**

CREAM CHEESE LAYER

- 1 **tsp. unflavored gelatin**
- 2 **Tbsp. cold water**
- 1 **pkg. (8 oz.) cream cheese, softened**
- ⅓ **cup whole milk**

BERRY LAYER

- 2 **pkg. (3 oz. each) strawberry gelatin**
- 2 **cups boiling water**
- 1 **can (14 oz.) whole-berry cranberry sauce**
   Optional ingredients: Thawed whipped topping, lime wedges and fresh strawberries

1. Dissolve lime gelatin in boiling water; stir in pineapple juice. Stir in pineapple. Pour into an 11x7-in. dish; refrigerate until set.

2. In a small saucepan, sprinkle unflavored gelatin over cold water; let stand 1 minute. Heat over low heat, stirring until gelatin is completely dissolved. Transfer to a small bowl. Beat in cream cheese and milk until smooth. Spread over lime layer; refrigerate until set.

3. Dissolve strawberry gelatin in boiling water; stir in cranberry sauce. Cool for 10 minutes. Carefully spoon over cream cheese layer. Refrigerate until set.

4. Cut into the gelatin into squares. Serve, if desired, with whipped topping, lime wedges and fresh strawberries.

1 piece: 267 cal., 8g fat (5g sat. fat), 26mg chol., 139mg sod., 46g carb. (39g sugars, 1g fiber), 5g pro.

TEST KITCHEN TIP

Homemade whipped cream topping truly tastes best: Beat 1 cup heavy whipping cream on high until slightly thickened, then add 3 Tbsp. confectioners' sugar and ½ tsp. vanilla extract and beat until soft peaks form.

APPLE PANDOWDY

This comforting dessert comes from a very old cookbook. It's so tangy and delicious.
—Doreen Lindquist, Thompson, MB

- -

Prep: 25 min. • **Bake:** 55 min.
Makes: 9 servings

- 1 cup packed brown sugar
- 1¼ cups all-purpose flour, divided
- ½ tsp. salt, divided
- 1 cup water
- 1 tsp. lemon juice
- 2 tsp. baking powder
- 5 Tbsp. butter, divided
- ¾ cup whole milk
- 5 cups sliced peeled apples
- ½ tsp. plus ⅛ tsp. ground cinnamon, divided
- ½ tsp. ground nutmeg
- 1 tsp. vanilla extract
- 1 Tbsp. coarse sugar
  Whipped cream, optional

1. In a saucepan, combine brown sugar, ¼ cup flour and ¼ tsp. salt. Add water and lemon juice; cook and stir over medium heat until thick. Cover and set aside.

2. In a bowl, combine the baking powder and remaining flour and salt. Cut in 3 Tbsp. butter. Add the milk and mix just until moistened (a few lumps will remain); set aside.

3. Arrange apples in a 1½-qt. baking dish; sprinkle with ½ tsp. cinnamon. Add nutmeg, vanilla and remaining butter to sauce; pour over apples. Drop dough by spoonfuls over sauce. Combine remaining cinnamon and coarse sugar; sprinkle over dough. Bake at 350° until the top is brown and apples are tender, about 55 minutes. Serve warm, with whipped cream if desired.

1 serving: 260 cal., 7g fat (4g sat. fat), 20mg chol., 304mg sod., 47g carb. (33g sugars, 2g fiber), 3g pro.

HOMEMADE STRAWBERRY ICE CREAM

What could be better than a bowl of luscious homemade ice cream made with fresh strawberries? Having an ice cream social at church with more of the same!
—Esther Johnson, Merrill, WI

Prep: 20 min. + cooling
Process: 20 min./batch + freezing
Makes: about 1½ qt.

- 6 large egg yolks
- 2 cups whole milk
- 1 cup sugar
- ¼ tsp. salt
- 1 tsp. vanilla extract
- 2 cups heavy whipping cream
- 2 cups crushed fresh strawberries, sweetened

1. Place egg yolks and milk in the top of a double boiler; beat. Add sugar and salt. Cook over simmering water, stirring until mixture is thickened and coats a metal spoon. Cool.
2. Add the vanilla, cream and strawberries. Pour mixture into the cylinder of an ice cream freezer and freeze according to the manufacturer's directions. When ice cream is frozen, transfer to a freezer container; freeze for 2-4 hours before serving.

½ cup: 265 cal., 19g fat (11g sat. fat), 166mg chol., 88mg sod., 22g carb. (21g sugars, 1g fiber), 4g pro.

> "This ice cream is very easy. It turns out perfect every time."
> —DIEBLENDER, TASTEOFHOME.COM

CARAMEL RHUBARB COBBLER

I came up with this recipe after hearing a friend fondly recall his grandmother's rhubarb dumplings. My son especially likes rhubarb, and this old-fashioned dessert lets those special stalks steal the show.
—Beverly Shebs, Pinehurst, NC

Prep: 25 min. • **Bake:** 35 min.
Makes: 6 servings

- 7 Tbsp. butter, divided
- ¾ cup packed brown sugar
- ½ cup sugar, divided
- 3 Tbsp. cornstarch
- 1¼ cups water
- 6 cups chopped fresh or frozen rhubarb, thawed
- 3 to 4 drops red food coloring, optional
- 1¼ cups all-purpose flour
- 1½ tsp. baking powder
- ¼ tsp. salt
- ⅓ cup whole milk
  Cinnamon-sugar
  Whipped cream or ice cream, optional

1. In a saucepan over medium heat, melt 3 Tbsp. butter. Add brown sugar, ¼ cup sugar and cornstarch. Gradually stir in water and rhubarb; cook and stir until thickened, 5-8 minutes. Add food coloring if desired. Pour into a greased 2-qt. baking dish and set aside.
2. In another bowl, combine flour, baking powder, salt and remaining sugar. Melt the remaining butter; add to dry ingredients with milk. Mix well. Drop by tablespoonfuls onto rhubarb mixture. Bake at 350° for 35-40 minutes or until the fruit is bubbly and the top is golden brown. Sprinkle with cinnamon-sugar. Serve warm with whipped cream or ice cream if desired.

1 serving: 429 cal., 14g fat (9g sat. fat), 38mg chol., 357mg sod., 73g carb. (47g sugars, 3g fiber), 4g pro.

PEACH COBBLER

I created this recipe myself with a few tips from my mom and grandma. Because it's so quick and easy, this cobbler can be made in minutes to suit any occasion. I've used it for a dinner dessert, snack or even a fruity side dish at breakfast.
—Martha Betten, North Manchester, IN

Prep: 15 min. • **Bake:** 25 min.
Makes: 8 servings

½ cup butter, melted
1 can (15¼ oz.) sliced peaches, drained
1¼ cups sugar, divided
1 cup all-purpose flour
1 cup whole milk
2 tsp. baking powder
¼ tsp. salt

Pour butter into a shallow 2-qt. baking dish; set aside. Drain peaches, reserving ¼ cup juice. In a saucepan, bring the peaches and juice just to a boil. Meanwhile, in a bowl, combine 1 cup sugar, flour, milk, baking powder and salt; mix well. Pour over butter in baking dish. Spoon hot peaches over batter. Sprinkle with remaining sugar. Bake at 400° for 25 minutes or until cake tests done. Serve warm.

¾ cup: 328 cal., 13g fat (8g sat. fat), 34mg chol., 282mg sod., 52g carb. (40g sugars, 1g fiber), 3g pro.

MINI CHERRY CHEESECAKES

These little cheesecakes make a fun dessert that's just right for cooks who don't have a lot of time for fussy recipes. Plus, you get to eat a whole cheesecake by yourself! What could be better?
—Kay Keller, Morenci, MI

- -

Prep: 20 min. + chilling
Bake: 15 min. + cooling • **Makes:** 12 servings

- 1 cup crushed vanilla wafers (about 30 wafers)
- 3 Tbsp. butter, melted
- 1 pkg. (8 oz.) cream cheese, softened
- ⅓ cup sugar
- 2 tsp. lemon juice
- 1½ tsp. vanilla extract
- 1 large egg, room temperature, lightly beaten

TOPPING

- 1 lb. pitted canned or frozen tart red cherries
- ½ cup sugar
- 1 Tbsp. cornstarch
  Red food coloring, optional

1. Preheat oven to 350°. Combine crumbs and butter; press gently onto bottoms of 12 foil-lined muffin cups. In another bowl, combine cream cheese, sugar, lemon juice and vanilla. Add egg; beat on low speed just until combined. Spoon over crusts.

2. Bake until the centers are almost set, 12-15 minutes. Cool completely.

3. For the topping, drain cherries, reserving ½ cup juice in a saucepan; discard remaining juice. To reserved juice, add cherries, sugar, cornstarch and, if desired, food coloring. Bring to a boil; cook until thickened, about 1 minute. Cool; spoon over cheesecakes. Refrigerate, covered, at least 2 hours.

1 mini cheesecake: 213 cal., 12g fat (6g sat. fat), 44mg chol., 127mg sod., 26g carb. (21g sugars, 1g fiber), 2g pro.

TEST KITCHEN TIP

Give these a sweet-salty spin and use crushed pretzels instead of vanilla wafers. You can substitute strawberries for the cherries—an especially tasty option when they're in season and you can buy locally grown berries.

CARAMEL-APPLE SKILLET BUCKLE

My grandma used to make a version of this for me when I was a little girl. She would prepare it with fresh apples from her tree in the backyard. I've adapted her recipe because I love the combination of apple, pecans and caramel.
—Emily Hobbs, Springfield, MO

- -

Prep: 35 min. • **Bake:** 1 hour + standing
Makes: 12 servings

½	cup butter, softened
¾	cup sugar
2	large eggs, room temperature
1	tsp. vanilla extract
2	cups all-purpose flour
2½	tsp. baking powder
1¾	tsp. ground cinnamon
½	tsp. ground ginger
¼	tsp. salt
1½	cups buttermilk

TOPPING

⅔	cup packed brown sugar
½	cup all-purpose flour
¼	cup cold butter
¾	cup finely chopped pecans
½	cup old-fashioned oats
6	cups thinly sliced peeled Gala or other sweet apples (about 6 medium)
18	caramels, unwrapped
1	Tbsp. buttermilk
	Vanilla ice cream, optional

1. Preheat oven to 350°. In a large bowl, cream butter and sugar until light and fluffy. Add 1 egg at a time, beating well after each addition. Beat in vanilla. In another bowl, whisk the flour, baking powder, cinnamon, ginger and salt; add to creamed mixture alternately with buttermilk, beating well after each addition. Pour into a greased 12-in. cast-iron or other ovenproof skillet.
2. For topping, in a small bowl, mix brown sugar and flour; cut in butter until crumbly. Stir in pecans and oats; sprinkle over batter. Top with apples. Bake until the apples are golden brown, 60-70 minutes. Cool in the pan on a wire rack.
3. In a microwave, melt the caramels with buttermilk; stir until smooth. Drizzle over cake. Let stand until set. If desired, serve with ice cream.

1 slice: 462 cal., 19g fat (9g sat. fat), 64mg chol., 354mg sod., 68g carb. (42g sugars, 3g fiber), 7g pro.

RUSTIC CRANBERRY TARTS

For gatherings with family and friends, we love a dessert with a splash of red. These two beautiful tarts are filled with cranberry and citrus-packed flavor and are easy to make and serve.
—Holly Bauer, West Bend, WI

- -

Prep: 15 min. • **Bake:** 20 min./batch
Makes: 2 tarts (6 servings each)

- 1   **cup orange marmalade**
- ¼   **cup sugar**
- ¼   **cup all-purpose flour**
- 4   **cups fresh or frozen cranberries, thawed**
- 1   **pkg. (14.1 oz.) refrigerated pie crust**
- 1   **large egg white, lightly beaten**
- 1   **Tbsp. coarse sugar**

1. Preheat oven to 425°. In a large bowl, mix orange marmalade, sugar and flour; stir in the cranberries.

2. Unroll 1 pie crust onto a parchment-lined baking sheet. Spoon half of the cranberry mixture over crust to within 2 in. of edge. Fold edge over filling, pleating as you go and leaving a 5-in. opening in the center. Brush folded crust with egg white; sprinkle with half of the coarse sugar.

3. Bake for 18-22 minutes or until crust is golden and filling is bubbly. Repeat with the remaining ingredients. Transfer the tarts to wire racks to cool.

1 slice: 260 cal., 9g fat (4g sat. fat), 6mg chol., 144mg sod., 45g carb. (24g sugars, 2g fiber), 2g pro.

CHOCOLATE BAVARIAN TORTE

Whenever I take this torte to a gathering, I get so many requests for the recipe.
—Edith Holmstrom, Madison, WI

Prep: 15 min. + chilling
Bake: 30 min. + cooling • **Makes:** 12 servings

- 1 pkg. devil's food cake mix (regular size)
- 1 pkg. (8 oz.) cream cheese, softened
- ⅓ cup packed brown sugar
- 1 tsp. vanilla extract
- ⅛ tsp. salt
- 2 cups heavy whipping cream, whipped
- 2 Tbsp. grated semisweet chocolate

1. Prepare and bake cake according to the package directions, using two 9-in. round baking pans. Cool the cakes in pans for 10 minutes before removing to wire racks to cool completely.
2. In a large bowl, beat the cream cheese, sugar, vanilla and salt until smooth. Fold in the cream.
3. Cut each cake horizontally into 2 layers. Place bottom layer on a serving plate; top with a fourth of the cream mixture. Sprinkle with a fourth of the chocolate. Repeat layers 3 times. Cover and refrigerate for 8 hours or overnight.
1 piece: 495 cal., 33g fat (16g sat. fat), 111mg chol., 475mg sod., 45g carb. (27g sugars, 1g fiber), 6g pro.

STRAWBERRY PRETZEL DESSERT

Here's a classic people can't get enough of. It's always potluck perfect!
—Aldene Belch, Flint, MI

Prep: 20 min. • **Bake:** 10 min. + chilling
Makes: 16 servings

- 2 cups crushed pretzels (about 8 oz.)
- ¾ cup butter, melted
- 3 Tbsp. sugar

FILLING
- 2 cups whipped topping
- 1 pkg. (8 oz.) cream cheese, softened
- 1 cup sugar

TOPPING
- 2 pkg. (3 oz. each) strawberry gelatin
- 2 cups boiling water
- 2 pkg. (16 oz. each) frozen sweetened sliced strawberries, thawed

Optional: Additional whipped topping and pretzels

1. In a bowl, combine the pretzels, butter and sugar. Press into an ungreased 13x9-in. baking dish. Bake at 350° for 10 minutes. Cool on a wire rack.
2. For filling, in a small bowl, beat whipped topping, cream cheese and sugar until smooth. Spread over the pretzel crust. Refrigerate until chilled.
3. For topping, dissolve gelatin in boiling water in a large bowl. Stir in strawberries with syrup; chill until partially set. Carefully spoon over filling. Chill until firm, 4-6 hours. Cut into squares; serve with additional whipped topping and pretzels if desired.
1 piece: 295 cal., 15g fat (10g sat. fat), 39mg chol., 305mg sod., 38g carb. (27g sugars, 1g fiber), 3g pro.

BERRY BLISS COBBLER

A little bit sweet, a little bit tart and topped off with golden sugar-kissed biscuits, this cobbler is summer perfection.
—*Taste of Home* Test Kitchen

Prep: 10 min. + standing • **Bake:** 20 min.
Makes: 6 servings

    3   cups fresh strawberries, halved
 1½   cups fresh raspberries
 1½   cups fresh blueberries
    ⅔   cup plus 1 Tbsp. sugar, divided
    3   Tbsp. quick-cooking tapioca
    1   cup all-purpose flour
    1   Tbsp. sugar
    2   tsp. baking powder
    ¼   tsp. salt
    ¼   cup cold butter, cubed
    1   large egg, room temperature
    ¼   cup plus 2 Tbsp. 2% milk
        Coarse sugar

1. Preheat oven to 400°. Toss strawberries, raspberries and blueberries with ⅔ cup sugar and tapioca. Transfer to a greased 10-in. cast-iron or other ovenproof skillet; let stand 20 minutes.
2. Meanwhile, whisk flour, 1 Tbsp. sugar, baking powder and salt. Cut in butter until the mixture resembles coarse crumbs. In another bowl, whisk together egg and milk; stir into crumb mixture just until moistened. Drop by tablespoonfuls onto fruit. Sprinkle with coarse sugar.
3. Bake, uncovered, 20-25 minutes or until filling is bubbly and topping is golden brown. Serve warm.

1 serving: 335 cal., 9g fat (5g sat. fat), 52mg chol., 298mg sod., 60g carb. (34g sugars, 5g fiber), 5g pro.

RHUBARB CUSTARD TREATS

Once I tried these rich, hearty bars, I just had to have the recipe so I could make them for my family and friends. The shortbread-like crust and rhubarb and custard layers seem to inspire people to find rhubarb they can use to fix a gooey batch for themselves. Grab yourself a fork and enjoy!
—Shari Roach, South Milwaukee, WI

- -

Prep: 25 min. • **Bake:** 50 min. + chilling
Makes: 3 dozen

- 2   cups all-purpose flour
- ¼   cup sugar
- 1   cup cold butter

FILLING
- 2   cups sugar
- 7   Tbsp. all-purpose flour
- 1   cup heavy whipping cream
- 3   large eggs,
      room temperature, beaten
- 5   cups finely chopped fresh or frozen
      rhubarb, thawed and drained

TOPPING
- 6   oz. cream cheese, softened
- ½   cup sugar
- ½   tsp. vanilla extract
- 1   cup heavy whipping
      cream, whipped

1. In a bowl, combine the flour and sugar; cut in butter until the mixture resembles coarse crumbs. Press into a greased 13x9-in. baking pan. Bake at 350° for 10 minutes.

2. Meanwhile, for filling, combine sugar and flour in a bowl. Whisk in cream and eggs. Stir in the chopped rhubarb. Pour over the crust. Bake at 350° 40-45 minutes or until custard is set. Cool.

3. For topping, beat cream cheese, sugar and vanilla until smooth; fold in whipped cream. Spread over top. Cover and chill. Cut into bars. Store in the refrigerator.

1 bar: 198 cal., 11g fat (7g sat. fat), 52mg chol., 70mg sod., 23g carb. (16g sugars, 1g fiber), 2g pro.

TEST KITCHEN TIP
Pump up the flavor of this rhubarb treat simply by adding the seeds of 1 vanilla bean or 1 tsp. rosewater to the filling. Both flavors pair beautifully with rhubarb and take these already fabulous bars to a whole new level.

ROASTED BANANA & PECAN CHEESECAKE

We keep bananas on hand, but with just two of us in the house they ripen faster than we can eat them. That makes them perfect for baking into this cheesecake. We love the nutty crust.
—Patricia Harmon, Baden, PA

Prep: 45 min. + cooling
Bake: 45 min. + chilling
Makes: 12 servings

- 3 medium ripe bananas, unpeeled
- 1¾ cups crushed pecan shortbread cookies
- 3 Tbsp. butter, melted

FILLING

- 2 pkg. (8 oz. each) cream cheese, softened
- 1 pkg. (8 oz.) reduced-fat cream cheese
- ½ cup sugar
- ¼ cup plus 2 Tbsp. packed brown sugar, divided
- 1 tsp. vanilla extract
- 2 Tbsp. spiced rum, optional
- 4 large eggs, room temperature, lightly beaten
- ½ cup chopped pecans
- ½ tsp. ground cinnamon
- 12 pecan halves, toasted Chocolate syrup

1. Preheat oven to 400°. Place unpeeled bananas in an 8-in. square baking dish. Bake until banana peels are black, 10-12 minutes. Cool to room temperature. Reduce oven setting to 325°.

2. Place a greased 9-in. springform pan on a double thickness of heavy-duty foil (about 18 in. square). Wrap foil securely around pan. Place on a baking sheet.

3. In a small bowl, mix cookie crumbs and melted butter. Press onto bottom and 1 in. up sides of prepared pan. Bake until set, 8-10 minutes. Cool on a wire rack.

4. In a large bowl, beat cream cheese, sugar and ¼ cup brown sugar until smooth. Beat in vanilla and, if desired, rum. Add the eggs; beat on low speed just until blended. Remove ½ cup cream cheese mixture to a small bowl. Pour remaining filling into crust.

5. Peel and place roasted bananas in a food processor; process until smooth. Add to reserved cream cheese mixture; stir in chopped pecans, cinnamon and remaining brown sugar. Pour over plain cream cheese mixture. Cut through cream cheese mixture with a knife to swirl.

6. Place springform pan in a larger baking pan; add 1 in. of hot water to larger pan. Bake until center is just set and top appears dull, 45-55 minutes. Remove springform pan from water bath. Cool cheesecake on a wire rack 10 minutes. Loosen sides from pan with a knife; remove foil. Cool 1 hour longer. Refrigerate overnight, covering when completely cooled.

7. Carefully remove rim from pan. Top cheesecake with pecan halves; drizzle with chocolate syrup.

Note: To toast nuts, bake in a shallow pan in a 350° oven for 5-10 minutes or cook in a skillet over low heat until lightly browned, stirring occasionally.

1 slice: 430 cal., 30g fat (14g sat. fat), 126mg chol., 308mg sod., 33g carb. (24g sugars, 2g fiber), 8g pro.

MAPLE-ORANGE PEAR CRISP

In the fall, my family loves to kick back after dinner and dig into big bowls of this spiced crisp. It isn't too sweet, but still satisfies a sweet tooth.
—Noreen McCormick Danek, Cromwell, CT

- -

Prep: 15 min. • **Bake:** 30 min.
Makes: 8 servings

½ cup chopped pecans
¼ cup butter, cubed
3 Tbsp. brown sugar
3 Tbsp. all-purpose flour
1 tsp. grated orange zest
½ tsp. ground cinnamon
¼ tsp. salt
¼ tsp. ground ginger
⅛ tsp. ground cloves
1 tsp. butter, softened

FILLING
6 medium ripe Bosc pears
2 Tbsp. lemon juice
⅓ cup maple syrup
1 Tbsp. butter
2 tsp. grated orange zest
1 tsp. ground cinnamon
  Ice cream or whipped cream

1. Preheat oven to 375°. Place the first 9 ingredients in a food processor; pulse until crumbly. Grease an 8-in. square baking dish with 1 tsp. butter.
2. Peel, core and cut each pear lengthwise into 8 wedges; toss with lemon juice. Place in prepared baking dish.
3. In a small saucepan, combine the syrup, butter, orange zest and cinnamon; bring to a boil, stirring constantly. Pour over pears. Sprinkle with crumb mixture. Bake until golden brown and the pears are tender, 30-40 minutes. Serve with ice cream.
1 serving: 254 cal., 12g fat (5g sat. fat), 19mg chol., 135mg sod., 38g carb. (26g sugars, 5g fiber), 2g pro.

BANANA SPLIT DESSERT

Here's a mouthwatering make-ahead dessert that looks scrumptious—and tastes as good as it looks!
—Elmer Thorsheim, Radcliffe, IA

- -

Prep: 30 min. + freezing
Makes: 25 servings

- 3½ cups graham cracker crumbs
- ⅔ cup butter, melted
- 4 to 5 medium bananas
- ½ gallon Neapolitan ice cream (block carton)
- 1 cup chopped walnuts
- 1 cup (6 oz.) chocolate chips
- ½ cup butter
- 1 pint heavy whipping cream

1. In a small bowl, combine crumbs and melted butter. Set aside ½ cup; press the remaining crumbs into a 15x10x1-in. pan. Slice bananas widthwise and layer over the crust. Cut the ice cream widthwise into 10 slices; place over bananas. Spread edges of ice cream slices to cover banana and form a smooth layer. Sprinkle with nuts. Cover and freeze until firm.

2. In a large saucepan, melt chocolate chips and butter; stir until smooth. Pour over ice cream; freeze until firm.

3. In a large bowl, whip cream until stiff peaks form; spread over chocolate layer. Top with reserved crumbs. Store in freezer (will keep for several weeks). Remove from freezer about 10 minutes before serving.

Note: Purchase a rectangle-shaped package of ice cream for the easiest cutting.

1 piece: 406 cal., 26g fat (14g sat. fat), 66mg chol., 204mg sod., 41g carb. (20g sugars, 1g fiber), 5g pro.

FIGGY APPLE BRIE TART

Our family gatherings often included baked Brie. I transformed it into a dessert that's savory and sweet. It makes a wonderful appetizer, too.
—Kristie Schley, Severna Park, MD

- -

Prep: 25 min. • **Bake:** 15 min. + cooling
Makes: 8 servings

- 3 Tbsp. butter, softened
- ¾ cup sugar
- 2 large apples
- 1 cup dried figs, halved
- ½ lb. Brie cheese, rind removed, sliced
- 1 sheet refrigerated pie crust

1. Preheat oven to 425°. Spread butter over the bottom of a 10-in. ovenproof skillet; sprinkle evenly with sugar.

2. Peel, quarter and core apples; arrange in a circular pattern over sugar, rounded side down. Place figs around apples. Place skillet over medium heat; cook until the sugar is caramelized and apples have softened slightly, 10-12 minutes. Remove from heat; top with cheese.

3. Unroll crust; place over apples, tucking under edges. Place skillet in oven on an upper rack; bake until the crust is golden brown, 15-18 minutes. Cool in skillet for 5 minutes. Carefully invert onto a serving plate; serve warm.

1 piece: 394 cal., 19g fat (11g sat. fat), 45mg chol., 315mg sod., 50g carb. (33g sugars, 2g fiber), 8g pro.

BREAD PUDDING WITH NUTMEG

I always make this bread pudding recipe for my dad on his birthday and holidays. He says it tastes like the nutmeg-flavored bread pudding he enjoyed as a child.
—Donna Powell, Montgomery City, MO

Prep: 15 min. • **Bake:** 40 min.
Makes: 6 servings

- 2 large eggs, room temperature
- 2 cups whole milk
- ¼ cup butter, cubed
- ¾ cup sugar
- ¼ tsp. salt
- 1 tsp. ground cinnamon
- ½ tsp. ground nutmeg
- 1 tsp. vanilla extract
- 4½ to 5 cups soft bread cubes (about 9 slices)
- ½ cup raisins, optional

VANILLA SAUCE
- ⅓ cup sugar
- 2 Tbsp. cornstarch
- ¼ tsp. salt
- 1⅔ cups cold water
- 3 Tbsp. butter
- 2 tsp. vanilla extract
- ¼ tsp. ground nutmeg

1. In a large bowl, lightly beat the eggs. Combine milk and butter; add to eggs along with sugar, salt, spices and vanilla. Add the bread cubes and raisins if desired; stir gently.
2. Pour into a well-greased 11x7-in. baking dish. Bake at 350° until a knife inserted 1 in. from edge comes out clean, 40-45 minutes.
3. Meanwhile, for sauce, combine the sugar, cornstarch and salt in a saucepan. Stir in cold water until smooth. Bring to a boil over medium heat; cook and stir until thickened, about 2 minutes. Remove from the heat. Stir in the butter, vanilla and nutmeg. Serve with warm pudding.
1 piece: 419 cal., 19g fat (11g sat. fat), 118mg chol., 534mg sod., 56g carb. (40g sugars, 1g fiber), 7g pro.

MAMA'S BLACKBERRY COBBLER

Fifty years ago my mama headed out to pick blackberries to make a cobbler, but she ended up going to the hospital to have me instead. This is her recipe.
—Lisa Allen, Joppa, AL

Prep: 15 min. • **Bake:** 45 min.
Makes: 6 servings

- ½ cup plus 2 Tbsp. melted butter, divided
- 1 cup self-rising flour
- 1½ cups sugar, divided
- 1 cup 2% milk
- ½ tsp. vanilla extract
- 3 cups fresh blackberries or frozen unsweetened blackberries

1. Preheat oven to 350°. Pour ½ cup melted butter into an 8-in. square baking dish. In a small bowl, combine flour, 1 cup sugar, milk and vanilla until blended; pour into prepared dish. In another bowl, combine blackberries, remaining ½ cup sugar and the remaining 2 Tbsp. melted butter; toss until combined. Spoon over batter.
2. Bake until topping is golden brown and fruit is tender, 45-50 minutes. Serve warm.
¾ cup: 491 cal., 21g fat (13g sat. fat), 54mg chol., 421mg sod., 75g carb. (56g sugars, 4g fiber), 5g pro.

TEST KITCHEN TIP
Be sure to disperse the berry mixture evenly and all the way to the edges of the dish.

CRANBERRY-ORANGE CRUMB TART

After my sister took the family to the local cranberry festival, my mother bet me that I couldn't make a holiday pie out of cranberries and oranges. Considering the pie was gone before the holidays arrived, I think I won!
—Heather Cunningham, Whitman, MA

- -

Prep: 35 min. + standing
Bake: 10 min. + cooling • **Makes:** 12 servings

- 2 cups crushed cinnamon graham crackers (about 14 whole crackers), divided
- ½ cup sugar, divided
- 6 Tbsp. butter, melted
- ¼ cup all-purpose flour
- ¼ cup packed brown sugar
- ¼ cup cold butter, cubed

FILLING

- 1 large navel orange
- 1 cup sugar
- 3 Tbsp. quick-cooking tapioca
- ¼ tsp. baking soda
- ¼ tsp. ground cinnamon
- ⅛ tsp. ground allspice
- 4 cups fresh or frozen cranberries, thawed
- 2 Tbsp. brandy or cranberry juice

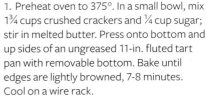

1. Preheat oven to 375°. In a small bowl, mix 1¾ cups crushed crackers and ¼ cup sugar; stir in melted butter. Press onto bottom and up sides of an ungreased 11-in. fluted tart pan with removable bottom. Bake until edges are lightly browned, 7-8 minutes. Cool on a wire rack.

2. For topping, in a small bowl, mix flour, brown sugar, and the remaining crushed crackers and sugar; cut in cold butter until crumbly. Refrigerate while preparing filling.

3. Finely grate enough zest from orange to measure 1 Tbsp. Cut a thin slice from the top and bottom of the orange; stand the orange upright on a cutting board. Cut off peel and outer membrane, starting from the top. Holding orange over a bowl to catch juices, remove orange sections by cutting along the membrane. Squeeze membrane to reserve additional juice.

4. In a large saucepan, mix sugar, tapioca, baking soda, cinnamon and allspice. Add the cranberries, brandy, grated zest and reserved juice; toss to coat. Let stand for 15 minutes. Preheat oven to 425°.

5. Bring the cranberry mixture to a full boil, stirring constantly. Add orange sections; heat through. Pour into crust; sprinkle with topping. Bake 10-15 minutes or until topping is golden brown. Cool on a wire rack.

1 slice: 332 cal., 11g fat (6g sat. fat), 25mg chol., 207mg sod., 56g carb. (38g sugars, 3g fiber), 2g pro.

BAKED CUSTARD WITH CINNAMON

My mother used to make this comforting custard when I was growing up. It was wonderful after a chilly evening of doing chores on our farm. Now I fix it for my husband and four sons. Best of all, the satisfying dessert only calls for a few items that I usually have on hand.
—Mary Kay Morris, Cokato, MN

Prep: 10 min. • **Bake:** 50 min. + cooling
Makes: 4 servings

- 2   **large eggs, room temperature**
- 2   **cups whole milk**
- ⅓   **cup sugar**
- ¼   **tsp. salt**
  Dash ground cinnamon
  Dash ground nutmeg

1. In a small bowl, whisk the eggs, milk, sugar and salt. Pour into 4 ungreased 8-oz. custard cups; sprinkle with the cinnamon and nutmeg.
2. Place in a 13x9-in. baking pan; pour hot water in pan to a depth of ¾ in. Bake, uncovered, at 350° until a knife inserted in the center comes out clean, 50-55 minutes. Remove cups to a wire rack to cool. Serve warm or chilled. Store in the refrigerator.

1 serving: 177 cal., 7g fat (3g sat. fat), 123mg chol., 239mg sod., 23g carb. (22g sugars, 0 fiber), 7g pro.

COOKIE SWIRL COBBLER

An extra-rich, chocolate chip cookie dough and crescent roll topping provide a tasty twist on a classic cherry cobbler. Serve it with a scoop of vanilla ice cream.
—Jeanne Holt, Mendota Heights, MN

- -

Prep: 20 min. • **Bake:** 25 min. + cooling
Makes: 12 servings

- 1 **cup (about 8 oz.) refrigerated chocolate chip cookie dough, softened**
- 2 **Tbsp. brown sugar**
- ⅓ **cup white baking chips**
- ¼ **cup plus 2 Tbsp. toasted sliced almonds, divided**
- 1 **can (21 oz.) cherry pie filling**
- ½ **tsp. almond extract, divided**
- 2 **cups fresh or frozen unsweetened raspberries**
- 1 **tube (8 oz.) refrigerated crescent rolls**
- ¾ **cup confectioners' sugar**
- 3 **to 4 tsp. 2% milk**
  Vanilla ice cream, optional

1. Preheat oven to 350°. Combine cookie dough, brown sugar, baking chips and ¼ cup almonds. Set aside. In a large saucepan, heat the cherry pie filling over medium heat until bubbly. Remove from heat; stir in ¼ tsp. almond extract. Fold in raspberries. Transfer to a greased 13x9-in. baking dish.

2. Unroll the crescent dough into 1 long rectangle; press perforations to seal. Drop small spoonfuls of cookie dough mixture over top; spread gently to cover. Roll up jelly-roll style, starting with a long side; pinch seam to seal. Cut crosswise into 12 slices; arrange the slices cut side up on cherry mixture.

3. Bake until golden brown, 25-30 minutes. Cool 10 minutes. Meanwhile, combine the confectioners' sugar, the remaining almond extract and enough milk to make a medium-thick glaze. Drizzle rolls with glaze; sprinkle with remaining toasted almonds. Serve warm, with ice cream if desired.

Note: To toast nuts, bake in a shallow pan in a 350° oven for 5-10 minutes or cook in a skillet over low heat until lightly browned, stirring occasionally.

1 serving: 308 cal., 11g fat (4g sat. fat), 2mg chol., 224mg sod., 49g carb. (22g sugars, 2g fiber), 3g pro.

BANANA BREAD PUDDING

With its crusty golden top, custard-like texture inside and smooth vanilla sauce, my grandmother's bread pudding is a real homespun dessert. Today, I enjoy making it for my own grandchildren.
—Mary Detweiler, Middlefield, OH

- -

Prep: 10 min. • **Bake:** 40 min.
Makes: 6 servings

- 4 **cups cubed day-old French or sourdough bread (1-in. pieces)**
- ¼ **cup butter, melted**
- 3 **large eggs, room temperature**
- 2 **cups whole milk**
- ½ **cup sugar**
- 2 **tsp. vanilla extract**
- ½ **tsp. ground cinnamon**
- ½ **tsp. ground nutmeg**
- ½ **tsp. salt**
- 1 **cup sliced firm bananas (¼-in. pieces)**

SAUCE
- 3 **Tbsp. butter**
- 2 **Tbsp. sugar**
- 1 **Tbsp. cornstarch**
- ¾ **cup whole milk**
- ¼ **cup light corn syrup**
- 1 **tsp. vanilla extract**

1. Place the bread cubes in a greased 2-qt. casserole; pour butter over top and toss to coat. In a medium bowl, lightly beat eggs; add milk, sugar, vanilla, cinnamon, nutmeg and salt. Stir in bananas.

2. Pour over bread cubes and stir to coat. Bake, uncovered, at 375° until a knife inserted in the center comes out clean, about 40 minutes.

3. Meanwhile, for sauce, melt butter in a small saucepan. Combine sugar and cornstarch; add to butter. Stir in milk and corn syrup. Cook and stir over medium heat until the mixture comes to a full boil. Boil for 1 minute. Remove from the heat; stir in the vanilla extract. Serve warm sauce over warm pudding.

1 piece: 439 cal., 21g fat (12g sat. fat), 157mg chol., 561mg sod., 56g carb. (38g sugars, 1g fiber), 9g pro.

"Bread pudding has always been a favorite in my family. This recipe takes it to the next level for me because of the bananas. Absolutely delicious! I'm making a second pan with chocolate chips thrown in with the bananas. That was my son's suggestion."
—PIP31453, TASTEOFHOME.COM

CARAMEL-PEAR DESSERT

It's nice to have a tempting fall treat that puts the season's best pears to excellent use—just don't expect this old-fashioned dessert to last long! The delicate pears and yummy caramel topping make it a winner whenever I serve it.

—Sharon Mensing, Greenfield, IA

- -

Prep: 15 min. • **Bake:** 45 min.
Makes: 8 servings

1	cup all-purpose flour
⅔	cup sugar
1½	tsp. baking powder
½	tsp. ground cinnamon
¼	tsp. salt
	Pinch ground cloves
½	cup whole milk
4	medium pears, peeled and cut into ½-in. cubes
½	cup chopped pecans
¾	cup packed brown sugar
¼	cup butter
¾	cup boiling water
	Optional: Vanilla ice cream or whipped cream

1. Preheat oven to at 375°. In a large bowl, combine the first 6 ingredients; beat in milk until smooth. Stir in the pears and pecans. Spoon into an ungreased 2-qt. baking dish.
2. In another bowl, combine the brown sugar, butter and water; pour over batter. Bake, uncovered, for 45-50 minutes. Serve warm, with ice cream or whipped cream if desired.

1 serving: 359 cal., 12g fat (4g sat. fat), 17mg chol., 223mg sod., 63g carb. (46g sugars, 3g fiber), 3g pro.

TURTLE PRALINE TART

This rich, comforting dessert is easy enough to make for everyday meals but special enough to serve guests.
—Kathy Specht, Clinton, MT

Prep: 35 min. + chilling • **Makes:** 16 servings

- 1 sheet refrigerated pie crust
- 36 caramels
- 1 cup heavy whipping cream, divided
- 3½ cups pecan halves
- ½ cup semisweet chocolate chips, melted

1. Preheat oven to 450°. Unroll pie crust on a lightly floured surface. Transfer to an 11-in. fluted tart pan with removable bottom; trim edges.
2. Line pie crust with a double thickness of heavy-duty foil. Bake 8 minutes. Remove foil; bake 5-6 minutes longer or until light golden brown. Cool on a wire rack.
3. In a large saucepan, combine caramels and ½ cup cream. Cook and stir mixture over medium-low heat until caramels are melted. Stir in pecans. Spread filling evenly into crust. Drizzle with melted chocolate.
4. Refrigerate until set, about 30 minutes. Whip remaining cream; serve with tart.

1 slice: 335 cal., 24g fat (4g sat. fat), 4mg chol., 106mg sod., 31g carb. (19g sugars, 3g fiber), 4g pro.

LEMON PUDDING DESSERT

After a big meal, folks really go for this light lemon treat. The shortbread crust is the perfect base for the fluffy top layers. I've prepared this sunny dessert for church suppers for years and I still get requests for the recipe.
—Muriel DeWitt, Maynard, MA

Prep: 20 min. + chilling • **Bake:** 20 min.
Makes: 16 servings

- 1 cup cold butter, cubed
- 2 cups all-purpose flour
- 1 pkg. (8 oz.) cream cheese, softened
- 1 cup confectioners' sugar
- 1 carton (8 oz.) frozen whipped topping, thawed, divided
- 3 cups cold whole milk
- 2 pkg. (3.4 oz. each) instant lemon pudding mix

1. Preheat oven to 350°. Cut butter into flour until crumbly. Press into an ungreased 13x9-in. baking dish. Bake until light brown, 18-22 minutes. Cool on a wire rack.
2. Meanwhile, beat the cream cheese and sugar until smooth. Fold in 1 cup whipped topping. Spread over cooled crust.
3. Beat milk and pudding mix on low speed for 2 minutes. Carefully spread over cream cheese layer. Top with remaining whipped topping. Refrigerate at least 1 hour.

1 piece: 348 cal., 20g fat (13g sat. fat), 49mg chol., 305mg sod., 35g carb. (22g sugars, 0 fiber), 4g pro.

ALMOND-FILLED STOLLEN

I've been making this stollen for nearly 50 years. When we flew to Alaska to spend Christmas with our daughter's family, I carried one on the plane!
—Rachel Seel, Abbotsford, BC

Prep: 1 hour. + rising
Bake: 30 min. + cooling
Makes: 3 loaves (12 slices each)

- 1¾ cups chopped mixed candied fruit
- ½ cup plus 2 Tbsp. rum, divided
- 2 pkg. (¼ oz. each) active dry yeast
- ½ cup warm water (110° to 115°)
- 1½ cups warm 2% milk (110° to 115°)
- 1¼ cups butter, softened
- ⅔ cup sugar
- 2½ tsp. salt
- 2 tsp. grated lemon zest
- 1 tsp. almond extract
- 7 to 8 cups all-purpose flour
- 4 large eggs, room temperature
- ⅓ cup slivered almonds
- 1 can (8 oz.) almond paste
- 1 large egg yolk
- 2 tsp. water
- 2 to 2¼ cups confectioners' sugar

1. In a small bowl, combine candied fruits and ½ cup rum; let stand, covered, 1 hour.
2. In a small bowl, dissolve yeast in warm water. In a large bowl, combine milk, butter, sugar, salt, lemon zest, almond extract, remaining rum, yeast mixture and 4 cups flour; beat on medium speed until smooth. Cover and let stand in a warm place, about 30 minutes.
3. Beat in eggs. Stir in enough remaining flour to form a soft dough (dough will be sticky). Drain candied fruit, reserving rum for glaze. Reserve ½ cup candied fruit for topping. Stir almonds and remaining candied fruit into dough.
4. Turn dough onto a floured surface; knead until smooth and elastic, 6-8 minutes. Place in a greased bowl, turning once to grease the top. Cover and let rise in a warm place until doubled, about 1 hour.
5. Punch down the dough; divide into 3 portions. On a greased baking sheet, roll each portion into a 12-in. circle. Crumble one-third of the almond paste over one-half of each circle. Fold dough partially in half, covering filling and placing top layer within 1 in. of bottom edge. Cover with kitchen towels and let rise in a warm place until doubled in size, about 1 hour. Preheat oven to 375°.
6. In a small bowl, whisk egg yolk and water; brush over loaves. Bake for 30-35 minutes or until golden brown. Cover loosely with foil if tops brown too quickly. Remove from pans to wire racks to cool completely.
7. In a small bowl, mix reserved rum with enough confectioners' sugar to make a thin glaze. Drizzle over stollen. Sprinkle with reserved candied fruit.

1 slice: 278 cal., 10g fat (5g sat. fat), 44mg chol., 241mg sod., 43g carb. (21g sugars, 2g fiber), 5g pro.

CHOCOLATE-COVERED STRAWBERRY COBBLER

This cobbler came about because I love chocolate-covered strawberries. Top it with whipped cream, either plain or with a little chocolate syrup stirred in.
—Andrea Bolden, Unionville, TN

Prep: 15 min. • **Bake:** 35 min. + standing
Makes: 12 servings

- 1 cup butter, cubed
- 1½ cups self-rising flour
- 2¼ cups sugar, divided
- ¾ cup 2% milk
- 1 tsp. vanilla extract
- ⅓ cup baking cocoa
- 4 cups fresh strawberries, quartered
- 2 cups boiling water
  Whipped cream and additional strawberries

1. Preheat oven to 350°. Place the butter in a 13x9-in. baking pan; heat pan in oven until butter is melted, 3-5 minutes. Meanwhile, in a large bowl, combine the flour, 1¼ cups sugar, milk and vanilla until well blended. In a small bowl, mix cocoa and remaining sugar.
2. Remove baking pan from oven; add batter. Sprinkle with strawberries and cocoa mixture; pour boiling water evenly over top (do not stir). Bake 35-40 minutes or until a toothpick inserted into cake portion comes out clean. Let stand 10 minutes. Serve warm with whipped cream and additional fresh strawberries.
1 serving: 368 cal., 16g fat (10g sat. fat), 42mg chol., 316mg sod., 55g carb. (41g sugars, 2g fiber), 3g pro.

STRAWBERRY SCHAUM TORTE

This schaum torte features an easy-to-make strawberry gelatin filling.
—Geraldine Sauke, Alberta Lea, MN

Prep: 25 min. • **Bake:** 45 min. + cooling
Makes: 12 servings

- 6   large egg whites
- 2   tsp. water
- 2   tsp. white vinegar
- 2   tsp. vanilla extract
- 1   tsp. baking powder
- ¼   tsp. salt
- 2   cups sugar

FILLING

- 1   pkg. (3 oz.) strawberry gelatin
- ½   cup boiling water
- 1   cup fresh or frozen sliced strawberries
- 1   tsp. lemon juice
      Dash salt
- 1½ cups whipped cream

1. Place egg whites in a large bowl; let stand at room temperature for 30 minutes. Add the water, vinegar, vanilla, baking powder and salt. Beat on medium speed until soft peaks form. Gradually beat in sugar, 2 Tbsp. at a time, on high until stiff glossy peaks form and sugar is dissolved.

2. Spread evenly into a greased 13x9-in. baking pan. Bake at 300° for 45 minutes. Turn off oven and do not open door; let crust dry in oven overnight.

3. For filling, in a bowl, dissolve gelatin in boiling water. Stir in the strawberries, lemon juice and salt (mixture will thicken quickly). Fold in cream. Spread over crust. Store in the refrigerator.

1 piece: 222 cal., 5 fat (3g sat. fat), 17mg chol., 150mg sod., 41 carb. (41g sugars, 0 fiber), 3g pro.

VANILLA CREAM PUFF DESSERT

Inspired by classic cream puffs, this recipe is a wonderful treat. I've served it at Cub Scout banquets, birthday parties and holidays. I'm a regular baker, and this dessert is one of my all-time favorites.
—Denise Wahl, Homer Glen, IL

- -

Prep: 45 min. • **Bake:** 30 min. + cooling
Makes: 15 servings

- 1 cup water
- ½ cup butter
- ¼ tsp. salt
- 1 cup all-purpose flour
- 4 large eggs, room temperature

FILLING
- 1 pkg. (8 oz.) cream cheese, softened
- 2½ cups cold 2% milk
- 2 pkg. (3.4 oz. each) instant vanilla pudding mix

TOPPING
- 1 carton (8 oz.) frozen whipped topping, thawed
  Chocolate syrup

1. In a large saucepan over medium heat, bring the water, butter and salt to a boil. Add flour all at once and stir until a smooth ball forms. Continue beating until smooth and shiny. Remove from the heat; let stand for 5 minutes. Add 1 egg at a time, beating well after each addition.

2. Pour into a greased 15x10x1-in. baking pan. Bake at 400° until puffed and golden brown, 28-30 minutes. Cool on a wire rack.

3. For the filling, in a large bowl, beat the cream cheese, milk and pudding mixes until smooth. Spread over the crust; refrigerate for 20 minutes. Spread whipped topping over filling. Store in the refrigerator. Just before serving, drizzle the dessert with chocolate syrup.

1 piece: 248 cal., 17g fat (11g sat. fat), 95mg chol., 273mg sod., 18g carb. (9g sugars, 0 fiber), 5g pro.

TEST KITCHEN TIP
A small offset spatula is your friend when you are spreading layered desserts. Don't have one? No problem; the back of a spoon works well, too.

DOWN EAST BLUEBERRY BUCKLE

This buckle won a contest at my daughter's college. They shipped us four lobsters, but the real prize was seeing the smile on our daughter's face.
—Dianne van der Veen, Plymouth, MA

Prep: 15 min. • **Bake:** 30 min.
Makes: 9 servings

2	cups all-purpose flour
¾	cup sugar
2½	tsp. baking powder
¼	tsp. salt
1	large egg, room temperature
¾	cup 2% milk
¼	cup butter, melted
2	cups fresh or frozen blueberries

TOPPING

½	cup sugar
⅓	cup all-purpose flour
½	tsp. ground cinnamon
¼	cup butter, softened

1. Preheat oven to 375°. In a large bowl, whisk flour, sugar, baking powder and salt. In another bowl, whisk the egg, milk and melted butter until blended. Add to flour mixture; stir just until moistened. Fold in the blueberries. Transfer to a greased 9-in. square baking pan.
2. For topping, in a small bowl, mix sugar, flour and cinnamon. Using a fork, stir in softened butter until mixture is crumbly. Sprinkle over batter.
3. Bake 30-35 minutes or until a toothpick inserted in center comes out clean (do not overbake). Cool in pan on a wire rack. Serve warm or at room temperature.

Note: If using frozen blueberries, use without thawing to avoid discoloring batter.

1 piece: 354 cal., 12g fat (7g sat. fat), 49mg chol., 277mg sod., 59g carb. (32g sugars, 2g fiber), 5g pro.

PEACH CRISP PARFAIT POPS

My little ones simply love Popsicles and fruit crisps, so I created a healthy and delicious treat that combines the two. For a sweet addition, use cinnamon sticks in place of the pop sticks.
—Carmell Childs, Clawson, UT

Prep: 15 min. + freezing • **Makes:** 8 servings

2	cartons (5.3 oz. each) fat-free vanilla Greek yogurt
2	tsp. brown sugar
¼	tsp. ground cinnamon
	Pinch ground nutmeg
1	cup granola without raisins
8	freezer pop molds or paper cups (3 oz. each) and wooden pop sticks
1	can (15 oz.) sliced peaches in extra-light syrup or juice, drained and chopped

In a small bowl, combine yogurt, brown sugar, cinnamon and nutmeg; fold in the granola. Divide half of the yogurt mixture among molds or paper cups. Top with half of peaches; repeat layers. Top molds with holders. If using cups, top with foil and insert sticks through foil. Freeze until firm.

1 pop: 167 cal., 3g fat (0 sat. fat), 0 chol., 40mg sod., 28g carb. (15g sugars, 5g fiber), 10g pro. **Diabetic exchanges:** 1½ starch, ½ fat-free milk.

CHOCOLATE TART WITH CRANBERRY RASPBERRY SAUCE

A little of this tart goes a long way, with its rich chocolate and fruit flavors. If you want to make this dessert even more special, top it with whipped cream.
—Diane Nemitz, Ludington, MI

Prep: 40 min. • **Bake:** 40 min. + cooling
Makes: 12 servings

- 1 cup all-purpose flour
- ½ cup old-fashioned oats
- ¼ cup sugar
- ½ cup cold butter, cubed
- 1½ cups unblanched almonds
- ½ cup packed brown sugar
- ½ cup dark corn syrup
- 2 large eggs, room temperature
- 4 oz. bittersweet chocolate, melted
- 2 Tbsp. butter, melted

SAUCE
- 2 cups fresh raspberries, divided
- 1 cup fresh or frozen cranberries, thawed
- ¾ cup sugar
- 2 Tbsp. port wine or water

1. Preheat oven to 350°. Process flour, oats and sugar in a food processor until oats are ground. Add butter; pulse until crumbly. Press onto bottom and 1 in. up sides of an ungreased 10-in. springform pan. Bake until lightly browned, 14-16 minutes. Cool on a wire rack.

2. Process almonds in a food processor until coarsely chopped. Beat brown sugar, corn syrup, eggs, chocolate and melted butter; stir in almonds.

3. Pour into prepared crust. Bake until center is set and crust is golden brown, 25-30 minutes. Cool completely on a wire rack.

4. Meanwhile, in a small saucepan, combine 1 cup fresh raspberries, cranberries, sugar and port wine. Bring to a boil, stirring to dissolve sugar. Reduce heat to low; cook, uncovered, 4-5 minutes or until cranberries pop, stirring occasionally. Remove from the heat; cool slightly.

5. Press berry mixture through a fine-mesh strainer into a bowl; discard the seeds. Refrigerate sauce until serving.

6. Remove rim from pan. Serve tart with sauce and remaining raspberries.

1 slice with 4 tsp. sauce: 462 cal., 24 fat (9g sat. fat), 56mg chol., 115mg sod., 55g carb. (39g sugars, 4g fiber), 7g pro.

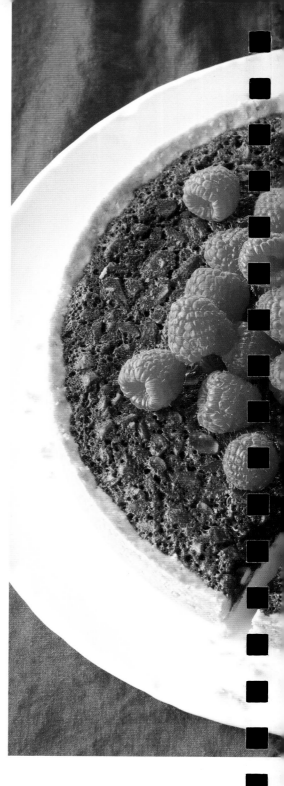

CARAMEL PECAN ICE CREAM DESSERT

My mother passed this old-fashioned recipe on to me because she knew I'd want to make it. I love desserts—especially this frosty one!
—Mary Wright, Morriston, ON

- -

Prep: 35 min. + freezing
Makes: 15 servings

1¾ cups all-purpose flour
1 cup quick-cooking oats
1 cup chopped pecans
1 cup packed brown sugar
1 cup butter, melted
1½ cups caramel ice cream topping
2 qt. vanilla ice cream, softened

1. In a large bowl, combine the flour, oats, pecans and brown sugar. Add butter; mix well. Spread in a thin layer in a 15x10x1-in. baking pan. Bake at 400° for 15 minutes or until golden, stirring occasionally. Crumble while warm; cool.

2. Press half of the crumb mixture into a 13x9-in. dish. Drizzle with half of caramel sauce; spread with ice cream. Top with remaining caramel sauce and crumb mixture. Cover and freeze until firm. Remove from the freezer 10 minutes before serving.

1 piece: 515 cal., 26g fat (13g sat. fat), 64mg chol., 300mg sod., 68g carb. (48g sugars, 2g fiber), 6g pro.

GRANDMA'S ORANGE MILK SHERBET

My dear grandma made this sherbet for my birthday party in the 1930s. She squeezed whole oranges to get the juice for it. I often double the recipe because it's so refreshing on a hot summer day.
—Marilynn Engelbrecht, Harrisonville, MO

Prep: 20 min. + freezing • **Makes:** about 2 qt.

- 3 **cups whole milk**
- 1½ **cups orange juice**
- ¾ **cup sugar**
- 2 **cans (8 oz. each) unsweetened crushed pineapple**

1. In a large saucepan, heat the milk over medium heat until bubbles form around sides of pan. Set aside to cool.

2. In a large bowl, combine orange juice and sugar thoroughly. Stir in milk. Transfer to an 11x7-in. dish; freeze until mushy.

3. Transfer mixture to a bowl and whip. Add pineapple and juices. Return mixture to dish and freeze.

½ cup: 97 cal., 2g fat (1g sat. fat), 6mg chol., 23mg sod., 20g carb. (19g sugars, 0 fiber), 2g pro.

CARAMEL CREME BRULEE

This recipe comes out perfect every time, and it's always a crowd-pleaser! A torch works best to get the sugar caramelized while keeping the rest of the custard cool. You may want to use even more sugar to create a thick, even crust on top.
—Jenna Fleming, Lowville, NY

- -

Prep: 20 min. • **Bake:** 40 min. + chilling
Makes: 14 servings

4½	cups heavy whipping cream
1½	cups half-and-half cream
15	large egg yolks, room temperature
1⅓	cups sugar, divided
3	tsp. caramel extract
¼	tsp. salt
⅓	cup packed brown sugar

1. Preheat oven to 325°. In a large saucepan, heat the whipping cream and cream until bubbles form around sides of pan; remove from heat. In a bowl, whisk egg yolks, 1 cup sugar, extract and salt until blended but not foamy. Slowly stir in hot cream mixture.
2. Place an ungreased broiler-safe 13x9-in. baking dish in a baking pan large enough to hold it without touching the sides. Pour egg mixture into dish. Place pan on oven rack; add very hot water to pan to within 1 in. of top of dish. Bake until center is just set and top appears dull, 40-50 minutes.

Immediately remove dish from water bath to a wire rack; cool for 1 hour. Refrigerate until cold.
3. Mix brown sugar and remaining sugar. To caramelize topping with a kitchen torch, sprinkle custard evenly with sugar mixture. Hold torch flame about 2 in. above custard surface and rotate it slowly until sugar is evenly caramelized. Serve immediately or refrigerate up to 1 hour.
4. To caramelize topping in a broiler, let custard stand at room temperature for 30 minutes. Preheat broiler. Sprinkle the custard evenly with sugar mixture. Broil 3-4 in. from heat 2-3 minutes or until the sugar is caramelized. Serve immediately or refrigerate up to 1 hour.
Note: This recipe was tested with Watkin's caramel extract in a broiler-safe Staub cherry ceramic rectangular baking dish.
½ cup: 452 cal., 35g fat (21g sat. fat), 298mg chol., 86mg sod., 28g carb. (27g sugars, 0 fiber), 6g pro.

"My first creme brulee, and it was so easy and worthy of a repeat! Two thumbs-up with my picky eaters, and it was restaurant-worthy!"
—TKUEHL, TASTEOFHOME.COM

CHERRY-ALMOND STREUSEL TART

Brimming with fresh cherries and topped with a crunchy streusel, this tempting tart will end dinner on a sweet note. It is fast to fix, looks elegant and tastes delicious.
—Marion Lee, Mount Hope, ON

Prep: 20 min. • **Bake:** 30 min. + cooling
Makes: 8 servings

Pastry for single-crust pie (9 in.)
⅔ cup sugar
3 Tbsp. cornstarch
Dash salt
4 cups fresh or frozen pitted tart cherries, thawed
⅛ tsp. almond extract

TOPPING
¼ cup quick-cooking oats
3 Tbsp. all-purpose flour
2 Tbsp. brown sugar
1 Tbsp. slivered almonds
2 Tbsp. cold butter

1. Press pastry onto the bottom and up the sides of an ungreased 9-in. fluted tart pan with removable bottom; trim edges.
2. In a large saucepan, combine the sugar, cornstarch and salt. Stir in cherries; bring to a boil over medium heat, stirring constantly. Cook and stir mixture for 1-2 minutes or until thickened. Remove from the heat; stir in extract. Pour into crust.
3. For topping, combine the oats, flour, brown sugar and almonds. Cut in butter until mixture resembles coarse crumbs. Sprinkle over filling. Bake at 350° until topping is golden brown, 30-35 minutes. Cool on a wire rack.
1 piece: 298 cal., 11g fat (5g sat. fat), 13mg chol., 143mg sod., 49g carb. (27g sugars, 2g fiber), 3g pro.

PRESSURE-COOKER CHOCOLATE-APRICOT DUMP CAKE

Years ago, I prepared this dessert in the oven. I converted it to my one-pot cooker, and now we enjoy it even on busy nights.
—Joan Hallford, North Richland Hills, TX

Prep: 10 min. • **Cook:** 35 min. + standing
Makes: 8 servings

1 can (21 oz.) apricot or peach pie filling
2 cups devil's food cake mix
½ cup chopped pecans, toasted
½ cup miniature semisweet chocolate chips, optional
½ cup butter, cubed
Vanilla ice cream, optional

1. Place trivet insert and 1 cup water in a 6-qt. electric pressure cooker. Spread pie filling in the bottom of a greased 1½-qt. baking dish. Sprinkle with cake mix, pecans and if desired, chocolate chips. Dot with butter. Cover baking dish with foil.
2. Fold an 18x12-in. piece of foil lengthwise into thirds, making a sling. Use the sling to lower the dish onto the trivet. Lock lid; close pressure-release valve. Adjust to pressure-cook on high for 35 minutes. Quick-release pressure. Press cancel. Using the foil sling, carefully remove baking dish. Let stand 10 minutes. If desired, serve warm cake with ice cream.
1 serving: 360 cal., 18g fat (9g sat. fat), 31mg chol., 436mg sod., 49g carb. (26g sugars, 0 fiber), 2g pro.

OLD-WORLD RICOTTA CHEESECAKE

I reconstructed this dessert based on an old recipe that had been in the family for years but was never written down. The subtle cinnamon flavor of the zwieback crust and the dense texture of the ricotta cheese are reminiscent of the cheesecake I enjoyed as a child.
—Mary Beth Jung, Hendersonville, NC

- -

Prep: 20 min. • **Bake:** 1 hour + chilling
Makes: 12 servings

1⅔ **cups zwieback, rusk or**
     plain biscotti crumbs
  3 **Tbsp. sugar**
  ½ **tsp. ground cinnamon**
  ⅓ **cup butter, softened**
FILLING
  2 **cartons (15 oz. each) ricotta cheese**
  ½ **cup sugar**
  ½ **cup half-and-half cream**
  2 **Tbsp. all-purpose flour**
  1 **Tbsp. lemon juice**
  1 **tsp. finely grated lemon zest**
  ¼ **tsp. salt**
  2 **large eggs, room temperature,**
     lightly beaten
TOPPING
  1 **cup sour cream**
  2 **Tbsp. sugar**
  1 **tsp. vanilla extract**

1. Combine zwieback crumbs, sugar and cinnamon; mix in butter until mixture is crumbled. Press onto bottom and 1½ in. up sides of a greased 9-in. springform pan. Refrigerate until chilled.
2. Preheat oven to 350°. Beat all of the filling ingredients except eggs until smooth. Add eggs; beat on low until combined. Pour into crust. Place pan on a baking sheet.
3. Bake until center is set, about 50 minutes. Remove from oven; let stand 15 minutes, leaving oven on. Combine the topping ingredients; spoon around edge of the cheesecake. Carefully spread over filling. Bake 10 minutes longer. Loosen sides from pan with a knife; cool 1 hour. Refrigerate 3 hours or overnight, covering when completely cooled. Remove rim from pan. Refrigerate leftovers.
1 slice: 260 cal., 14g fat (9g sat. fat), 83mg chol., 191mg sod., 25g carb. (16g sugars, 0 fiber), 7g pro.

MUST-HAVE TIRAMISU

This is the perfect guilt-free version of a classic dessert. My friends even say that they prefer my lighter recipe over other, more traditional, tiramisu.
—Ale Gambini, Beverly Hills, CA

Prep: 25 min. + chilling • **Makes:** 9 servings

½   cup heavy whipping cream
2   cups vanilla yogurt
1   cup fat-free milk
½   cup brewed espresso or
     strong coffee, cooled
24   crisp ladyfinger cookies
     Baking cocoa
     Fresh raspberries, optional

1. In a small bowl, beat cream until stiff peaks form; fold in yogurt. Spread ½ cup cream mixture onto bottom of an 8-in. square dish.
2. In a shallow dish, mix milk and espresso. Quickly dip 12 ladyfingers into espresso mixture, allowing excess to drip off. Arrange in 8-in. dish in a single layer, breaking to fit as needed. Top with half of the remaining cream mixture; dust with cocoa. Repeat the layers.
3. Refrigerate, covered, at least 2 hours before serving. If desired, serve tiramisu with fresh raspberries.

1 piece: 177 cal., 6g fat (4g sat. fat), 41mg chol., 80mg sod., 25g carb. (18g sugars, 0 fiber), 6g pro. **Diabetic exchanges:** 1 starch, ½ fat-free milk, 1 fat.

RECIPE INDEX